D1251849

THE EDUCATED MAN

THE EDUCATED MAN:

STUDIES IN THE HISTORY OF EDUCATIONAL THOUGHT

Paul Nash   Boston University

Andreas M. Kazamias   University of Wisconsin

Henry J. Perkinson   New York University

JOHN WILEY & SONS, INC.

New York · London · Sydney

Library of Congress Catalog Card Number: 65-19587
Printed in the United States of America

To Robert Ulich: An Educated Man

Preface

Whatever the ideals of education may be, they surely have been created by men. Education, then, is best understood through its history, or, more precisely, through the study of the thought of the men who have created these ideals through the ages. This book contains the educational thought of fifteen of the most fertile minds from the fourth century B.C. up to the second half of the twentieth century. Since nothing captures the intellectual flavor of any age better than its ideal of the educated man, this book is not only an educational history but, at the same time, an introduction to the intellectual history of Western civilization.

The essays are not intended to be comprehensive expositions of the thought of the fifteen figures we have chosen, nor are they intended to be definitive interpretations of these thoughts. Each essay presents a point of view. Our purpose is to begin a dialogue—a dialogue that will include the reader, the authors of the essays, and the men about whom they have written. To enter fully into this dialogue the reader must have some familiarity with the original works of these men. The bibliographical note following each essay should serve as an introduction to the relevant original writings—many of which are available in cheap paperback editions.

The work involved in the editing of this book has happily resulted in the deepening of a friendship among us that began when we were all students of Robert Ulich of Harvard University, to whom this book is dedicated.

H.J.P.
P.N.
A.M.K.

Contents

THE EDUCATED MAN

INTRODUCTION: *Concepts of the Educated Man*

In a rather general sense, education has been a characteristic of man ever since he existed on this planet. But it was not until the time of the ancient Greeks that it was established on a more rational basis in formal institutions known as schools. From the archaic Homeric period to the flowering of the classical civilization, the Greeks explicitly sought through education to train the young in the skills and values necessary for participation in the society and for attainment of what they conceived to be ideal manhood. Underlying all their educational activities there was an image of the ideal man and there was an inner conviction that the welfare of the society rested on the education of its members. This inner conviction has pervaded Western civilization to the present time. With us as with the Greeks, this conviction has invested education with a nobility and grandeur, but at the same time has given it a tragic note. For although man has constantly striven to create a better society and better human beings through education, we seem today to be confronted with the same problems and paradoxes as were the ancients. We offer different solutions, we construct different theories, but many fundamental questions are still as unanswerable as ever. Yet perhaps we can find solace in the belief that it is the pursuit of our goals—the constant quest for something that brings its own rewards rather than the attainment of it—that is the essence of education and cultural development. As one modern poet has said, it is the journey to Ithaca that matters, not the arrival.

The ideas of the thinkers included in this volume, spanning the history of Western man since ancient times, are examples of this Odyssean theme, in a sense. With uneasy minds, all have articulated both contemporary and universal ideas about man, society, and the universe. All of them have reacted against prevalent ideas and practices related to how man orders his life, performs his functions as a citizen, and educates his children. They have been intellectual and pedagogical gadflies; at the

1

same time they have sought to lay the foundations of a better society inhabited by better human beings. And all of them have conceived of education as the vitalization of their vision of man and society. It is truly impossible to understand the philosophical outlook of these men without understanding their ideas about education. They represent greatness as leaders in the evolution of man's thought and greatness as educators whose ideas are a continuing source of inspiration and means of intellectual development.

H. I. Marrou, the distinguished French classical scholar, provides us with the basic justification of the approach of this book. In his monumental *History of Education in Antiquity*, Marrou wrote, "The fruitfulness of historical knowledge is to be found primarily in the dialogue which it generates within us between the Self and the Other." Such a dialogue, according to him, enlarges our perspective, and strips us "of that naïve self-sufficiency which prevents us from imagining that anyone could be different from ourselves." Although historical knowledge may not necessarily change our course of action, it forces us to think, it compels us "to test the validity and cogency of the reasons for our choices— it makes our decisions conscious ones."

It was partly in recognition of this fundamental conviction that we engaged in this undertaking. The key figures included in this volume were chosen with a view to representativeness as to time and place and with a view to diversity of viewpoints and impact on educational thinking and practice. Although it was not our purpose to provide historical connecting links, the authors have sought, as far as possible, to place each individual within the historical context of his ideas.

In addition we were guided by another consideration—the usefulness of comparing the past and the present. Although in many respects the past is a different world from the present, with its own connotations and guiding principles, both past and present are part of man's total experience. We can only see the past through our human eyes and our present state of knowledge. In reconstructing the past and making it intelligible we cannot extricate ourselves from our present world of connotations nor from our assumptions that there are certain general principles of human behavior. When we examine the ideas and the world of historical figures, we unavoidably project upon them the external factors of our own ideas and world. "Uniqueness" in history is a matter of the historian's interest rather than an inherent quality of historical events. These essays show that each of the men whose ideas are discussed was a product of his environment, and yet each raised questions of a universal significance. We have tried to make certain comparisons in the hope of gaining a better understanding of the complexities of education and the changes that have taken place.

In seeking that perspective of which Marrou spoke, we have taken as our starting point the ancient Greeks. In all the essays the focus has been on interpretative analyses of key educational ideas. These range from the nature of knowledge and how it is acquired to the nature and function of the curriculum and the schools. Most of these questions, however, bear upon the central theme of the image that these representative thinkers had of the educated man: what attributes, intellectual, moral, or otherwise, he must possess, how he comes about possessing them, and what his relationships with his fellow men, as well as his duties toward society and the polity, should be.

HELLENIC ORIGINS

Homer presents us with the evidence necessary to reconstruct the origins of Greek education, the concept of excellence and virtue (*aretē*), and the image of one of the earliest ideals of manhood, the Homeric hero. Yet it was not until the fifth century B.C., with the consolidation of the city-state, that education in the form we know it emerged as an organized activity of the people. Homeric culture in general was highly personal, and education in any formal sense was a personal kind of apprenticeship between a tutor and a young noble. There was no organized communal existence, and the concept of educating for political participation in the affairs of the community was totally alien. The Homeric nobleman was imbued with the ideal that he must excel over all others in military valor, speech, and action and that he must seek personal glory and renown. This was his duty in life to be pursued until death.

By the fifth century two rather distinct conceptions of education and *aretē* emerged, the Spartan and the Athenian. Both of them emphasized the collectivist nature of human existence and education, but it was Athens, not Sparta, that developed what Marrou has called a "scribe" culture, and built schools. The growing Athenian concept of goodness and virtue (*kalokagathia*) denoted much more than military prowess; it was a composite of intellectual, moral, and physical powers. Knowledge, wisdom, and justice—as well as bravery—became the basic desiderata of the good and virtuous man. It was in Athens also that the first professional "pedagogues"—the Sophists—appeared. They had the explicit task of training individuals in excellence and for future leadership of the society.

The Sophists departed from traditional ideas about education. Their views of education (*paideia*) clashed with traditional beliefs held by oligarchic elements in Athenian democracy. The Sophists' art of disputation, which frequently degenerated into eristic controversy, or arguing for the sake of arguing, was often utilized by the oligarchs in the courts of law in order to defend themselves against their democratic critics. It was paradoxical that the Sophists, who professed to educate leaders for democracy, furnished its opponents with the skills to become a greater threat to democracy. The clash between the new and the old ways of educating children was most poignantly dramatized in Aristophanes' comedy *The Clouds*. There Socrates, personifying the new education (the Wrong Logic), is satirically portrayed as one of the Sophists. Aristophanes was clearly exaggerating, for Socrates always sought to expose the fallacies and inadequacies in the thought and teaching of such great Sophists as Gorgias, Protagoras, Hippias, etc. Both Socrates and the Sophists exemplified the new spirit of inquiry, criticism, and examination (*elenchos*). This new spirit turned out to be too much even for the champions of democracy. Soon after 403 B.C., when the oligarchy of Critias fell, and democracy was restored, Socrates was indicted by his alleged friends, tried, and sentenced to death. The trial and death of Socrates demonstrated a fundamental concern and cleavage in the Athenian society of the time. It reflected fear of the power of a critical approach to life and to those who ruled the society, itself a result of a more professional and conscious way of educating the younger generation.

It was within such a climate that young Plato grew and sought to express his views. By temperament and background he belonged to what might be called the reactionary, oligarchic elements in the society, but by education he was exposed to the Socratic spirit of *elenchos*. In that turbulent period when Athens was humiliated in the face of Spartan discipline and military strength, when Athenian democracy degenerated into mob rule, or ochlocracy, or fell victim to demagogues and tyrants, when his beloved teacher was removed by the very champions of democracy, Plato lost faith in the existing forms of government and foundations of society. He embarked upon the task of proposing his visionary utopia in the *Republic* and of setting up a school to train potential leaders. In the *Dialogues*, in his excursions to Sicily, and in the halls of his Academy, Plato devoted himself to building a systematic social structure within which the concepts of knowledge, virtue, and justice would be correlated. Education was assigned an essential place in his inquiries about the nature of knowledge and its acquisition and about the welfare of the individual and the society. Plato was the first thinker who formulated a model of the meaning of education and its role in society. In doing so he went back to traditional beliefs and practices, he scrutinized the prevalent views of the Sophists, and he reached for the universal in man. A study of Plato's views about education, therefore, epitomizes not only one current of thought during a crucial period of Greek life, but it also represents a dialogue between that period and the periods that preceded it.

Many of the questions to which Plato addressed himself, and which are examined in Dr. Chambliss' essay, bear upon the central concept of the philosopher as the ideal man and ideal ruler in the perfect state. The philosopher, according to Plato, must possess such necessary moral attributes of all citizens as temperance, self-control, and courage. Beyond these, he must acquire an insight into knowledge and what is "good," and a love for them. Through meticulous training, he must climb the ladder of knowledge from the world of imagination (*eikasia*) and belief (*pistis*) to the world of understanding or reasoning (*dianoia*). He must reach the highest level of knowledge, the intelligible (*to noumenon*), that is, the world of "pure forms" (*eidē*). From that level he must finally reach into the first principle, the good (*to kalon*), through his power of intuition (*nous*). The philosopher's unique power to reach these highest forms of knowledge sets him apart from the rest of the people and justifies his position of pre-eminence in the ideal state. For with such knowledge not only does he know what the good is, but also he is the best-equipped man in the society to guide people's destinies and to lead them to a just and happy life. In his *Paideia* Jaeger summarized the attributes of the Platonic philosopher, who is equivalent to the ideally educated man, as follows:

He is a man of great intellectual power, quick apprehension, and real eagerness to learn. He is averse to all petty details; he is always anxious to see things as a whole; he does not prize his life, and cares little for external goods. Display is foreign to his character. He is magnanimous in everything, and has considerable charm too. He is a friend and kinsman of truth, justice, courage and self-control.

Such a type, according to Plato, was not a mere figment of the imagination. He could be produced, provided extreme care was taken in his education and upbringing from childhood to manhood. Plato paid particular attention to the content of the education of the future philosopher-statesman and to the kind of life he should live in order to attain the ideal that Plato had in mind. Education in the Platonic framework was not only an essential basis of the virtuous life; it also performed the selective function of sorting people for their appropriate walks in life, and most important, selecting the future rulers.

Historians of educational ideas, with but few exceptions, in their treatment of the classical Greek period have taken Plato and Aristotle as their most representative examples. Influenced, perhaps, by the tremendous impact that these philosophers have had on Western thought, these historians have virtually ignored one of the greatest educators of antiquity, Isocrates, Plato's contemporary. Isocrates was pre-eminently an educationalist. Like Plato, he grew up during that tempestuous and uncertain period of Greek history when Spartan militarism triumphed and Pericles' eulogy rang a tragic sound. Isocrates' life spanned a period of social and political unrest and of conflicting views about man, society, and the best way to educate children. Like Plato, he fell under the influence of the Sophists, but he, too, rejected their excesses and their utilitarian proclivities. Unlike Plato, however, Isocrates was not a system builder or an inveterate seeker of the nature of things, of the essence of knowledge and of virtue. His faith in the power of education, although great, was also more "realistic." As Dr. Proussis has shown, Isocrates felt that inquiries into perfect knowledge and the way to attain it were fruitless and perhaps useless enterprises. He believed that man should concentrate on what is possible, attainable, and of practical value. There was less of the imaginative speculator and "mystic" in Isocrates than in Plato, and more of the down-to-earth practitioner. After all, Isocrates argued, the educator or teacher must contend with the individual's ability to face problems in the society in which he lives and with the caliber of students under his charge. All that the teacher can do is to seek to develop in the future leader or citizen wise judgment or judicious insights, and certain moral attributes, in order that he may live his life more successfully.

Yet with all its simplicity, pragmatism, and focus on the citizen or leader of the Greek world of his time, the Isocratean view of education and of the educated man was another example of that persistent stream in classical Greek thought dramatized by the playwrights, sung by the poets, and expressed in various forms by the artists. That stream had to do with the universality of man, the Promythean theme of the importance of those human potentials which only man can realize, the constant striving to reach beyond the ephemeral and the temporal, the humanism that inheres in all men and not in animals, and invests man with grandeur and nobility. Both Plato and Isocrates, in their own ways, were concerned with the good ruler who could save or restore the glory of Greece. Implicit in the Platonic philosopher and the Isocratean orator was the sense of the completeness of man in general. Although one might accuse them of being rather ethnocentric, because both Plato and

Isocrates essentially defined the universality of man by what the Greeks had done or dreamed of doing, one cannot but admire their noble quest. This is perhaps why their ideas have been a source of inspiration through the ages and why they are as much alive today as they were in their own time.

In the hands of Isocrates the rhetorical school, which had its beginnings with the Sophists of the fifth century, reached its most mature and accomplished form. As it was with Plato's Academy, the main purpose of Isocrates' school was to train talented youth for political leadership. To be successful in high office, the future statesman needed to become well versed in the oratorical skills, to become eloquent, logical, and "philosophical" or "cultured." Oratorical success could be attained either through native talent or through exercise, but the combination of both would produce a man "incomparable among his fellows." Isocrates placed most of his emphasis on practice or exercise, and in this respect he felt education could play its most important role. There was less of the Socratic or Platonic method of dialectical discourse, contemplation, and inquiry into the essence of reality, and more of the paradigmatic, the imitative, and the practical in the Isocratean school.

Isocrates' greatest contributions were in the art of oral and written expression and in his pedagogical ideas and methods. The emphasis on rhetorical education, as the most important ingredient of the training of political leaders, survived the collapse of the city-states and the Hellenistic kingdoms, and was revivified under the Romans. It was the rhetorical school of Isocrates, more than the philosophical school of Plato or Aristotle, that motivated the Roman Emperor Vespasian to bring Latin and Greek teachers of rhetoric into the service of the Roman state and to endow chairs of rhetoric in Rome. And it was as a holder of the first endowed "professorship" of Latin rhetoric that the famous Roman educator Quintilian developed the ideas that, upon his retirement, he expressed in his famous *Institutio Oratoria*. In the prefatory letter to the editor, Quintilian wrote that the purpose of the book was "the Education of the Orator" whom he later described as follows:

The orator whom we are educating is the perfect orator, who can only be a good man: and therefore we demand of him, not merely an excellent power of speech, but all the moral virtues as well. Nor am I prepared to admit (as some have held) that the science of a righteous and honorable life should be left to the philosophers: for the man who is a true citizen, fit for the administration of private and public business, and capable of guiding cities by his counsels, establishing them by his laws and reforming them by his judgements, is none other than the orator.

There was no substantial difference between Quintilian's and Isocrates' conceptions of the orator, except, of course, that the latter preceded in time and influenced the former. Isocrates' views were the model upon which the Romans based their own ideas of the orator. Indeed, there was very little, if any, difference between the rhetorical schools of Greece and those established in Rome during the so-called Greco-Roman period of its history (31 B.C.–A.D. 284). Yet one should note that Quintilian also injected the "philosophic" element in his ideal "orator." He wrote:

Let the orator, then, be the kind of man who may truly be called a philosopher: not merely perfect in character (which, despite the opinion of some, is clearly not enough), but also skilled in Knowledge and eloquence—such a man, it may be, as we have never yet seen.

The Roman orator, the epitome of the Roman practical genius, was the cultured man who, as Cicero tells us in *De Oratore*, must combine training in rhetoric with all other branches of knowledge. Oratory included virtually everything in Roman life except agriculture; it was the route to public office, to the Senate, the Forum, the practice of law, as well as to demagoguery and the haranguing of multitudes. There may be an element of truth in the characterization of the Roman orator as combining the functions of a modern preacher and newspaper editor.

It is important at this juncture to emphasize that the Greeks, as well as the Romans, were primarily concerned with the education of leaders or rulers. Whatever variations there were in the content of the curriculum or in the methods of teaching, the primary concern of all of these great educators was the education of political leaders, which, considering the contemporary historical context, also meant the aristocratic classes. Thus the origins of Western education were essentially aristocratic in nature, and the image of the educated man was identified with the image of the aristocrat.

This combined image was seen even more distinctly during the Renaissance, and it underlay a great deal of educational thinking and practice until quite recently. Before we comment on this development it will be appropriate to look at another movement that, unlike the Isocratean-Roman oratorical one, had more connection with the Platonic and Neoplatonic strands in Western thought. This movement was associated with the emergence of Christianity and was exemplified by the views of St. Augustine and St. Thomas Aquinas.

CLASSICAL CHRISTIAN SYNTHESIS

All contemporaneous currents of thought found a confluence in St. Augustine. He was the earliest thinker in the West (in contrast to the

Fathers of the Eastern Christian Church) to succeed in reconciling pagan learning with the Christian religion. Because he was born in North Africa, which then spanned the world of the Eastern and Western Mediterranean, he was exposed to Semitic, Roman, and Greek influences, as well as to such heretical doctrines as those of the Manichees. From his mother, an ardent Christian, he absorbed Christianity, and through his schooling he learned of the culture and excesses of the Roman world. Unlike other Christians of the period, Tertullian, for example, Augustine was not uncompromising in his attitude toward the pagan thinkers of antiquity, and in the philosophical system of the Neoplatonists (Plotinus, Origen, etc.) he found a basis upon which to build his own essentially Christian philosophy and system of values. The Neoplatonists furnished him with a framework to view the universe as a whole, a cosmology. Also, and this is most important, they provided Augustine with the cardinal concept of the One, the Absolute, the infinitely perfect and good, as well as the notions of the immateriality of Truth, of the Soul, and of an otherworldly existence. There were, of course, important differences as well. To the Christians, God was a personal God and the Creator. To the Neoplatonists, God was perfect Unity and Goodness but not an ultimate Being; all existence was "a procession of intelligences from the One down to the material world"; and creation was taking place through intermediaries. The Christian view was based as much on the world of actual existence as on the "other world"; the Neoplatonists viewed matter and the body as impediments to spirituality.

As to the question of knowledge, Augustine rejected the Platonic doctrine of "reminiscence" and the Aristotelian doctrine of abstraction from sense experience. The key concept in the Augustinian theory of knowledge was "Divine Illumination," by which he meant that the soul or the mind could not know or be illumined except by the grace of God. There is a parallel between Augustine's Divine Illumination and Plato's *nous* and concept of the Good. Plato defined Good as "that which imparts truth to the known and the power of knowing to the knower." But there is also a slight difference. *Nous* was an aptitude or faculty of man; and man had the power to perceive and understand that which was rendered "radiant with intelligence." Augustine certainly did not use the metaphor of Divine Illumination to refer to a supernatural process, nor would he say that God would do man's thinking in his arrival at universal truths; but he did say that man could know truth, absolute, unchanging, eternal truth, only through the help of the source of all Truth, that is, through Divine Illumination.

Augustine's general philosophical orientation cast a nonpolitical light upon his educational views and his conception of the educated man. The overriding consideration of creating leaders of worldly polities, be they orators or philosopher-kings, was absent from the Augustinian ideal scheme. Augustine's ideal kingdom was the "City of God" inhabited by educated men who were so deeply developed as Christians that they might be called "saints." A saint could use pagan sources (Latin and Greek), but these would be used in the all-encompassing service of God. The man who possessed saintly wisdom would be the one who had transcended the world of paganism and had freed himself from its spiritual bondage. It is not paradoxical, therefore, that in the education of youth, Augustine included somewhat the same areas of study—the so-called liberal arts—as did Cicero, Quintilian, and, to some extent, Isocrates, Plato, and the Sophists. These studies were essentially of the literary-Humanistic variety. Augustine had some qualms about the inclusion of astronomy, although he felt that it could be useful in determining Easter and other Church festivals. Other studies involving written signs would serve the purpose of understanding the Holy Scripture and the Apostolic tradition as it was received from Christ. The purpose of any type of education, however, should be the pursuit of truth, identified with revealed truth, which could only be comprehended through faith and the will and grace of God.

In developing or educating the Christian saint, Augustine was very explicit as to the limits of the power of the teacher. In *De Magistro* he said that the teacher could not really impart knowledge, for only God, the real teacher, was capable of doing so. The truth of what the teacher said to the pupil would have to be discovered by the pupil himself. It could not be communicated by the teacher. The pupil would discover the truth of what the teacher told him through his own past or future experience. The pupil, of course, could believe what the teacher said was true, but this was belief, not knowledge. The experience of truth came from God, either directly (Divine Illumination), or indirectly (interaction with His creation), according to Augustine.

The belief in revelation and faith, so characteristic of Christian thought, pervaded the entire intellectual world of the ages following St. Augustine. But the revival of Aristotelian modes of reasoning in the medieval period and the growth of universities to train future theologians, "scientists," and men in the various professions inevitably raised religious questions about the possible incompatibility of theological and "scientific" modes of thinking and pedagogical questions concerning methods of acquiring knowledge and of educating the people. This ferment of ideas produced "Scholasticism" and the Scholastic method of teaching. It was Peter Abelard who first sought to apply philosophical concepts and methods to a reconciliation of the conflict between faith and reason; but it was Thomas Aquinas, pre-eminent representative of the Scholastic school of thought, who wedded Aristotelian logic with Catholic Christian theology.

Scholasticism was both a method of disputation in order to arrive at truth and a philosophy in its own right. The Scholastic, therefore, was both an inquirer and a system builder. In the essay on Aquinas, in whose hands Scholasticism flowered, Father Donohue cautions the reader against seeing too much of strictly educational import in the essentially theological treatises of Aquinas, against isolating the parts without considering the panoramic whole, and against treating Thomistic philosophy as a "Christianized version of Aristotle." Yet, as the author points out, an educational ideal was implicit in Aquinas' views of God, man, knowledge, intelligence, and ethical behavior. And, although Aquinas' knowledge encompassed Platonic and Neoplatonic elements, it found its greatest affinity to pagan learning in Aristotle, the philosopher. Several basic Aristotelian concepts, particularly relevant to a theory of education and the educated man, appeared in the Thomistic framework. For example, Aquinas expounded on the basic Aristotelian distinctions between the theoretical and the practical, between body and soul, between intellection and habituation, and between potentiality and actuality. Like Aristotle, Aquinas conceived the ultimate goal of man to be happiness (*eudemonia*) and the goal of education to be virtue. Yet, as is clearly shown in Father Donohue's analysis, Aquinas did not clothe Aristotelian language and meanings with the Christian Scholastic garb; his vision and scheme were as original as they were derivative. In many respects Aquinas went beyond Aristotle, as, for example, when he placed certain limitations upon the speculative sciences and human intelligence in the pursuit of perfect happiness. In other respects his order of priorities differs, as, for example, when he placed moral virtue ahead of intellectual accomplishments. The similarities and differences between St. Thomas and Aristotle, as well as the other pagan thinkers, are most clearly revealed in Aquinas' views bearing upon education and the educated man. Aquinas, in true Aristotelian fashion, held the end of man to be perfect happiness or beatitude pursued through "theorizing" or "contemplation of the divine"; he held human intelligence or wisdom to be both theoretical (or speculative) and practical; he held that moral virtue, despite Plato, could not be taught; and he believed habituation to be basic to the acquisition of virtue. On the other hand, Aquinas, being a Christian and a theologian, accounted faith and revelation as sources of knowledge, as well as experience and intellection; and, like St. Augustine, he believed that human salvation, the end of life and education, could not be attained without the service of God. Unlike the ancients, Aquinas viewed manual work as an important "human" activity, and he would not deprecate a vocational type of education. In addition, therefore, to the classical virtues of courage, wisdom, and liberality, Aquinas added faith, charity, and hope as characteristic ingredients of his educational ideal. As a Christian, he placed charity at the top of his list of virtues whereas Plato, for example, placed justice first.

The difference between the Platonic concept of justice and the Thomistic concept of charity (*agapē*) points up a basic distinction between ancient and Christian thought. Justice, the supreme virtue of man and society in ancient thought, was defined by Plato as giving each and every man his due; an individual would be respected according to his ability and merit. Charity, on the other hand, the supreme Christian virtue, was not premised on merit, but conceived as an outpouring of love bestowed on everybody, whether he deserved it or not. In fact the notion of "deserving it" would be irrelevant to the virtue of charity in Christian doctrine—one would love one's fellow men for the love of God. The educated man, therefore, according to this basic Christian belief, must also possess the capacity to love. In addition to the intellectual and moral attributes, which could be developed through education, there were also those Christian qualities that man could receive only through the power of the divine grace. Implicit in this attitude another basic distinction between the pagan and the Christian view of man may be seen. To Plato, human nature was essentially sound and innately "good"; man could be reformed through secular means and through education. In contrast, the Christian view was that man was born in sin; since man had corrupted himself through the fall, he could not save himself through education or other secular means. There had to be a supernatural intervention of the divine grace.

In the hands of its greatest master Scholasticism both as a method of disputation and as a philosophy reached the zenith of its glory. The reconciliation of pagan modes of reasoning and Christian religion furnished the basis of Roman Catholicism, and Scholastic theology became the queen of the sciences in medieval learning. To us many of the questions which occupied medieval thinkers, teachers, and students may seem to be pedantic or so exclusively theological as to be suitable only for preachers or priests. They may seem somewhat outside the mainstream of intellectual life and the everyday concerns of man. But to the medieval people discussions centering on religious dogma, the universals, sin, redemption, or the Holy Trinity were vital matters not only in intellectual and clerical relationships, but also in relationships of government and people, and their regulation. The Christian religion, in short, was the most important element in life, an integral part of the emerging civilization of the West. It was inevitable, therefore, that the "redis-covery" of pagan literature and the arts during the Renaissance would raise conflicts and intellectual upheavals as momentous as those that occurred when Aristotelian logic entered the religious tradition in the early medieval period. It was also inevitable that Christian thought would permeate the new views about man, society, government, and education.

When one looks at the Renaissance, especially in its later years (after about 1450), one notices some striking parallels with previous periods to which we have alluded. It was a time of political and social unrest. In the East the Byzantine Empire disintegrated, and with it the last bastion of Christendom and Western culture against Islam; in the West feudal-ism was being undermined, and with it the universality of the medieval culture. In Italy powerful city-states emerged, bringing about changes in economic and political activities. The Crusades, although a failure, opened up new intellectual and commercial routes, as did the various other exploits of navigators and explorers. The Renaissance was also a time of intellectual commotion. Old ways of thinking and believing were being challenged, and once again, as in classical Greece in the time of the Sophists, education became a major focus. If the Athenians of the fifth and fourth centuries "rescued" man from the "fetters" of the archaic aristocratic tradition, the men of the Renaissance "rescued" man from the "fetters" of what had become a stultifying medieval Scholasti-cism, and ascetic "otherworldliness," and an ecclesiastical tyranny over the intellect. Once again man, the free thinker, the inquirer, the rebel, with all his strengths and weaknesses, cast himself as the chief protago-nist. The Renaissance raised the curtain on a new act in this unending drama of human existence as modern man entered the stage. Like fifth-century Athens, from which the Renaissance drew so much of its inspira-tion, this new era accorded human intellect and the intellectuals the highest positions; but like its intellectual prototype, it also revealed weaknesses and tragic elements. This was typified in the lives and thoughts of those who best articulated the new ideas, the Humanists, and particularly in one of their greatest representatives, Desiderius Erasmus of Rotterdam.

Erasmus in many respects personified the Humanistic ideal that under-lay his own writings and those of many other Renaissance Humanists. In Erasmus himself, as presented in Dr. Schacht's essay, one sees the exemplar of the Humanistic ideal, the passionate devotee of man's intel-lectual independence, the erudite classicist who would gaze from above on man's folly and intemperance, who would strive to educate lay and ecclesiastical princes according to those higher ethical standards that would free them from the bondage of fanaticism, intolerance, war, and uncurtailed passion and unite them in a sort of rational cultural cosmopolis.

Like the ancients, Erasmus' belief was that man was "basically good," and that through proper education he could attain a virtuous life. There was in Erasmus that same confidence in the power of knowledge and proper upbringing that we encountered in Plato. The educated man, according to Erasmus, was also a civilized and cultured man who was not capable of resorting to brute force and fanaticism, who controlled his animal passions, who settled his disputes through moderation—"erasmically," as Stefan Zweig called it—and who in all cases of conflict sought to find the common element in man that would unite everybody. The educated man exercised reason and the golden mean in all his affairs. The heart of Erasmus' humanism lay in the belief in the perfectibility of man through education; herein also lay its cardinal weakness. To quote from Stefan Zweig's *Erasmus of Rotterdam*:

In their overevaluation of the effects of civilization, the humanists failed to take account of the basic impulses and their untamable strength; in their facile optimism they overlooked the terrible and well-nigh insoluble problem of mass-hatred and the vast and passionate psychoses of mankind. Their view was too simple. For them there existed two layers, an upper and a lower: in the latter were to be found the uncivilized, rough, and passion-ridden masses; in the former lived the educated, the penetrating, the humanistic, the civilized.

The overconfidence in the power of education to secure a life of virtue was also revealed in Erasmus' social philosophy, that an educated aristocracy, or a meritocracy to use Michael Young's modern term, would insure justice and peace in the society. Like Plato, Erasmus placed limitless faith in government by the excellent (*aristoi*) and said relatively little about the masses. The Humanists' intellectual aristocrat would be the one who would combine erudition (*eruditio*) and eloquence (*eloquentia*), who would be deeply versed in the Greco-Roman literary classics and imbued with their spirit, who would combine pagan wisdom with the highest form of Christian morality.

Although the Humanistic spirit in education could very well apply to all the people in the society, it was essentially aristocratic in nature. Erasmus' ideal was part of the general knightly and aristocratic ideal of culture which, in some form, characterized most of the significant writings on education throughout the entire Renaissance. Thus, for example, Vittorino da Feltre (1378–1446) at his school in Mantua educated princes, noblemen, and rich merchants; Sir Thomas Elyot (1490–1546) addressed his work to the education of the "Governour"; Erasmus wrote on "The Education of a Christian Prince"; and Montaigne (1533–1592) designed his educational program for the nobleman who would not have to earn a living. Thus the revival of classical learning was also accompanied by the revival of many of the social assumptions upon which it was based.

In an age such as ours when democratic and equalitarian ideologies pervade much of our political and educational thinking, and science has triumphed, we might scoff at the aristocratic aloofness, the intellectual arrogance, and the literary classicism of the Humanists. Yet in an age such as ours with its ideological splits as momentous as those of the Renaissance and Reformation, its international conflicts, and its spectre of annihilating wars, Erasmus' simplest of thoughts acquires new significance. This was the thought that it was mankind's duty to strive to be more humane, more sympathetic, more tolerant, more understanding, and more spiritual. Erasmus' vision of a cultural cosmopolis, governed by reason and moderation, and sustained by a humanely educated citizenry, continues to be as viable an ideal as it was in sixteenth-century Europe; so does his ideal of a balanced individual, independent in spirit and thought, freed from ignorance and from the excesses accruing from unbridled passions. Erasmus and the Humanists may have been addressing themselves to a small group of people who had the leisure to pursue Humanistic studies; but the liberal and Humanistic spirit that pervaded their writings could be applied to the masses as well as to the leaders of an industrial and complex civilization.

In discussing the Renaissance we must guard against reducing the entire period to simple generalizations and against assuming that Humanism can be defined exclusively in terms of the Erasmic philosophy. At about the same time that Erasmus wrote the *Education of a Christian Prince*, Niccolo Machiavelli, a Latin scholar, penned his own *De Principatibus* (The Prince), the first "modern" scientific treatise on politics. Unlike Erasmus, Machiavelli viewed human nature as "corrupt," at least in political behavior, and man as naturally inclined to be wicked, therefore requiring compulsion to be good through education or other means. The Prince, according to Machiavelli, must possess virtue (excellence in understanding politics) so that he could constantly adapt himself to "fortune"; he must be what we would call a good "propagandist"; and for "reasons of state" he could utilize any kind of measure or policy. Clearly some of the characteristics of the Prince and of "Machiavellism" were antithetical to Erasmus' pious Christian Humanism. On the other hand, like Erasmus, Machiavelli built his philosophy on classical models; moreover, he followed the tradition of the Humanists in breaking away from the strictly religious orientation of the medieval thinkers, thus paving the way for a secular approach to politics.

Erasmus and Machiavelli represented two important catalysts in the intellectual ferment of the postmedieval world. Personifying another, more violent reaction to the dogmatism, the theological excesses, and the practices of the medieval church was the Augustinian friar, Martin Luther. Luther was in many respects the complete opposite of Erasmus— nonconciliatory, fanatical, nationalistic. And the Reformation, which he was instrumental in bringing about, was in many ways hostile to the ideas of the Humanists and the Renaissance in general. Yet, Luther was as much a part of the anti-Scholastic movement as the Humanists were; and he was part of the spirit of independence and individualism that characterized the whole Renaissance period. The cleavages, however, between Humanism and Protestantism were irreconcilably deepened not only by differences concerning religious matters, but also by the political and social associations of the two movements. Luther's "liberalism" reached farther down the social ladder than Erasmus'. Originally it appealed to princes, the middle bourgeois interests, and the peasant groups. And it substituted nationalism for a disintegrating cosmopolitanism.

Luther and his followers, notably Calvin, succeeded in splitting the Christian church and in shattering the cosmopolitan pacifist vision of Erasmus. In time, however, Lutheranism and Calvinism came to be as authoritarian, inflexible, antirationalist, politically theocratic, and socially aristocratic as the old religious order, which, in conjunction with the Humanists they sought to supersede. Luther placed unquestioned reliance upon faith and the Bible rather than upon man's reason, which he called "God's worst enemy." He sanctioned the ruthless suppression of people's revolts against established authority. He accepted social divisions in society as divinely ordained. And he rejected the Renaissance hellenistic Humanism as well as the "worldliness" of man. Yet Lutheranism and Protestantism, as has often been pointed out, did contribute to the breaking down of excessive authority, and the Lutheran "protest" opened the way for other protests in the religious, economic, political, and educational realms.

SCIENTIFIC PROGRESS AND REACTION

The spirit of the classical revival and the challenge to authority were also reflected in the emergence of a new mode of "scientific" inquiry emphasizing inductive experimental methods of investigation. The new scientists turned their attention to nature and natural philosophy instead of theology and inquired into natural rather than supernatural causes. With the genesis of the "modern" scientific method, educational thinking entered a new phase. The confidence of Erasmus' Humanism in the power of classical literary knowledge and education gave way to confidence in scientific knowledge. This attitude gradually enveloped all aspects of life including ethics, politics, and education. Yet scientists like Francis Bacon, and later T. H. Huxley, scientific pedagogues like Comenius, and political scientists like John Locke were as much influenced by the Humanism of the Renaissance as they were motivated by the new scientific spirit and method. It was not until our own age that science became more specialized and divorced from literary Humanism. The separation of "cultures," in C. P. Snow's sense, is a modern phenomenon.

John Amos Comenius is probably one of the best representatives of that aspect of the new pedagogy combining the intellectualism of the Greeks, the moralism and idealism of the Neoplatonists and the Humanists, Christian pietism, Protestant Scripturalism and faith, Baconian sense realism, and Christian equalitarianism. The synthesis of all these elements may be found in Comenius' concept of "pansophia," which epitomized his view of the components of an ideal type of education. In the lengthy title of his *Great Didactic*, Comenius described his pansophic ideal as learnedness in science, purity in morals, training in piety, and instruction "in all things necessary for the present and for the future life." The all-wise (*pansophos*) was not merely the encyclopedic man with an inexhaustible fund of knowledge or information; he was rather the man who possessed, in addition to knowledge, virtue and wisdom. In the heritage of the Socratic-Platonic ideal, the *pansophos* was the man who had attained an inner perfection, or harmony, of the various parts of his psychological nature, the rational, the vegetative, and the animal. Comenius, however, was also an heir of the Christian tradition of the Renaissance and the Reformation. Thus, as Dr. Clauser notes, although he placed intellectual enlightenment as an important element in man's spiritual salvation, Comenius believed that ultimate happiness could only be attained in some other form of life. Like Erasmus, Comenius envisioned a world order that proper education would set free from vice, ignorance, and conflict; but, unlike his classical and Renaissance intellectual mentors, he felt that the pansophic spirit could be infused in all the children of all social classes. This basic belief in "democracy" and in the limitless possibilities of human nature was a departure from traditional pedagogical thought and was far ahead of Comenius' times. Seventeenth-century Europe was still enmeshed in aristocratic assumptions about man and society, as well as about government and education.

More in accord with contemporary social and political conditions than Comenius was the Englishman John Locke, who was, in Bertrand Russell's words, "the most influential though by no means the most profound of modern philosophers." With the contributions of John Locke, a representative of the era of the Enlightenment, the view that education is an integral part of statecraft acquired added significance and dimensions. As a philosopher of the new scientific spirit, with its emphasis upon experience in the acquisition of knowledge, Locke systematized British empiricism. As an apostle of political liberalism and parliamentary government, Locke provided a rationale for British parliamentary democracy.

In the portrait of the Lockian concept of the "gentleman," Dr. Benne observed that Locke's ideal had its roots in the Renaissance; and of course the idea of a polity governed by an elite dates back to the classical period. But Locke's "gentleman," Dr. Benne emphasizes, was enmeshed in the Whig tradition of 18th century England and in the emergent English bourgeois culture.

In addressing himself to the education of a special social class, Locke invested his educational ideal with class connotations. He assumed that there were different types of education befitting different social classes; and since he was concerned with a privileged aristocracy the Lockian image of the educated man was closely tied up with the image of the aristocrat, or the landed Whig gentry. The Lockian gentleman-ruler, however, unlike the Platonic philosopher-king, was bound to the governed by a contractual arrangement. The governed possessed certain natural rights (life, health, liberty, possessions), and if the rulers usurped such rights, the people could interfere to overthrow the government. The purpose of civil government, according to Locke, was not to curb individual freedom and equality arbitrarily, but to protect them, and to do so with the minimum of interference by the state. Unlike previous theoretical polities, Locke's ideal government would resemble a "research establishment" run by political scientists who would discover the laws of human nature, and govern accordingly. Next to this possibility, the best group capable of becoming the leaders would be the gentleman class. Although Locke considered education important for all classes in his laissez-faire democratic state, he claimed that it was more important for the upper classes from which the future leaders would be recruited. His basic assumption, stated in his dedicatory epistle prefacing *Some Thoughts Concerning Education,* was that if those belonging to the "gentleman's calling" were "by their Education once set right, they will quickly bring all the rest into Order."

The Lockian image of the gentleman was not a normative concept of what should be; it was, rather, a synthesis of characteristics derived from the demands made upon the eighteenth-century English gentlemanly class. Of course these demands were different from those made upon the fifth-century statesmen or the Roman patrician class. The heritage of Christianity had been a potent force in shaping ideologies and in regulating man's life. Thus, according to Locke, the wise and virtuous gentleman would be the man who had faith in God, who could "get along with others," who was truthful, tolerant, and well-mannered, and who was prudent in the management of personal as well as of civic affairs. Locke subordinated knowledge or learning to the qualities of virtue, wisdom, and breeding, in his design for the education of the gentleman. The Lockian gentleman was to be an amateur in the field of "learning," very much like the statesman of the Periclean age, but quite unlike the Platonic philosopher; and he would avoid theological disputations about such matters as the nature of God, preferring simply to be a good Christian.

The Lockian concept of wisdom had nothing of the Augustinian or the Thomist concept of contemplative knowledge of God (*sapientia*). Yet the Lockian concept of wisdom was as imbedded in the classical-Renaissance tradition as it was related to the new empiricism. Wisdom was a virtue based on common-sense experience. Locke explicitly stated that wisdom was as much the product of a "good natural temper" and "experience" as it was the result of the "application of mind." The human mind, or human understanding, would "direct wisely," it would take the "right way." Herein, therefore, lay Locke's similarity to the Renaissance concept of wisdom as an active, natural virtue, naturally acquired. Locke believed that the cultivation of man's reasoning "faculties" would free him from intolerance, prejudice, presumption, passion, narrow specialization, and outdated rules; it would lead man to examine principles in terms of their foundations, and to make wise decisions. In extolling the power of human mind and reason and in putting major emphasis upon education, Locke transcended the boundaries of his era and eulogized man in general. In his own words, "The next and principal Business is, to set the *Mind* right, and on all Occasions it may be dispos'd to consent to nothing but what may be suitable to the Dignity and Excellency of a rational Creature."

The gentleman ideal in all its aspects (political, social, and educational) has always been a pervasive element in English educational thought and practice. The aristocratic conception of democracy and education, as well as the assumptions upon which it was based, was not successfully challenged until the latter part of the nineteenth century. Even today—the period of equalitarian ideologies and expanded educational opportunities—aristocratic speech, manners, and type of schooling are important factors in attaining positions of leadership in the political hierarchy. However, since Locke's time there have also been important and far-reaching developments. One such development of particular relevance here has been in the content of formal education.

In stating his views about "learning," Locke was reacting against the prevalent curriculum of the schools, especially of the classically oriented public schools and the two ancient universities. His own personal experiences at Westminster and Oxford so revolted him that he turned away from school education and advocated private education under a tutor. He attacked the undue emphasis placed upon the classics, upon Scholastic theological pedantry and Aristotelian logic, and he criticized the neglect of mathematics, the sciences, and the new empirical scientific spirit. He called for the expansion of the curriculum to include mathematics (one of the best tools to make people "reasonable creatures"), natural philosophy ("the knowledge of the principles, properties, and operations of things as they are in themselves"), as well as "rational experiments and observations," geography, history, ethics, French, English, and Latin. Rhetoric and logic would be of little advantage to young people, and Greek more properly belonged to "the scholar," according to Locke.

The schools for gentlemen, however, continued to provide the same type of education as before. Indeed, until the nineteenth century the education of the gentleman was defined almost exclusively in terms of the classical literary tradition. The study of classics was associated with high status as Greek had been in the Roman period, and Latin in the period of the Renaissance. However, the claims of science for a legitimate position in any scheme of liberal education were upheld by many, and after the appearance of Darwin's *Origin of Species* received added impetus. In the scientific educational revival that characterized the latter part of the nineteenth century, two figures particularly stand out— Herbert Spencer and T. H. Huxley.

Of the two new apostles of scientific culture, Spencer has received more attention from historians of education. Yet, although Spencer provided the initial jolt to traditional beliefs through his flair for exaggeration, it was Huxley, the professor, who popularized science and who actively participated in enlightening his Victorian countrymen on the value of what came to be known as scientific culture. In Huxley's conception of education we see the blending of the traditional literary type of education with the emerging scientific type; and this advance was made, as Dr. Bibby pertinently remarks, more than one hundred years before C. P. Snow's famous pamphlet *The Two Cultures*. Moreover, Huxley sought to elevate science from the inferior status it had held both as a school subject and as a way of looking at man and the world. The value of science, according to Huxley, lay as much in its contribution to the mental and moral development of man as it did in its immediate utility. Huxley believed that science (natural and social) could liberate man from traditional and fallacious beliefs, could give him the right ideas, could bring him into closer contact with nature and society, and could contribute to man's realization of himself as a human being and as a citizen. Huxley, in short, expanded the traditional view of a "humanistic education" by including science as one of its most important ingredients. Yet, unlike many modern partisans of science, Huxley was also conscious of its limitations in education. In words that have more relevance today than in his time, Huxley cautioned, "Unless we are led to see that we are citizens and men before anything else, I say it will go very badly with men of science in future generations, and they will run the risk of becoming scientific pedants when they should be men, philosophers, and good citizens."

In its social aspects, Huxley's scientific humanism was applied over a wider segment of the population than was classical humanism and the Lockian educational ideal. Huxley, Dr. Bibby emphasizes, envisaged a more universal scheme of education; he scoffed at the Victorian social and educational dichotomies and the laissez-faire liberal doctrines. He himself sought to instruct the common man who, he fervently believed, was as capable of reaping the fruits of education as was the more privileged Victorian aristocrat. In the same vein Huxley actively participated in the movement toward the expansion of educational opportunities.

In spite of the ferment created by the advocates of science in the decades following Darwin's *Origin of Species*, the progress of scientific instruction in schools was rather slow in England where it was not until after World War I that science effectively challenged the supremacy of the classics. In the United States, on the other hand, Spencer's and Huxley's ideas of a scientific culture seem to have had a more favorable immediate reaction. Spencer's ideas about education, stemming from an analysis of man's actual activities rather than from absolutist and metaphysical doctrines, found a more fertile ground in a pioneer and experimental society untrammeled by traditional institutional and ideological constraints. In the United States the evolutionary hypothesis was utilized by John Dewey, one of the greatest modern champions of the development of man's intelligence and the scientific method.

Dewey, as Dr. Holmes's essay shows, rejected many of the assumptions and doctrines of the various "classical" theories of education discussed in this book: the Platonic views of change, mind, reason, knowledge, freedom, and society; Lockian laissez-faire liberalism; medieval religious individualism; and the numerous dualisms (mind-body, theoretical-practical, liberal-vocational, etc.) that underlay many of the traditional conceptions of education. Yet Dewey, like many of his predecessors, placed human reason and intelligence at the very center of his conceptual scheme. Contrary to the views of many critics, Dewey was as strong a supporter of the cultivation of intellect, or of "mental discipline," as any of the classical theorists. He may have stripped his theories of absolutist and metaphysical elements; he may have substituted a unified and dynamic meaning of experience and knowledge; he may have considered science and the scientific method as central in the acquisition of knowledge and in morality. In short, he may have rejected traditional views about epistemology, methodology, and human nature; but he still regarded the rational element in man as the most important and he had an unswerving faith in the power of education to develop a free and moral individual. The thinker, synonymous to him with the "scientific" man, was his image of the ideally educated man, the man, that is, who could solve the various problems encountered in his life through reasoned inquiry, who made choices after deliberation and a foresight of the possible consequences. The educated man would act intelligently. Dewey interpreted intelligence not as an abstract entity independent of man's social experience but as the capacity that develops through the dynamic interaction of the individual and the environment. Dewey defined "manness" in terms of the degree to which man had developed his capacity for reflective thinking. In itself, this was not a particularly revolutionary idea. But—and here was where Dewey deviated from other thinkers— "manness" was realized not in the isolation of man from other human beings or from the world; rather, man realized his individuality through cooperation, and in a social context, according to Dewey.

Dewey's conception of individuality and freedom seems to be in direct contrast to that of earlier modern thinkers and notably to that of Rousseau. That "eccentric," revolutionary Frenchman was not only unsociable as a person (something which irritated his contemporaries, especially the *philosophes*), but he was also a vitriolic critic of the social and political institutions of his time, including education. Rousseau, with a literary flair for hyperbole, saw the entire civilization of his day as degenerate, oppressive, stultifying, evil, and deleterious to personal freedom, goodness, and civic virtue. His venomous thrusts spared few aspects of his contemporary civilization; education, schools, the arts, and the sciences received their proper share. Rousseau felt that man was by nature good and free (an obvious contrast to the Christian view), and that it was his environment that brought about his degeneration and curtailed his freedom. Goodness was man's natural endowment. Yet it was a necessary part of man's existence that he live in society. Therefore, the best and surest way to preserve his dignity, his freedom, and his "rights" was to organize society so that his freedom and moral goodness might be realized. Thus, in fact, Rousseau's ideal of man's returning to a state of nature was not an individualistic, "noble savage" ideal; upon closer examination, the "natural man" turns out to be nothing less than the ideal citizen. The chained man to whom Rousseau referred was the individual living in eighteenth-century society. As G. D. H. Cole pointed out in his Everyman edition of the *Social Contract,* Rousseau did not mean literally that man "is born free," but rather that man "ought to be free," or perhaps that man "is born for freedom," the fulfillment of which can take place only *in society.*

In the same way that he criticized his contemporary social and political institutions, Rousseau castigated the prevailing educational practices. His ideas, examined in detail by Dr. Ballinger, were based on the assumption that education should follow the natural development or "maturation" of the child. But, as in the case of his social philosophy, Rousseau did not advocate a libertarian, uncontrolled type of education. Here again, he held that the environment should be so organized that the child's natural capacity "for freedom" would be preserved unspoiled and that he would be equipped to fulfill his functions as a citizen. It was Rousseau's conception of "education from nature" that was the major afflatus of the "nature school" of pedagogy developed by Basedow, Salzmann, von Rochow, and Richter in Germany, and the great Pestalozzi in Switzerland. Rousseau's views of the "child as a child" with his own world and his peculiar problems were what gave Rousseau an important position in modern pedagogical thought and strong similarities to Dewey.

Dewey, however, unlike Rousseau, was speaking about man in a complex, industrial, urban civilization. His reassertion and reinterpretation of the basic liberal and democratic tenets concerning freedom, intelligent behavior, and the individual were at no other time in human history more pressingly necessary, for education and the school were called upon to perform a most demanding task.

Dewey's concern was the concern of most other thinkers of the modern, complex, industrial civilization. The differences lay in the types of suggestions given for the transformation of society and the moral uplift-ing of modern man, as well as in the type of education that would bring about these results. Karl Marx, for example, Dr. Nyberg reminds us, sought to build a world order in which industrial man, who had become alienated and "dehumanized," would realize his essential human at-tributes. Marx's ideal society was a classless society reached through changes in the economic and social conditions rather than through spiritual or rational development. Marx assumed that in this classless utopia man would make such complete identification with the collective character of the society that any conflict between the individual and the collective would disappear, alienation and exploitation would disappear, and dignity and social justice would be realized.

A concern for man's seeming alienation and "dehumanization" is also reflected in the thought of existential theologians like Tillich and Buber, philosophers like Jaspers and Heidegger, social psychologists like Erich Fromm, and social scientists like Reisman. Dr. Friedman's discussion of Martin Buber's ideas illustrates a different interpretation of man's predicament in the impersonal modern world from that of Marx, and a different view of the process of education. Buber's philosophy is centered in the "I-Thou" relationship, the "interhuman" interaction between man and man, the recognition of "otherness," as well as of uniqueness in each individual. Education that emphasizes cultural transmission, classical or scientific knowledge, the unfolding of the creative powers of the indi-vidual, or the cultivation of reason is considered quite inadequate. Such education ignores that human interaction between teacher and pupil, that dialogistic relationship necessary for the development of responsi-bility, character, and self-realization, according to Buber. The educated individual is the one who has developed "his own unique relation to truth," who has become his own unique judge of what is right and wrong, in Buber's view. The perfection of one's reason is not, of itself, a guarantee that the individual will attain this felicitous state. Buber con-siders that the individual must be immersed in the totality of human existence and, through interpersonal interaction, develop his own sense of personal responsibility.

Like Buber, T. S. Eliot provides an example of reaction against the contemporary condition of man and the supremacy of science. Eliot went farther than any modern social thinker in his critique of the pres-ent state of society and culture. Not only did he find modern society "neutral" in terms of ultimate values, but also he found it uncreative and in a deplorable state of cultural decline. His views about the "educa-tive society," "high culture," a "community of Christians," and a reli-gious basis for education, may sound too reactionary, too romantically unrealistic, too withdrawn, too aristocratic, and perhaps too pessimistic in countries that are dominated by secular, equalitarian, utilitarian ideologies, by the spirit of science, and by an almost irrational belief in the perfectibility of man. Yet, Eliot's ideal of the creative artist, the poet, the man who is not circumscribed by the exigencies of the present but assimilates the values of tradition and the past and is aware of the limitations of his environment, afforded a challenge to what have developed to be sacred cows in our thinking. There is a reality and a relief in Eliot's thinking; and this, in Dr. Bantock's words, "stems from a realization that his [Eliot's] view of experience represents something more permanent in the human condition, more true about human beings, than that implicit in so much of the vapid social theorizing of our times." Paradoxically, in being traditional and reactionary, Eliot's views provided that jolt necessary to strike for balance and sanity.

In contrast to Buber's "existentialism" and Eliot's views, and closer to Dewey's emphasis upon reasoned intelligence and scientific inquiry, is B. F. Skinner's conception of the planned society, the conditioned man, and the application of science in the regularization of human activity. In concluding these studies with Skinner we are reminded of the man with whom we started, Plato. There are marked similarities between Plato's *Republic* and Skinner's *Walden Two*: both utopias envisage an ideal society where people would know themselves and their potentialities, where they would be happy, secure, and productive; both are based on the value of knowledge as a guide to human action; both have assigned education a most central part; both have been the subject of intensive criticism as denying human freedom and dignity and as being contrary to the concept of an open society. Of course, as may be gathered from Dr. Aschner's analysis, there are also important differences regarding the nature of knowledge and how it is acquired, the theory of valuation, and the implications of these for education.

What is the ideal of the educated man? Is there *one* ideal that emerges from the study of the history of Western education? Or are there merely ideals—ideals relative to specific times and specific places? Our questions can be asked in another way: Is there a Western man? Or are there merely Western men? Has Isocrates anything in common with Skinner, or Augustine with Dewey?

Whether there is one Western ideal of the educated man or whether there are only Western ideals, it is patent that one cannot go about the business of education without some ideal of the educated man. Else, how can education take place? The formulation of the ideal of an educated man is not the work of a class period, nor even of a semester. More likely the formulation of such an ideal is the work of a lifetime, since there are always different questions to be answered concerning that ideal. Some of these questions are raised in this book, and some of the answers of some of the men who wrestled with these questions are here too.

Isocrates, in opposition to Plato, claimed that it was not possible to have certain knowledge concerning the affairs of men. Who today is the educated man: the student of the social sciences (the true heir of Plato) with his "cold," demonstrable knowledge of human behavior, or the student of the humanities (the true heir of Isocrates) with his "warm," right opinions about human behavior?

Most would probably agree that the educated man today is a moral man. Western educational thinkers from Plato to Skinner have all affirmed this. But how do we educate a man to be moral, to be good, or at least to be a better person? Is it a matter of the intelligence, as both Plato and Dewey would have it? Or is it more a matter of the examples set by the great men and great deeds of the past, as both Isocrates and Erasmus would have it? Or perhaps the more efficacious examples are those of the teacher and of the companions of our student, as Locke avowed. Perhaps the power to make another human being better is beyond the teacher and ultimately resides in God, or Divine Grace, as SS. Augustine and Aquinas aver, or perhaps such power resides in the cultural milieu in which one is born and nurtured, as T. S. Eliot seemed to be saying. If our question is purely a question of method, a question of "how to," then B. F. Skinner would seem to have the only scientifically grounded answer. And yet we can ask: Is it good (moral) to condition another to be good (moral)?

Is the educated man to be identified by the role he plays, by the function he fulfills? Is that function rooted in his society, as is held by most of our Western thinkers, or is the educated man one who transcends the limitations of specific time and specific place, as the Stoics taught, as the Christian saints taught, and as Martin Buber teaches? If the educated man is one who has a duty or a responsibility to his society, then what is that responsibility? Is it, as Eliot says, to conserve what is worthwhile in society? Or was Marx right when he held that the educated man was to lead in the reconstruction of his society? Or perhaps Dewey had the answer to the question of societal responsibility: the educated man is he who confronts and tries to solve the continually changing problems of his society. What, then, ought to be the attitude of the educated man toward change? Should he resist it, promote it, or adjust to it?

Finally, is our ideal of the educated man an ideal for everyman? Can anyone become an educated man? Plato did not feel that there were very many potential guardians in any random sampling of the population, and most Western educational thinkers have tended to follow

Plato in conceiving the educated man as a rather exceptional person, definitely not everyman. Does this mean that only our gifted children can hope to approach our ideal of the educated man? Yet, if we are committed to mass education, is it not incumbent upon us to conceive an ideal of the educated man that encompasses every man?

A. M. K.
H. J. P.
P. N.

PLATO (427?–347 B.C.) was born in Athens of an aristocratic family. His father traced his ancestry to the last king of Athens; his mother was a descendant of Solon. As a youth of twenty Plato came under the influence of Socrates, who was twenty years his senior. Following the execution of Socrates in 399 B.C., Plato left Athens and went on a series of travels in Greece, Italy, and Sicily. During this time he seems to have acquired a knowledge of the philosophy of Pythagoras as well as that of Heraclitus. Returning to Athens in 387 B.C., he founded his school of mathematics and philosophy, called the Academy. For the rest of his life Plato presided over the Academy, making it the intellectual center of Greek life. His career as a teacher was interrupted on two occasions by trips to Sicily, where he tried without much success to advocate and advise Dionysius the Younger. Plato's most famous pupil was Aristotle, who studied with him for twenty years and embodied many Platonic views in his own philosophy. From the comments of Aristotle it appears that Plato lectured without manuscript, and problems were propounded for solution by the joint researches of the students. The Academy continued as a school of philosophy until closed by Justinian in A.D. 529. The works of Plato are chiefly in the form of dialogues, twenty-five of which have been preserved. The Platonic theory of education, based on a drawing out of what is already dimly known to the learner, can be found in: *Meno, Republic* (II–VII), *Theatetus,* and *Laws.*

1

THE GUARDIAN: *Plato*

BY J. J. CHAMBLISS

A legend has it that the young Plato wrote tragedies but burned them after meeting Socrates, who did not write but taught solely by conversing with his students. Plato's holiday from writing was short-lived. After Socrates died in the cause of philosophy, Plato turned his dramatic abilities to that cause, creating dialogues in imitation of his master's method of inquiry.

In Plato's early dialogues, Socrates inquires about the definitions of such concepts as courage and self-control. The procedure is for Socrates to get another person to make a statement about the virtue under consideration. By careful questioning, it is found that no agreement can be reached; and so the dialogues end with the particular question left unanswered. To an impatient observer, the outcomes of this procedure would make it appear that Socrates is not getting anywhere; but this is so only if one thinks that people do know the nature of the subjects they commonly talk about, or that the way to find out is to ask those who say they know. And this is what Socrates finds out: that most people do not really know what they think they know; that every opinion can be countered by another in such a way that eventually numerous opinions are offered; that about no single opinion is there agreement that it constitutes knowledge.

In an important sense, then, Socrates is learning something. He finds out that common-sense opinions about subjects will not hold up under careful examination. But this does not leave him helpless; it suggests that, if he would know, he must look elsewhere. Armed with an understanding of the limitations of opinions gained from sensory experience, Socrates learns to guard against deceiving others and, what is equally important, he learns to guard against deceiving himself.

In the *Protagoras*, Plato pitted Socrates against one of the greatest of the Sophists. Protagoras had written that man is the measure of things; and, since he was a teacher by profession, it seemed quite proper to expect him to answer questions as to whether men could be educated and whether virtue could be taught. But even the great Protagoras is unable to establish his claim that the collective common-sense opinions of civilized men set appropriate standards for education. Protagoras' sociological considerations of man turn out to be no more certain as a measure of virtue than were the opinions of ordinary individuals in the early dialogues. And here Socrates gets a firmer hold on what he seeks. Now he can state that what passes as virtue can scarcely be "taught" (in the Sophistic way of passing on particular knowledges or arts to another), since not even those reputed to be the greatest teachers know what virtue is. How can one "teach" something that he does not know? Or, if there is a sense in which he does, it is scarcely firm enough to be a standard compelling agreement by all. So the inquiry shows that a prior question needs to be asked: what is virtue in itself—not what are the separate virtues, such as courage and self-control, but what is a virtue that, if known, would enable its knower to know its parts? To have this virtue would be to know it. Therefore, it appears that virtue is knowledge of a kind that not even the greatest teachers of Greece seem to have. If anyone had it, this knowledge would provide the kind of standard not understood by ordinary men nor by the Sophists who profess to teach.

In the *Meno*, Socrates says:

I have no knowledge about virtue at all. And how can I know a property of something when I don't even know what it is?[1]

He continues to press the point that it is one virtue he is after, not many, saying:

What is that character in respect of which they don't differ at all, but are all the same? . . . While the nature of virtue as a whole is still under question, don't suppose that you can explain it to anyone in terms of its parts, or by any similar type of explanation. Understand rather that the same question remains to be answered; you say this and that about virtue, but what *is* it?[2]

Socrates makes it clear that he is not merely holding back his knowledge from Meno, but is genuinely seeking it himself:

It isn't that, knowing the answers myself, I perplex other people. The truth is rather that I infect them also with the perplexity I feel myself. So with virtue now. I don't know what it is. You may have known before you came into contact with me, but now you look as if you don't. Nevertheless I am

---

[1] Plato, *Meno*, trans. W. K. C. Guthrie, Penguin Books, Baltimore, 1956, 71b, pp. 115–16.
[2] *Ibid.*, 72c, 79d–e, pp. 117, 127.

ready to carry out, together with you, a joint investigation and inquiry into what it is.[3]

But if the teacher doesn't know, how can knowledge come about? Meno asks how one can set something he doesn't know as the object of his search? And furthermore, if one happens to stumble against the object of his search, how will he recognize it? This familiar puzzle does not stop Socrates, nor is it answered at this point. It does, however, point to the necessity for coming to know; and it indicates the possibility that one can come to know something previously unknown to him and not yet known by anyone now living—neither teachers nor learners. Socrates is both a learner and a teacher; he is engaged in teaching himself. He offers a hypothesis to account for the possibility of knowledge:

The soul, since it is immortal and has been born many times, and has seen all things both here and in the other world, has learned everything that is. So we need not be surprised if it can recall the knowledge of virtue or anything else which, as we see, it once possessed. All nature is akin, and the soul has learned everything, so that when a man has recalled a single piece of knowledge—*learned* it, in ordinary language—there is no reason why he should not find out all the rest, if he keeps a stout heart and does not grow weary of the search; for seeking and learning are in fact nothing but recollection.[4]

To demonstrate his notion that there is no such thing as teaching in its usual sense, but only recollection, Socrates calls in a slaveboy who has not studied geometry; and, by asking him questions, leads the boy to discover the theorem of the square on the hypotenuse. In doing so, Socrates takes care not to give instruction or explanation but only to elicit the boy's own opinions. The boy is reminded by the words Socrates uses in such a way that he recollects what his soul has previously learned.

In light of this demonstration, what is virtue? If it is some sort of knowledge, it must be "teachable" in the sense just described, that is, "recollectable." And if virtue is somehow present in the soul—to be learned, to be recollected—then men are not born virtuous; for virtue will come to men, if at all, by a kind of education. Virtuous men are made, not born.

It must be emphasized that Socrates has not come across anyone who really knows what virtue is, nor has he found any teachers of virtue. But he thinks he has found some men with "right opinion," that is, men who believe the truth but do not know it. The point with respect to

---

[3] *Ibid.*, 80c–d, p. 128.
[4] *Ibid.*, 81c–d, pp. 129–30.

right opinion about virtue still does not answer the fundamental question, since one cannot *know* which opinion is the right one without the standard of knowledge. But it suggests at least this: in an existing state of affairs, it is possible for men to act in accordance with virtue, if their opinions are in keeping with what *would be found to be virtue,* if it were known. The fact remains, however, that in the present state of affairs, there is no one wise enough (that is, no one who *knows*) to distinguish truly between "false opinion" and "right opinion."

Can virtue be learned as the square on the hypotenuse was learned? Is knowledge of virtue attainable in such a manner that the same slave-boy, by a Socratic reminding, could recollect the knowledge of virtue which he has in his soul? Socrates' experience has taught him that this knowledge is not so easily demonstrated, and he is not going to surprise us with any sudden answer. The incident of the slaveboy is not to be taken as a model to be imitated for every kind of knowledge. Socrates knows what the theorem of the square on the hypotenuse is, though he does not know what virtue is. And so the hypothesis of recollection does not enable us to answer finally the question of what virtue is. It does enable us to gain an insight into the possibilities of knowledge without telling us what constitutes certain kinds of knowledge. "We shall not understand the truth of the matter until, before asking how men get virtue, we try to understand what virtue is in and by itself."[5]

JUSTICE AS A PART OF VIRTUE

A long discussion of this question, what virtue is in and by itself, and of the conception of education that aims to take us farther along the way toward answering it, is to be found in the *Republic.* This dialogue is central to Plato's treatment of educational theory in two significant ways. First, in it Socrates departs substantially from his role of interrogator and answers the challenge to elaborate his conception of virtue. It will be made clear that Socrates does not become a dogmatic system builder; for, at important junctions in the dialogue, he professes not to know certain answers in a final sense and states that further understanding must wait for another occasion. Second, Plato had Socrates set forth lines of inquiry that could not be settled immediately but would serve as points of departure for discussion in later dialogues. Questions with respect to the nature of knowledge, the kinds of laws proper to a state, the relationships among statesman, Sophist, and philosopher are raised but not finally answered here. In fact, Plato spent a great portion of the rest of his life writing on these subjects.

---

[5] *Ibid.,* 100b, p. 157.

It would be an error to suppose that Plato approached these questions in a didactic manner. With his flair for the dramatic and his sense of the meaning of the dialogue as an educational document, he placed the characters in a position of familiarity with some of his earlier writings and, therefore, ready to press on with the discussion. The discussion begins, in a manner characteristic of the early dialogues, with Socrates eliciting different definitions of justice and disposing of them in turn as it is found that they do not really tell what justice is. But the participants will not allow Socrates to stop after showing how the current views of justice will not do. One of the young men, Adeimantus, concludes a speech by saying to Socrates:

You have agreed that justice belongs to that highest class of good things which are worth having not only for their consequences, but much more for their own sakes—things like sight and hearing, knowledge, and health, whose value is genuine and intrinsic, not dependent on opinion. So I want you, in commending justice, to consider only how justice, in itself, benefits a man who has it in him, and how injustice harms him, leaving rewards and reputation out of account. I might put up with others dwelling on those outward effects as a reason for praising the one and condemning the other; but from you, who have spent your life in the study of this question, I must beg leave to demand something better. You must not be content merely to prove that justice is superior to injustice, but explain how one is good, the other evil, in virtue of the intrinsic effect each has on its possessor, whether gods or men see it or not.[6]

Pedagogically, Adeimantus' challenge marks a significant turning point, not just in the *Republic* but in the development of Plato's thinking about the meaning of virtue and the possibility of knowing it in the course of the dialogues written earlier than the *Republic*. As we have seen, the question of the meaning of virtue in itself is not new to Plato's thought. What is different about the question in the *Republic* is that someone other than Socrates asks it. In other words, not only the conversations in the *Republic* but those in earlier dialogues, with which Adeimantus must have had some acquaintance, remind the young man of something of which he was previously unaware. Adeimantus, by making explicit the question which he needs to ask for the development of his own understanding, is now ready to press the discussion further; the time may be ripe for his mind to be reminded of something else. But what is more, he is challenging Socrates to subject himself to his own method, to try to remind himself by his own words of what is in his mind.

---

[6] Plato, *Republic*, trans. F. M. Cornford, *The Republic of Plato*, Oxford University Press, New York, 1954, 367, pp. 52–3.

It is significant that Adeimantus does not ask Socrates to deliver an oration, as if Socrates knew the answer and simply could tell someone. Rather, Socrates is asked to "step into the breach and carry through our inquiry into the real nature of justice and injustice." Socrates proceeds by first inquiring what justice means in a state and then looking for its counterpart written small in the individual. In the imaginary state he builds, Socrates discusses the kinds of occupations essential to its well-being and the nature of the citizens who will best serve the ends of the occupations. First are the occupations of farming, weaving, shoemaking, building, and others—each trade to be filled by men who are naturally fitted for the particular skill, art, or technique. Then there are those who "keep guard" over the state and who, likewise, are naturally fitted for their particular occupation. It becomes clear at the outset that, for Plato, each citizen must be well educated for his own occupation and must be kept free from the work of other occupations. Early in the building of the imaginary state, Socrates says:

The nature required to make a really noble Guardian of our Commonwealth will be swift and strong, spirited, and philosophic. . . . Given those natural qualities, then, how are these Guardians to be brought up and educated? First, will the answer to that question help the purpose of our whole inquiry, which is to make out how justice and injustice grow up in a state?[7]

And the tentative answer at this point in the inquiry is that the aim of finding out how justice and injustice grow up is to be furthered by an education which finds and develops the natures of those men who carry out the state's occupations. How to build a just state and how to educate citizens in justice are two ways of stating the same problem.

As the discussion proceeds, it becomes imperative that the educative process perform a selective function in order to ascertain the natural fitness of individuals for the necessary occupations of society. Those who guard, the Guardians (earlier described as having both spirited and philosophic natures), are to be divided by rigorous tests in the course of their education so that those whose natures are more philosophic will rule over those having mainly spirited natures. One order—the smallest in number, the Philosophers—is to rule. A second order, the Auxiliaries, is to fight and otherwise carry out the executive decisions of the rulers. A third order, the Craftsmen, is to produce the food, clothing, and shelter, as well as practice various other arts of the state.

Wisdom is the characteristic of the highest order of the state.

If a state is constituted on natural principles, the wisdom it possesses as a whole will be due to the knowledge residing in the smallest part, the one

---

[7] *Ibid.*, 376, p. 66.

which takes the lead and governs the rest. Such knowledge is the only kind that deserves the name of wisdom, and it appears to be ordained by nature that the class privileged to possess it should be the smallest of all.[8]

Courage, "a power of constantly preserving, in accordance with our institutions, the right conviction about the things which ought, or ought not, to be feared,"[9] is the quality of the second order.

A third quality, temperance, is not like wisdom and courage which make the state wise and brave by dominating the character of certain citizens. Rather, it is a characteristic of all citizens, producing a "unanimity or harmonious agreement between the naturally superior and inferior elements on the question which of the two should govern."[10]

It remains to characterize justice, which, as Socrates says, has been under the inquirers' noses all along. Since it has been determined that everyone ought to perform that function in the state suited to his nature, a just society would exist "when each order—tradesman, Auxiliary, Guardian—keeps to its own proper business in the commonwealth and does its own work."[11] And, conversely, when any order attempts to do the work of another order, there is injustice.

And what of justice written small in the individual? One can think of the above-mentioned qualities as existing analogously in the individual. A man is wise if he has "the knowledge of what is good for each of the three elements and for all of them in common,"[12] and so can rule over the others. He is brave if the spirited part of his nature "holds fast to the injunctions of reason about what he ought or ought not to be afraid of."[13] He is temperate if his soul agrees that reason should rule. And justice in the soul, "though evidently analogous to this principle, is not a matter of external behavior, but of the inward self and of attending to all that is, in the fullest sense, a man's proper concern."[14]

It is now becoming evident that Plato used the discussion of the nature of justice to bring Socrates back to (or, more properly, *up to in a different way*) the question remaining at the close of the *Meno*—what is virtue in and by itself? For it becomes increasingly obvious that the conception of justice in the individual—whether gods or men see it or not—is a part, not the whole. For justice, the same as other virtues discussed in the early dialogues, can be likened to courage: *it is a virtue, not virtue in and by itself.*

---

8 *Ibid.*, 428–9, p. 122. 11 *Ibid.*, 434, p. 129. 13 *Ibid.*

9 *Ibid.*, 430, p. 123. 12 *Ibid.*, 442, p. 140. 14 *Ibid.*, 443, pp. 141–2.

10 *Ibid.*, 432, p. 126.

THE MIND AND THE WORLD IT KNOWS

The discussion of justice served as a means for Plato to take aim again at the question of knowledge. The philosopher is to be a wise man and he is to know what is good. What appears to be a rather innocent statement, using common-sense ordinary language about the characteristics of the ruler of a just state, is developed into a more technical discussion of the nature of knowledge itself and of its objects. Socrates introduces a distinction between knowledge, which has as its object the perfectly real, and belief, which is something intermediate between knowledge and ignorance. What are the objects of belief? They are the multitude of things around us in the world of everyday life; they are the objects considered real by men who are unable to agree upon the true conception of justice, courage, beauty, or virtue. One who understands justice solely in terms of his view of the multitude of things, people, and actions involved in daily life only believes. But one who understands justice in terms of his vision of an unchanging reality knows. Most people "believe," but the name "Philosopher" is reserved for those who "know." One is reminded of the introduction in the *Meno* of the notion of right opinion—the power of believing the truth but not knowing it. Some may come to have right opinions, that is, beliefs which happen to agree with knowledge. But Plato was not satisfied with right belief. He wanted *to know*; this was a way of saying he thought that philosophers, by knowing a certain kind of object, could distinguish between false belief and right belief.

Plato made a distinction "between the multiplicity of things that we call good or beautiful or whatever it may be and, on the other hand, Goodness itself or Beauty itself and so on."

He explained:

Corresponding to each of these sets of many things, we postulate a single Form or real essence, as we call it . . . the many things, we say, can be seen, but are not objects of rational thought [they are objects of belief]; whereas the Forms are objects of rational thought, but invisible.[15]

By now, meaning has been gained for Socrates' aim to know what virtue is, in and by itself. The previous suggestion, that we shall not know the separate virtues until we know that object by which they can be recognized as one, now shifts ground somewhat by postulating an object of knowledge "corresponding" to each virtue. In this sense, the possibility of knowing each virtue is held forth. Even so, the earlier

---

[15] *Ibid.*, 507, pp. 217–8.

hungering for "virtue in and by itself" still remains though now expressed as a Form, the Form of the Good, or Goodness itself.

Plato pointed out:

This, then, which gives to the objects of knowledge their truth and to him who knows them his power of knowing, is the Form or essential nature of Goodness. It is the cause of knowledge and truth; and so, while you may think of it as an object of knowledge, you will do well to regard it as something beyond truth and knowledge and, precious as these both are, of still higher worth.[16]

Thus, to know the Form of Goodness is the ultimate objective of the philosopher.

Since knowledge of the Good will come, if at all, only after a long, arduous, educational process (good men are made, not born), one objective of education is to produce philosophers who know the Form of the Good. Those who have in their souls the capacity to remember the Form of the Good must have the kind of education that will "teach" them to remind themselves in order to recollect it.

Further distinctions of meaning made by Plato, concerning kinds of objects of the mind, can serve as a point of departure for examining the kind of education Plato thought would develop men's minds. Plato divided the world of objects into two orders of things, the visible order and the intelligible order. He then divided the visible order into two sections, images, such as shadows or reflections in polished surfaces, and actual things, mainly things in the everyday world that have images, such as animals or trees. The intelligible order was likewise divided into two sections. In one of these "the mind uses as images those actual things which themselves had images in the visible world; and it is compelled to pursue its inquiry by starting from assumptions and traveling, not up to a principle, but down to a conclusion."[17] For example, students of geometry begin with postulates and adopt them as assumptions. These assumptions, taken as self-evident, are used to arrive at conclusions. The point of the investigation is not to prove the assumptions but to use them in establishing proofs. And he explained the other division of the intelligible order thus:

By the second section of the intelligible world you may understand me to mean all that unaided reasoning apprehends by the power of dialectic, when it treats its assumptions, not as first principles, but as *hypotheses* in the literal sense, things "laid down" like a flight of steps up which it may mount all the way to something that is not hypothetical, the first principle of all; and having grasped this, may turn back and, holding on to the con-

---

[16] *Ibid.*, 508, p. 220.   [17] *Ibid.*, 510, p. 224.

sequences which depend upon it, descend at last to a conclusion, never making use of any sensible object, but only of Forms, moving through Forms
from one to another, and ending with Forms.[18]

Plato used the following terms to represent states of mind corresponding to the objects in the four sections: imagining, belief, thinking, and
intelligence or knowledge. Quite literally, the mind imagines with respect
to images, believes with respect to things, thinks with respect to postulated assumptions, and "intelligences" (knows) Forms. However, this is
at best suggestive rather than axiomatic, and one must not limit Plato's
meaning by restricting oneself literally to Plato's examples. Plato meant
that as the mind moves from imagination toward intelligence, it moves
from lower to higher degrees of certainty and clarity in correspondence
with the degrees of certainty and clarity possessed by the mind's objects.
He seems to mean that the possibility of true knowledge is the possibility of having knowledge of Goodness itself. In coming to knowledge,
one's mind would have passed through the lesser degrees of certainty
and clarity with respect to its objects. Only a man of worldly experience
can hope to rise to a knowledge of Forms, which are eternal, changeless,
timeless, and spaceless; a knowledge of Forms is possible only to those
who have learned in the everyday world about those objects which
change, are of time, and are in space.

THE PHILOSOPHER'S QUEST FOR WISDOM

Imagination and belief are states of mind that accept appearances. They
are characteristic of people who lack the quality of justice and are less
certain than they believe themselves to be. Even thinking, a process less
uncertain of its objects than imagining and believing, can deceive if the
thinker tries to make more of the objects than is appropriate to them.
Thus, all states of mind, except knowing, are susceptible to misuse if they
exist in persons who lack justice. Plato was far from being critical of
imagining and believing, let alone thinking, when the state of mind is
performing its proper function. Each has a function, and that function
is just what it is. Injustice results, not from any shortcomings in the
functions themselves but from malfunctioning when people try to make
imagination, or belief, or thinking attend to something other than its
proper concern, or to do something not in its nature.

Plato's criticism of the Sophists, the professional teachers of his day,
was aimed mainly at their claims to teach virtue rather than at the inherent nature of the subjects taught. By pretending that they knew when

---

[18] *Ibid.*, 511, pp. 225–6.

they did not know, by pretending wisdom when they were not wise, the Sophists were making false claims. In a later dialogue, the *Sophist*, Plato defined characteristics of various Sophists. There were the hired hunters, the merchants, the retail dealers, and the makers and sellers of information, such as the lecturers on rhetoric and other advanced subjects who "sold" their alleged knowledge and the arts of getting along in life. In Plato's day, as in ours, there was no shortage of Sophists who made a business of selling all sorts of arts of living, often making extravagant claims for their powers to have the buyer become wise, good, happy, or at least prosperous. Then there were the eristics, those contentious Sophists who argued for the sake of victory and not for truth. (Socrates' questioning was not eristic according to Plato.) But the characteristic of Sophists identifying the fundamental spirit of their work and constituting the essence of Sophistry is the inability to distinguish appearance from reality. This inability has the effect of falsely claiming that there is a wisdom in imagination, belief, and thinking, whereas it is only in genuine knowledge that wisdom can be attained. It is no injustice to imagine, to believe, and to think; but it is injustice for persons with these states of mind to pretend to know, and this is the injustice of Sophistry.

Although the Forms are the only genuine objects of knowledge, and are the highest in the order of objects of the mind, it should be emphasized that Forms are not the only objects worthy of men's attention, in Plato's way of thinking. Plato did not deny the place of other goods in men's lives, although the highest good attainable was held to be knowledge of the Form of the Good, Goodness itself. In fact, even for those who may have it in their souls to know the Form of the Good (the potential philosophers), that knowledge will come only after an active life of imagining, believing, and thinking. In educational development, these three activities of body and mind occur prior to the functioning of intelligence. Activities of imagining, believing, and thinking are necessary means to the ultimate end of philosophers, the activity of knowing.

While the pedagogical thinking expressed in the *Republic* is aimed explicitly at the education of those whose gradual successes in passing the rigorous tests of the curriculum seem to qualify them as philosopher-candidates, it must not be supposed that Plato would neglect the education of the Auxiliaries and the Craftsmen. Not only the childhood education described in the *Republic*, with which all children would enter the selective process, but much of what Plato said about the kinds of education involving imagining, believing, and thinking would be relevant to the education of those citizens in the state other than philosophers.

Since there can be no guarantee that anyone will, in fact, become a true philosopher in the full sense of knowing Goodness itself, there remains the possibility that no effort of the mind will enable it to rise above the level of thinking. It is definitely in the realm of possibility that no prospective philosopher will become an actual philosopher. And even if he did so, he could not convey his knowledge to the world of everyday life, for his knowledge would be of Forms which are not thought, believed, or imagined, but truly known. The essential nature of Forms makes them peculiarly free from thinking, believing, and imagining: as a knower of Forms, a philosopher does not think, believe, or imagine, but really *knows*.

Granting the possibility of producing a philosopher, Plato was not content to let him remain apart from objects of appearance—the things which come into being and pass away. He is somehow to use his wisdom in ruling over the predominantly spirited and appetitive life of the state. The philosopher—who has learned to turn the gaze of his soul away from images, things, and, perhaps, even from postulated assumptions, in order to fulfill his just function in the state—must come back with the fruits of his wisdom to rule among the objects that his long, arduous education has enabled him finally to escape. Plato cautioned:

The law is not concerned to make any one class specially happy, but to ensure the welfare of the commonwealth as a whole. By persuasion or constraint it will unite the citizens in harmony, making them share whatever benefits each class can contribute to the common good; and its purpose in forming men of that spirit was not that each should be left to go his own way, but that they should be instrumental in binding the community into one.[19]

The definition of justice in the state and in the individual has now taken on a further dimension of meaning: attending to one's proper nature turns out to be a rigorous disciplining of one's soul to the requirements demanded by that nature. The philosopher finds that he has learned to look beyond the world of appearance in order that he may return to it with the knowledge gained in his quest. Now, by virtue of having known Goodness itself, he can ascertain which are the right opinions. He now knows, rather than merely believes, or even thinks, what is the truth of any matter. He knows and in so knowing is virtuous.

Plato was unable to define the Form of Goodness. Words could not explain its nature. Plato turned to images, allegories, and myths that might serve to remind the soul of Forms, if Forms were in the soul to be recollected and if one's soul were at the proper stage of its develop-

---

[19] *Ibid.*, 519–20, p. 234.

ment to be reminded by images, words, things, or postulates. In the *Republic*, as formerly in the *Meno* with "virtue in and by itself," Plato could not explain a Form in the sense that one can explain the theorem of the square on the hypotenuse. The analogy between mathematical objects and other objects of thinking, on the one hand, and the Forms as objects of knowing, on the other hand, is at best suggestive. The very nature of Forms forbids their being really known by any of the customary states of mind—even by thinking, which uses postulates.

Is it necessary to restrict the objects of thinking to mathematical ones, which were to Plato the best models for thought? In the *Republic*, a rigorous and long study in mathematics is required in the higher education imagined for prospective philosophers; and it is historically true that Plato prized the study of mathematics in his school, the Academy. But Plato did not explicitly deny the possibility that subjects other than mathematics could be objects of thought. Surely it is possible, in Plato's way of thinking, to include rhetoric, literature, Socratic discussions, and other arts as subjects appropriate for thought, rather than only for belief and imagination. Although these other arts have not achieved the beauty of precision possessed by geometry, they stand above mere acceptance of belief or seeing of images. To interpret Plato most suggestively would be to recognize that many subjects have possibilities for thought. An essential aim of education is to raise such subjects above the state of mere acceptance to a consideration of the consequences of viewing them first in one way and then in another. It is obvious that his own dialogues are models illustrating the possibility of learning by discussion. Things take on different meanings according to the contexts in which they are stated; or, to put it another way, different meanings arise as different contexts become possible and then actual.

To those who think that there is an easy way or a short route to genuine growth of the mind, Plato would reply that there is a great deal of catharsis in the kind of discussion characteristic of Socrates, discussion in which the soul expels what is worse in order that it may get ready to recollect what is better and ultimately learns to distinguish false opinion from true opinion. There is a passage near the end of the *Theaetetus* incomparable for its demonstration of the value of a certain kind of failure. In this dialogue Socrates and young Theaetetus attempt at great length to define knowledge. But failure is freely admitted:

S: Are we in labour, then, with any further child, my friend, or have we brought to birth all we have to say about knowledge?

T: Indeed we have; and for my part I have already, thanks to you, given utterance to more than I had in me.

S: All of which our midwife's skill pronounces to be mere wind-eggs and not worth the rearing?

T: Undoubtedly.

S: Then supposing you should ever henceforth try to conceive afresh, Theaetetus, if you succeed, your embryo thoughts will be the better as a consequence of to-day's scrutiny; and if you remain barren, you will be gentler and more agreeable to your companions, having the good sense not to fancy you know what you do not know. For that, and no more, is all that my art can effect; nor have I any of that knowledge possessed by all the great and admirable men of our own day or of the past. But this midwife's art is a gift from heaven; my mother had it for women, and I for young men of a generous spirit and for all in whom beauty dwells.[20]

Failure of this kind, as it was pointed out with respect to Socrates' inquiry in the early dialogues, does not necessarily mean ultimate failure. Purging one's soul of "wind-eggs not worth the rearing" helps open up the soul to further inquiry. At the same time, however, the success of further inquiry does not necessarily follow. Whether or not success comes depends on what is in one's soul to recollect and on the power of the art brought to bear in the inquiry. It may come to pass that one will have only wind-eggs or it may be that future eggs will be fertile. The viability of one's conception will be for experience to determine— an experience of inquiry. One should not fear the consequences of further inquiry, even though it takes courage to "hold fast to the injunctions of reason about what he ought or ought not to be afraid of." One needs courage if he genuinely inquires, as much if he is able to come to knowledge as if he is only able to think. The only imperative is to continue inquiry—it is false to suppose that the consequences can be understood ahead of the inquiry yielding them.

Will anyone come to knowledge of the Good, according to Plato? Since to answer this question would be to presume to know prior to the very inquiry necessary for one to come to know (or for one not to come to know), Plato went only so far as to say that the plan for education in the *Republic*, if practicable, would be the best. He said, "Our institutions would be the best, if they could be realized, and to realize them, though hard, is not impossible."[21] The courage called for, then, is the courage to proceed in inquiry, the highest outcome of which cannot be guaranteed, with the possibility held forth for producing a philosopher— one who knows the Good.

[20] Plato, *Theaetetus*, trans. F. M. Cornford, *Plato's Theory of Knowledge*, The Liberal Arts Press, New York, 1957, 210b–d, p. 163.
[21] Plato, *Republic*, op. cit., 502, p. 211.

EDUCATION FOR JUSTICE

It is appropriate here to consider the course of education proposed by Plato that might possibly produce Philosophers and, for justice in the state and in the individual, must produce Auxiliaries and Craftsmen. If achieved, justice written small in the soul of each citizen would function as follows:

It will be the business of reason to rule with wisdom and forethought on behalf of the entire soul; while the spirited element ought to act as its subordinate and ally. The two will be brought into accord, as we said earlier, by that combination of mental and bodily training which will tune up one string of the instrument and relax the other, nourishing the reasoning part on the study of noble literature and allaying the other's wildness by harmony and rhythm. When both have been thus nurtured and trained to know their own true functions, they must be set in command over the appetites, which form the greater part of each man's soul and are by nature insatiably covetous. They must keep watch lest this part, by battening on the pleasures that are called bodily, should grow so great and powerful that it will no longer keep to its own work, but will try to enslave the others and usurp a dominion to which it has no right, thus turning the whole of life upside down.[22]

Plato would begin childhood education with storytelling, including legends, myths, and narratives in poetry and prose. Since the stories used are to begin molding character, many existing stories will not do, for they mislead young minds by such devices as presenting gods as wicked. Stories appropriate to the emotional nature of children should be written to replace these. Plato said, "The first principle to which all must conform in speech or writing is that heaven is not responsible for everything, but only for what is good."[23] Those authors who willfully practice deception would not be allowed to publish; the only ones allowed to practice deception are the rulers acting for the benefit of the state. In dramatic studies children are to be prevented from playing several parts, for in Plato's state people should not try to be jacks of all trades— instead, they are to learn well the one task they are fitted for by nature. In music, also, the works expressing images of noble character are to be used for cultivating grace of body and mind.

The end in view in all works of literature and music is to present the soul with whatever is most lovely and gracious—the noblest images of beauty and form apprehensible by children's emotions—in order to arouse the noblest elements of the soul to imitate them. Although the

[22] *Ibid.*, 441–2, p. 140.   [23] *Ibid.*, 380, p. 72.

images and forms used by poets and musicians are far removed from the Forms which are objects of knowledge, and can be likened to the shadows and mirror-images discussed earlier as objects of imagination, their educational function is to serve as a reminder for the souls of children, opening them up to the possibilities of beauty therein. To cultivate the emotions and the senses in preparation for their next higher stages, childhood subject matter is not selected from the highest stages of the mind's possibilities, because the plan is to find objects appropriate to each stage of development.

There is a sense in which physical education is musical, in that it harmonizes the ferocious quality with the gentleness in children's natures. Thus, physical education, properly carried out, is not only of the body but also of the soul. And music, since it influences the soul's tendencies toward acting in different ways, is not only of the soul but also of the body. Activity of the soul and of the body and harmony of the body and of the soul are means to the end of developing the spirited and philosophic elements of the soul. Plato put it this way:

There are, then, these two elements in the soul, the spirited and the philosophic; and it is for their sake, as I should say, and not (except incidentally) for the sake of soul and body, that heaven has given to mankind those two branches of education [physical training and music]. The purpose is to bring the two elements into tune with one another by adjusting the tension of each to the right pitch. So one who can apply to the soul both kinds of education blended in perfect proportion will be master of a nobler sort of musical harmony than was ever made by tuning the strings of the lyre.[24]

Childhood education, consisting mainly of literature, music, and physical training, is to perform the selective function of determining which children appear to have the abilities to become Guardians. At about the age of twenty, after further physical and military training, young people will be given rigorous tests in an effort to find those who appear to have the abilities to be educated for the occupation of Philosopher-ruler. Those deemed worthy will be educated intensively in mathematics for ten years, since mathematical subjects are models of the purest thought—that is, of the thought that is farthest removed from imagination and belief. Plato conceived astronomy and harmonics as branches of pure mathematics and as peculiarly appropriate to the mathematical education. To understand Plato's attempt to reach knowledge beyond any dependence upon shadows and material things, one should recognize that Plato's fascination with mathematics is related to its nonempirical nature. Mathematics is not a discipline attempting study of the sensible world of observation and experiment; instead, it

---

[24] *Ibid.*, 411-2, pp. 101–102.

works with axioms and postulates accepted by reason alone and having
no necessary bearing on things of the sensible world. Yet, to think, to
discipline the mind with mathematical objects, is not the highest end
for the prospective philosophers, just as the study of harmonics is also a
means and not a final end. Plato said, "I would rather call it a 'useful'
study; but useful only when pursued as a means to the knowledge of
beauty and goodness."[25] F. M. Cornford explained, "Each mathematical
science is a separate chain of deductive reasoning, self-consistent but not
linked at the upper end to any absolutely self-evident and unconditioned
principle."[26]

And so, after ten years of discipline in mathematics, there will be
another selection of those who can rise above mathematical reasoning
to the highest study of all—dialectic. For five years, these prospective
philosophers are to engage in procedures with the aim of acquiring
knowledge of Forms. We may suppose that something like the Socratic
method suggests the meaning of dialectic: "hypothetical" attempts are
made at defining Forms and rendering an account of the definitions,
and this rendering is amended by further questioning, and so on and on.
Again, Plato could give a detailed account that can be understood; but,
as with the difficulty in rendering intelligible the Form of Goodness
itself, his inability is understandable. By its very nature, the end sought
by dialectic is beyond the world in which things are only understood,
and thus, any attempt at *understanding* dialectic will necessarily miss its
mark. In talking about the method of dialectic, Plato restated the notion
discussed earlier in connection with genuine knowledge. He said that
dialectic is a method that does away with assumptions (as in pure mathematics) and travels to the first principle of all; one who can do this
would have an account of the essence of each thing. Of a dialectician,
he said:

He must be able to distinguish the essential nature of Goodness, isolating it
from all other Forms; he must fight his way through all criticisms, determined to examine every step by the standard, not of appearances and opinions, but of reality and truth, and win through to the end without sustaining
a fall. If he cannot do this, he will know neither Goodness itself nor any
good thing; if he does lay hold upon some semblance of good, it will be
only a matter of belief, not of knowledge.[27]

The prospective philosophers, after the five years of education in the
method of dialectic, are to gain practical experience for about fifteen
years in public service. Then, at the age of fifty, the best among them, it

---

25 *Ibid.*, 531, p. 250.
26 F. M. Cornford, *The Republic of Plato, op. cit.*, p. 251.
27 Plato, *Republic, op. cit.*, 534, p. 255.

is hoped, will reach the Form of the Good. It is then that the rulers will have become Philosophers. In the meantime, those whose nature it is to be auxiliaries will have become Auxiliaries; and those whose nature it is to be craftsmen will have become Craftsmen. And when all this will have come to pass, there will be justice written large in the state and written small in each citizen.

PLATO'S PARADOX

There is a paradox in Plato's thought. It appears in the early dialogues as the possibility of a teacher's teaching what he does not know and in the *Republic* as the possibility of a philosopher-ruler's having knowledge not found in the world he is to rule. These discussions relate to the difficulties of understanding the objects of dialectic and of defining the Form of Goodness itself. The paradox appears to be resolved only by conceiving the nature of a philosopher-ruler as beyond our usual conceptions of understanding and definition. Analogously, in earlier dialogues teaching was conceived as something other than the usual concept of the art. Yet, the resolution of this paradox is apparent and not real. Or perhaps one should say that the resolution could come about only in the real world, not in the one which appears, and that is the paradox. Unless men become godlike, that is, unless they participate in the reality of Forms, there will not be justice; but—and this is an all-important qualification—to become more nearly god-like, they must go beyond the world of beliefs and imaginings of ordinary men.

As has been pointed out, Plato was so completely an inquirer that he could not guarantee that a genuine philosopher would emerge, and would go only so far as to say that producing one was not impossible. In the *Laws*, his last work, he took seriously the alternative possibility that no philosopher-ruler would be developed, and described a "second-best" state. In a passage in the *Laws* evidently referring to the state described in the *Republic*, Plato wrote:

That State and polity come first, and those laws are best . . . As to this condition,—whether it anywhere exists now, or ever will exist . . . no one will ever lay down another definition that is truer or better than these conditions in point of super-excellence. In such a State,—be it gods or sons of gods that dwell in it,—they dwell pleasantly . . . Wherefore one should not look elsewhere for a model constitution, but hold fast to this one, and with all one's power seek the constitution that is as like to it as possible.[28]

[28] Plato, *Laws*, trans. R. G. Bury, Harvard University Press, Cambridge, 1952, 739c–e, I, p. 363.

And he went on to say that the state to be discussed in the *Laws* "would be very near to immortality"—that is, would be second in order of excellence to a state where either men become gods or gods come down to dwell among men. He proposed, also, to investigate the nature of a third-best state but did not live to do this.

What all this means as to Plato's methodology is not that he gave up the ideals for education set forth in the *Republic* but, rather, that he was proposing a different educational program for a situation in which realization appeared unlikely for certain of those ideals. And he was willing to propose yet another program for a third kind of situation. In terms of the method of inquiry for which his dialogues are models, the discourse in the *Republic* suggests certain possibilities and the means necessary to realize them. If one considers other possibilities—for instance, that a particular situation in the world of appearance is unlikely to produce a philosopher-ruler—then one would need means suited to *its* ends. Viewed specifically in terms of the second-best state, in the *Laws*, the means will be those needed to approximate justice. Plato said, "Education is the process of drawing and guiding children towards that principle which is pronounced right by the law and confirmed as truly right by the experience of the oldest and the most just."[29] What is confirmed as right "by the experience of the oldest and the most just" is wisdom in its highest sense—knowledge of the Good—only if the oldest and most just have become divine, that is, have achieved knowledge of the Good. But that which makes a state second-best is lack of knowledge of the Good. In admitting the possibility of states wherein the most just remain in the world of thought in order to approximate perfection without achieving it, Plato was admitting that men of thought must take responsibility for proposing educational plans for second-best, third-best, and, within the realm of possibility, others as well. Although Plato thought a knowledge of reality would make one truly a philosopher, he did not back away from the task of inquiring into the nature of images, things, and objects of thought, and was able to face the possibility that these could be the only objects achievable in a particular state.

Plato lacked a conception of the way in which change comes about. And so the states described by him—the best one of the *Republic* as well as the second-best one of the *Laws*—devote much attention to censoring the work of poets and stamping out the efforts of those who might question the existing order of things. The rulers are absolute in their judgments and unyielding in their answers to questions. Whether in a truly just state ruled by a philosopher who knows, or in a second-

---

29 *Ibid.*, 659d, p. 111.

best state ruled by elderly wise men who only approximate knowledge, the effect is virtually the same. The rulers are to act *as if* they have the wisdom to account for everything, a wisdom taking itself to be god-like. Acting as if they have such wisdom, the rulers try to prevent change of any kind. On the assumption that the existing state is perfect, as is the best state, or on the assumption that the existing state is as close to perfection as its nature allows, as is the second-best state, any departure from the existing situation can only be bad. The result is a subordination of everything to the conception of good held by the rulers.

R. G. Bury's comments about the *Laws* are apt:

[Plato] constantly insists on the entire subordination of the individual to the State, on the principle (which holds throughout the universe) that no *part* is independent, but every part exists for the sake of its whole. . . . The average citizen is given but little freedom, except the freedom to obey. . . . The saying vox *populi*, vox *dei* is, for Plato, the supreme lie.[30]

The second-best state, as seen in the *Laws*, would be a theocracy in which the laws would invoke the opinion of the rulers derived from their conception of the Good. The opinions of the rulers would be expressed as though they were conceptions of the Good—as though they knew the way God measures things. Plato declared, "In our eyes God will be 'the measure of all things' in the highest degree—a degree much higher than is any 'man' they talk of."[31] In this allusion to Protagoras, with his view that man is the measure of all things, Plato took a whack at the Sophist, warning any citizen of the second-best state not to be tempted in the direction of impiety by supposing that ordinary men might be able to give an account of things.

The intention here is not to dwell on the nondemocratic character of the states Plato described. Nor is it a claim that there is a contradiction between the suggestiveness of Plato's educational methodology and the conclusions he reached. Rather, it is partly to show how, by special use of his methodology, Plato did reach certain conclusions, among which are the preference for changlessness and the educational proposals reflecting that preference. The intention here is also to ask whether another person employing the Platonic method of inquiry will necessarily arrive at the particular results gained by Plato. Since Plato's own thinking took place in a context, it is subject to limitations that are inherently contextual and make any thinking subject to the requirements of particular times and places. However much Plato sought to attain principles enabling him to reason unhampered by the merely empirical character of his own time and place, it does not necessarily follow that one using

---

[30] *Ibid.*, xiii, xv–xvi.   [31] *Ibid.*, 716c, p. 295.

Plato's method of inquiry in different times and places would arrive at Plato's results. On the contrary, since the terms of inquiry are different according to particular times and places, one could expect different consequences—if the inquiry were genuine. It is possible, therefore, to treat Plato's writings as suggesting, fundamentally, a method of inquiry; it is possible, also, to see them as offering certain doctrines. The contention here is that Plato's greatest contribution to the history of educational thought lies in the method of inquiry, and that the suggestiveness of his method offers more genuine alternatives to the possibilities of men's activities of the soul than do the particular conclusions reached by Plato himself. Indeed, it would be an example of the worst kind of sophistry to treat the thinking of Plato as though its results were necessarily the highest wisdom; perhaps no greater injustice to Plato's thought could be rendered.

DIALECTIC—THE ART OF SELF-EDUCATION

What remains is to make explicit a central meaning in Plato's educational writings—his belief that the problems of men could be dealt with by education. By this it is meant that education is a process in which various subjects are taught, and that whatever passes for imagination, belief, thought, and knowledge can come into being only if there is a genuine education. Education is a process that creates its subject matter. Men literally subject themselves to matter that enables the process to go on. Plato's theory of knowledge, political theory, psychology, ethical theory, and theology can be seen as subjects developed within a context of primarily educational questions.

Werner Jaeger argued that in the *Republic* the highest virtue of the state is education. He claimed that the interpretation of a distinguished historian of philosophy, who thought Plato's discussion of education in the *Republic* was a pretext for displaying Plato's philosophy, is a common misunderstanding of the centrality of educational problems in Plato's thought. Jaeger pointed to this historical context in which the misunderstanding arose:

Philosophy and scholarship had soared too high above the scholasticism of the humanists, and had come to despise all "pedagogy" so arrogantly that they forgot their own origins. . . . philosophers were now incapable of realizing the scope [the problem of education] had had in Plato's day and in the classical period generally—when it was the center of all spiritual life and the source of all the deepest significance of human existence.[32]

---

[32] *Paideia: The Ideals of Greek Culture*, trans. Gilbert Highet, Oxford University Press, New York, 1943, II, p. 200.

John Dewey made essentially the same point in writing, "It is suggestive that European philosophy originated (among the Athenians) under the direct pressure of educational questions."[33] And, with reference to Plato's thought, Dewey wrote:

It would be impossible to find in any scheme of philosophic thought a more adequate recognition on one hand of the educational significance of social arrangements and, on the other, of the dependence of those arrangements upon the means used to educate the young. It would be impossible to find a deeper sense of the function of education in discovering and developing personal capacities, and training them so that they would connect with the activities of others.[34]

All this is a way of illustrating how Plato's thinking was aimed, fundamentally, at educational ends, with the consequence that a variety of means was developed. And it was as a conception of education that these means, including the subject which came to be called philosophy, were developed. This is quite different, historically and psychologically, from deducing implications for education from a philosophical position held independently of educational problems. To understand the educational means that were developed, one must take them as hypotheses or as points of departure for the development of further meanings.

Plato's dialogues are educational in this sense: they are not presented as treatises claiming to have final answers for the questions raised. Pedagogically, they are examples of an educational method, a dialectic. Philosophically, they set forth a way of thinking that has a development of its own. The dialogues, then, stand as a way of treating educational questions as well as of providing for a certain growth in the understanding of those questions. As has been said above, it would be an injustice to the spirit of Plato's pedagogic methodology to take his results as dogmatic doctrine that could be learned, in the absence of a dialectical development, by the one who is coming to understand.

Plato was well aware of the limitations of written and spoken words when the art of dialectic is lacking. Both the grammarian and the rhetorician, if lacking in the dialectic art, fall short of what a teacher might be. In the *Phaedrus* Plato tells a myth of how the god Theuth invented the art of writing and took it to the king Ammon, saying that it would provide a recipe for memory and wisdom. But the king, not so enthusiastic about the possibilities of the art of writing, says:

If men learn this, it will implant forgetfulness in their souls: they will cease to exercise memory because they rely on that which is written, calling things

---

33 John Dewey, *Democracy and Education*, The Macmillan Company, New York, 1916, p. 385.   34 *Ibid.*, p. 104.

to remembrance no longer from within themselves, but by means of external marks; what you have discovered is a recipe not for memory, but for reminder. And it is no true wisdom that you offer your disciples, but only its semblance; for by telling them of many things without teaching them you will make them seem to know much, while for the most part they know nothing; and as men filled, not with wisdom, but with the conceit of wisdom, they will be a burden to their fellows.[35]

Written discourse, like any other semblance of wisdom, cannot guarantee that wisdom will come about. The sort of discourse that is of unquestioned legitimacy is "the sort that goes together with knowledge, and is written in the soul of the learner: that can defend itself, and knows to whom it should speak and to whom it should say nothing."[36] What finally can be relied upon is neither the written nor the spoken word but, Plato said:

. . . the serious treatment of them, which employs the art of dialectic. The dialectician selects a soul of the right type, and in it he plants and sows his words founded on knowledge, words which can defend both themselves and him who planted them, words which instead of remaining barren contain a seed whence new words grow up in new characters; whereby the seed is vouchsafed immortality, and its possessor the fullest measure of blessedness that man can attain unto.[37]

Thus, it is by a method akin to dialectic that a teacher uses words so that students may remind themselves of what is in them to be thought, and, for some, to be known. Whether one can only think or whether one can know, as well, cannot be determined prior to the dialectic by which one learns to think and, perhaps, to know. A teacher of dialectic is also a student, since one who thinks engages in discourse with himself and may remind both himself and others by the words he uses. And a student is also a teacher, since the words he uses may remind both others and himself. No matter what means may be placed before one by others and by oneself, the inward beauty and justice and goodness will be found, if at all, by an activity of the mind that grasps the means in such a manner that one is reminded of ends not previously envisaged—in some sense they were previously there but not in the way they were eventually found. And so each grasping affords one the leverage for carrying the dialectic farther, for finding justice in one's soul, and for continuing to educate oneself.

---

[35] Plato, *Phaedrus*, trans. R. Hackforth, *Plato's Phaedrus*, The Liberal Arts Press, New York, n.d., 275a–b, p. 157.
[36] *Ibid.*, 276a, p. 159.   [37] *Ibid.*, 276e–277a, p. 160.

BIBLIOGRAPHICAL NOTE

Plato's most important work on education is the *Republic*. F. M. Cornford's translation, *The Republic of Plato*, published by Oxford University Press, New York, in 1954, is nearer to the modern idiom than most; this volume has an introduction to Plato's life and times as well as interpretive notes. Another quite readable translation is H. D. P. Lee's *Plato: The Republic*, published by Penguin Books, Baltimore, in 1962, also with an introduction and notes. Other dialogues of particular value to the student of education are the *Protagoras*, *Gorgias*, and *Meno*. In addition, the *Laws* may be consulted for a statement of Plato's thinking on education late in his life: R. G. Bury's translation in the Loeb Classical Library includes in its introduction a brief analysis of the dialogue. A somewhat advanced student might well consider Plato's discussion of knowledge in the *Theaetetus* and *Sophist*. F. M. Cornford's translation of these, with a lengthy analysis and interpretation, is *Plato's Theory of Knowledge*, published by The Liberal Arts Press, New York, in 1957.

One of the fundamental studies of Greek culture, putting Plato's educational thought in the context in which it arose, is Werner Jaeger's *Paideia: The Ideals of Greek Culture*, translated by Gilbert Highet, published in three volumes by Oxford University Press, New York, in 1943 and 1944. Volumes II and III discuss Plato's educational dialogues at length. The work by Richard Lewis Nettleship, *The Theory of Education in the Republic of Plato*, published by University of Chicago Press, Chicago, in 1906, has long been valuable for students of its topic. See Chapter VI in H. I. Marrou, *A History of Education in Antiquity*, translated by George Lamb, published by Sheed and Ward, New York, in 1956, for a discussion of Plato as one of the masters of the classical tradition in education. John Dewey's discussions of Plato's educational thought, though brief, are insightful and suggestive. See Dewey's *Democracy and Education*, published by The Macmillan Company, New York, in 1916, pages 102 to 106, and "Plato" in *Cyclopedia of Education* (edited by Paul Monroe), published by The Macmillan Company, New York, in 1918, Volume IV, pages 722 to 725. For works of wider scope not aimed mainly at Plato's educational thought, see A. E. Taylor, *Plato: The Man and His Work*, seventh edition, published by Methuen, London, in 1960, and G. M. A. Grube, *Plato's Thought*, published by Beacon Press, Boston, in 1958. The latter includes a chapter on education. The student who wishes to read a critical appraisal of Plato is referred to Karl R. Popper, *The Open Society and Its Enemies*, published by G. Routledge & Sons, London, in 1945, in which Plato is viewed as one of the enemies of an open society.

✿ ISOCRATES (436–338 B.C.) was the fourth of the famous ten Attic orators. The son of a wealthy proprietor of a flute manufactory in Athens, Isocrates received an excellent education, numbering Protagoras, Gorgias and Socrates among his teachers. In the calamitous years that closed the Peloponnesian War his family's wealth was lost. As a means of earning a livelihood Isocrates turned to composing forensic speeches for others. His own weak voice and bashfulness prevented him from taking part in public life. After having taught rhetoric at Chiòs (probably about 404 B.C.), he returned to Athens in 403. For the next ten years he wrote occasional speeches for the law courts, although he claimed to have despised this branch of his work. In 392 B.C. he founded his famous school near the Lyceum, where, for the rest of his life, he attracted students from the entire Greek-speaking world and gained for himself considerable wealth. Isocrates kept himself completely aloof from any personal share in the public life of his day, but he attempted to influence the political world by a series of rhetorical declamations intended primarily to be read rather than delivered. The dominant subject of his public writings was the policy of uniting Greece in a concerted attack on Asia. Isocrates died a few days after the battle of Chaeronea. He is said to have died of voluntary starvation because of his despair at the downfall of Greek liberty. There were sixty compositions bearing his name known to antiquity, but only twenty-one have come down to us. The two orations *Against the Sophists* and *Antidosis* contain his conception of the training of an orator. His most famous political orations are *Panegyricus, Areopagiticus,* and *Panathenaicus;* this last he composed in his ninety-eighth year.

2

THE ORATOR: *Isocrates*

BY COSTAS M. PROUSSIS

Greece, during the long lifetime of Isocrates, experienced great political and social changes affecting her cultural and moral climate and, consequently, her educational attitude. Successive internal wars—the long Peloponnesian War (431–404 B.C.) and many shorter ones during the fourth century—undermined the power of the city-state. At the same time, these conflicts brought about financial and social upheavals with sad results for individual life and for national behavior. Political instability led to social discontent, which, in turn, created new and difficult problems for which the individual was unprepared. In his struggle for self-assertion the individual sought to escape from his adversity by turning to his inner self or by concentrating on personal satisfactions alone. Earlier the individual had regulated his actions according to the aims of the city-state, but now he became more inclined to neglect his city duties, to pursue his own personal needs and ends, and to try to find his own way amidst conflicting beliefs and tendencies. This, of course, produced no solution; on the contrary, it created a vicious circle of new problems and complications in the political, social, intellectual, and moral aspects of life. It was at this point that education could enter and fill the vacuum. Indeed, during the fourth century Greek education responded to the changing conditions of the times and developed progressively to attain its mature and final form, moving out of the confines of the city-state to become universal.

Educational trends toward that end had started primarily in Athens in the second half of the fifth century B.C. with the advent of the Sophists. These men were itinerant teachers who professed to teach everything for a fee, especially how to become successful in the conduct of life. Oratory was almost always included among the subjects of instruction, since excellence in oratory was of prime importance for success in democratic states like Athens. However, the Sophists, by training their students to be able to argue for any point of view, irrespective of its truth, and by placing emphasis on material success, were actually encouraging skepticism rather than positive beliefs concerning truth and morality. Both Socrates and Plato attacked and condemned them and their educational system for corrupting youth. The term "sophist" thus came to acquire the disparaging connotation of "quibbler" that it has today. Plato established his own educational system, as did other Socratics, but the teaching of the Sophists lingered through the fourth century B.C. and, in a way, gave birth to the educational system of Isocrates.

Isocrates was a pupil of Gorgias and of other Sophists, but he also felt the impact of Socrates' teaching, especially in ethical beliefs. He was primarily interested in Athenian and even Greek politics, but like Plato— although for different reasons—he did not take an active part in the political affairs of his city. During all his life he remained a secluded observer of Athenian political conditions and never held public office, although he faithfully performed all the public functions required of him. However, his interest in politics remained steadfast, and he strove to influence and reshape the political life not only of Athens but also of Greece.

The Peloponnesian War was disastrous for Isocrates. During the war he lost his father's property, and to earn a living he became a logographer, that is, a speech writer for litigants. He abandoned this profession to become a teacher. In 392 B.C. he opened his own school in Athens and he directed it for more than fifty years. Here he accepted young men of aptitude for instruction in the art of oratory. He tried to give them an education that would enable them to get the best out of life and to achieve excellence. His school was a pronounced success, with pupils from all over the Greek world gladly paying the high tuition for Isocrates' teaching. Indeed, many renowned men in politics and letters of the fourth century B.C. were pupils of Isocrates.

The success of his school was the result of his educational system, which appeared as an answer to the problems of his day. It provided an education that cultivated the whole man, preparing him for political, intellectual, and moral leadership. Isocrates believed that at the roots of Greece's troubles in the fourth century was the lack of suitable leaders in various fields, primarily the political. He believed in the intrinsic value and power of example. He reasoned, therefore, that a wholesome change in the political and moral climate of Greece could be achieved only by educating leaders who could become decisive examples for the common people. If this could be brought about, then Greece and the individual Greek not only would prosper but also would fulfill Greece's civilizing mission in the world. This ideal of Greece's mission is one of Isocrates' characteristic beliefs underlying all his work and illuminating his preoccupation with politics and the political character of his education.

ISOCRATES' REACTION TO EXISTING EDUCATION

Isocrates' teaching career was not an easy one. He had to struggle all his life for his own educational system, for there were many misunderstandings and disagreements concerning education at that time. Before he started his school, there were other teachers in Athens, the minor Sophists and the minor Socratics, and a few years later (387) the Academy of Plato was opened. Each teacher had his own ideas about education, his own methods and final aims. The teachers differed among themselves sharply, and Isocrates' views on education differed from theirs still more sharply. An educational multiplicity, therefore, was created, and professional rivalry, confusion, and mistrust predominated in education. From the beginning Isocrates had not only to define his own system of education but also to oppose and expose the education offered by others. He tried to put educational matters straight. When he started his school, he published a tract with the title *Against the Sophists*, which was a manifesto against other teachers as well as a proclamation of the principles and methods of his school. (Only the first part, in which he attacks other systems of education, has survived.) About forty years later (353) he wrote *On the Antidosis*, a long discourse in defense of himself and of his educational system. These two essays are the main sources for the study of his educational system, but in many of his other discourses he frequently refers to educational matters.

The "false" teachers against whom Isocrates protested were, first, the eristics, who devoted themselves to critical disputations in the field of ethics. According to Isocrates they professed to teach their prospective students (for a small fee) virtue and perfect knowledge that would enable them to act and behave rightly in any circumstance. He condemned them because, as he said:

They pretend to search for truth, but straightway at the beginning of their professions attempt to deceive us with lies. For I think it is manifest to all that foreknowledge of future events is not vouchsafed to our human nature (*Against the Sophists* 1–2).[1]

Commenting on this passage, Norlin said:

There is, according to Isocrates, no "science" which can teach us to do under all circumstances the things which will insure our happiness and

---

[1] The translations from Isocrates' discourses used in this study are those of George Norlin (Vols. I–II) and Laure Van Hook (Vol. III) of the three-volume edition of Isocrates' text with translation in the Loeb Classical Library, (London 1928, 1929, and 1945).

success. Life is too complicated for that, and no man can foresee exactly the consequences of his acts—"the future is a thing unseen." All that education can do is to develop a sound judgement (as opposed to knowledge) which will meet the contingencies of life with resourcefulness and, in most cases, with success. This is a fundamental doctrine of his "philosophy" which he emphasizes and echoes again and again in opposition to the professors of a "science of virtue and happiness."

Isocrates also censured the teachers of "political discourse" who taught practical oratory, deliberative and forensic. He labeled them impostors, because they claimed that they could make anyone a good speaker by teaching him the tricks of the profession and the mechanical formulas of composing a speech. They had no interest in truth, he noted. Their main effort was to display their oratorical ability in artificial speeches concerning mythical or paradoxical topics that had no relation to truth or to life. Isocrates was convinced that training alone could not make one a good speaker. He named three elements needed for a good speaker—nature, experience through exercise, and proper instruction—and of these he thought natural talent by far the most significant, training the least important.

He then assailed "those who lived before our time and did not scruple to write the so-called arts of oratory," because "although exhorting others to study political discourse, they neglected all the good things which this study affords, and became nothing more than professors of meddlesomeness and greed" (*Against the Sophists* 19, 20). According to Isocrates, they chose the least esteemed branch of oratory, the forensic, which was false and immoral, dealing with trivial disputes and not with noble and great ideas.

Isocrates did not show great regard for teachers of geometry, astronomy, and other definite sciences, because, he claimed, these sciences have no practical value in life. However, he condescended to accept them as a mental discipline, "a gymnastic of the soul" for young students only.

Finally, he did not approve of the speculative philosophers who were interested in the nature of things and served no useful purpose in practical life. Especially because they did not agree among themselves, they proved to Isocrates that it was impossible to find the truth in such matters as these and, therefore, futile to search for it.

ISOCRATES' VIEWS ON EDUCATION IN GENERAL

By assailing the extravagant promises, deceptive methods, and futile aims of all whom he thought to be false teachers, Isocrates showed what was opposite to his educational system. His own position was clearly stated in the *Antidosis* and other discourses. There he first laid down the theoretical foundations of education in general and of his educational system in particular and then proposed and described his own program. It must be noted, however, that although Isocrates may seem to speak generally about education in all its stages, from the child to the adult, he actually referred only to what interested him most, the higher education of young men. This was very natural, for the chief aim of ancient Greek education, and specifically of Isocrates' system of education, was the formation of adults and not the development of children. In fact, throughout his writings Isocrates seldom spoke about the two first stages of education, elementary and high school, although he thought of them as an important and necessary preparation for any kind of higher education. Another reason why he did not deal in detail with them is that he accepted, almost without any objection, the then established system of child and adolescent education.

Isocrates viewed education as a continuous process of developing the innate qualities of a young man through sustained and calculated effort and exercise under the guidance of a properly qualified person. He named nature as the most important ingredient in this process, with exercise and training following in that order. However, the power of training, although limited, could be considerable, as evidenced by the benefit that even the animals derived from it. The aim of education was the cultivation of the whole man so that his conduct in life as an individual and as a citizen would always be the right one. This depended greatly upon the content and method of instruction, about which Isocrates had definite ideas. He sought to explain the nature and character of education, its power, its relation to other arts, its benefits, and the claims he himself made for it. His examination of these specific educational topics was detailed and descriptive, though sometimes naïve and often repetitious.

He first described how and why education appeared in human society. His concept of the beginnings of education was simple, based on the nature of man as a unit of body and soul. The body was to serve the soul and execute what the soul decided was proper and useful. Both soul and body must be trained to do their respective jobs properly. For the training of the body, the art of gymnastics was invented; for the training of the soul and mind, "philosophy"—a term used by Isocrates for education and culture in general—was invented. The one would supplement the other, and together they would accomplish their common aim of preparing a man for an intelligent and useful life. In this connection, Isocrates' own description is very interesting:

It is acknowledged that the nature of man is compounded of two parts, the physical and the mental, and no one would deny that of these two the mind comes first and is of greater worth; for it is the function of the mind to decide both on personal and on public questions, and of the body to be servant to the judgements of the mind. Since this is so, certain of our ancestors, long before our time, seeing that many arts had been devised for other things, while none had been prescribed for the body and for the mind, invented and bequeathed to us two disciplines, 'physical training for the body, of which gymnastics is a part, and, for the mind, philosophy, which I am going to explain. These are twin arts—parallel and complementary— by which their masters prepare the mind to become more intelligent and the body to become more serviceable, not separating sharply the two kinds of education, but using similar methods of instruction, exercise, and other forms of discipline (*Antidosis* 180–182).

"Philosophy" for Isocrates meant not only general culture but, more specifically, education in discourse. He proceeded to show how an educator, especially the teacher of discourse, worked. In school, he said, the teacher first instructed his students theoretically, presented to them the various kinds of discourse, and explained their form and content and the proper composition for each kind. After that the students would begin the most important part of their schooling—even more important than theoretical teaching itself. They would apply in practical exercises the things that they learned from their teachers:

. . . in order that they may grasp them more firmly and bring their theories into closer touch with the occasions for applying them—I say "theories," for no system of knowledge can possibly cover these occasions, since in all cases they elude our science. Yet those who most apply their minds to them and are able to discern the consequences which for the most part grow out of them, will most often meet these occasions in the right way (*Antidosis* 183f.).

Here Isocrates took the opportunity to declare once more his belief that education could play only a subsidiary rôle in one's attainment of excellence, the first place belonging to nature, with exercise and training following. He said that he was candid with his prospective students and from the very beginning explained to them the indispensable qualities for success in any field and the limitations of education:

I say to them that if they are to excel in oratory or in managing affairs or in any line of work, they must, first of all, have a natural aptitude for that which they have elected to do; secondly, they must submit to training and master the knowledge of their particular subject, whatever it may be in each case; and, finally, they must become versed and practised in the use and application of their art; for only on these conditions can they become fully competent and pre-eminent in any line of endeavour (*Antidosis* 187).

In this process, he said, master and pupil each had his place: only the pupil could furnish the necessary capacity, and only the master would have the ability to impart knowledge. Both had a part in the exercise of practical application, for the master must diligently direct his pupil, and the latter must rigidly follow the master's instructions.

Isocrates considered these observations relevant to the teaching of any subject. He said:

If anyone, ignoring the other arts, were to ask me which of these factors has the greatest power in the education of an orator I should answer that natural ability is paramount and comes before all else (*Antidosis* 189).

Isocrates supported this view with the argument that follows. Suppose that a man had a mind capable of finding out and learning the truth and of working hard and remembering what he learned; that he had a strong, clear, and pleasant voice, and was able to captivate an audience not only by what he said but by the music of his words; and that he had a self-assurance that, tempered by sobriety, so fortified the spirit that he was at ease in addressing all his fellow-citizens: then it would be evident that this supposed man might, without the advantage of an elaborate education, be an outstanding orator. Furthermore, he said, there have been men of no great natural talent but excellent experience and practice who not only improved upon themselves but surpassed gifted men who had been too negligent of their talents. The argument showed that either one of these factors—natural talent or practical experience—might produce an able speaker or an able man of affairs, but both of them combined in the same person might produce a man incomparable among his fellows.

These were his views as to the relative importance of native ability and practice. He said, however, that he could not make a like claim for theoretical education, because he believed that its powers were not equal or comparable to theirs. He suggested, that if a man had taken lessons in the principles and forms of oratory and had mastered them thoroughly, he might become a more pleasing speaker than others; but if he lacked one thing only, the natural ability of assurance, he would not be able to utter a word before a gathering of people.[2]

ISOCRATES' EDUCATIONAL PROGRAM AND ITS OBJECTIVES

These were his general theoretical views about the nature and character of education, its power and benefits, and the claims he made for it. With these general principles and contemporary Greek conditions in mind, Isocrates proposed his own educational program, which aspired to produce eminent men in all fields of endeavor.

---

[2] Isocrates' last statement was based on his own bitter experience; he was compelled to abstain from public speaking because of his lack of good voice and self-assurance.

His program emphasized a broad and useful culture, which he termed "philosophy." It is worth pointing out again that he used the term "philosophy" to mean cultivated life, general culture, and a higher liberal education appropriate for a free man. His usage was consistent with the meaning of the word "philosophy" at that time. In a narrower sense Isocrates also identified "philosophy" with the cultivation of the art of discourse, which was the main object of his school.[3]

At first sight Isocrates' program was very simple and not novel; it did not seem to be different from that of the other teachers of rhetoric, since rhetoric was the basic subject of his school. But rhetoric for Isocrates was a much broader discipline than that of the other rhetoricians and Sophists: it was a cultivation of the mind as well as a training in speech; it was culture in morals as well as education in practical politics. He defined his "philosophy" as an education in thought and its rational expression (*logos*), that is, culture in discourse. For him *logos* was not limited to speech or the spoken word but included the inward thought, the logical thought properly expressed. *Logos* for him was a mark of an understanding mind, a reflection of character, an outward image of inward virtues of soul, the faculty governing the conduct of personal and public affairs; it was that special element of human nature that raised man above animals and enabled man to create civilization by the founding of cities, the establishment of laws, and the invention of arts. With these powers and functions that Isocrates attributed to speech, education in speech was for him no mere training in clever oratory but a broad and sound cultural education covering almost all those fields that form what we call humanistic culture. It was the cultivation of expression, reason, feeling, and imagination, the cultivation of the whole man so that he might live a civilized life.

He proposed to cultivate in his students the parts and qualities of discourse that would "turn them out to be good men in their relations to the state, to their friends, and to their own households" (*Antidosis* 99). This aim, however, could not be achieved through the limited scope of forensic oratory, which confined itself to petty controversies in court cases concerning private interests, nor by the vanity of "epideictic" (exhibitionistic) discourses dealing with silly and insignificant themes. Isocrates was against the teachers of these kinds of oratory; he never ceased to point out that the most important thing for a speaker or writer was the greatness of the subject with which he had to deal. He believed that discourses not only must be well composed as literary prose but also

---

[3] His concept of philosophy differed from that which has come down to us from the time of Plato.

must be practical and concerned with great causes and large ideas. The orator must choose "causes which are great and honourable, devoted to the welfare of man and our common good" (*Antidosis* 276) and must write "discourses which deal with the world of Hellas, with affairs of state, and are appropriate to be delivered at the Pan-Hellenic assemblies." Furthermore, he must write:

. . . discourses which are more akin to works composed in rhythm and set to music than to speeches which are made in court. For they set forth facts in a style more imaginative and more ornate; they employ thoughts which are more lofty and more original, and, besides, they use throughout figures of speech in greater number and more striking character (*Antidosis* 46f.).

Such discourses, he continued, would please and benefit the listener, would not be easily forgotten, and, because they were distinguished by their noble and moral tone and dealt with subjects of permanent interest, they would have a timeless value. Isocrates cited his own discourses as exemplary models of the characteristics of form and content that he demanded of an orator.

Now, how could his students—merely from exposure to such discourses and from demands that they produce similar ones—become good orators, just and honest men, and good citizens? Isocrates did not believe that justice and honesty and virtue and other moral or intellectual qualities could be taught. But he strongly believed in the power of education to improve its adherents, in the beneficial power of example and imitation, and in the innate desire of the individual for excellence and well-meant advantage. He was particularly convinced that constant practice in conversing with good and noble discourses would inspire a man to imitate the good human qualities in them until eventually he would become good, honest, and virtuous. He based this belief on the assumption that good speaking implied right thinking, and, therefore, right acting. Thus, Isocrates was sure that training his pupils in the art of rhetoric prepared them for an honest and successful life.

His ideas on the entire matter are summed up in these words:

I consider that the kind of art which can implant honesty and justice in depraved natures has never existed and does not now exist, and that people who profess that power will grow weary and cease from their vain pretensions before such an education is ever found. But I do hold that people can become better and worthier if they conceive an ambition to speak well, if they become possessed of the desire to be able to persuade their hearers, and, finally, if they set their hearts on seizing their advantage—I do not mean "advantage" in the sense given to that word by the empty-minded, but advantage in the true meaning of that term (*Antidosis* 274f.).

In further clarification of this, Isocrates said that when anyone elected to speak or write discourses worthy of praise and honor, he would not support causes that were unjust or petty or devoted to private quarrels. Rather, he would concentrate his efforts on causes that were great and honorable, devoted to the welfare of man and the common good. He added:

> He will select from all the actions of men which bear upon his subject those examples which are the most illustrious and the most edifying; and, habituating himself to contemplate and appraise such examples, he will feel their influence not only in the preparation of a given discourse but in all the actions of his life (*Antidosis* 227).

It followed that the man who approached the art of discourse with love of wisdom and honor would acquire not only the power to speak well but also the power to think well. Furthermore, the man who wished to persuade people would not neglect virtue. On the contrary, he would do his best to establish a most honorable name among his fellow citizens, because words are more convincing when spoken by good men than when spoken by men of bad reputation, and because the proofs that come from a man's life carry more weight than those furnished by words. Therefore, the more strongly a man desired to persuade his hearers, the more fervently would he strive to be good and righteous and earn the esteem of his fellow citizens, according to Isocrates.

There is no doubt, however, that in addition to the benefit that his students were supposed to derive from training themselves and practicing with good and noble discourses, Isocrates gave them general moral instruction, exemplified in all his orations, particularly the hortatory ones. The virtue that he taught was "that recognized by all men." He disdained the futile attempt of the theoretical moralists (the "eristics"), who "exhort their followers to a kind of virtue and wisdom which is ignored by the rest of the world and about which they themselves dispute." Isocrates preferred the practical morality of average people, instilling it with his own sincere sentiment and lofty intentions. Often he even adopted maxims of popular prudence without attempting to connect them to any doctrine of transcendental ethics. Isocrates was a man of this world who loved and respected generous and noble ideas and despised and disapproved of mean and wrong ones. And this, considering the times in which he lived, was an extraordinary quality that distinguished him from his contemporaries. Selfishness in public and private life was rampant, and Isocrates' life, teaching, and writings were a strong and healthy protest against it. Ernest Havet, a French scholar, in his introduction to *Antidosis* in 1862, extolled the nobility of Isocrates' moral tone as follows:

Isocrates' spirit is marked by respect and love for all worthy sentiments; by the habit of moderation, by a just dislike for dishonest agitations; by antipathy alike for the brutal force of despots and for the brutal passions of mobs; by distance from superstition; by faithful attachment to what he called "philosophy" . . . lastly, by the faculty of admiration,—the finest gift of his genius,—and by that lively feeling for the great aspects of his country in which we can still rejoice with him. . . . His serene eloquence, free from all precipitation and all rashness, selects its thoughts as well as its words, has never to lend itself to offensive sentiments, never degrades itself or those who listen to it, is nourished only on generous ideas, and thus reflects the human spirit always on its nobler side.

A middle-of-the-road, common-sense attitude characterized Isocrates' views on knowledge and the possibility of learning absolute truth. In contrast to other thinkers who believed that absolute knowledge and truth could be achieved through strict dialectic, Isocrates believed that absolute knowledge was unattainable, and, even if achieved in a limited field, useless except for the specialist. He did not subscribe to the idea of seeking knowledge for knowledge's sake but held that study was only useful to the extent that it improved character and prepared one for life. He believed that people should be satisfied with what it is possible for them to learn. Therefore, he recommended that instead of seeking perfect knowledge, people limit themselves to well-founded opinion and to sound conjecture, which are attainable, commonly accepted, and, in most cases, effective in the proper conduct of life. For Isocrates, conjecture was not irresponsible opinion but a working theory based on practical experience, wise judgment, or judicious insight in dealing with the uncertain situations of human life. He wrote:

Since it is not in the nature of man to attain a science by the possession of which we can know positively what we should do or what we should say, in the next resort I hold that man to be wise who is able by his powers of conjecture to arrive generally at the best course, and I hold that man to be a philosopher who occupies himself with the studies from which he will most quickly gain that kind of insight (*Antidosis* 271).

For this reason he believed that the main function of education was to provide a training by which pupils would most quickly and safely acquire such "powers of conjecture." He also believed that those who sought after perfect knowledge and exact science neither reached practical results nor rendered any useful service to anyone. They even disagreed among themselves, and their theories were refuted. Therefore, he advised:

They ought to pursue the truth, to instruct their pupils in the practical affairs of our government and train to expertness therein, bearing in mind that likely conjecture about useful things is far preferable to exact knowledge of the useless, and that to be a little superior in important things is of greater worth than to be pre-eminent in petty things that are without value for living (*Helen* 5).

This down-to-earth attitude toward the practical realities of life was typical of Isocrates' educational program and methods from beginning to end. Education, he believed, would not work miracles but was the art of the possible, an art that must be well founded to achieve even the possible. He stated again and again that education was based, first and foremost, on the capacity of the student, on his natural talent, his natural ability to become something and learn something and derive beneficial results from learning. Besides natural talent, the student must have leisure, the necessary time and means to pursue higher studies successfully. Since, because of differences in people's circumstances and for other reasons, it would be neither possible nor useful to direct all people into the same occupation, Isocrates deemed it advisable to assign to each one a vocation in keeping with his means. The needier might be directed toward farming and trade, while those with sufficient means might devote themselves to higher studies. His students, Isocrates said, were those young men who, of all the Hellenes, led the most untroubled lives, had sufficient means, and were able to take the time to embrace an education and a training of this sort.

Not all students were equally prepared to sustain the pains of learning, to learn fast and thoroughly, or to practice successfully what they learned. There were not only financial but also psychological and mental differences among them. Some were indolent while others were industrious; some were lacking in natural ability while others were blessed with vigorous minds. They could not all benefit equally from their studies nor all excel after they finished. Knowledge yields itself to us only after great effort on our part, or, as Isocrates said elsewhere, using a popular maxim, "The roots of education are bitter but its fruit is sweet." And he confessed, "From all our schools only two or three students turn out to be real champions, the rest retiring from their studies into private life" (*Antidosis* 201). However, the beneficial influence of education was felt and experienced by all students, not only those who became excellent orators, statesmen, or teachers, for even "those who have preferred to live in private have become more gracious in their social intercourse than before, and keener judges and more prudent counsellors than the great majority" (*Antidosis* 204). These qualities were regarded by Isocrates as the main characteristics of a truly educated man. Since the education he described was not a specialized, technical training but a general education, liberal in scope and meant to cultivate the good qualities of students so that they might become good men and citizens, one may well understand why Isocrates prided himself on those average students who became good men in private life as well as on those who distinguished themselves as statesmen, teachers, or writers.

Isocrates offered us the opportunity to glance often into his classroom and see what and how he taught. He told us, for example, that his students stayed with him three to four years and attended his courses in "philosophy." He first gave his students theoretical instruction in rhetoric and presented them with model discourses as examples for imitation. He then demanded of them intensive practice on what they had learned. His teaching in discourse was thorough and detailed, going into such minute things as how to read a speech or a treatise, how to enunciate and make it understandable to oneself and one's audience. However, his students did not spend all their time in acquainting themselves with the rules, forms, and practice of oratory. In his school they received a much wider and more diverse education, for Isocrates' "philosophy" and his concept of *logos* covered, as has already been observed, a much larger area and many more themes than the narrow technical oratorical preparation.

From many relevant references in his speeches it is evident that a course in politics occupied a prominent place in Isocrates' curriculum. His strong personal opinions on state, national, and world politics are noted briefly below to the extent that they relate to his educational system and its aims. It is certain that for his students they embodied an important part of Isocrates' political education. One may cite here the passage in the *Antidosis* (see especially 117–120, 132) concerning the direct advice he gave to his most famous student, the general and statesman Timotheus, about the qualifications and duties of the good statesman and general.

Together with politics two other topics, ethics and history, were intimately connected in Isocrates' teaching. As we have already seen, the moral instruction given by Isocrates was primarily the traditional ethics of the average Greek and was based on poetry and popular wisdom. He frequently urged his students to acquaint themselves with the best things in the poets and learn from other wise men whatever useful lessons they had taught, "because a number of poets of earlier times have left precepts which direct us how to live" (*To Nicocles* 3). He even intended at the age of ninety-seven to "speak on the poets at another time provided that my age does not first carry me off" (*Panathenaicus* 34). It was an intention he did not live to fulfill.

His ethical teaching was about the practical, everyday ethics applied by the common man. It concerned conduct toward gods, parents, children, friends or enemies, society in general—in distress or happiness, in poverty or prosperity. It asked many questions. Which are the really best things in life and how should one pursue them? What are the duties of the private citizen and the holder of public office? What is the power of example and culture? These and similar topics were examined and discussed in his school as well as in his writings. The combination of this plain, unaffected, and commonly accepted ethics with Isocrates' lofty but practical intentions was a major factor in making his teaching and influence so effective. From the "commonplaces," according to Marrou, arose the "general ideas" for great moral themes with eternal import which formed one of the most characteristic features of humanistic culture and which were also responsible for its profound human values. In fact, Isocrates prided himself more upon the sound moral influence of his work and teaching than upon anything else.

As for history, it served Isocrates as an inexhaustible source of examples. He used it abundantly to illustrate his views and frequently urged his students and listeners to turn to history as the safe guide for the present and future. Besides the teachings of the poets, the works of Herodotus and Thucydides were part of his teaching material. Certainly his approach to history was not objective. It was, rather, rhetorical and dramatic and full of edifying examples. He presented historical events carelessly and interpreted them according to his personal political predilections. However, Isocrates was the first educator to introduce history as an academic discipline. It is worth remembering that the historians Ephorus and Theopompus were his pupils, and that many later historians were deeply influenced by him in their attitude to history and historiography.

In addition to proper teaching material, an expert teacher is a very important factor in education, according to Isocrates. He had high criteria. A competent teacher must turn out good and worthy pupils. A teacher must influence his pupils not only by his thorough knowledge and skilled teaching but also through his example, his work, his manners, and his life in general. By his special techniques of training and by his living habits, the teacher must inspire his pupils with the principles that he himself practices in his life and in his professional field. Also, he must be on friendly terms with his pupils, take them into his confidence, and make them love and respect him. Only in such an intimate atmosphere could a teacher develop in full a genuine teaching activity which would exert a profound personal influence on his disciples, Isocrates believed. Isocrates was a master in creating such atmosphere. Many times he even shared with his pupils his problems of composing a new speech and asked for their frank opinion. Upon graduation they were reluctant to leave. "So happy did they feel in their life with me, that they would always take their leave with regrets and tears" (*Antidosis* 88). One of them, Timotheus, even dedicated a bronze statue of Isocrates at the sanctuary of Eleusis as a token of his love and respect for his sage teacher.

ISOCRATES' CONCEPT OF "PAIDEIA" AND THE EDUCATED MAN

Isocrates' immediate concern as an educator was the preparation of men who might live and act properly and successfully in the changing conditions of fourth-century B.C. Greece. He attained this immediate goal by the simple educational program that he had devised. His real purpose, however, was much wider and more far-reaching. His foremost and constant concern was the political and moral regeneration of Greece so that she might perform effectively her great civilizing rôle in the world. For the realization of this mission of Greece, he advocated that the Greek states end their rivalries and wars and join in a confederacy of free states united under a single leadership (preferably of Athens) in a common cause, to wage war against Persia. He envisioned such a Pan-Hellenic crusade as a revenge upon the Persians for their earlier expeditions against Greece. Also, it would be a means for considerable practical gains for Greece: the Asiatic Greeks would be liberated; the poor and socially troublesome Greeks of the mainland could immigrate to Asia; and a considerable amount of wealth would pour into Greece and alleviate her financial plight.

Much more important than these tangible gains, it seemed to Isocrates, was the idea that this would be "the only war that is better than peace: more like a sacred mission than a military expedition" (*Panegyricus* 182). In other words, it would be a cultural expedition, an assertion of the superiority of Greeks over barbarians. This had no racial overtones, since, for him, barbarian meant merely uneducated. He considered as Greeks all those who accepted and practiced in their lives Greek culture, *paideia*, rather than considering as Greeks only those of Greek blood. He declared in a very celebrated passage of his greatest work, the *Panegyricus* (50):

So far has Athens distanced the rest of mankind in thought and in speech that her pupils have become the teachers of the rest of the world; and she has brought it about that the name "Hellenes" suggests no longer a race but an intelligence, and that the title "Hellenes" is applied rather to those who share our culture than to those who share a common blood.

It appears that for Isocrates Greek culture was a kind of saving religion, of which Athens was the central shrine, and that the "sacred mission" of a united Greece was to expand and bring it everywhere. In Norlin's words, Isocrates conceived "of Hellenism as a brotherhood of culture, transcending the bounds of race . . . an outpost of culture, a lamp to be kept burning amid the surrounding darkness."

This is not the proper place to follow further the political views of Isocrates and the methods he periodically used in his futile endeavors to have his ideas put into action. Indeed, through his political and educational pamphlets he was able to reach the Greek people, but he was pragmatic enough to realize that in the unstable and even dangerous political, social, intellectual, and moral climate of fourth-century Greece only a few selected individuals could be beneficially affected. He rightly perceived that the political problem was basically an educational problem. So, he turned to the education of leaders, particularly of political leaders, precisely because it is the political leaders "who train the multitude in the ways of virtue and justice and great sobriety and who teach through the manners of their rule this very truth, namely, that every polity is the soul of the state, having as much power over it as the mind over the body." He believed that "it is this which deliberates on all questions, seeking to preserve what is good and to avoid what is disastrous, and is the cause of all the things which transpire in states" (*Panathenaicus* 138).

And he emphasized the role of education thus:

I suppose that you are not unaware of the fact that the government of the state is handed on by the older men to the youth of the coming generation; and that since the succession goes on without end, it follows of necessity that as is the education of our youth so from generation to generation will be the fortune of the state (*Antidosis* 174).

By keeping in mind what Isocrates meant by "philosophy" and what breadth and depth and powers he attributed to *logos*, we may understand why he was not hesitant about the theoretical soundness of his program. For him (it is worth repeating), "philosophy" was culture in general, and, more specifically, the art of speaking and writing well on large political and other subjects was a preparation for advice or action in political affairs. And *logos* (word, reason, discourse, the logical and artistic speech), the principal element of the *paideia* he was teaching, was for him the central cause of progress, improvement, and the civilization in general of mankind. He described *logos* as:

. . . that power which of all the faculties that belong to the nature of man is the source of most of our blessings. . . . Because there has been implanted in us the power to persuade each other and to make clear to each other whatever we desire, not only have we escaped the life of wild beasts, but we have come together and founded cities and made laws and invented arts; and, generally speaking, there is no institution devised by man which the power of speech has not helped us to establish. For this it is which has laid down laws concerning things just and unjust, and things base and honourable; and if it were not for these ordinances we should not be able to live with one another. It is by this also that we confute the bad and extol the good. Through this we educate the ignorant and appraise the wise; for the power to speak well is taken as the surest index of a sound understanding, and discourse which is true and lawful and just is the outward image of a good and faithful soul. . . . And, while we call eloquent those who are able to speak before a crowd, we regard as sage those who most skillfully debate their problems in their own minds. And, if there is need to speak in brief summary of this power, we shall find that none of the things which are done with intelligence take place without the help of speech, but that in all our actions as well as in all our thoughts speech is our guide, and is most employed by those who have the most wisdom (*Nicocles* 5–9).

Because Isocrates attributed these sweeping qualities and functions to *logos*, education in discourse was for him the cultivation of the whole man. Isocrates really aimed at what was good, permanent, and universal in Greek culture, especially as it was found in Athens. What Athens "revealed" to mankind was described by Jaeger as "this universal striving after intellectual possessions, after knowledge and wisdom, that made the Athenians what they were, and attuned them to that peculiar gentleness, moderation, and harmony that is the mark of civilization." It was because of this "universal striving" that, although Isocrates' educational program may appear narrow and one-sided, it was actually very broad and diversified, embracing the whole man—not only the Athenian or the Greek, but the universal man. For, although the character of Isocrates' education was essentially national, it was also universal in scope. The general conditions in Greece, particularly in Athens, were favorable to this trend of intellectual and political universality during the fourth century B.C. The increasing dissolution of the bonds between the individual and the state, estranging the individual from traditional beliefs and ideas and turning him to the pursuit of personal happiness, tended to lead him toward a contemplative citizenship of the world. And indeed, even before the end of the fourth century, philosophers like the Stoics preached cosmopolitanism and the brotherhood of all men, while Alexander the Great made universal citizenship a reality. Even earlier, in 380 B.C., Isocrates himself, when he was writing his most important oration, the *Panegyricus*, declared that "Greek" is defined not by race but by culture.

Isocrates' educational system met with high success during his lifetime and prevailed in later centuries. It became, in a sense, the foundation upon which liberal education was built, primarily because it aimed at the cultivation of the whole man and at universality. Another reason for its success was Isocrates' position against the "false" teachers of his time, the quibblers, the specialists, the utopians, against all those who gave excessive promises or professed impractical aims. Another very important reason for his success was the fact that he preached the "golden mean"; he advocated values that were generally accepted as right and correct, that were not likely to generate controversy, and that might be found as good and attainable by almost everyone. Finally, he did not exaggerate the power of education and he acknowledged the limitations of man. He was against absolutes—against any absolute concept. This relativistic attitude showed him to be a true pupil of the Sophists.

His education was really intended for the upper-middle and the ruling class, with the aim of preparing youth for eventual leadership, primarily in the political field. Many of his students became political leaders. Three of his speeches were entirely concerned with the theme of how a king should be educated in order to discharge his duties (*To Nicocles, Nicocles*, and *Evagoras*). The advice that Isocrates gave in these speeches and elsewhere to prospective governors of states could be profitably heeded and used by any politician, even by any common citizen. Only the angle of perspective was different. The finished product expected by Isocrates was always the educated man as defined in the following famous passage:

Whom, then, do I call educated, since I exclude the arts and sciences and specialties? First, those who manage well the circumstances which they encounter day by day, and who possess a judgement which is accurate in meeting occasions as they arise and rarely misses the expedient course of action; next, those who are decent and honourable in their intercourse with all with whom they associate, tolerating easily and good-naturedly what is unpleasant or offensive in others and being themselves as agreeable and reasonable to their associates as it is possible to be; furthermore, those who hold their pleasures always under control and are not unduly overcome by their misfortunes, bearing up under them bravely and in a manner worthy of our common nature; finally, and the most important of all, those who are not spoiled by successes and do not desert their true selves and become arrogant, but hold their ground steadfastly as intelligent men, not rejoicing in the good things which have come to them through chance rather than in those which through their own nature and intelligence are theirs from the very beginning. Those who have a character which is in accord, not with one of these things, but with all of them—these, I contend, are wise and complete men, possessed of all the virtues (*Panathenaicus* 30–32).

Isocrates' concept of an educated man may seem meager today, because of the increased demands upon an educated man in modern times. Isocrates did not believe that an educated man had to be a scholar, a specialist, a person isolated in laboratory or study for research in the sciences, speculative philosophy, theoretical politics, or any other special area. He wanted his educated man to practice without affectation what he had learned in school; he wanted him to be first of all a *man*, a good and efficient man in his relations to society and the state. Isocrates' *paideia* was aiming at what in England is traditionally termed a *gentleman*.

THE IMPACT OF ISOCRATES: AN ASSESSMENT

Certainly Isocrates was not a great or original thinker. His ideas often seem commonplace and superficial, and most of them were borrowed from other sources. But the versatility and adaptability of his mind and the effectiveness of his work entitle him to a special position in the world's cultural history. He has exerted an especially great influence on posterity in two areas, prose composition and education. Isocrates was a master of prose; his discourses are models of beauty of expression and soundness of thought. He accomplished this perfection because he believed that prose must be artistic, sensibly ornate, full of meaning, serene and dignified. He introduced various stylistic refinements that made prose a form of art almost as definite and exacting as poetry. He worked with special care on the building up of the "period of speech" by giving prominence to the essential points and subordinating the lesser ones, while not neglecting important detail; thus his "period of speech" became really an exercise in logical thinking. Also, he paid attention to the refinement of taste by choosing properly and using temperately the right embellishments, while not ignoring the music and rhythm of the phrase. Isocrates established a style that became the norm of literary prose, because through his works, his pupils, and their tradition it profoundly influenced Cicero, and through him and his imitators, all subsequent literature. We may cite the pertinent conclusion of R. C. Jebb:

The Isocratic style has become the basis of the rest. That style, in its essential characteristics of rhythm and period, passed into the prose of Cicero; modern prose has been modelled on the Roman; and thus, in forming the literary rhetoric of Attica, Isocrates founded that of all literatures (*The Attic Orators*, II, 432).

Isocrates' undeniable influence on the formation of literary prose is, of course, educational in character, but it is his specific contribution to education proper that is examined here. This was considerable; it has been recognized since ancient times by Cicero, Quintilian, and many other ancient as well as modern authorities. Dionysius of Halicarnassus declared, "Isocrates was the most illustrious teacher of his day; he educated the best youths of Athens and of all Greece—distinguished, some as politicians, some as advocates, some as historians; and made his school the true image of Athens." H. I. Marrou writes, "Isocrates became the educator first of Greece and then of the whole ancient world." Professor Moses Hadas admits, "At all events Isocrates is the greatest educationist of antiquity," and emphasizes, together with many other modern scholars, the bearing that Isocrates has had on education, humanistic education in particular. Many modern scholars even maintain that Isocrates is the father of modern liberal education.

One may not entirely agree that Isocrates is the father of liberal-arts education as we understand it today. However, it is history that the educational system he invented greatly influenced later educational systems from which our modern liberal education has developed. Surely, this is sufficient accomplishment to warrant one to occupy an honorable place among the world's great educators.

A brief comparative examination of the development of higher education since Isocrates will make the point clearer. Isocrates gave to rhetoric a high cultural and civic responsibility, and his school was a rhetorical school in contrast to the philosophical schools of his and later times. But the formal higher education in Hellenistic and later times was, under the influence of Isocrates, basically rhetorical with the gradual addition of some courses in dialectic and science that Isocrates had recommended as being preparatory to the serious study of discourse. On the other hand, even the opponents of rhetorical education, beginning with Aristotle in Plato's Academy and in his own Lyceum later, soon deemed it necessary—probably in order to survive the competition and most certainly because the times demanded it—to add the formal study of rhetoric to their curriculum. This rhetorical trend continued during the Roman period—as the educational ideas of Cicero, Quintilian, and others show—and later through the Middle Ages, when the Seven Liberal Arts of higher education were established, with grammar, rhetoric, and dialectic (the *trivium*) and geometry, arithmetic, astronomy, and music (the *quadrivium*) as the embodiment of the most essential part of our modern liberal education. Even today, students, before they specialize, are required to learn to think logically for themselves, to articulate with both the spoken and written word, and, when faced with decisions, to make the one that is right or wisest—just as Isocrates wanted.

But, beyond and above the typical courses, it is the spirit of liberal education that is markedly Isocratean. Liberal education is general, not specialized, is education of the whole man, cultivation of his most human and humane qualities, just as Isocrates' *paideia* embraced all the relations of human existence. Liberal education is a humanistic education, and humanistic studies have their origin in Isocrates' educational system. As Professor Hadas correctly observes:

Humanistic education is not an exclusive possession of Hellenes but accessible to all men who wish to participate in what the Greeks regard as education. Education is not training for a craft or profession or any specialty but familiarity with a traditional library of books—the same library, in effect, which continued to be the mainstay of liberal education in the Hellenistic world, in Rome, and, with vicissitudes of fortune, in Europe to this day (*Humanism* 89).

Isocrates' system, more than any other ancient Greek educational system, provided the appropriate educational climate for the expansion of Greek culture into the Hellenistic and later periods and was largely responsible for the promulgation of a new and universal concept of culture. One might say that what Alexander the Great attempted to do in the political field for a short time, Isocrates achieved in the cultural field through his educational system, and with more lasting results. Greece's "cultural conquest" of the world for centuries seems to have its origins, to a great extent, in the educative effectiveness of Isocrates' *paideia*.

BIBLIOGRAPHICAL NOTE

The main source for the study of Isocrates' educational system is his work. A good and handy edition of his writings is that in the Loeb Classical Library, *Isocrates*, in three volumes, with an English translation by George Norlin (Vols. I–II) and Laure Van Hook (Vol. III), London, 1928, 1929, 1945.

From the many works on Isocrates the following may be cited for their bearing on the subject of this study and for their further bibliographical information.

R. C. Jebb, *The Attic Orators.* Especially Vol. II, London, 1893. Reprinted recently by Russel and Russel, New York, 1962.
A. Cartelier and E. Havet, *Antidosis.* Paris, 1862.
A. Burk, *Die Pädagogik des Isokrates.* Würzburg, 1923.
A. G. Amatucci, "Isocrate Pedagogista," *Atene e Roma,* 4(1923), pp. 113–118.
W. Jaeger, *Paideia: The Ideals of Greek Culture.* Translated by Gilbert Highet. Especially Vol. III. Blackwell, Oxford, 1947.
H. I. Marrou, *A History of Education in Antiquity.* Translated by George Lamb. Sheed and Ward, New York, 1956.

H. LL. Hudson-Williams, "A Greek Humanist," *Greece and Rome*, 9 (1940), pp. 166–172.

S. E. Smethurst, "Cicero and Isocrates," *Transactions and Proceedings of the American Philological Association*, 84 (1953), pp. 262–320.

B. Laourdas, *Isocrates and His Time*. Athens, 1944 (in Greek).

E. B. Castle, *Ancient Education and Today*. Penguin Books, Baltimore, 1961.

Moses Hadas, *Humanism: The Greek Ideal and Its Survival*. Harper & Brothers, New York, 1960.

Frederick A. G. Beck, *Greek Education 450–350 B.C.* Barnes & Noble Inc., New York, 1964.

ZENO (334–262 B.C.) was born at Citium, on the island of Cyprus. His father was a merchant, but, noticing in his son a strong bent toward learning, he early encouraged him to study philosophy by securing for him the writings of the most eminent Socratic philosophers. At the age of thirty Zeno traveled to Athens where, according to legend, he met Crates the Cynic philosopher in the shop of a bookseller. Although he became a disciple of Crates, Zeno attended the lectures of other philosophers. After making himself master of the views of others, Zeno determined to become the founder of a new sect. The place where he located his school was called the *Stoa Poikilē*, or "Painted Porch," a public portico deriving its name from the pictures of Polygnotus and other eminent masters with which it was adorned. This portico became the most famous in Athens and was called by way of distinction, Stoa, "the Porch." It was from this circumstance that the followers of Zeno were called Stoics, or "men of the Porch." As a teacher Zeno obtained a considerable vogue, and even enjoyed the favor of the great; Antigonus Gonatus, King of Macedon, while residing in Athens, attended his lectures. Among the Athenians, Zeno was held in high esteem for his integrity, so much so that they deposited the keys of their citadel in his hands. They also honored him with a golden crown and a statue of bronze. His writings, a list of which have been given by Diogenes Laertius, have all been lost. They treated of the state and of the life according to nature.

3

THE STOIC: *Zeno*

BY JOHN E. REXINE

Stoicism, though it has been called a second-rank philosophy, certainly became one of the most important philosophies of Hellenistic and Roman times (both republican and imperial) and has been described as one of the world's most significant religious forces. From the point of view of education, it had a teaching purpose; it had ideals, which, though perhaps never literally carried out, served as guidelines to help the educated man to conduct his life; and it had teachings that, at least if practiced precisely, could presumably have been achieved within a man's lifetime. Zeno, the founder of Stoicism, believed that Stoicism could liberate man from the degenerate and degenerating demands of this life by providing him with real freedom from desire and fear. Stoicism as a philosophy promised the individual who became educated in its principles and practices independence from the stifling anxieties, doubts, and apparent difficulties of this world. Through this philosophy man could find that he was a significant element in the over-all pattern of things. This "liberating" feature is built into the traditional "liberal-arts" system of education, which emphasizes this same liberating element, though it may not be clear exactly from what one is freed (ignorance is the obvious answer that some would give). At any rate, it is significant to note that Stoicism satisfied a widespread need at a time when the collapse of the traditional political structures of the then known world forced the individual man to reassess his place in the totality of things.

In Hellenistic times the Greek city (*polis*) was superseded by the larger Hellenistic kingdoms in which the individual as such no longer had the meaning, the rights, or the power that he had exercised in the small city-state where his participation in governmental, civic, and social activity had been the keystone of the direct democratic process. Individual freedom was no longer the hallmark of the ideal citizen. The education of the Athenian of the fifth century had stressed the freedom of the individual and his worth. It was a precious heritage that was no longer characteristic of the times. Still, man was man, and his innermost urgings insisted that he did have a place somewhere in the total picture, even though his area of public activity had diminished. The large imperial state, the national state, replaced the smaller, more personal city-state. The limitations on individual freedom were considerable, and these limitations were even more pronounced in Roman imperial times when republican forms were preserved but were lacking in democratic content. In a circumscribed world such as this, it was important that an all-embracing philosophy or religion be able to provide the people, the rulers, and the slaves with a meaningful guide to life; it was the aim of Stoicism to do this and to do it adequately.

It is very difficult for modern man, familiar as he is with public and private systems of education at the elementary, secondary, and higher (university) levels, to project himself back into a time in the history of the West when education was primarily privately administered and primarily a matter of parental responsibility and private tutors. Schools in the modern sense of large administrative and teaching establishments catering to thousands of students at a time did not exist. The teacher was generally a slave—the lowest status in the social structure—a status that, it would seem, has only recently seen improvement. State interest in schools was, as a rule, nonexistent. There was neither state supervision nor state aid to education. Originally, and for a long time, the aim of education was primarily moral. The interest was less in producing scholars than in developing good, solid citizens. In some ways, this goal has not changed substantially.

In early Greek times, the works of Homer and Hesiod constituted the material of higher education. Put more generally, from Homeric times down to the period of the fifth century B.C., the so-called Golden Age of Greek civilization, the education of the Greeks came from the poets. The conflict between poetry and philosophy, culminating in the persons of Plato and Aristotle, resulted in the triumph of philosophy over poetry and of the written over the oral word. This conquest meant the replacement of the symbolic language of poetry by the abstract language of philosophy as the means of education. The power of poetry as an educational instrument in ancient Greece may be summarized in the famous reference to Homer as "the school of Greece."

Enough has been said to show that the philosopher became the principal teacher and philosophy became the chief educational tool. One need only conjure up the picture of the master teacher Socrates or the first professional teachers, the Sophists. One sees how the young disciples gathered round a teacher—this was the essence of education more than going to a school—to hear from the teacher, to talk, to discuss, to explore with the teacher fundamental problems, questions, and issues. One notes how important was the give and take of the "discussion method" to the ancient system of education, although the lecture method was to become equally important later.

Zeno was certainly in the tradition of the Greek philosopher of colorful eccentricities and determined individualism. He went from Citium in Cyprus to Athens, presumably on business, but he was soon to give up business for philosophy. And where but in Athens could he pursue the study of philosophy more relentlessly? He had read *The Memorabilia* of Xenophon and was impressed by its portrayal of Socrates. He sought to find such a man and soon came under the influence of Crates the Cynic who preached the mysteries of the higher life to him. Under Crates, Zeno received the fundamentals of his philosophic education. He was required to memorize Plato, Aristotle, and Antisthenes, and he did this with honors. Other schools exerted such an influence over Zeno that he was later called an eclectic, but it is fair to say that Zeno was more concerned with truth than he was with the school that presumed to teach that truth. From the Megarians, and in particular from Stilpo, he learned logic and eristics; from the Cynics he learned the doctrine of passionlessness; from the Academics he acquired a rigorous knowledge of the ethereal notions of Plato; from Heraclitus he inherited physics; and from the Aristotelians he learned formal logic, metaphysics, and natural science. He also came into contact with Polemo, Xenocrates, and Diodorus. But with all his borrowing, his dominant desire was still simply to learn the truth. *Veritas* is still the motto of many a university, no matter how elaborately it may be phrased. Zeno's ideal of the educated man, if he could have expressed it in this way, would undoubtedly have been the dedicated seeker of truth.

It is vital to point out that never do we find Zeno expounding a theory of education, as we understand the term. Education is a concern of every philosopher, and Zeno was no exception, but education for the ancient philosopher was the training of the student in a particular philosophy. For Zeno this was Stoic philosophy, and he saw the educated man as the one whose training in and practice of Stoic principles made him a "free man." "Wise," "free," "virtuous" would have been the terms used, rather than "educated," because the primary purpose of education even for the Stoic was the leading of the good life, a life of virtue and harmony with nature.

The reader should be warned that none of the works of Zeno has survived the ravages of time. A few scraps have been gathered, but our knowledge of Zeno rests upon secondary sources. His disciples were numerous. His influence was enormous. Though later Stoics developed and modified some of Zeno's teachings, Zeno's doctrines were the fundamental groundwork upon which Stoicism was built. As H. Vernon Arnold so aptly puts it in his *Roman Stoicism* (London, 1911, p. 66), "From that foundation neither Zeno nor his true followers ever departed, and thus stoicism embodied and spread the fundamental dogmas of Cynicism, that the individual alone is really existent, that virtue is the supreme good, and that the wise man, though a beggar, is truly a king." Early, while studying under the Cynics, Zeno wrote a book in criticism of Plato's *Republic*. Zeno's book bore the same title and preached cosmopolitanism, law by nature, no images or temples of deity, no law courts, no statues, no gymnasia. This perfect Zenonian state would be completely virtuous, and men and women in perfect equality would all possess wisdom. Love would be dominant as a deity who provided for the good of all.

Zeno is credited with dividing the interests of his Stoic movement into logic, ethics, and natural science (*physis*). In 294 B.C. he is reported to have opened his own school. His practice of teaching from a portico, the *Stoa Poikilē*, gave the name to the school.

Zeno was a man of great virtue. His character has been compared with that of Socrates. Zeno was a Phoenician and so a Semite. It has often been noticed that certain schools of Greek thought were repugnant to him; in fact, the whole tone of Zeno's thinking has been called un-Greek. He was concerned with the concrete, the intuitive, and the morally conscious "ought," a preoccupation dominating the Semitic approach to life. It has been said that he preached like a prophet and that he did not reason like a Greek philosopher. Whereas the Greek philosopher was an intellectual dealing with ideas, mathematics, and abstract reasoning, Zeno was basically a practical man. His manners were more like those of an Old Testament prophet. Not a single follower, it is said, was an Athenian; most were Semites. In the East it was the prophet who was also the teacher; among the Greeks it was the philosopher. One scholar, Edwyn Bevan in his *Stoics and Skeptics* (Oxford, 1913), went so far as to say that Zeno expressed the intense convictions of a teacher—convictions that were essentially dogmatic and authoritative but not necessarily based on reason. He surmised:

If men received it, it was not because they were convinced in a cold intellectual way, but because behind his affirmations there was a tremendous personal force, because something deep in their own hearts rose up to bear witness to the things he affirmed. It was a way of faith.

We can add that Zeno was astute enough to see that man lived not by reason alone but also by faith. It certainly would seem that a great part of the Stoic appeal lay in its being a religion as well as a philosophy; it was something that men could believe in, because it provided them the means by which they could believe in themselves. To be able to find oneself, to discover the authentic self, to use the modern expression that has grown popular in interpreting J. D. Salinger's *Catcher in The Rye*, is to be educated. If education is truly to "know thyself," as Socrates urged and as modern educators would echo, then Stoicism, too, was an educational system, created by Zeno and brilliantly developed by Chrysippus and others, for it provided man with the wherewithal to know himself not merely superficially but as part of a total cosmic structure that was explainable and reasonable.

Presumably then, the Stoic ideal of the educated man, as expounded by Zeno, would mean a person well versed in Stoic physics, ethics, and logic. These three "subjects" would constitute the basic elements of any Stoic education and would certainly explain everything for the educated Stoic man, at least. Modern educational curriculums tend to specialize, to serve up portions of knowledge in different disciplines that offer different views. The Stoic system, like most ancient philosophies, strove to explain all that was worth knowing—the totality of knowledge, not just a part of it.

To understand the Stoic concept of an educated man, therefore, one should understand Stoicism as a philosophical system. To begin with, the universe was viewed as running in a circuit of numbers with a clockwork whirring and purring of cosmic harmony. The natural was rational and harmonious, and this harmony possessed purpose, moving according to the plan of the Logos (the rational principle in the universe) and proceeding under divine and logically perfect patterns. Zeno obviously found the world orderly and explainable. His cosmology contained nothing that Aristotle and Heraclitus did not include in their Logos. It is necessary, at this point, to say something about the Stoic Logos.

According to Zeno, the cosmos was constantly experiencing change, but the change followed reason and cosmic law. This reason or Logos was divine and possessed an intelligence that was immanent in nature and in man. In his famous syllogism he reasoned, "What is more rational is more excellent than what is irrational; nothing is more excellent than the universe; therefore the universe is rational and exercises reason." To prove that nature possessed consciousness, he argued, "Nothing destitute of consciousness and reason can produce out of itself beings endowed with consciousness and reason; the universe produces beings endowed with consciousness and reason." It becomes abundantly clear that though Zeno spoke of the Logos or reason, of the universe, he did not treat it in the traditional way of the Greek philosophers. It is essential to note that all Stoic ontology was subordinate to Stoic ethics.

Therefore, we should not be too critical of logical inconsistencies in Stoic ontological and cosmological doctrines. All of Zeno's metaphysical arguments were partly ontological, partly ethical. Even though he lucidly asserted that the ultimate reality would be known in the Logos, he transformed a metaphysical concern into a moral "ought." He said, "Having hearkened not unto me but to the Logos, it is wise to confess all things are one." He believed that the Logos always existed but that men did not always recognize it, even though men knew that everything happened through this Logos. He observed:

There is but one wisdom: to understand the knowledge by which all things are steered. . . .

Intelligence is common to all things; those who speak with understanding must strongly cleave to that which is common to all things, even as a city cleaves to a law. . . .

Although the Logos is universal, most men live as though they had an intelligence of their own. . . .

Men are at variance with the Logos, even though it is their constant companion.

He felt that all being was circumcentric to the Logos and dependent on its will. Men consequently would have no existence or intelligence of their own but would be extensions of that divine will which was their constant companion. Ironically enough, even though men lost their being without the Logos, still they did not know or acknowledge its power, according to Zeno.

With this system nothing was evil in itself since intelligence was universal. If men considered an object evil, it was because they were making it metaphysically concentric to themselves, when they should have been relating evil to the Logos, to whom both good and evil were known. Only in this respect could good and evil exist, namely, in relation to the cosmos.

For Zeno the universe or cosmos was a living being (*zōion*). As to the Logos' realization of its potentiality, he said, "It is not concentrated in the whole of matter but in the finest part of it." The finest part was described as "fiery ether," which Zeno, like Heraclitus, equated with pure reason. Some of the fire became "common" fire and so became one of the four elements—fire, air, earth, and water. The pure fire that was left acted upon the remaining matter, which contained common fire. Because fire underlay all things, it was the vital force of cosmic reason

After Zeno saturated the universe with fire, he went on to add proportionate parts of Aristotelian teleology. All things in the universe must have a purpose or end (*telos*). The end would come (or the purpose would be consummated) when all things met in the "furnace of being," since all things found being in the Logos. The Logos, which was absolute being, would then be left alone to contemplate his thoughts. As pure reason, or Logos, had granted all being, so all being would reunite with him. Once all things were united with the one, the Logos would commence to re-form all things. He would recharge the universe with being from out of the ether, and the cosmos would re-emerge from it.

We are told by Cicero that sometimes Zeno called the universe itself God, while at other times he gave this name to the soul and spirit of all nature. Therefore, the Logos of the cosmology of Zeno was God, a God who filled the world with his ethereal spirit and charged life with his soul. Zeno said, "In all things is the divine; the law of nature is divine." For Zeno, Zeus was the absolute God who existed and whose existence was demonstrable from the harmony of the universe. This was the so-called argument by design. The orderliness of the cosmos presupposed a creator. Zeno further argued that "whatever exists must act and be acted upon; action implies contact and therefore body." So, God, as an acting force in the cosmos, as virtually the acting cosmos itself, had to be corporeal. Furthermore, Zeno added that since there was nothing that neither acted nor was acted upon, all things were corporeal. God could only be found in nature. God was a part of nature, and nature itself was found in this world.

An ineluctable result of Zeno's pantheism was the exclusion of popular Greek polytheistic deities from Zeno's system. Only their names remained and these were explained as natural objects. God was one— Zeus. All other so-called gods either were mortals or could be explained as natural phenomena. For Zeno, the educated Stoic had to know the source of his own existence, and this source was God, the supreme Logos, the cosmos, the eternal fire.

Having established the place of God, Zeno realized it would then be necessary to assign nature (*physis*) its position in his system. Zeno's own knowledge about natural science was not original but derived from Heraclitus and Aristotle. Zeno's conception of physical nature is known as hylozoism, the doctrine that matter is animated. The stuff underlying the sensible world was "physis," a natural substance possessing "the character of life." Heraclitus had previously described this stuff as fire and had identified it with pure reason. The fire kept substance vital, kept all things in flux. Because the fire was reason, flux and change followed a rational order. We might most easily discover that order in mathematics, music, and the movement of the stars. Contrary to the philosophy of Plato, which demanded that fire be transcendent, Zeno held that the soul, synonymous with fire, was corporeal. The soul of matter was "living being" (zōion) rather than a "Good" transcending the empirical world. If this view made Zeno a materialist, it made him a vital materialist. Zeno's system of physics was teleological, so if we call it materialism at all, we must consider it a materialism ruled by vital principles, the "entelechies" and life spirit (elan vital) of Bergson.

Matter was divided by Zeno into two categories: the passive, which was unqualified and known as matter; and the active, which was the Logos, the reason in matter. These corresponded to the substance and form of Aristotle. The kinds of matter were fire, air, water, and earth, respectively qualified as hot, cold, moist, and dry. Fire and air were light substances, because they sought to fulfill their inherent inclinations of rising; earth and water were heavy substances, because they sought to fulfill their inherent inclination of falling. What caused the rise and fall, flux and change was prime matter. The prime matter or fire or formative power might be either constructive or destructive. It was referred to as ether, an aery vapor surrounding the earth in the outermost layer, preceded by layers of air and water over the earth.

The natural tendencies of fire opposed to earth stabilized the world. Outward-moving fire and air counterbalanced inward-moving water and earth, and thus the opposite pressures kept the world in harmonious equilibrium. The curious conclusion that Zeno reached was that the universe had no weight and eternally remained at rest: the outward motion and weight negated the inward motion and weight, leaving the earth motionless and weightlessly fixed between two pressures.

From defining the physical nature of matter, Zeno proceeded to explain the nature and cause of bodies. As to their nature, bodies were capable of extension into three dimensions. Bodies were the only possible mode of existence and were recognized as the things that acted and were acted upon. Zeno conceived the physical world as a plenum. Geometrical solidity did not characterize body, but only the qualities of passivity (matter) and activity (form). Thus the nature of bodies was evident in the character of their causation and not in their atomic characteristics. Zeno had defined the physis as possessed of fire and had defined this vital fire as the source of all motion and, therefore, of causation ("the fire is the source of all flux"). He did not define fire in terms of static qualities, but in terms of dynamic qualities. Had he realized that, in combining quantitative mathematics with his dynamic view of the nature of things, he had removed the aesthetic qualities from his science, he could have advanced empirical science well past Aristotle. Because of Zeno's dynamic view of nature, we must look back to him and to Heraclitus for the original terrestrial mechanics rather than to Aristotle.

In Zeno's explanation of cause, the interaction of bodies was causation. The contact of one body with another was the efficient cause. All bodies might be moved and modified; all bodies were thus subject to causation. Since only a body could act on a body, all causation was strictly corporeal. Void was the absence of body; place was the presence of body; and space was the combination of void and place. In all this there was actually no need for teleological causation. Were it not for the influence of Aristotle, Zeno might perhaps have developed an entirely material system. As it was, Zeno adopted Aristotelian teleology: he described motion and causation in terms of the Logos and the animated fire.

Zeno's concept of time and infinity perplexed his whole generation with its paradoxes. From the assumption of time as motion that is extended, Zeno proposed the paradox that Achilles could not beat a turtle in a foot race. He said that Achilles would run half the distance of the race course; then he would reach the point halfway between there and the end of the course; then he would get halfway between that point and the part of the course that was left; and finally he would be running the infinitely diminishing half-distances of what remained. Achilles could never reach the finish because he would forever be running those half-distances. Of course, the turtle would do the same thing, and neither would win. Both would take the same time to run the course—infinity. The error in Zeno's paradox was his concept of time as a series of quantitative units rather than as a continuum. Zeno thought of time as mathematical divisions of distance in terms of absolute quantity, while we believe that it is actually relative and continuous.

Having established the nature of matter and bodies, Zeno placed them into four categories, derived from those of Aristotle but decreased in number by six. These categories may be outlined as follows: (1) simply as body; (2) as a body of a particular kind; (3) as a body of a particular state; and (4) as a body in a particular relation. One critic (St. George Stock) has reduced these to the following philosophical terms: (1) substrate; (2) suchlike; (3) so disposed; and (4) so related. Zeller's clearer and more accurate divisions follow: (1) subject matter (substance); (2) property (form); (3) variety; and (4) variety of relation. One can fit all bodies and relations between bodies neatly into these categories and thus give to Zeno's physics a final order and coherence.

His systemization of the nature of the physical world prompted Zeno to explain how man could know this physics. This study comprised his epistemology and psychology. For Zeno, the mind was as deep as the cosmos. He said, "In our inner life there is also a universe . . . that you cannot measure, for that every step is in the infinite." His inquiry into the nature of the mind and its understanding was not skeptical, as were the inquiries of his predecessors. He used the dialectic as a weapon against his enemies. He did not use the dialectic to seek transcendental truth, for he had a strong aversion to the Platonic Theory of Ideas.

Zeno was sure that the mind could apprehend with certainty and that material reality might be known through "presentations." He believed that a presentation was impressed on the mind from a real object, correctly representing it. The wise man was he who could tell grasping impressions (presentations on the senses) from ambiguous ones. A grasping impression "takes hold of us by the hair and drags us to assert," he said. Zeno compared simple sensations with the extended finger; assent, "first activity of the power of judgment," with the closed hand; conception with the fist; and knowledge with one hand firmly grasped on the other.

Though the idea is usually attributed to Locke, the concept of the mind as a clean sheet of paper (*tabula rasa*) was originated by Zeno. Impressions of sense were the first character on the mind. Unreality resulted from false impressions; the objects did not change, but remained the same; only impressions changed. Because delusions arose from faulty sense perceptions, most men of Zeno's time despaired of all knowledge; sense perceptions very often left no room for doubt. Once indubitable "impressions of the soul" or "phantasies" were known, then the apprehension of the truth could be logically deduced from these premises.

The chain of certainty linked the mind to the thing. Impressions stamped on the mind formed perception; this combined with memory, made up experience; and experience understood by thinking led to universal conception. Primary conceptions were not innate but might be deduced from thought or experience. Zeno believed that knowledge was gained when "the activity of the understanding is allied with sensation." Traces of transcendental thought still remained in the empiricism of Zeno but its prominence was considerably lessened. Conceptions of good and evil were not allied to sensations, he asserted, but those other than primary moral conceptions must not be considered reality. This peculiar empiricism was called the "Doctrine of Irresistibility." It had a dualism of innate ideas and ideas from experience, both dominated by realism that claimed that perceptions presented ideas of objects as the objects really were. Zeno, with many well-placed lapses in logic and florid rhetoric, asserted that the mind could empirically know things in themselves. With that assertion, epistemological certainty was made possible.

Had Zeno been able to establish an epistemological foundation for knowledge, very little in Stoicism would have changed. What he said, he said with an unflinching dogmatism, a certainty so pronounced that one may wonder why his method is called logic at all. Even though his logic was unnecessary and the principles stood without its aid, Zeno felt a need to clothe his ideas in a logic to give them the force of "rationality." Later in Stoic history Seneca would tire of the "rigid monotony of Zeno's paradoxes," and others would become annoyed at his "repellent technical terminology." Nevertheless, the logic of the Stoics did give their doctrine some coherence and the air of authority, if nothing else.

Their logic included rhetoric and dialectic. Zeno expressed the difference between rhetoric and dialectic by comparing rhetoric with the palm and dialectic with the fist. Presumably the palm was used to persuade the listener by the gentle pat on the head, and if he still would not believe the argument, the fist would convince with a pounding. More abstractly, dialectic concerned argument by means of questions and answers, and rhetoric concerned excellence in speaking.

Rhetoric was divided into the judicial, the demonstrative, and the deliberative; its parts comprised invention, style, arrangement, delivery, and memory. Speeches were given a format of preface, narration, controversial matter, and conclusion.

Dialectic was divided into poetics (meaning) and grammar (structure). The subject of poetics included amphibology (ambiguity), meter, and music. Grammar included alphabet, parts of speech, solecism, and barbarism. The parts of speech were designated as common and proper nouns, verbs, conjunctions, and articles. Solecism was an offense against syntax; barbarism was an offense against accidence (inflection); both corresponded to the fallacies in logic. The five virtues of speech were considered to be Hellenism, clearness, conciseness, property, and distinction.

Formal logic was primarily concerned with fact, tautology, and contradiction. The correction of fallacies arising from contradiction was made by reference to empirical knowledge. Stoic reasoning used the following scheme of argument, or syllogism:

Major Premise: If A, then B;
Minor Premise: But A;
Conclusion: B.

Though this may seem simple, it was extremely complex compared with the more crystalline Aristotelian logic in which the syllogism took the form: "If A is predicated universally of B, and B of C, A is necessarily predicated universally of C." Thus,

All cats are animals (A=B);
All kittens are cats (C=A);
All kittens are animals (C=B).

If applied carefully, this method of reasoning could produce valid demonstrations. Zeno, however, used it poorly, as in the following instance:

One does not commit a secret to a man who is drunk;
One does commit a secret to a good man;
Therefore a good man will not get drunk.

This was flimsy logic, because it contained no necessarily connected logical clauses leading to a conclusion but instead offered only three major premises. His chain logic was even weaker, as, for example:

The wise man is temperate;
The temperate is constant;
The constant is unperturbed;
The unperturbed is free from sorrow;
Who so is free from sorrow is happy;
Therefore, the wise man is happy.

This form of logic consisted of a chain of major premises linked together, one following the other; if all the premises were correct, the conclusion would be correct. What use is a logic of this sort, though? There are so many major premises that the logical form is useless except as dogma; furthermore, the conclusion is a tautology, since it was stated in the premises.

Another of these dogmatic syllogisms ran thus:

It is reasonable to honor the gods;
It would not be reasonable to honor nonexistent beings;
Therefore, the gods exist.

The argument had such an impossible major premise that it might as well have not been logic. Actually, it was not logic, nor was it intended to be logic. It was intended as a kind of prophetical saying. Zeno would not have said, "It is reasonable that . . ." He would have said, "Thus saith reason." His utterances were laconic and paradoxical dogma set in the form of syllogism, but more Biblical than Greek. Zeno formed the logic and set the tone, but it was for Chrysippus to create the logical systems.

The Greeks, apparently, found Zeno's dogma very comforting in their "shivering and naked age." Values had distintegrated with the rise of tyranny, and the life of Platonic reason had lost all meaning. When people no longer care about anything, they desire to cling unquestioningly to a single moral force. Zeno provided that force for the Greek people and injected it into his logic. He did not intend to convince by reason. His witticisms and sayings "caught on" because of a people's desperate necessities. Stoicism created a logic to suit the urgent need; the necessities preceded all its complex meanings. And from the same need arose Stoic physics with its overriding purpose of demonstrating the rationality of the universe.

Once God and the physical world were explained, it became necessary for the educated Stoic to ask, "How is man to live in this Universe?" Zeno's ethical thesis was that if nature were as described above, and man were a part of nature, then man must live according to nature.

Zeno taught that the divine was in all things, that the law of nature was divine, and that the fulfillment of a man's life was to live in accordance with nature. Virtue of itself was sufficient for happiness; things, neither good nor evil, were indifferent. The indifferent things included life and death, good and ill repute, pain and pleasure, riches and poverty, and like matters. And men were of two sorts: the upright and the wicked. Only the wise were beautiful.

Men lived by passionate loves and desires, according to Zeno, and the result of this turmoil was not happiness. A man was happy only when what he willed came to pass. Zeno believed, "I am happy when I do not want things any other than they are." He warned that if a man willed what went against nature, fate would flow over him; therefore man must adjust his will to divine reason.

Since man could not change nature, then in the face of nature's torment the most noble thing he could do would be to remain impervious to all disturbance. The only thing a man could really achieve would be to control his own will. Here the Stoics looked for a basis of conduct in absolute reason. Man should not allow his transient passions to obscure true value; the true value consisted of living according to nature and of being impervious to human passion.

The value of morality was that it controlled the will. The internal will determined good and evil in relation to man, a good and evil independent of externals. The external cosmos was inherently good; it was only men's wills that were evil. Though external actions were necessary, they were irrelevant. The internal should remain tranquil, impervious to the tumultuous outer world; it was only in the tranquil soul that virtue could be found.

The rational life must follow a harmonious plan. The purpose of life was to live in conformity with nature, which meant to live a life of virtue, since nature lead to virtue. Living this way amounted to an official duty. The natural man must adapt his action to the arrangement of nature, to consistency and harmony, and to the dictates of reason. Duty consisted solely of conformity to nature and reason. And all the moral trappings we attach to it were Roman in origin.

Zeno introduced the term "value" into ethics. Value demanded substitution for an undesirable and unpreferred agent by an agent that was desirable and preferred. A man could discover whether he were making moral progress by examining his dreams. If the dreams dwelt upon the undesirable "impure delights," it was a sure sign of moral laxity, but if the images in his dreams were pure, he was moving toward virtue. The preferred values were wisdom, altruism, moderation, and detached tranquillity.

Wisdom, according to Zeno, was the good sense to be temperate. For only in moderation was a man unperturbed and free from frustration. The wise man knew when to speak and when to be silent, knew how to hold firm his passion in order to "conquer his own action," and knew what was preferred or indifferent. He knew that happiness depended solely on the will, that value depended upon intention, that sin carried punishment with it, that virtue was action in conformity with reason, and that nothing external could dishonor a man. He knew that the greatest art was to heal the sickness of the mind. He knew how to be simple and straightforward; he knew how to be independent and self-contained. He knew, no matter what might happen, no matter how tragic life might seem, that all things flowed with the cosmic good and that he must face it with optimism. But most of all he knew that there was hope beneath the endless phases of the sun. Zeno believed, "We are not so poor in anything as in time, but though life is short, art is long." And only in art was there hope.

For Zeno, art was more than the creation of poetry or golden statues; art was embodied in service to mankind: the art of a moral physician. The wise man, who was the Stoic ideal of the educated man, became a healer among men simply because he was a man. For man was not an isolated unit; he was a social animal and a particle of divine reason. As a member of the great city of humanity, man was intended in nature to devote himself to the service of society. The true philosopher, unless prevented, would serve the state.

Zeno visualized "one flock feeding in one pasture," saw all men united into one government, with one way of life, with no nationalities, with no discriminations between Greek and barbarian, and with no bondsmen or slaves. In his own *Republic*, Zeno made Plato's *Republic* juster still. His altruism would bring order into a crumpled civilization, create values in a valueless society, and unite the peoples of an ancient world.

Zeno's altruism was wholly un-Christian, and Bevan suggests that this is why Stoicism was never assimilated into Christianity. Zeno insisted that man must serve but that he must never feel compassion, for that would disrupt his internal and external tranquillity. Breakage of his inner calm was the worst tragedy man could endure. Even when the Stoic sighed, he did not sigh from the heart. If he ever sighed, it would be because he had reasoned that it was a preferable action, not because he had felt an emotion. No emotion was compatible with the Stoic ideal. Emotions caused frustration; therefore, the Stoic was detached and aloof. And because detachment and love were incompatible, Stoicism and Christianity were incompatible.

The real purpose of education, Zeno would argue, was to foster the moral conduct of man. Philosophy could serve to educate man in the exercise of the highest art—virtue (*aretē*). All knowledge was useful and important only to the extent that it converged on ethics. For the Stoic, as for all liberal educators, it was not the mere acquisition of knowledge that was central. It was Zeno's contention that the educated man, the "wise man," could conduct his own life in accordance with a system that would guarantee him not only a good life but a happy, peaceful life. Though many features of the Stoic system were careless, illogical, and even unoriginal, its central purpose was taken seriously by very large numbers of people for many years. The Stoic saint was no accident—he was the product of an educational system that promised him happiness if he lived in accordance with nature and reason. In order to live in this way, he had to learn to know what this meant. What is crucial to the success of any educational system is what the students of that system do with their lives, how they conduct themselves as human beings. In this sense Stoicism was eminently successful.

BIBLIOGRAPHICAL NOTE

This chapter obviously owes a great deal to the many scholars who have done a good deal of work on Stoicism. Generally, it may be said that there has not been as much done in recent times on Stoicism as in the past. The following list, though not complete, will give the interested student a basic working bibliography of Stoicism.

Hans von Arnim, *Stoicorum Veterum Fragmenta.* 4 Vols. Leipzig, 1905–1924. This work is indispensable for the scholar who can read the ancient languages and who wishes to deal with what has survived of the Stoics in the original.

E. V. Arnold, *Roman Stoicism.* London, 1958 (reprint). This is a substantial treatment of the subject with the emphasis placed upon the development of Stoicism into an international system under the Romans.

John W. Basore, *Seneca: Moral Essays.* 3 Vols. London and New York, 1928–1935. This is the Loeb Library translation with the Latin on the left hand page and the English on the right. Useful and valuable.

Edwyn Bevan, *Stoics and Skeptics.* Oxford, 1913. Often thought to be the best perceptive study of Stoicism.

W. W. Capes, *Stoicism*. London, 1880. Old but usable.

W. L. Davidson, *Stoic Creed*. Edinburgh, 1907. Fairly adequate.

G. M. A. Grube, *The Meditations of Marcus Aurelius*. Indianapolis and New York, 1963. Contains an excellent translation with a solid introduction, valuable glossary and biographical list.

R. M. Gummere, *The Epistles of Seneca*. 3 Vols. London and New York, 1918–1925. The *Epistulae Morales* of Seneca in the Loeb Library translation.

R. M. Gummere, *Seneca the Philosopher and His Modern Message*. Boston, 1922. An appreciative study by a man who has devoted a good deal of his life to Senecan scholarship.

Moses Hadas, *The Stoic Philosophy of Seneca*. New York, 1958. In this paperback edition Professor Hadas has written a brief but fine introduction and translated some of the more representative selections from the Essays and Letters to illustrate Senecan views.

R. D. Hicks, *Stoic and Epicurean*. New York, 1962 (reprint). One of the more important books on the subject.

M. Holland, *Reign of the Stoics*. Boston, 1874. Old but contains some useful comments.

P. E. Matheson, *Epictetus: The Discourses and Fragments*. Oxford, 1916. Translation in the Oxford series.

W. J. Oates, *The Stoic and Epicurean Philosophers*. New York, 1940. The Epicurean and Stoic philosophers edited and translated by a famous American educator.

St. George Stock, *Stoicism*. New York, 1908. A helpful account.

R. M. Wenley, *Stoicism and Its Influence*. Boston, 1924. Useful for tracing the impact of Stoicism on history.

E. Zeller, *Stoics, Epicureans, and Skeptics*. New York, 1962 (reprint). A very important study by the German scholar. Moral in tone but penetrating in detail and knowledge.

The Oxford Classical Dictionary. Oxford, 1949. For general articles on all Stoics and all aspects of Stoicism.

🌿 AUGUSTINE (354-430) was born in Tagaste, a small town in the Roman province of Numidia, near what is now the eastern border of Algeria. His father, though not wealthy, was an official in the Roman administration of the village and was then still a pagan. His mother, Monica, was already known as a fervent Christian. At the age of eleven or twelve he was sent some twenty miles south to Madaura to study grammar and literature. He did so well that at the age of sixteen he was able to go to Carthage to study rhetoric for three years. After completing his studies, he taught first in Tagaste, then in Carthage. In 383 Augustine left Africa for Italy, staying first in Rome, then Milan. In Milan he came under the influence of St. Ambrose. After having been attracted successively to Manichaeanism, Skepticism, and Neoplatonism, Augustine found intellectual and moral peace in conversion to Christianity in his thirty-fourth year. Returning to Africa, he sought to lead a kind of monastic life with a few friends and pupils. He was made a priest in 391 and in 395 was made Bishop of Hippo. He died during the Vandals' siege of the town of Hippo in 430. Augustine was a prolific writer. In addition to many letters, sermons, and tracts, he composed a number of books, the most famous of which are *The Confessions, On the Trinity, The City of God,* and *On Christian Doctrine.* This last contains Augustine's appraisal of the place of pagan learning in Christianity.

4

THE CHRISTIAN: *Augustine*

BY PEARL KIBRE

In addition to his fame as a Father of the Roman church and as a renowned Christian teacher, St. Augustine is noted as one of the most significant transmitters of Roman culture and educational practices to succeeding generations. He was an able student and a gifted and skillful teacher of grammar and rhetoric in the imperial schools of the fourth century. Like most Roman intellectuals, he held the view that in the training of the Christian as well as of the pagan intellectual, the liberal arts, grammar, rhetoric, and logic, and the four mathematical disciplines, arithmetic, geometry, music, and astronomy, were essential. He insisted, particularly in his *Confessions* (I,15), upon the early study and mastery of the lessons of reading, writing, and arithmetic, even if, as in his own case, "in boyhood . . ." the student "loved not study and hated to be forced to it." But that he was forced he acknowledged was good, since by such studies he obtained and retained the power to read what was written and to write what he wished.

Although Augustine conceded that those who forced him to study in his youth had done well toward him, he also maintained in the *Confessions* (I,17) that from his own experience, "a pleasurable encouragement has more force in learning . . . than a frightful enforcement." He attributed his own dislike of Greek not only to his difficulty and failure to understand the foreign tongue but also to being forced by "cruel threats and punishments" to continue its study. He pointed out that "although Latin too was a foreign tongue," he learned this easily "without pressure of punishment" amid the smiles and the encouragement of his friends.

Augustine held that the benefit of these studies came largely from the skills that they developed rather than from the precepts of pagan grammarians or the poetic fictions of Aeneas. For Augustine, especially after his conversion, moral guidance was most important. And in the *Confessions* he pointed again to his own early career in which this was ignored, while care was taken to have him "learn to speak excellently, and to be a persuasive orator." He believed the best discipline of all to be moral science, which provides an understanding of both virtues and vices. However, he approved any instruction that causes to be learned or acquired the certain knowledge of things of all kinds, especially the "liberal arts." But the usefulness of these studies was to be measured by their service to God. They were to be studied not for the attainment of specific ends or to maintain opinions but to serve God. Therefore, in the *Confessions* (I,21–22) he held up to scorn the view current in his own day that a teacher or learner of the laws of pronunciation gives greater offense when he speaks without an aspirate, "of a uman being," contrary to the laws of grammar, than when he hates another human being, "contrary to God's will." And he insisted that "no science of letters could replace the record of conscience . . . that he is doing to another what from another he would be loth to suffer." He also derided the man who, seeking for fame in eloquence and appearing before a judge amidst a huge crowd, "declaiming against his enemy with fiercest hatred," would take the greatest care to avoid "by an error of the tongue" the "murder of the word 'human being' " but would take little care lest, through the fury of his pride, he murder a real human being.

With the above qualifications, Augustine continued to be an advocate of a general education in the seven liberal arts, which had been the bulwark of Roman education. He frequently quoted from his storehouse of reading in the classics and demonstrated that Christians could learn something from reading them. He recorded in the *Confessions* (III,40) that reading Cicero's *Hortensius* (apparently no longer extant), led him to the study of philosophy and to the first step in his quest for the wisdom that would eventually lead him to the Scriptures and to God. In his tract *The Happy Life* (2.8), Augustine asserted that "the souls of people not scientifically trained and unfamiliar with the liberal arts are, as it were, hungry and famished." Moreover, in the *Divine Providence and the Problem of Evil* (1.8.24), which together with *The Happy Life* was written shortly after his conversion, he held that "instruction in the liberal arts . . . produces devotees more alert and steadfast and better equipped for embracing truth." He further maintained, in the second book of the above work on *Divine Providence*, that since "order is a pathway leading to God," the aspirant for truth finds illustration and evidence for this order in the branches of learning that have come to be called liberal. For example, in music, with its sounds arranged in a fixed measure of time and in modulated variations of high and low pitch, in geometry, with its beauty in the design and dimensions of numbers, in astronomy, with the fixed and unerring movements of the stars, in the "constant alterations of the seasons," and in the fixed power and ratios of numbers, he will find that order reigns supreme. In Augustine's opinion, one who has acquired a knowledge of all these branches of learning, together with a knowledge of right reason, may then aspire to a knowledge of philosophy and may begin the search for things divine. The liberal arts were thus a means to an end. They were to be utilized in preparing one to gain an understanding of God. With this in mind, Augustine began work on an encyclopedia of the seven liberal arts, of which he apparently completed only the tracts on grammar and *On Music*. It is still not clear whether some recently discovered texts of the former are by Augustine. But the latter work is available both in Latin and in English translation.

In the tract *On Music* Augustine stressed particularly the rational and mental aspects of the art. As he elsewhere asserted, in *The Immortality of the Soul* (4.5–6), "It is evident, however, not only that art is in the mind of the artist, but also that it cannot be but in his mind, and inseparable from it." For if an art passed from one mind to another, no one would teach an art except by losing it, and no one would become skilled except by his teacher's loss of the skill or by his death. And he further observed that art does not exist "in a mind conspicuous for its forgetfulness and ignorance." Augustine concerned himself in the tract *On Music* with rhythm and meter, number, motion, and time. And he used these as vehicles to draw men of good natural capacity gradually from the consideration of changeable numbers in inferior things to a love of unchangeable truth, to the one God and master of all things.

The use of the arts as vehicles to truth and to God was further demonstrated by Augustine in his work *Concerning the Teacher*. There he utilized the liberal arts as a means for approaching the eternal and immutable principles of which the ultimate cause is truth and God. They were employed to exercise and sharpen the faculties of the mind so that it might be better equipped to reach the truth that leads to the happy life and hence to God. And their study, he indicated in this tract, was so to be conducted that it would raise the mind progressively from the contemplation of subject matter based on sense knowledge to that of the spirit. The mind would thus be directed from a consideration of the constantly changing, inferior, material realities upward toward the superior, invisible, nonmaterial, and unchanging realities. Furthermore, that grammar and rhetoric could be used to present the truth in a beguiling fashion, Augustine illustrated by the word-by-word explanation of a line of verse from Vergil.

Augustine also set forth in his tracts some sound educational precepts regarding both the method of teaching and the qualifications of the teacher. He dealt particularly with the Christian teacher in *Christian Instruction* and in *On Catechizing the Unlearned*. But his principles might well be applied in a more general sense. Since the aim of teaching is, he asserted, to expound what is good, to turn men from evil, and to lead them to God, the Christian teacher or orator should begin by winning the sympathy of those whom he is addressing. And he should also aim toward building up in them a cheerful attitude toward life. Then, after gaining their attention and respect, he should carefully and clearly explain the matter at hand. He should avoid excessive subtleties and discard nonessentials. He should also endeavor to resolve doubtful points and to move the wills of his listeners. But he should never do so for personal gain or for the mere entertainment of those addressed. The good teacher, Augustine held, is one who chooses words not for their elegance but because they reveal and make known what he wishes to express. He avoids all expressions that do not instruct. And he keeps ever in mind that it is his aim to teach, to please, and to persuade. Augustine set forth the above principles in his tract *Christian Instruction* (4.10.24). And he added the reminder that to make his words persuasive, the one who teaches should live uprightly and choose the good life (*ibid.*, 4.28.61).

Augustine gave some further pedagogical advice in his discussion of converts in the tract *On Catechizing the Unlearned*. He urged that each one be dealt with individually, because the disposition, the mental capacity, and the previous education of none were precisely the same. He also insisted that in the presentation of materials in actual teaching, the instructor should have a definite end in view for each lesson and should limit the subject matter so that a little could be taught thoroughly, while some might be done cursorily. Yet all the parts of the lesson should be fitted together to form a unity in which the main principles to be emphasized might always be kept clearly in view.

Moreover, Augustine demonstrated in *Christian Instruction* (2) the specific relation of each of the branches of knowledge that a Christian should have for an understanding of Scripture. He should first of all have a knowledge of grammar, particularly about the structure and use of language; he should also know not only Latin but also Greek and Hebrew, for a comprehension and appreciation of the terms used. He should know the natures of animals, minerals, plants, trees, and other things named in the Scriptures for the sake of analogy. For if he does not know, for example, the nature of the serpent he cannot comprehend the Lord's meaning when He directed that we be "wise as serpents" (Matt. 10:16). If he knows about the carbuncle that glitters in the dark, this knowledge will throw light on many obscure passages. The

Christian student of the Scriptures, Augustine continued, should not be ignorant of numbers. For if he is, he will misunderstand the figuration and mystical references in Scripture. He should also know certain elements of music to explain some figurative passages in the Bible; and he should recognize that it is important for him to know history and chronology. He should not entirely eschew astronomy, provided that it is not tied to prediction and that he does not attempt to learn from the stars about his own deeds but limits himself to what relates only to the stars themselves. Augustine insisted that the Christian should completely reject all the arts of superstition as either worthless or sinful. But he should not shun a knowledge of human institutions or of mechanics since these are useful not only in comprehending Scripture but for the daily course of life; and he should recognize the importance of the sciences of reasoning and of numbers. The science of reasoning in particular, Augustine held, is especially valuable in penetrating and finding answers to questions regarding disputed points in sacred writings. And finally, as a former teacher of rhetoric, Augustine did not fail to discuss rhetoric in his survey of the requisite branches of knowledge for the student of Scripture. However, he asserted, in his *Christian Instruction* (4.1–5), that while the use of language in the service of truth may well be guided by the principles of eloquence and oratory, these can better be acquired from reading and listening to the eloquence of orators than from time spent in the study of rhetoric. In short, Augustine acknowledged in *Christian Instruction* (2.40–41) that the Christian student of the Scriptures may with profit read the books of the pagans and appropriate from them those teachings that can be of service to truth. For, he asserted, although the works of the pagans may abound in superstitious and false notions, "they also contain liberal instructions . . . adapted to the service of truth" and some "useful principles about morals." But the Christian should be mindful, Augustine admonished, that all knowledge gained from the pagans, however useful, is inferior to the knowledge gained from the sacred Scriptures. Moreover, Augustine added, the student of Holy Scripture, after he has been instructed in all the arts, should reflect upon the observation of the Apostle: "Knowledge puffeth up, but charity edifieth" (I Cor. 8:1).

Augustine himself, as a Christian teacher and student of Holy Scripture, and an ardent defender of the truth, provided a personal example of one who had first developed and enhanced his natural endowment by acquiring the necessary knowledge and skills afforded by a study of the liberal arts before he embarked on his quest for truth. He had also been directed through the reading of a pagan work, Cicero's *Hortensius*, to the pathway that was eventually to lead him to truth and to God. The truth, he held, is ultimately attainable. And he clearly enunciated this conviction in the several treatises written shortly after his conversion and while he was at Cassiacum—*Answer to Skeptics*, *The Happy Life*, the *Soliloquies*, and *The Immortality of the Soul*. In the first of these, written in dialogue form, Augustine argued against the views of the Skeptics, or Academics, the fourth-century philosophers who held that although man is not able to discover truth, the search for it constitutes happiness. Augustine insisted that truth can be known and is attainable by man. And while happiness may be found in the conformity of man's instincts, desires, and wants to the dictates of reason, no true happiness is possible, in Augustine's opinion, if reason is incapable of satisfying the thirst for truth. Augustine admitted that one arrives at truth only after a long and painful search; but this search, he held, does have an intellectual appeal, and it is not fruitless. In the tract *The Happy Life*, Augustine further set forth his view that happiness consists in the knowledge and possession of God (which for him is synonymous with truth), and that this ought to be the goal of all human endeavor. However, in this work and in the *Soliloquies* (1.6.13), his dialogue with reason regarding the nature of God and of the soul, he maintained that the three virtues, faith, hope, and love, are prerequisites of the recognition of truth and the attainment of a happy life.

Besides demonstrating the role of the liberal arts in the discovery of the truth to which he was dedicated, Augustine also turned his attention, in the tract *Concerning the Teacher*, to the fundamental philosophical problem underlying all education and, in fact, all teaching. He confronted the question of how teaching is possible and whether, if at all, one man can transmit ideas to or produce ideas in another. Since the examination and discussion of this question together with the development of the theme of the "interior teacher" in the above tract constitute a major contribution of Augustine to educational thought, his thinking on this subject merits detailed consideration. The work, *Concerning the Teacher*, in the form of a dialogue between Augustine and his precocious son Adeodatus, directs attention first to the generally accepted assumption that teaching is accomplished through speech, that is, that the teacher transmits ideas to the pupil by the intermediary of the spoken word. Augustine began, therefore, with an examination of this assumption and a consideration of the purpose of speech: whether speech exists to teach or to remind; and whether words are the only signs or means of communicating. In the course of this discussion he tentatively concluded that teaching and learning take place when one uses speech to ask questions, and that there are two reasons for speaking: to teach and to remind others or even ourselves. Augustine demonstrated that the latter occurs also when we sing or pray (obviously God does not need to be reminded or taught by our spoken words in order to learn what is in our minds). Furthermore, even if we utter no sound, we may think the words themselves and thus speak within the mind. Hence words and speech do serve to remind and to stimulate the memory to recall the realities that the words signify.

Augustine next turned to the consideration of words as signs and to the question of whether signs other than words can be used to communicate ideas. He had elsewhere, in his *Christian Instruction* (2.1), defined a sign as something that, besides impressing its own form on the senses, brings to mind something else. For example, when one sees a footprint, he thinks not only of the footprint but also of the animal that walked there; or when one sees smoke, he thinks not only of smoke, but also of a fire nearby. However, in the tract *Concerning the Teacher*, Augustine used the exercise in grammar, the word-by-word examination of a line of verse in Vergil, mentioned earlier, to demonstrate that in order to explain the sense of a word, one must use other words or signs. Hence "if" is explained as signifying doubt, and "nothing" as signifying that which does not exist. In the case of the latter, it is made clear that what is signified does not exist, but that the word itself does. Augustine also demonstrated that signs other than words can be used to communicate or to signify things. One can call attention to a wall without speaking the word "wall," merely by pointing the finger. Similarly, one can do this for colors and for all other visible qualities of corporeal things, without the use of speech. One can indeed signify sound, weight, odor, and taste, pertaining to senses other than sight, without the use of spoken words. This is shown, Augustine asserted, when men communicate with the deaf by gestures and actors in the theatres portray and enact entire dramas, without the use of words but by pantomime. Hence, words are not the only signs that can be used to communicate.

This conclusion led Augustine to the question of whether there is anything that can be shown or taught without the use of a sign. In his answer, he tentatively agreed that the meaning of some words, such as "walking," can be shown without the use of a sign by performing the act signified when one is asked what walking is. This might also be done to explain such action words as eating, drinking, sitting, and innumerable others. However, if one were already doing what was asked, that is, if one were walking when asked what walking is, it would be impossible to answer the question without the use of signs. Hence, it appears that an activity that one is not doing when asked, or that one can do immediately after the inquiry, can be shown without the use of a sign, and this includes an activity that may be a sign itself, such as speaking. For when we speak, we utter words or signs—that is, we signify.

Augustine then returned to the consideration of signs. He pointed out that there are signs that signify other signs, and signs that signify words that are not themselves signs. For example, if one says "gesture" or "letter," the words are signs, and the things these two words signify are also signs. But if one says "stone," the word is a sign, because it signifies something, but the thing signified is not necessarily a sign. Augustine further directed attention to signs that signify each other, such as "noun" and "word." He pointed out that the signs that are spoken words pertain to the sense of hearing; the signs that are gestures pertain to the sense of sight; and that the written word is understood as a sign of a word rather than as a word, since the word is really that which is uttered by the articulate voice with some meaning. And this can be perceived by the sense of hearing alone. When a word has been written, it first conveys a sign to the eyes, and then, just as the spoken word comes to the ears, it comes into the mind. Related to the preceding, too, is the further discussion of the differences between noun and word, both of which are signs; but even though all nouns are also words, their meaning is not the same. Things are called words for one reason, Augustine noted, and nouns are called words for another; words (verba) are derived from vibration (verberando), while nouns (nomina) are from knowing (noscendo).

At this point in the dialogue, Augustine made it clear that the preceding intensive analysis and discussion of signs were undertaken to prepare, by the gradual stages suited to our comprehension, for progress on the road that leads to eternal truth. He had thus first considered not the things signified but rather their signs. And he had done this primarily to exercise the powers of the mind. Hence, Augustine demonstrated that he considered the exercises that involve the use of reason and the speculative faculties to be a preparation for the mystical contemplation that leads to a knowledge of God.

The discussion was then turned from words as signs to the things signified. Augustine pointed out that there can obviously be no reasonable discussion if the spoken words do not bring to mind the things of which they are the signs. When a word is uttered, one thinks both of the sign and of the reality that the word signifies. For example, when one hears the word "man" (homo), he thinks not only of the letters or syllables that make up the word but also of the reality signified. However, it is only the sign of the reality signified that comes from the mouth of the speaker. Augustine illustrated this by an amusing example. He told of the Sophist who forced his opponent to assert that everything one says comes forth from the mouth and thus obliged him to conclude that when he spoke the word "lion," the lion itself came forth from his mouth, whereas of course it was the word "lion," not a lion, that came out of his mouth. Hence what we say signifies the things of which we speak. And it is not the reality, but the sign by which it is signified, that issues forth from the mouth of the speaker. Whenever signs are heard, therefore, the attention is directed toward the things signified.

One may then inquire, Augustine indicated in the next part of the discussion, whether the realities signified are to be more highly valued than their signs. To illustrate the possibility that this may not always be the case, the word "filth" (*coenum*) was given as an example of a noun that is superior to what it signifies, since one hears the sign more cheerfully than one perceives the reality by any of the senses. Augustine demonstrated, however, that because the word is used for the purpose of teaching, it is the use of the word or sign that is superior to the word or sign itself. Words exist so that we may use them; and we use them for teaching. And just as teaching is superior to speaking, so the use of speech for instruction (doctrine) is far superior to words themselves. Hence, the knowledge or cognition of things is more precious than the signs of the things and is to be preferred to the cognition of the signs. A further illustration of this, Augustine noted, is the word "vice" (*vitium*), which is better than what it signifies, although the knowledge of the word is inferior by far to the cognition of vices.

After a further review of what, if anything at all, can be taught without the use of signs, verbal or otherwise, Augustine presented a hypothetical case of learning about an art from direct observation of its performance, without the use of signs. He related an instance of an individual, entirely ignorant of the art of fowling or ensnaring birds, who encountered a fowler equipped for his art, but not fowling at that moment. However, upon seeing himself observed, the fowler showed off his art by setting his snares and capturing a small bird nearby. Was not the fowler, in this instance, teaching his art to the spectator, not by signs, but by means of the activity itself? In reply, Augustine asserted that if the spectator is intelligent enough he may grasp the technique of the entire art from what he observes. And one may thus conclude that some men can be taught some things, though not all, without signs. In corroboration of this Augustine recalled innumerable things that can be shown through themselves without signs. Among these are the frequent spectacles of men in theatres exhibiting dramatic actions through their performance, without signs; and the revelations of God to the discerning, through nature and the realities themselves, through the sun and sunlight, the moon and the other planets, the stars, the earth and the seas, and everything that is generated in them.

Is it possible, therefore, Augustine asked, in regard to communication by words or signs, that there is nothing that can be learned by signs; and that it is not through signs that our understanding progresses? In answer to this question, Augustine suggested that although ideas can seemingly be communicated only by the use of signs, yet the one hearing the words, in order to understand them, must in fact already know the reality they signify. For when a sign is given, if the hearer does not kow of what it is a sign, he learns nothing from the sign. If, on the other hand, he does know of what it is a sign, he also learns nothing new from the sign. As an illustration, Augustine introduced the unfamiliar word *sarabarae* for head coverings. If one does not know that certain head coverings are signified by this name, he does not learn from hearing it either what a head is or what coverings are. After hearing the word repeatedly, however, and seeing the things of which it is a sign, one may recognize that it is a sign of something that one already knows. One thus learns the sign only after one has perceived that it refers to a reality one already knows. One does not learn the reality anew from the sign. Thus, with the word "head," one may learn the meaning of the word when it is used at the same time that the head is pointed out by the finger. The knowledge of what the head is, however, is already in the mind. Hence one does not learn it anew. Augustine concluded that, contrary to what was suggested earlier, we learn nothing through those signs called words. We learn the meaning of the word, that is, the signification that lies hidden in the sound, only after we perceive the reality by other means. In the case of the unfamiliar word *sarabarae*, if one signifies that they are head coverings by a gesture, by a sketch, or by showing something familiar to which they are similar, one may teach the signification of the name but not by words. If one looks at the head coverings at the same time that the word is called to his attention one may be reminded of the realities the word signifies, not through the words spoken but by seeing the things themselves. In this way one comes to know the meaning of the word; he does not learn anew the reality itself since he already knows it.

The chief value of words, therefore, according to Augustine, does not lie in their power to show us realities in order that we may know them, but lies, rather, in their power to remind us of realities we already know. Thus, Augustine pointed out, when one speaks to another, although he may believe that he is exchanging ideas, he is actually only exchanging words. The words received do not bring the ideas of the speaker.

They reveal those of the hearer who is given only what he already has. Moreover, when one who wishes to teach something presents to the eyes, to some other sense organ of the body, or even to the mind itself the things that he wishes to make known, he does not depend on words, because he recognizes that only words, or rather the sounds of words, can be learned from them. One does not indeed know that the sound one hears is a word until one knows what it signifies. And as of the realities themselves, one cannot be said to learn words one already knows, nor can one learn words one did not know earlier, unless their signification is perceived. Such perception occurs, Augustine maintained, not from hearing the sounds of the words but through the cognition of the realities signified. The words cannot therefore teach one to know physical realities unless one presently sees or experiences these realities through the senses. Augustine thus re-emphasized the point that we learn nothing by means of words. Perceptions, he continued, come either through the senses or the mind. If one is asked about a sensible object, one may reply that it is a thing one senses. For example, if while gazing at the moon, one is asked what the moon is, he replies that it is the object at which he is gazing. However, if the questioner does not himself see the thing about which he is asking, he may or may not believe the answer given. But in either case he learns nothing from the words used unless he himself sees the object. He can thus learn only from the reality itself and through his own senses, not by words. If the questioner asks about things that were sensed in the past but are not now present, the one asked speaks of the images impressed by the things themselves and committed to memory. When he hears the names of the things that he sensed before, he does not learn by the words but rather he is led to recall things to mind by the images hidden within himself. If, however, he has not sensed them before, he can believe what he hears but he does not learn by the words.

Moreover, as to things perceived by the mind, that is, by the intellect and reason, these, according to Augustine, have an immediate presence that can be contemplated in that interior light of truth by which the inner man is illumined and made joyful. The hearer of words, who sees with that hidden and pure eye the things signified, knows what is spoken of not through the words but through his own contemplation. Hence, when the teacher speaks, he does not teach the learner who is gazing at the true realities, for reality is taught not by the words but by that which is made manifest within by God. Occasionally, however, a learner is not aware that he knows, but when urged on by skillful questions, he finds that he does know what is asked. This discovery may occur because, on first hearing the question, he did not grasp its import. Then, guided by the teacher's questions, he may be enabled to discover the answer by himself and within himself.

Applying these concepts to the act of learning, Augustine concluded that no one can teach another an idea without making him see it or discover it in himself. The words of the teacher cannot, however, cause one to see intelligible realities within the mind. That can be brought about only by the power and wisdom of God. But the words of the teacher may remind the one being taught to consult the truth that resides within the mind itself. Hence, it is not the speaker or the teacher who expresses himself outwardly but the truth residing within the mind itself that one consults when reminded by words to do so. And the truth consulted is the "interior teacher," the immutable power and wisdom of God dwelling within man, consulted by every rational soul. Yet, if despite this "interior teacher," one should sometimes err, it is not because of a defect of the truth consulted, any more than it is because of a defect of the light outside that the eyes of the body are often deceived. And just as one consults this external light about visible things such as colors, and just as one consults the other senses employed by the mind to interpret physical things, so also one consults the interior truth, by means of reason, about those things that are to be understood.

In discounting the value of words, Augustine called attention further to the frequent failure of words to reveal what is in the speaker's own mind. For one thing, there are liars and deceivers. And even honest men sometimes do not speak about what they are thinking; this happens when a man has committed a speech to memory and, while delivering it, thinks of other things, or when the mind strays during the singing of a well-known hymn, or when, by a slip of the tongue, the wrong words are said. Words can be misleading even when the speaker does say what he is thinking, if the words that he utters do not signify the same thing to others that they do to him. He may call something by a name other than the one used for it by his listeners. Or he may mean something other than his listeners think he means. For example, if he should use the term *virtus* to denote physical prowess rather than moral or physical excellence, the more commonly accepted Roman definition, he might well offend his listeners. He would do this because of a difference in understanding of the term. To some extent, such misunderstanding might be overcome if the speaker were careful to define his terms, although, as Augustine added, it is not easy to find a good definer. Furthermore, the listener may not hear correctly what the speaker says, as Augustine illustrated from his own mistake in thinking Adeodatus used the Punic word for "faith" rather than for "piety." But still more distressing, Augustine asserted, is the inability to know or understand the thoughts of a speaker, even when one understands his language and clearly hears his words. Masters, indeed, do not profess that it is their own thoughts rather than those of their discipline that they transmit. And parents do not send their sons to school to learn the teacher's thoughts. Moreover, one cannot learn from the words the teacher uses that he is speaking the truth. Hence, when those who hear the words spoken by the so-called teacher ponder within themselves as to whether what they hear is true, they look for guidance not to the teacher outside but to the interior truth. Only when they find from within that the things said are true, do they learn. They can then more justly be called their own teachers.

Finally, Augustine concluded, no man on earth can be called a teacher because there is only one teacher of all, who is in heaven (Matt. 23: 8–9). And He himself will teach of heaven. He may communicate outwardly through men by means of signs but only to remind them that by turning inwardly to Him they may be taught. He will also teach men that to know and to love Him is the blessed or happy life that all are seeking, but few have found. In the dialogue *Concerning the Teacher* Adeodatus sums up the tenor of the tract. He has learned that words serve merely to remind the hearer that he may learn but that it is rarely through speech that much of the thinking of a speaker is made apparent. And whether the things said are true can be taught only by the "interior truth," which dwells within. Adeodatus declares that the more he progresses in learning the more ardently does he love God. This is the end toward which all learning, in Augustine's estimation, should be directed—the love of God.

In *Concerning the Teacher* Augustine belittled the importance both of words and of the human teacher in the communication of knowledge and in the teaching and transmission of truth. Knowledge and truth are already within each man through divine illumination. And Augustine indicated that the source of his view was Scripture. His concept of the interiority of knowledge and truth in the human intellect coincided to some extent with the Platonic view that no external teacher could "teach" or transmit knowledge or "truth" to his pupil, since truth is within each man; it resembled also the Platonic assertion that the aim of instruction is not to impart but to draw out the knowledge and truth already within, by skillful questioning. In Augustine's view, too, the spoken words of the teacher serve merely to admonish, to stimulate, and to remind the hearer to reflect upon what he has heard and to discover and consult the truth within himself.

Hence, according to both Plato and Augustine, learning is not obtained from a teacher but is rather a kind of remembering in which the teacher's role is that of helping the pupil to disinter or to draw out the knowledge he already has. However, Augustine differed from Plato in his explanation of the interiority of knowledge and truth. Whereas Plato held that the soul in its union with the present body has brought with it from a previous existence a store of innate ideas, Augustine offered his "light of the eternal mind" or doctrine of "illumination" to explain the soul's having the answers to questions not learned on this earth. Augustine's doctrine of the "interior teacher," who is none other than God himself residing within, replaced Plato's theory of pre-existence to explain innatism and memory. Augustine held that memory, in addition to being a storehouse of images of sense objects, contains the knowledge of the unchangeable principles by which one evaluates the truth of statements. And he maintained that while the soul is not explicitly and continuously aware of all the knowledge it has, it can under God's illumination bring it forth from that "memory," where it is latent, by means of recall.

In conclusion, it may be said that Augustine's advocacy of intellectual discipline and of a thorough and basic grounding in the liberal arts was of utmost importance for his own time as well as for the centuries that followed. In his own time he helped to resolve the dilemma of the Christians who had either to send their sons to the pagan schools or forego the preparatory training in the arts which for most Romans constituted the chief bulwark against encroaching barbarism. Augustine made clear both by example and precept the salient fact that the Christians were amply justified in utilizing all that pagan learning and the arts had to offer, provided they were supplemented by moral guidance. And he demonstrated how these might be employed in the service of God. Moreover, although Augustine held that God is the first and final cause of all learning, and that nature, too, as a part of God's creation is a teacher of the first order, he nevertheless exemplified the importance of the role of the human teacher. It was the latter who could guide, stimulate, and remind the learner to look within himself for the truth. This is shown clearly in *Concerning the Teacher*, the dialogue with his son, in which Augustine's well-chosen and skillful questions led Adeodatus by self-discovery from vague and even erroneous assumptions and conclusions to the light of truth. Yet to Augustine himself the true teacher is the "interior teacher," whom he held to be synonymous with truth and with God. And he attributed man's acquisition of the knowledge of truth to divine illumination. The human teacher as an instrument of God can, however, help to make this knowledge explicit. He can by his words and other outward signs admonish and remind his pupils to look within themselves to that "interior teacher." He can also make lucid, as Augustine has done, the means by which the search for truth and happiness may be carried forward; he can give emphasis to Augustine's conviction that the final goal of learning is love of God and the attainment of the happy life.

BIBLIOGRAPHICAL NOTE

St. Augustine's works cited in the preceding article are chiefly to be found in Latin in the *Opera omnia, Patrologia Latina,* edited by J. P. Migne, Volumes 32 to 47, and in the *Corpus scriptorum ecclesiasticorum latinorum,* published in Vienna in 1908 and subsequent years.

Collections of translations are in the *Nicene and Post-Nicene Fathers of the Christian Church,* first series, Volumes 1 to 8, published in New York, 1907–1909; in *The Works of the Fathers in Translation,* edited by John Quasten, S.J.D., and Joseph C. Plumpe, now in progress; and in *The Fathers of the Church. A New Translation,* Ludwig Schopp, Editorial Director, published by the Cima Publishing Company, New York, in 1947 and subsequent years.

The specific translations or Latin text of individual works of St. Augustine utilized in the above study follow.

On Catechizing the Unlearned (De catechizandis rudibus) Patrologia Latina, Volume 40. Paris, 1865.

Christian Instruction (De doctrina christiana), translated by John J. Gavigan, O.S.A., The Fathers of the Church, A New Translation. Cima Publishing Co., New York, 1947.

The Confessions (Libri confessionum), translated by E. B. Pusey. Carlton House, New York, 1949.

Divine Providence and the Problem of Evil (De ordine), translated by Robert P. Russell, O.S.A., The Fathers of the Church. New York, 1948.

The Happy Life (De beata vita), translated by Ludwig Schopp, The Fathers of the Church. New York, 1948.

The Immortality of the Soul (De immortalitate animae), translated by Ludwig Schopp, The Fathers of the Church. New York, 1947.

On Music (De musica), translated by Robert C. Taliaferro, The Fathers of the Church. New York, 1947.

Answer to Skeptics (Contra academicos), translated by Denis J. Kavanagh, O.S.A., The Fathers of the Church. New York, 1948.

The Soliloquies (Soliloquia), translated by Thomas F. Gilligan, O.S.A., The Fathers of the Church. New York, 1948.

Concerning the Teacher (De magistro), translated by G. G. Leckie, Appleton-Century-Crofts, Inc., New York, 1938. Another translation, by J. M. Colleran, C.SS.R., The Works of the Fathers in Translation. The Newman Press, Westminster, Maryland, 1950; reprinted 1964.

Some selected works on and relating to St. Augustine utilized in the above study follow.

Bourke, V. J., *Augustine's Quest of Wisdom. Life and Philosophy of the Bishop of Hippo*. The Bruce Publishing Co., Milwaukee, Wisconsin, 1945.

Chabannes, J., *St. Augustine*, translated by J. Kernan. Doubleday, New York, 1962.

Colleran, J. M., *The Treatises 'De magistro' of St. Augustine and St. Thomas* (diss. Pontif. Inst. 'Angelico'). Rome, 1945.

Cutts, Rev. E. L., *Saint Augustine*. (The Fathers for English Readers). London, 1897.

Gilson, E., *Introduction à l'étude de Saint Augustin* (Etudes de philosophie médiévale), XI. Paris, 1943 (Second Edition).

Gilson, E., *The Christian Philosophy of St. Augustine*, translated by L. E. M. Lynch. Random House, New York, 1960. This work contains an excellent bibliography.

Laistner, M. L. W., *Thought and Letters in Western Europe*. Cornell University Press, Ithaca, New York, 1957 (Second Edition).

Marrou, Henri-Irénée, *Saint Augustin et la fin de la culture antique*. Paris, 1958 (reprint).

Marrou, Henri-Irénée, *A History of Education in Antiquity*, translated by George Lamb. Sheed and Ward, New York, 1956.

🌰 THOMAS AQUINAS (1225–1274), the seventh and young-est son of Count Landulfo, was born at the castle of Roc-casecca near Aquino in the province of Naples. After receiving his elementary education at the Abbey of Monte Cassino, he went in 1239 to study in the arts faculty at the University of Naples. Five years later he entered the order of St. Dominic against the wishes of his family. In 1245 he went to Paris where he studied theology under Albert the Great, going with him to Cologne in 1248 to the newly opened studium generale of the Dominican order. In 1252 he returned to study in the faculty of theology at the University of Paris where at the age of thirty-one he was made a master in theology, after receiv-ing a papal dispensation from the university requirement that a master of theology be at least thirty-four years old. In 1259 he began teaching at the Papal Curia in Rome, returning to the University of Paris in 1268 to help battle against the Averroism of the arts faculty. In 1272 he left Paris once again, this time to teach at the University of Naples. He died on March 7, 1274 on the way to the Council of Lyons. Known as the "Angelic Doctor," this most famous of the medieval philosophers was canonized in 1322. In 1879 a papal encyclical directed that the teachings of St. Thomas should be taken as the basis of theology in the Roman Catholic Church. St. Thomas taught and wrote for twenty years. His most famous works include: *Summa Theologiae, Summa Contra Gentiles,* and *De Veritate* (On Truth). In this last work there is a short section on teaching.

5

THE SCHOLASTIC: *Aquinas*

BY JOHN W. DONOHUE, S.J.

Cardinal Newman once said that education, taken in the large sense of the word, had been his line from first to last. For all the differences between the world of thirteenth-century Paris and the world of nineteenth-century Oxford and Birmingham, St. Thomas Aquinas (1225–1274) might have said the same. When he was about five years old, his parents enrolled him as an oblate in the celebrated Benedictine abbey perched on Monte Cassino. The rest of his life was neatly divided into twenty-two student years, some at the abbey, some at the University of Naples, and some as a young Dominican doing his own studies, and then twenty-two years as a teacher and writer, for he began to lecture at Paris as a bachelor of theology in 1252. Teaching, moreover, was not for St. Thomas simply a means of livelihood. It was his way of fulfilling his Dominican vocation to the apostolic service of his fellow men.

This vocation involved him in proclaiming the Gospel message from pulpit and professorial chair. But to do that effectively required constant study of the Christian sources. It is hardly surprising, therefore, to find St. Thomas on several occasions defending teaching as an ideal blend of the active and contemplative "lives." (*S. Th.*, II–II, q. 181, a. 3, c. and *De Ver.*, q. 11, a. 4.)[1] For the teacher's energies converge upon two objects: the material that he teaches and the students to whom he teaches it. Consequently, the verb *docere*, like the English *teach*, takes a double accusative, and this itself suggests a resolution of any forced

---

[1] Some selected references to St. Thomas' writings are inserted into the text here and designated by conventional cues. Thus *S.Th.*, I, q. 1, a.1, c. refers to the First Part of the *Summa Theologiae*, question 1, article 1, the corpus or main portion of the article. References to the replies to objections following the body of the article are indicated by *ad* with the number of the reply. Other parts of the *Summa Theologiae* are abbreviated as: I–II (first section of the Second Part); II–II (second section of the Second Part); III (Third Part); and *Supp.* (The Supplement to the Third Part which was put together from earlier writings of St. Thomas after his death left the *Summa* unfinished). C.G. stands for the *Summa contra Gentiles* with book and chap-

antinomy between a pupil-centered and a curriculum-centered school. Insofar as the teacher must, by his own study, master the discipline he would teach, his life is contemplative. Yet it is even more properly called active, St. Thomas declared, since this study is ultimately directed toward helping one's neighbor, and the active life consists chiefly in a man's relations with his neighbor. (*S. Th.*, I–II, q. 69, a. 3, c.) St. Thomas himself, despite the staggering volume of his publications, was not one of those professors who sacrifice teaching to research. Indeed, his contemporary biographer, William of Tocco, claimed that Aquinas surpassed all his colleagues in the force and clarity of his lectures and in his ability to inspire students.

Nevertheless, the theme of the ideally educated man does not lead as easily and reliably to the center of St. Thomas' thought as it does to that of certain other subjects of this book. It will be useful, at the outset, to see why this is so, for otherwise it will be hard to grasp even what can be said about St. Thomas and education. To ask about the ideal of an educated man is, of course, to ask a twentieth-century question. It is a question, moreover, raised with particular insistence in industrialized democracies where universal formal schooling, as distinguished from education in the wide sense of initiating the young into their elders' way of life, is both an individual and a social necessity. Still, the response to this question will deliver the pith of an Isocrates but not of an Aquinas. The reasons for this are bound up with the sheer quantity of St. Thomas' scholarly production together with the distinctive character of this corpus and the need for considerable effort and technical skill if one is to appreciate its depth and originality.

Although his life was relatively short, St. Thomas left behind an enormous mass of writings, but only a tiny part of them has to do explicitly with what we think of as problems of education. A focus on this part, therefore, would be quite inadequate for suggesting the substance of St. Thomas' intellectual achievement, even supposing one could avoid distorting passages in separating them from their context. The cataloguing of Aquinas' works is not yet definitive, but the list compiled by I. T. Eschmann, O.P., and printed in Etienne Gilson's *The Christian Philosophy of St. Thomas Aquinas*, contains 98 items, of which nine

---

ter number indicated. *De Ver.*, q.11, a.1 refers to the eleventh of the *Quaestiones Disputatae de Veritate* (Academic Disputations concerning Truth), the first article. *In lib. Eth.*, b.I, lect. 1, signifies the first *lectio* or lecture of St. Thomas' commentary on the first book of the Nicomachean Ethics. To this is added the paragraph number in the edition of this commentary by A. M. Pirotta, O.P. (Turin: Marietti, 1934). In the references to other writings cited less often, sufficient detail is given at the point where the reference is inserted.

brief ones are of doubtful authenticity. Many of the authentic items, however, are multivolumed or are collections that might reasonably be divided into several books. Under the category of *Quaestiones Disputatae* (Academic Disputations), for instance, the treatise *De Veritate* (On Truth) is listed as a single entry, although its English translation runs to three stout volumes.

St. Thomas' principal writings can be classified, generically rather than chronologically, according to a serviceable, if somewhat rough, threefold division. There are the commentaries, chiefly on Scripture, on Aristotle, and on Boethius. There are the monographic treatments of special theological and philosophical issues, including the *Academic Disputations*, the *Quodlibet Questions*, and various short treatises known as *opuscula*. And there are three great theological syntheses: the early *Scripta super libros Sententiarum*, which is a commentary on the "Sentences" of Peter Lombard; the *Summa contra Gentiles*, a summary of the Christian faith with emphasis upon its defense against the Averroism of those Moslem thinkers who are the "Gentiles" of the title; and the *Summa Theologiae*, which is a synthesis or summary for students of theology. This last, commonly considered its author's major work, was left unfinished at his death.

As St. Thomas developed his principal theological and philosophical themes, he scattered along the way many brief references to education, usually in the form of asides or illustrations. These marginal notes are, consequently, rather oblique and fleeting. In the whole of the monumental Thomistic literature, only the eleventh of the *Quaestiones Disputatae de Veritate*, a short discussion sometimes called *De Magistro* (Concerning the Teacher), and the places in the *Summa Theologiae* that correspond to it deal to any extent with formal pedagogical matters. It is true that a good deal is said about education in the commentary on Aristotle's *Ethics*, and there are also some remarks in the part of the commentary on the *Politics* that St. Thomas himself actually wrote. But this part covers only the first two books of the *Politics* and some of the third. The remaining books, including the seventh and eighth in which most of Aristotle's material on education occurs, were done by a pupil of Aquinas, Peter of Auvergne. In any case, what St. Thomas mainly intended in all these commentaries was simply a faithful exposition of Aristotle for his own students. It is risky to ascribe the opinions expressed in the commentaries to the commentator himself, unless they clearly represent an addition to the Aristotelian text or are echoed in writings that professedly set forth St. Thomas' own views.

Students of Thomistic educational theory have, indeed, suggested that those vast stretches of the *Summa Theologiae* treating of the moral life should be considered as a kind of educational treatise. For these pages inquire into the nature of man's true and ethical self-realization along with the means for achieving it. And is not this the ultimate concern of education? No doubt it is, and perhaps Dewey was thinking in similar fashion when he said that all philosophy is philosophy of education. For Dewey thought the task of philosophy was to promote the conditions required in a democratic society for individual self-fulfillment or education. But when educational concepts are made this wide, they cease to be very useful for particularized problems. If we are going to ask here about St. Thomas' educational ideal, we must have in mind something more specific and delimited than the Christian portrait of the morally good man, although that ideal will certainly suppose the elements of this portrait.

Of course, the smallness of space that St. Thomas gave to strictly educational problems does not itself prove that such problems were only on the periphery of his interests. Marx also left behind him an imposing aggregate of writings in which there is relatively little about education. But in his case a quantitative measure would be misleading. For as the implications of Marxism are drawn out, the educational ideal emerges as highly important, since Marx was often preoccupied with the need to reshape man and society and he recognized the role education would play in this effort. But it is fair to say that St. Thomas adverted infrequently to educational issues because the problems that chiefly occupied him were not those of an educational theorist like Rousseau, or a physician like Freud, or a social reformer like Marx. Apart from the Aristotelian commentaries, St. Thomas generally wrote as a theologian. He was primarily concerned, therefore, with understanding as profoundly as possible and then with accurately expounding what the Christian faith had to say about God, about the origins of the universe, about the nature and destiny of man, and about the person and redemptive mission of Christ. But since St. Thomas was also the very flower of Scholasticism, he employed for this work of theological meditation, for his effort at systematization and defense, the resources of a realist and personalist philosophy. This philosophy may be described, at a rather high level of generalization, as continuous with the classical tradition of Plato and Aristotle.

The texture of a work like the *Summa Theologiae* is, therefore, very complex despite its cool surface lucidity. Sometimes, St. Thomas' method and assertions are strictly theological, that is to say, based ultimately on authority—the authority of God whom the Christian believes to have spoken during the course of human history and climactically in the Person of Jesus, the Word and Son. At other times, however, the

Thomistic lines of argumentation are strictly philosophical in character, although designed to advance the work of theological reflection somewhat as complex mathematical elucidations advance the understanding of problems in theoretical physics. To be valid, these philosophical assertions must be grounded, not on authority but on the facts of common experience as interpreted by the natural human intelligence. For outside the realm of theology, St. Thomas once observed, the argument from authority is the weakest possible one. (*S. Th.*, I, q. 1, a. 8, ad 2.) Or as he noted in his commentary on Aristotle's *De Coelo*, the purpose of philosophy is not to know the opinions of men but the truth of the matter. (*In lib. De Coelo et Mundo*, b. 1, lect. 22, n. 8.)

The methods of philosophy and theology are, therefore, different, and St. Thomas himself distinguished them clearly. But since he used both, it is possible to extract a philosophy from his library of theological speculation. One of the most keenly debated questions among twentieth-century Thomists, however, has to do with just how the autonomy of the philosophy thus extracted is to be understood. Some would maintain that it is Christian only in the sense of harmoniously coexisting with the Christian world view. Others insist that this philosophic dimension of St. Thomas' thought, though truly philosophical because it derives from contact with experience and not from faith, has nonetheless been intrinsically influenced by revelation. Faith, for instance, has sometimes raised questions for philosophical consideration that might otherwise have been overlooked. Howsoever this rather subtle debate is resolved, we need only note here that in his greatest works St. Thomas was writing theology and was proceeding according to what is called the theological order, that is to say, beginning with the divine and moving thence to a study of the universe of men and things.

His subject, therefore, is everything. The *Summa Theologiae* is a synthesis treating of God, man, and nature although, to be sure, not saying everything that might be said on these spacious topics. It is notably lacking, for instance, in our contemporary interest in historical process and in phenomenological descriptions of the conditions of concrete existence and of subjectivity. Perhaps the most striking aspect of St. Thomas' achievement is precisely this steady and impersonal orchestration of so many themes, some of them monumental and some relatively trivial, into a vast totality. The first and second parts of the *Summa Theologiae*, for instance, have a sort of symphonic progression. They begin with one tremendous theme, the question of God in Himself and in relation to all other things as they proceed from Him. Then several submotifs are introduced with the study of three levels of divine creation: that of the purely spiritual beings or angels; that of the infrahuman world; and that of man. Thereupon the discussion evolves into hundreds of variations as it proceeds through a multitude of questions about human existence and action from the most intricate speculation about intellection to such curious items, raised in the course of an examination of virtues and vices, as the lawfulness of women's use of cosmetics.

It is just this central characteristic of universal synthesis that is necessarily lost sight of in disengaging St. Thomas' observations about education, for these are tangential to the main line of his thought. One certainly can sift through his works and gather up all his passing comments on teaching and studying—of which there are, in fact, a good number. One might also focus on certain pivotal topics that St. Thomas himself developed at length and that have important implications for education. The metaphysical inquiries into the nature and conditions of knowledge or into the ontological structure of the intellectual habits that are significant learning products are two such topics. But with any such specialized focus one inevitably misses the total view of the forest by concentrating upon the trees or even upon the twigs. To take such a partial look at Aquinas is, therefore, quite different from doing so with Rousseau, since one would actually get hold of much of the Rousseauian substance in abstracting the program for Emile's education.

In addition to the limitations imposed by the bulk of St. Thomas' writings and by their nature as a theological, not a pedagogical, synthesis, there remains a third difficulty besetting the attempt even to deduce what St. Thomas might have said about the ideal of an educated man. A reader who comes to the *Summa Theologiae* after having struggled with a Heidegger or a Wittgenstein, is apt to think, at first, that these medieval pages are remarkably accessible even in translation. The prologue of the *Summa* actually observes that this work has been designed as a text for beginners, and it does move with a deceptive clarity and precision. But although the novice can derive a good deal, even from a first reading, he will indeed be deceived if he imagines that he can penetrate these discussions without carefully exploring their historical context and the meaning of the Thomistic language, and without some hard thinking about the arguments proposed. The professional Thomistic scholars have expended a great deal of effort on the exegesis of St. Thomas' writings and have by no means finished mining them. Nor have they reached general agreement on disputed points. For despite the apparent clarity of the text, the meaning of many passages and sentences has not yet been satisfactorily determined.

For these reasons one must be cautious about accepting the conventional generalizations concerning St. Thomas. The typical handbook (or textbook) summary, for instance, makes Thomistic philosophy a thirteenth-century, Christianized version of Aristotle. But this is over-simplification to the point of caricature. For one thing, although St. Thomas obviously employed Aristotelian elements, he also referred hundreds of times to Plato and the Platonists. Many contemporary scholars have concluded, not merely from these references but from close examination of his thought, that St. Thomas absorbed along with the main Aristotelian positions a good many of the Platonic and Neoplatonic insights. Others, on the contrary, think that his Platonism is more a matter of terminology than of substance. But whatever may be the truth of the matter, all serious students of the Thomistic text would agree that when St. Thomas took over the notions or the vocabulary of an Aristotle or an Augustine, he frequently so transmuted both that his philosophy, upon closer inspection, turns out to be at least as original as it is derivative.

He agreed with Aristotle, for instance, in rejecting the concept of man as a Platonic soul ruefully using a body and he substituted the concept of man as an incarnate spirit possessing the essential unity of an animated body. But strict Aristotelianism does not appear to have room for a substantial form capable of existing after the composite, which it helps to constitute, has broken up. St. Thomas, however, argued on philosophical grounds that the human soul, this substantial form, which is the principle whereby a man exists, eats, walks, feels and thinks, does remain in existence even after the body has corrupted. (*S. Th.*, I, q. 76, a.1, c. and ad 5.)

When it comes to deducing St. Thomas' concept of the educated man, one can easily be misled into supposing that this ideal has been faithfully constructed according to a blueprint found in the *Nicomachean Ethics*. For there are a number of texts that, if strung neatly together, appear to support such a conclusion. St. Thomas did, for instance, remark quite characteristically, that the body exists for the sake of the soul just as a tool (*instrumentum*) exists for the sake of the user. (*S. Th.*, I, q. 91, a. 3, c. and II–II, q. 55, a.1, ad 2.) The highest power of the soul, in turn, is intelligence, he said, and man is most himself when he is most rational. The lower animals also possess such qualities as material extension, sensation, and sexuality so that it is not in these elements that man's uniqueness is to be located but in his reason. (*S. Th.*, I–II, q. 55, a. 2, c.) Morality itself can be described as living according to right reason so that the stuff of one's life is rationally ordered. (*S. Th.*, II–II, a. 47, a. 7, c. and q. 168, a. 1, c.)

Now the goal of any human life is perfect happiness or beatitude, we are told. (*S. Th.*, I–II, q. 34, a. 3, *sed contra*.) But we also find the

Summa saying in good Aristotelian fashion that happiness consists principally in the speculative exercise of intelligence. (*S. Th.*, I–II, q. 3, a. 5, c.) This is the functioning of intelligence displayed when men by profound, often deductive reasonings uncover and contemplate in science, mathematics, metaphysics, and theology the deepest meanings implicated in nature and in human existence. The argument is that happiness must lie in the highest activity of which a man is capable and this must be the noblest operation of his noblest power centered upon its noblest object. Perfect happiness, therefore, will be obtained only in the life after death through the direct, beatifying vision of God in which the divine nature is known immediately or in itself. The highest degree of partial happiness available in this life consists in the sort of contemplation of things divine that is possible for those who give themselves to metaphysical and theological cogitation. Or, as St. Thomas put it elsewhere, contemplation is eminently suitable for man, because it engages the best in him, his mind in a pure concern for knowledge rather than for the external necessities that he shares, often enough, with the beasts. (*S. Th.*, II–II, q. 182, a.l, c.) Finally, St. Thomas noted that for this contemplation men need a certain repose or leisure, a certain freedom from sorrow and cares. (*S. Th.*, I–II, q. 37, a. 1, ad 3.)

The *De Magistro* (Concerning the Teacher) is concerned with education in the restricted sense of development of this speculative valence of intelligence. It discusses the means a teacher can use to help students acquire those learning products to which St. Thomas applied the term *scientia*. These are habits of knowledge in areas where deductive reasoning is customarily employed; *scientia* is defined as "the ability to demonstrate conclusions from principles." (*S. Th.*, I–II, q. 57, a. 2, ad 1.) Thus the geometer has the "habit" of geometry, which is a genuine ontological expansion of his personality, because he can prove the various propositions from the Euclidean postulates and does not merely parrot them. The theologian possesses the loftiest of "sciences," called wisdom, because he can demonstrate the conclusions of theology from revealed principles, which are accepted on faith, or from the philosophical principles that are derived from experience and used to expound or defend theological propositions.

Now, all this strongly suggests an intellectualistic educational ideal generically akin not only to the ideals of Plato or Aristotle but to those commonly honored in the contemporary university world. In twentieth-century America, these accents on the cultivation of intelligence and on the importance of leisure for that purpose are rather consistently defended by spokesmen for higher education. Modern theorists, of course, carefully link this emphasis to some acknowledgment of the social dimension of men and they like to underscore the social benefits of that Hellenic educational ideal. But then, St. Thomas also devoted a good deal of thought, including most of the massive second section of the Second Part of the *Summa Theologiae*, to detailing the individual's social obligations. And at one point in the Third Part of the *Summa*, he noted that the active life of a teacher, who shares with others the fruits of his thought, is more perfect than a life of contemplation alone. (*S. Th.*, III, q. 40, a. 1, ad 2.) There is good reason, therefore, to suspect that the strictly rationalistic model of the educated man is much too oversimplified to be that of St. Thomas.

Indeed, if one takes account of St. Thomas' full picture of man, one sees that it includes a crucial insistence upon the substantial unity of spirit and flesh in the continuum of human experience and upon the full register of human intelligence, which is not only speculative but also practical, not only rational but also capable of a certain intuitive grasp of reality. At first sight this picture seems quite Aristotelian, yet it is clear that St. Thomas was not saying the same thing as Aristotle or as some modern scholar extolling the pursuit of knowledge for its own sake. For the contemplation in which Aquinas located perfect happiness is not the same thing as the metaphysical speculation praised in the *Ethics* and *Politics*. Much less is it identified with those degrees of knowledge in the Aristotelian scale ranking below metaphysics—mathematics and the various scientific and literary humanities. In fact, St. Thomas explicitly assured the followers of these disciplines that perfect happiness could not be found in the pursuit of the "speculative sciences." (*S. Th.*, I–II, q. 3, a. 6, c.) The intellectual fulfillment in which, to his way of thinking, beatitude is found is that ultimate, face-to-face sight of God; the possibility of such a vision is a datum of religious belief, not metaphysics. (*De Ver.*, q. 14, a. 10, c.)

So far as man's earthly life is concerned, then, St. Thomas would very much qualify an exuberant celebration of the primacy of intelligence. In this world, a man's knowledge of God is mediate, since his own conceptual constructs, the scaffolding of his own thought about God, always stand between him and the Divine. "We cannot grasp what God is," said St. Thomas in a much-quoted sentence, "but what He is not and how other things stand to Him." (*CG*, b. I, c. 30.) But when a man loves God, according to Aquinas, then he is directly united to Him, even though he does not yet "see" Him. For love always unites the lover to the beloved. In our present existence, therefore, this highest operation of love is more exalted and more powerful than anything of which the mind is capable. (*S. Th.*, I–II, q. 28, a. 1 ad 3 and I, q. 108, a. 6, ad 3.) At one point in the *Summa contra Gentiles*, St. Thomas ranked the values of life hierarchically in terms of their proximity to ultimate beatitude. Here he placed moral virtue ahead of intellectual attainments, because it promotes ethically good action, which leads, in turn, to the happiness of heaven. (CG, b. III, c. 141.) In this connection, it is worth noting that Aquinas used the term *educatio* not for intellectual development but for what we would call character formation. In his *Commentary on the Sentences* he defined education as the "advancement of the child to the state of specifically human excellence, that is to say to the state of virtue." (Bk. IV, dist. 26, q. 1, a.l and *S. Th.*, *Supp.*, q. 41, a.l, c.) This is a usage that "progressive" educators would regard sympathetically.

But if St. Thomas' ideal of the educated man cannot be simply equated with Aristotle's notion of the philosopher-citizen, what is it like? We have already indicated that St. Thomas himself did not spell the answer out in detail. Every theory of education is obviously based upon some general philosophy of the cosmos and of man and his life and values. But the reverse is not true. Not every philosophy of truth, beauty, and goodness has had tacked on to it by its author a statement of its implications for education. In the last fifty years, however, a good many essays have been written to expound what might be called a Thomistic theory of education. These have usually been one of two sorts. Sometimes a writer has marshaled St. Thomas' comments upon education and perhaps added to these an indication of what Aquinas might have said, if he had woven these scattered remarks into a fully articulated statement. Sometimes a writer who has been inspired by the Thomistic synthesis has developed certain of its nuclear themes into a personal contribution to educational theory. Jacques Maritain has done this on several occasions and notably in *Education at the Crossroads*.

The remainder of the present essay will make some modest use of both these approaches. We shall underline certain basic positions of St. Thomas from which we think deductions about his presumptive formula for the ideally educated man may be made. At the same time, we shall be helped in this deduction by hints that St. Thomas' own comments on educational matters afford. For these comments often represent the application of fundamental elements of his thought to those pedagogical affairs in which he had considerable professional interest. We shall first ask what hints for education may be derived from St. Thomas' theory of human nature, which is itself a theological-philosophical anthropology. Then we shall ask what conclusions can be drawn from his concept of the processes and products of learning. Finally, we shall note briefly the significance of man's state as both a person and a social being. In each instance we shall only point up the conclusions, since there is not space for the arguments adduced in their support.

THEMES FROM ST. THOMAS' PORTRAIT OF MAN

Since St. Thomas usually wrote as a theologian, questions about God are logically the core of his centripetal study of universal reality. Nevertheless, questions about man constitute the dominant problem of this study. The *Summa Theologiae*, for instance, devotes far more than half its pages to inquiries about man: his nature; his characteristic activities and their goals; his exercise of freedom; and the consequences of his existence in a world where God, according to Christian belief, has decisively intervened to establish a new relationship of men to Himself through the gift of His love, which is called grace. It has been remarked, therefore, that St. Thomas' thought is, in one sense, profoundly anthropocentric, although when he analyzed human nature he intended, of course, to set out what his theology as well as what his philosophy had to say about man.

There is one conclusion of this analysis of human nature that deserves first mention because of its fundamental importance for education. It is not only central in Christian thought but is also a thesis asserted by some philosophers on the evidence naturally available to them. St. Thomas occasionally epitomized this particular thesis in a formula brushed with an unwonted glint of imagery. Man is unique, he wrote, because he is composed of a corporeal and a spiritual substance and is therefore set between two worlds with his soul situated on the boundary between heaven and earth. (*Quaestio Unica de Anima*, a.l, c. and *S. Th.*, I, q. 75, a.l, Prologue.)

Perhaps no key position of theistic realism is harder to understand correctly than this classic statement that man is essentially a composite of matter and spirit. St. Thomas, following Aristotle, described the spiritual soul as the first principle of life: not a body but the form or act of the body. Yet, it requires a good deal of philosophical reflection to appreciate what this expression even intends, for it is all too easy to be misled by the imagination into picturing the soul as a "Ghost in the Machine." It is not our business here to venture upon such philosophical reflection. We must note, however, that the Thomistic thesis means that man has two dimensions but is not two things, because his two essential factors are related to one another as components of a single being. It is clear enough that man is material and animal. He breathes, digests, walks, and thinks, but his soul is understood as precisely that principle whereby he exists, lives, and acts in these many styles. Yet because man is one being, St. Thomas remarked, we do not say that the soul acts but rather that man does. (*S. Th.*, I, q. 75, a. 2, ad 2.)

This composite condition has resonances for every zone of human life. Two of these implications need emphasis because they bear particularly upon the notion of an ideally educated man. First, since this man is not a disembodied intelligence, his learning is vitally linked to his experience in the world. Experience is taken here to mean both sense contact with the encompassing milieu and, more broadly, the funded wisdom that comes from living one's life. Second, because man is corporeal as well as spiritual, he is necessarily laced into the context of space and time where he interacts with his environment. Strictly speaking, not even the hermit can be the spectator of a passing show, for the very nature of his being makes him an actor in it. The man of fully developed intelligence not only understands the world to some extent but also changes it to some extent. These two points are worth a bit of expansion.

For St. Thomas, the approach to reality through knowledge was pluralistic. Like any thinker in the tradition of the perennial philosophy, he recognized two chief natural sources of knowledge, the intelligence and the variety of cognitive powers which are lumped together under the term "sense." (As a Christian, Aquinas would also account his faith a source of knowledge but a supernatural one. He would believe that acceptance of the divine revelation put him in possession of many truths beyond the reach of his natural powers. Indeed, he remarked in his explanation of the Apostles' Creed that none of the ancient philosophers knew as much about God as, following upon the revelation of Christ, one old woman knows through faith.)

What the educator will note is the importance attached by Thomistic philosophy to sense experience, through which we have an immediate conjunction with reality. St. Thomas particularly emphasized the senses of sight, hearing, and touch and once noted that we have experience when we know individual objects through our senses. (*S. Th.*, I, q. 54, a. 5, c.) Elsewhere he remarked that the existence of things other than ourselves can be known if they fall directly under our senses or if their existence can be inferred from sense data, as when we surmise that there is fire where we see smoke. (*Scripta super libros Sententiarum*, Bk. III, d. 23, q. 1, a. 2.)

Of course, St. Thomas did not think either that sense knowledge is the only kind of cognition or that intellection is simply a matter of shuffling and regrouping sense images. His theory of knowledge maintains that intellection penetrates more deeply than the senses are capable of doing into the sense data, in order to grasp intelligible or transsensible aspects of reality imbedded or somehow implied in these data but beyond the reach of the senses themselves. Through his senses, which are bodily powers, a man knows individual, singular objects of a material nature—the color and scent of this rose. But through his mind, which is itself immaterial, he grasps "universal" aspects. These can be applied to many specific instances because, in the process of intellection, they have been liberated from the concrete materiality that ties them down to one or other particular. Thus we have an idea of a rose or a man, and it expresses, though not completely, the true nature of the thing. These concepts can, therefore, be predicated of many roses or many men. It is in such predications, moreover, that the fullness of truth is obtained. However, the process which culminates in this possession of truth, though it has a certain freedom from sense experience, still begins with that sense awareness. One of St. Thomas' most virtuoso metaphysical performances is a subtle theory devised to explain how this intellectual knowledge arises out of the interpenetrating action of senses and intelligence. The standard summaries of Thomism all sketch the main lines of this theory, but the Thomistic scholars have not ceased to debate its complexities and to carry on the work of refining and modifying them. They would all agree, however, that St. Thomas himself emphasized the importance of sense experience for the life of reason.

He adverted to this importance from various points of his philosophic compass. He would remark, for instance, that the better a man's bodily structure, the better his understanding. Those with finer bodies have more powerful intelligences, he thought. (*S. Th.*, I, q. 85, a. 7, c.) He would note that since we naturally acquire knowledge through our senses, our powers of reasoning and learning would be impeded or suspended if the senses were ligated. He would often echo Aristotle's conviction that touch is the foundation of the other senses, and that consequently those who have a refined sense of touch have better bodies and better minds. (*S. Th.*, I, q. 76, a. 5; q. 91, a. 1, ad 3; q. 101, a. 2, c.) He would observe that strong emotions or pain deprive us of the power to learn, because of their bodily repercussions. But most significant is the central role he allotted to sense images in the whole process of intellectual learning. What color is to sight, he remarked, the phantasms (sensible images formed and retained by sense consciousness from the data of the external senses) are to the intellect. Tad W. Guzie, S.J., in an extended study of this point, *The Analogy of Learning*, has shown that in the Thomistic philosophical psychology, learning is understood, in general, as the acquisition and organization of images, while intellectual learning in particular is a process terminating ideally in judgments, not about abstractions but about the concrete realities of immediate experience.

St. Thomas observed that learning through one's own sensible contact with reality is preferable to being taught by another who must make considerable use of verbal signs pointing to that reality. (S. Th., III, q. 12, a. 3, ad 2; De. Ver., q. 11, a. 2, ad 4.) If one should learn through being taught (*disciplina*) rather than through one's own research (*inventio*), this would be only because the teacher exploited some sense knowledge to help one form appropriate intellectual concepts and judgments. For after all, as St. Thomas noted, the teacher's words are objects that are sensed, whether they are heard or read. They are *signs*, that is, sensible objects that lead to knowledge of things not yet known. (S. Th., I, q. 117, a. 1, ad 3; De. Ver., q. 11, a. 1, ad 11.) The teacher's signs indicate the thing, and the student learns when he passes from a superficial verbalism to a knowledge of the reality itself.

Very likely St. Thomas would have agreed with a modern writer, William Walsh, who remarked in his book *The Use of Imagination* that the best indication of a teacher's quality is his use of language. At least, for Aquinas the teacher's art consists largely in his ability to select and propose tellingly the most effective signs. The skillful teacher is a fertile source of examples that help his students to generate understandings of their own. (S. Th., I–II, q. 111, a. 4, c. and I, q. 117, a. 1, ad 3.) Of course, these signs will be ineffective unless the learner comprehends their elements either from his own experience or from some earlier lesson. A student who does not know what a grizzled wombat is can obtain some notion when the teacher tells him it resembles a small, grayish bear, provided he does know what is meant by *gray* and *bear*.

An educator guided by these convictions of St. Thomas would surely place thinking about things well ahead of thinking about words. The ideally educated person would prefer knowledge drawn from his own experience to abstractions derived from the experiences of others. To be sure, this is not always possible, but at least one may say that an excessively bookish training is incompatible with the implications of St. Thomas' analysis of human nature and of the origins of knowledge. This emphasis upon the importance of experience also appears in many passages where Aquinas wrote deprecatingly of the period of youth, just because the limited experience of young people necessarily means intellectual immaturity. Young men abound, indeed, in ardor and hope, simply because they have so little acquaintance with the checks that reality will impose upon their aspirations. (S. Th., I–II, q. 40, a. 6, c.) But for this same reason, and because youth is distracted by the impact of rapid growth and the awakening passions, it is not the suitable period for such studies as ethics and metaphysics. (CG, b. I, c. 4; In lib. Eth., b. VI, lect. 7, n. 1210 and b. VIII, lect. 3, n. 1571.) Aquinas agreed with

Aristotle in doubting that young men could know much about moral science, because this study requires a considerable experience of life. For him, the educational ideal could be achieved only in the plenitude of maturity.

It would be achieved, moreover, by men in whom the life of knowledge and contemplation issues in effective action. For men are not angels, but dwellers in a material universe where the sustenance and development not of the body only but of the spirit depend upon fruitful interaction with the natural and social environments. If St. Thomas could remark that contemplation is man's greatest joy, still he did not say that this is the only human joy. Indeed, he pointed out that none can live without some sensible and bodily pleasure. (*S. Th.*, I–II, q. 3, a. 5, c. and q. 34, a. 1, c.) Then too, to cite another instance, men need to work. On several occasions, St. Thomas underscored this in quite modern and even instrumental and evolutionary terms. In the seventh of the *Quaestiones Quodlibetales*, sometimes entitled *De opere manuali* (On Manual Work), he argued that work is an eminently connatural activity for men. "As is clear from the very structure of his body," he wrote, "man has a natural orientation to manual work. For this reason it is said in Job 5, 7: 'Man was born to labor and the bird was born to fly.' Nature has adequately provided all the other animals with whatever they require in the way of food, weapons, and covering for the maintenance of life. Man is not thus equipped because he is gifted with intelligence wherewith to supply himself with these things. Consequently, in their place man has hands which are adapted to fashioning all sorts of products answering to his mental conceptions." (*Quodlibet* VII, a. 17, c. See also *S. Th.*, I–II, q. 95, a.1, c.)

This union in man of reason (*ratio*) and hand (*manus*) was characteristically emphasized by St. Thomas, perhaps because it neatly mirrors man's composite condition. For, as contemporary Thomists have pointed out, work means that an idea has been embodied in matter and it is, therefore, an activity peculiarly proper to man who is himself an incarnate spirit. Out of a block of wood the cabinetmaker fashions a chest; out of some acres of underbrush the farmer makes a garden. For each, an idea has been realized in the objective order, and nature has been humanized.

Unlike his great Greek predecessors, then, St. Thomas did not ignore the humanizing power and the moral value of those practical and vocational pursuits in which the majority of men spend most of their time. He also praised the typical virtues of the successful man of action. The second section of the Second Part of the *Summa Theologiae* offers a detailed examination of the theological and moral virtues that ennoble a man and enhance his action. Here one finds St. Thomas analyzing and commending not only faith, hope, and charity but also liberality, courage, large-mindedness, confidence, tenacity, reasonable ambition, and a due love of honor. It is noteworthy, as Gilson once remarked, that this eulogy of the right uses of wealth and fame comes not from a Renaissance prince but from a thirteenth-century mendicant friar.

His appreciation of the practical as distinguished from the speculative dimension of life and of reason prompted St. Thomas to make another Aristotelian position his own. In the sixth book of the *Nicomachean Ethics*, Aristotle argued from manifold instances of mental activity to a fundamental division between two archetypical functions of intelligence, the practical and the speculative, neither one of which can be reduced to the other. This is not a distinction between two minds but between two expressions of the root power. The practical or deliberative mode shows itself in the arts and technics as well as in scientific experimentation, and in the solving of not a few problems in human relationships. These deliberations involve the choice of means for desired ends. St. Thomas agreed with Aristotle that the validation of these choices would lie in their actual success. For in the realm of practical judgments on concrete measures, the truth of a plan of action does indeed lie in its success. My judgment that this car will provide me with the service I want is true if the car really does perform as anticipated. (*S. Th.*, I–II, q. 57, a. 5, ad 3; *In lib. Eth.*, b. VI, lect. 2, nn. 1129–1132.) It may be concluded, therefore, that for St. Thomas the ideally educated man would be deft in the practical as well as the speculative employment of intelligence. If for no other reason, this is desirable simply because, as St. Thomas once noted, human life consists in actions to be performed and the purely speculative life is quite beyond the present condition of men. (*S. Th.*, II–II, q. 51, a.l, c.)

This sketch of an educational ideal is not, however, complete at this point. We have begun by summarizing the traits that were more likely to be overlooked. The scales must be balanced now by adding that if St. Thomas saw man as a composite of matter and spirit, still he allotted the primacy to the spiritual. If he emphasized the importance of sense knowledge and experience, still he criticized those who rely too heavily upon their sense and imagination as well as those who simply experience phenomena without trying to understand their origins. If he praised the virtues of the successful man, still as a Christian he would acknowledge the service of God leading to salvation to be the final goal of life and education. If he recognized the practical valence of intelligence, still he most esteemed the insightful exercise of the mind that is variously called speculative, theoretical, or contemplative. In this exercise, the mind manifests itself as a prehensive power penetrating to a true, though by no means exhaustive, understanding of things as they really are. The resulting knowledge is "scientific" in the sense of a knowledge of the causes of some aspect of the real. It may well be useful. Yet even if it were not, it would still constitute an immanent enrichment of the learner and a value or end in itself. Finally, if St. Thomas appreciated the thinking that deals with concrete determination of ways to an objective, still he also honored and practiced the other kind of thinking that determines the ethical validity of both the goal and the means antecedently to observed consequences.

The primacy awarded to the spiritual provides a philosophical base for those who would direct schooling chiefly to the development of intelligence through mastery of subject matter. For while St. Thomas maintained that man is a composite of material body and immaterial soul, he also argued that this situation is precisely for the benefit of the soul. Aristotle had explained how the soul was united to the body—that is, as the form of the composite. St. Thomas added that this union is for the enrichment of the soul as well as for the completion of a human nature. He rejected the Platonistic view of Origen who held that the soul was in the body as though in a prison. To be joined with a body is no loss to the soul, said Aquinas. Rather, it perfects it. (*Quaestio Unica de Anima*, a. 1, ad 7; a. 2, ad 14.) More than once St. Thomas described a graduated scale of spiritual creatures, in which the pure spirits, the incorporeal angels, are at the top of the ladder, and the human soul on the bottom rung. This human spirit is precisely the kind of intellectual substance that needs the society of a body if it is to achieve its own distinctive intellectual development. For man's soul does not naturally possess innate knowledge. It must learn from its encounter with the limited beings accessible, because they can be sensed. But if men are to derive knowledge from the sensible, they need senses and hence bodily organs. Still, this is, in the Thomistic perspective, something of a weakness in the human condition, and the angels' mode of intellection is judged to be more perfect. (*S. Th.*, I, q. 76, a.5, c.)

Those who bear down strongly on this particular theme will prefer to think of man as a basically spiritual being. Of course, he is that sort of spiritual being whose soul needs embodiment and a temporal existence in history with its day-by-day advance, if he is to actuate his own most distinctive potentialities for knowledge and love. Nevertheless, some Thomists are inclined to define the educational ideal in severely intellectualistic terms and to accent the acquisition of as much knowledge and intellectual skill as possible. For human perfection will be thought of as fundamentally a mental growth. The self is realized through knowledge and moral virtue, which consists in the domination of behavior by what St. Thomas called right reason (*recta ratio*). On this reckoning, schooling should emphasize knowledge of those several aspects of reality that are severally explored by the characteristic approaches of mathematics, the physical and social sciences, the literary humanities, philosophy, and theology. In his commentary on Boethius's tract on the Trinity, St. Thomas subscribed at one point to the curricular fashions of his own day. He wrote that the traditional seven liberal arts were the best preparation for the study of philosophy, and presumably his well-educated man would have followed that program. At least, this was the sequence at Paris where the young bachelor of arts was formed by the *trivium* of language disciplines and the *quadrivium* of mathematical disciplines. The master's course concentrated, in its turn, upon philosophy, which included material that nowadays would belong to the physical sciences. (*Expositio super librum Boethii De Trinitate*, q. 5, a.1, ad 3.)

If St. Thomas does provide support for those who make intellectual formation the chief purpose of schooling, still this theme receives some important modifications when set within the total context of the Thomistic synthesis. It has already been indicated that the full register of intelligence includes more than scientific and philosophical thinking. It includes practical thought ordered either to action or to the making of things and it includes the joy which comes from the vision of the beautiful. For the beautiful, said St. Thomas, fulfills desire not by being possessed but simply by being known. (*S. Th.*, I–II, q. 27, a. 1, ad 3.) Granted these qualifications, one can agree that St. Thomas would very likely have expected the well-educated man to be, in the first place, a man of wisdom and erudition, with as thorough a knowledge of as many significant areas as possible. At the same time, he would presume that in such a person the pursuit of wisdom would itself be rationally controlled. For he noted the danger of the ruinous vice of *studiositas*. This is an inordinate appetite for sheer learning, which disregards the hierarchical order obtaining among things more or less useful to know. The human good does indeed consist in a knowledge but not just any knowledge. It is in the knowledge of God, the supreme truth, that supreme happiness is found. (*S. Th.*, II–II, q. 167, a. 1, c.) St. Thomas did not canonize an unprincipled avidity for learning, which is careless of the uses to which knowledge is put and of its suitability to the moral capacities of the learner. He would have understood the contemporary fear that knowledge of the physical world may outrun the wisdom to use this knowledge ethically.

SOME IMPLICATIONS OF THE LEARNING PROCESS

St. Thomas' remarks about the learning process suggest some further lineaments of the ideally educated man. On several occasions, for instance, he drew a distinction between two methods of acquiring the habits of knowledge that are the distinctive products of intellectual learning. Both methods presuppose a basic conception of knowledge as a process of becoming, in a certain sense, the thing that one knows. A man looking out the window sees a rose upon its stem in his garden. The flower remains untroubled where it is and yet somehow it is now within him, for he knows it. Consequently, knowledge was understood by St. Thomas as an actualization of the subject's capacity for a cognitive union with the form or essence of the object known. This requires that the rose achieve a new mode of intentional existence within the knower. No doubt these formulas strike readers unacquainted with the Aristotelian-Thomistic framework as simply mystifying. The distinction between the two approaches to this cognitive union is, however, easy enough to appreciate. One can learn, said St. Thomas, through one's own investigation and experience, as when one knows an orange by seeing it or discovers the best way to tie a knot or solve a mathematical problem. This is the *inventio* or research that was noted previously. A man can also learn through the assistance of a teacher who has himself previously acquired the knowledge that the student is seeking. This is *disciplina*, which may be somewhat awkwardly translated as learning-through-teaching.

Of these two ways, the first, as was indicated before, is the primary and the best. The ability to employ it shows that a person is more gifted than those who depend upon another's teaching. This second method, however, is often necessary if learning is to be reasonably economical, since even the most talented inquirer would require too much time if he had to learn everything on his own. (*S. Th.*, I, a. 117, a.l; *De. Ver.*, q. 11, a. 2, ad 4.) St. Thomas' preference for the method of personal research was underlined when he recommended that teachers adopt the same procedures that an independent investigator uses to acquire knowledge by himself. For teaching is an art, and when effects can be produced either by art or by nature, the artist should follow nature's method. (*De Ver.*, q. 11, a.l, c.) In this crisp formula St. Thomas anticipated one of Rousseau's favorite themes. No doubt Aquinas' concept of nature and the logical framework he provided for this basic recommendation were very different from Rousseau's, but the radical insight was the same. In explaining the need to imitate nature's way, St. Thomas highlighted another significant theme in his theory of learning. He compared the work of a teacher with that of a physician, since the most that either of these agents can do is to strengthen the internal resources of student or patient. A sick man is really healed, St. Thomas believed, by his organism's own curative powers. The doctor's medication only reinforces this natural restorative power. In like fashion, a teacher helps others to learn by expediting the efforts that they make themselves. (De. Ver., q. 11, a.l, c.) This is another way of saying that the primary agent of all learning is the learner himself and that teachers are secondary and instrumental causes. They help but they are not indispensable. We can conclude that for St. Thomas an educated man was one capable of independent intellectual inquiry. His mental powers have been matured, either with or without much formal schooling, and thereby have been liberated for free and effective action in a life of continuing learning.

Whether a man learns by himself or with a teacher's aid, however, learning always implies growth. We are not born with innate ideas, said St. Thomas, but with a mind, which, of its nature, has an innate capacity and desire to know. When this power develops, it means, to use a term from St. Thomas' commentary on Aristotle's Posterior Analytics, that habits of knowledge are generated in the learner. He wrote:

What is generated does not exist fully before generation. It exists in a way, and in a way it does not. It exists in potency but not actually. Generation is the reduction from potency to act. What is learned, then, was not fully known beforehand, as Plato maintained, nor fully unknown . . . But it was known potentially or virtually in the knowledge of universal principles. As knowledge in the strict sense, it was actually unknown. And so to learn means to be brought from the condition of potential, virtual, or general knowledge to actual knowledge in the proper sense (In lib. Post. Anal., b. I, lect. 3, n. 6).

St. Thomas was speaking here of the learning that builds up the intellectual habits he called "science." We have noted that this term is applied to academic disciplines that have conclusions demonstrable in terms of fundamental principles—whether these be the principles of mathematics, physics, philosophy, or theology. As a rule, St. Thomas reserved the word "teaching" for those situations in which intellectual habits of this sort are "generated." He agreed with Aristotle in rejecting Plato's conviction that moral virtue could be taught. In the geometry class, indeed, the student is taught when he is brought to see for himself that two parallel lines never meet in the Euclidean universe. When he understands it, the specific work of the teacher is done, for the student is, in this respect, a "geometer." The teacher might also conduct the same pupil to a theoretical appreciation of the meaning, necessity, and value of truthfulness, but that does not insure his being honest. Speaking once of character training, therefore, St. Thomas did not use *docere* (to teach) but made a significant change of verbs and remarked that the child should be accustomed (*assuescere*) to acting virtuously; he should be taught, as it were, through the practice of personal action. (*In lib. Eth.*, b. II, lect. 1, n. 254.)

It is clear, nonetheless, from St. Thomas' fundamental philosophical analysis of habits, that all learning—practical, scientific or ethical— involves transit from potentiality to actuality and is, therefore, a growth. An emphasis upon the dynamic character of human nature is a central Thomistic theme. While man lives, he acts. If his mental and moral actions are systematic and effective, then the capacities of mind and will are enlarged by genuine entitative additions. In the Aristotelian terminology these expansions of personality are called habits. They include not only scientific skills but such practical intellectual "virtues" as prudence, which governs ethical action, and skills in the arts, which perfect man's creative powers. And they also include the moral virtues, so that the man who has acquired the habit of courage is, in this respect, more fully a man than a coward is. A painter or a composer, as well as a plumber or a chef, is a man whose intelligence has been so enriched by his habitual art that he can control his material and produce excellent effects consistently rather than by chance. Those who have developed sound ethical character are persons whose potentiality for moral action has been perfected by an habitual inclination to conform behavior to right moral principle. In Thomistic terms, then, the ideally educated man is more completely human and exists with a higher degree of intensity than he would have, if he had remained uneducated. For that growth, besides, he has paid the honorable price of steady effort. For the intellectual and moral virtues are normally acquired only by assiduous practice. (*S. Th.*, I–II, q. 63, a. 2, c.)

In the process of this growth, intellectual, moral, and physical development are interrelated and mutually influential. It has been noted already that St. Thomas made a good deal of the physical organism's effect upon mental maturation. He was similarly convinced that the moral life has significant implications for intellectual development. This conviction was part of his broader emphasis upon the interplay between the effective and cognitive powers. The mind and the will, he remarked in the *Summa Theologiae* at one point, are mutually inclusive of one another. (*S. Th.*, I, q. 16, a. 4, ad 1.) This suggests once again that St. Thomas would not have drawn an exclusively rationalistic diagram of the ideal school.

In fact, in his analysis of human action, he concluded that the cause of all uncoerced activity is love in the sense of a fundamental seeking for some value. Every agent, said St. Thomas, acts for an end. But every end is a good, which the agent finds lovable and desirable in some aspect. If a man acts, therefore, he does so out of some love. (S. Th., I–II, q. 28, a. 6, c.) Indeed, even when he is coerced, he acts because he desires to save himself. One is not surprised, therefore, to find St. Thomas ratifying Aristotle's comment that we do best those things that we delight in doing. (S. Th., II–II, q. 15, a. 3, c.) Or, as he remarked common-sensically: What is willed out of love is willed more intensely than what is willed out of fear. (CG, b. III, c. 116.) Thomistic scholars like Rousselot have pursued this theme and have shown how effective dispositions can heighten perception, so that love, far from being blind, actually makes it possible for the lover to see further and understand more profoundly than can those who do not love. Unexceptionally enough, St. Thomas suggested that teaching would be more effective if students could acquire a love for their work. He granted that knowledge is desirable in itself but noted that it might become hateful by accident should it obstruct a man from something he loves even more. (S. Th., II–II, q. 15, a. 1, ad 3.) A strong motivation, moreover, would help to overcome the obstacles tossed into the path of learning by lack of talent or the distraction of life's cares or sheer laziness—the torpor addiscendi. (S. Th., II–II, q. 2, a. 4, c.)

Not the least of such obstacles, St. Thomas believed, is the impediment of an evil life. Here, too, he acknowledged the impact of bodily factors. He was persuaded that the somatic disposition, or complexio corporis, as he called it, might even predispose (though not predetermine) a man to certain virtues or vices. (S. Th., I–II, q. 51, a. 1, c.) In any case, the material side of nature contributes to the inclination to sense pleasure and to the vehement recoil from pain, even when this pain necessarily accompanies a good that benefits the whole man. (S. Th., II–II, q. 138, a. 1, c.) Both the child and the intemperate adult, St. Thomas thought, find learning difficult, because each naturally follows the motions of sensual appetite and refuses to listen to reason. (S. Th., II–II, q. 142, a. 2, c.) But in his commentary on Aristotle's Physics, he suggested that impediments of this sort could be overcome if young people would develop moral virtues. (In lib. Phys., b. VII, lect. 6.)

This was a characteristic theme of St. Thomas. On the one hand, he observed that a good moral life, by subduing the passions and quieting the clamor of external businesses, disposes a man to intellectual pursuits. (S. Th., II–II, q. 180, a. 2, c.) On the other hand, he noted that vice impedes learning. Carnal sins blunt the senses, he thought, and produce a consequent mental blindness. They do not alter the intellect but they do inhibit its range by tying it down to images of food or sex. (*S. Th.,* II–II, q. 15, a. 3, c.) Envy, anger, excessive sadness, and pride are all, in varying degrees, obstacles to the intellectual life. It is not that immoral people are incapable of brilliant achievements upon occasion, but that vice prevents them from realizing their full potentiality. (*S. Th.,* II–II, q. 15, a. 3, ad 1.) Knowledge, after all, is both speculative and affective. Your proud man may be a theologian of vast erudition, but an authentic affective knowledge is denied him, because pride, which is self-love, leaves no room for love of truth. (*S. Th.,* II–II, q. 162, a. 3, ad 1.)

From these and many other instances, it is clear that St. Thomas' recipe for an educated man would count as essential ingredients both the moral and the intellectual virtues. He would agree, to borrow Gordon Allport's terms, that the mature personality must be marked by a variety of psychogenic interests transcending the mere viscerogenic. He would agree with Aristotle that to enjoy the goods of the soul, one must exercise rational control over external goods and the goods of the body. But as a Christian, St. Thomas would then go further in two ways. He would put the essence of human perfection in charity, which is love of God and love of the neighbor for the sake of God. And he would maintain that this perfection is only possible through the divine gift of grace, which is a dynamic principle of a new life and love. He wrote:

A thing is perfect insofar as it achieves the appropriate end which is its ultimate perfection. But it is charity, which unites us to God, our ultimate end . . . and so the perfection of a Christian life is determined principally by love (*S. Th.,* II–II, q. 184, a. 1, c.).

Here, of course, it was the Christian believer and theologian who spoke rather than the Aristotelian commentator and philosopher.

This theme of charity leads to a last, though scarcely a least, element in the Thomistic ideal of the well-educated man. Because this man is endowed with intelligence and is capable of freedom and love, he is not simply an individual item in a mass but a *person*. This term, said St. Thomas, signifies what is most perfect in all of nature. (*S. Th.,* I, q. 29, a. 3, c.) A person cannot be completely subordinated, therefore, to the elements below him nor even to the human community, since by virtue of his spiritual dimension he transcends that community to some degree. At the same time, the person has an essential social dimension. In fact, St. Thomas observed, it is natural for a good man to risk his life for the republic, because it is natural for him to be part of civil society. (*S. Th.*, I, q. 60, a. 5, c.) Moreover, the plenitude of human excellence is actually verified not in any single person but in the collectivity. It is the community as a whole that needs and has the perfections of farmers, builders, and contemplatives, although each individual member only specializes in one of these offices. (*S. Th., Supp.*, q. 41, a. 2, c.)

Political philosophers point out that the social views of St. Thomas occupy a middle lane between those theories in which civil society is reduced to a sheer convention or useful tool and those in which man is no more than the citizen and, consequently, totally ordered to the community's purposes. In a searching study, *Between Community and Society*, Thomas Gilby, O.P., has developed this Thomistic philosophy and theology of the state. He shows that on its terms a man can be understood as wholly social, yet more than a simple social unit. Indeed, because men are persons, they are capable not only of citizenship but of the noblest sort of community. This is the ideal community of friendship that is made possible by knowledge and love. In this life, said St. Thomas, a man cannot be happy without friends because friends sustain one another in fidelity to the values of both action and contemplation. (*S. Th.*, I–II, q. 4, a. 8, c.) We can conclude, therefore, that the ideally educated man is a man who leads the life of a good citizen and a true friend.

BIBLIOGRAPHICAL NOTE

A brief, scholarly presentation of St. Thomas' life and work is that of Angelus Walz, O.P., *Saint Thomas Aquinas: A Biographical Study*, translated by Sebastian Bullough, O.P., and published by the Newman Press, Westminster, Maryland, in 1951. A good short introduction to the thought of St. Thomas, particularly to his philosophical ideas, is F. C. Copleston's *Aquinas*, published by Penguin Books, Baltimore, in 1955. Outstanding among longer studies is Etienne Gilson's *The Christian Philosophy of St. Thomas Aquinas*, translated by L. K. Shook, C.S.B., published by Random House, New York, in 1956. This volume contains a descriptive catalogue of St. Thomas' works, which provides full information about the various editions of the original Latin text. An introduction, through English translation, to the wide range and flavor of St. Thomas' writings is furnished by two volumes of texts, generally brief ones, selected and gracefully translated with notes and an introduction by Thomas Gilby: *St. Thomas Aquinas: Philosophical Texts*, published by Oxford University Press, London, in 1951, and *St. Thomas Aquinas: Theological Texts*, published by Oxford University Press, London, in 1955. A two-volume collection of longer passages is that edited by Anton C. Pegis, *Basic Writings of St. Thomas*, published by Random House, New York, in 1945. The English Dominican Fathers translated the entire *Summa Theologiae*, which was published in 22 volumes by Burns, Oates and Washbourne of London. This translation is also available in a large, three-volume American edition published by Benziger, New York, in 1947 and 1948. The English Dominicans also translated the *Summa contra Gentiles*, and there is an American translation of the same work prepared by James F. Anderson, Vernon J. Bourke, Charles J. O'Neill, and Anton C. Pegis and published by Hanover House, Garden City, in 1955 and 1957. This is in five volumes under the title *On the Truth of the Catholic Faith*. The *Quaestiones Disputatae de Veritate* have been translated by Robert W. Mulligan, S.J., James V. McGlynn, S.J., and Robert W. Schmidt, S.J., and published in three volumes under the title *Truth* by Henry Regnery, Chicago, in 1952 and 1954. From this same translation the eleventh of the questions, the *De Magistro*, has been issued separately as *Thomas Aquinas: The Teacher*, published by Henry Regnery, Chicago, in 1954. At the present time, a team of scholars under the general editorship of Thomas Gilby is engaged in a fresh translation of the *Summa Theologiae*. The first volumes in this series were published by McGraw Hill, New York, in 1964, with the Latin text and the English translation on facing pages.

For a full bibliography of books and articles on Thomistic educational theory, see Tad W. Guzie, S.J., *The Analogy of Learning: An Essay Toward a Thomistic Psychology of Learning*, published by Sheed and Ward, New York, in 1960, pages 1 to 25 and 225 to 236. For a very full, general bibliographical guide to the study of St. Thomas, see Vernon J. Bourke, *Thomistic Bibliography: 1920–1940*, published by The Modern Schoolman, St. Louis, in 1945. To this listing the following items may be added.

Pierre H. Conway, O.P., and Benedict M. Ashley, O.P., *The Liberal Arts in St. Thomas Aquinas*. The Thomist Press, Washington, D.C., 1959.

Pierre H. Conway, O.P., *Principles of Education: A Thomistic Approach*. The Thomist Press, Washington, D.C., 1960.

W. Lawson, S.J., "Neo-Thomism," in A. V. Judges (ed.), *Education and the Philosophic Mind*. George G. Harrap, London, 1957, pp. 43–59.

Jacques Maritain, "Thomist Views on Education," in Nelson B. Henry (ed.), *Modern Philosophies and Education: The Fifty-fourth Yearbook of the National Society for the Study of Education*, Part I, University of Chicago Press, Chicago, 1955, pp. 57–90; "On Some Typical Aspects of Christian Education," in Edmund Fuller (ed.), *The Christian Idea of Education*, Yale University Press, New Haven, 1957, pp. 173–198; extracts from these essays and other educational discussions in Donald and Idella Gallagher (ed.), *The Education of Man: The Educational Philosophy of Jacques Maritain*, Doubleday, Garden City, 1962.

※ DESIDERIUS ERASMUS (1465–1536) was born in Rotterdam, the illegitimate son of a priest, Gerhard De Praet. Erasmus received his early education in the famous school of the Brethren of Common Life in Deventer, where he acquired the love of letters that was to be the ruling passion of his life. Left an orphan at thirteen, Erasmus was defrauded of his inheritance by his guardians who then compelled him to enter a monastery. He was ordained a priest in 1492. In 1494 he was granted permission to leave the monastery in order to enter the service of the Bishop of Cambria, under whose patronage he was able to study at the University of Paris. Leaving Paris, he embarked on a career of writing and travel that took him to almost every country in Europe and brought him into contact with most of the leading scholars. Erasmus was a prolific writer: his collected works fill eleven volumes; a separate edition of his letters alone fills five volumes. Erasmus was the leader of the movement to apply the skills of the Humanist to the editing and translating of sacred literature. His most famous works in this area are his editions of the works of a number of the early church Fathers and his edition of the New Testament in his own Latin translation. Erasmus' concern with Humanist education led him to produce two textbooks for the teaching of Latin in the schools, the *Adagia* and the *Colloquies*. As an advocate of what he called Christian Humanism, he wrote educational treatises for the Christian Prince, the Christian Soldier, and the Christian Priest: *Institutio principis christiani* (The Education of a Christian Prince), *Enchiridion militis christiani* (Handbook for the Christian Soldier), *Ecclesiastes* (On the Way to Preach).

6

THE CLASSICAL HUMANIST: *Erasmus*

BY FRANK E. SCHACHT

The year is 1509, and the first decade of the century in which the educational dynasty of Humanism will reach its greatest power is drawing to a close. The Western world, which has yet to discover its true physical extent and knows but little about its material qualities, is going through a stage of spiritual reshaping—rebirth as it will be known in the future— one of those mysterious revolutions that, true to the name, bring to mankind reversal and reflection of thought, and afterward progress with renewed energy. In this year Erasmus of Rotterdam is returning from a three-year sojourn in Italy. Now forty-three years old, he is very much a child of his times: his intellect has mastered the learning of past and present, has endowed him with prophetic vision into the future, and has brought him ever closer to the eminent position that history will eventually give him—Prince of the Humanists. But physically he experiences at this point mostly the dire discomfort of the journey: day after day "spent on horseback in dull and unlettered gossiping," as he describes it in one of his many revealing letters, "the gait of the horse giving me excruciating pains in the kidneys . . . with my whole body in a state of unbelievable agony. . . ."

Not that all his journey had been this bad! On the contrary. In Italy he had enjoyed the hospitality of the most influential people, cardinals, and even "the present Pope (Leo X), not to mention bishops, archdeacons, and men of learning." From the latter especially he had received ample information, first-hand and long-sought, about his primary field of interest. From the time of his boyhood as an orphan, for all practical purposes, receiving home and tutelage from the Augustinian Fathers, his agile mind had retraced the thoughts of Greek and Roman writers and tried to discover their meaning and usefulness for his own times. His intimate communication with the Italian Humanists had thus been, to a large extent, a crowning achievement of his early academic endeavor.

In order to pursue and perfect its ideals of culture and education, the Early (fifteenth-century) Humanist School of Italy had gone back to its earliest sources and, in setting its main goal as the "perfection of the man as citizen," had successfully combined the primarily individualistic ethics of Aristotle with the social ideals of Cicero, the actual founding father of the School. *Cum sibi tum communibus studere commodis, et prodesse quam pluribus cupere* (to study for one's own as well as for the community's sake, and to desire to help as many as possible) was the aim, as Vergerius, a Humanist who lived in 1400, had put it in one of his letters.

From this general aim, there followed logically the intensive study of classical philosophy—especially the Stoics—and literature (Vergil, Ovid, Horace, Plautus, Plutarch and, of course, the works of the "Fathers") that was considered the basic necessity of Humanist education. But, especially among the Early Humanists, this study was not only pursued for its own sake, that is, for the development of literary culture, knowledge, and skill. It was also considered essential in helping to develop "practical judgment in public affairs" and was regarded as the best possible preparation for specialized studies in law, medicine, theology, and even banking.

The formal education of youth, according to the pedagogical planners of the Humanist School, should proceed in definite stages and should be the logical preparation for the eventual attainment of selected goals. Very young children should be trained at home by their mothers in the development of courteous manners, good speech, and healthy personal habits of eating and drinking. Good playmates as well as the exemplary conduct of parents and adults were considered of great importance during this first stage of child development.

Actual school instruction should begin no later than the age of ten. Classes should, wherever possible, be conducted by skilled laymen. Contrary to the educational practices of the later Humanist period, the Early Humanists advocated and practiced "friendly personal relations of teacher and pupil." They generally disapproved, and even condemned openly, the application of corporal punishment, which, they believed, always carried with it servile connotations. A teacher should have in his class only as many students as he could know and guide individually. To students of normal intelligence he should present the prescribed subject matter, including classical literature, works of the Fathers, and also mathematics, astronomy, music, and rhetoric. To the less gifted "the teacher must provide the constant stimulus of oral teaching and questioning," according to Vergerius. "Let him study carefully the particular interests of such students in order that they may devote themselves to those studies which they are likely to pursue with most pleasure and profit." To this liberal opinion Maffeo Vegio, about 1450, added, in his very important work *De educatione liberorum*, that "we may not count upon capacity of letters in every child. . . It is obvious that business, agriculture, or the professions of arms are careers for which due preparation may be made in other ways."

The Early Italian Humanists may be considered as literary aristocrats and as intensely practical Romans. The practicality showed itself clearly when they discussed certain additional educational goals, the three most important of which were summarized by W. H. Woodward as excellence in conversation, resourcefulness in the use of leisure time, and dignified passing of old age. With regard to conversational skill the Humanist Leonardi Bruni inquired, "What advantage is it to possess varied and profound learning unless one can convey it in a language worthy of the subject?" And Aeneas Sylvius, Bruni's Scholastic associate, specified that conversation should show "ease and lightness of touch, courtesy, and willingness to listen," whereas "vehemence, loss of temper, arrogance, and exaggeration are destructive of all conversation."

The correct use of leisure time was another mark of a man who, in the Humanist sense, was truly educated and truly free—truly educated because his education had resulted in useful and appreciable activity and truly free because he would then not be slave to all sorts of lower-ranking pleasures. The "correct use" of leisure was by no means restricted to literary activity, or "literary leisure," as Erasmus liked to call it. Music and certain outdoor activities were considered equally useful accomplishments.

There is no doubt that Erasmus, during his tedious return journey from Italy, had ample time to reflect upon these and many other teachings of the Italian Humanists whom he had just inspected and studied so intently. There can also be no doubt that he agreed with many of their ideals, for, as we shall see, he incorporated them into his own educational writings. Perhaps, as he was riding along uncomfortably, their mentioning of certain outdoor activities as a mark of a truly educated man brought an occasional smile to his lips—the thin, critical, and almost painful smile that the painter Hans Holbein has so well portrayed in his numerous pictures of Erasmus.

Yet, many more important things went on in the rider's restless mind—thoughts that brought him not smiles but scruples and the urgent feeling, as he wrote two years later, "that I must at all hazards do *something*." Certainly, it had been a pleasure to converse so intimately with his Italian friends, to study their schools and plans, to learn with and from them. But what about the rest of society, especially in his own sphere, north of the Alps? Was it not rapidly moving in the wrong direction, away from the original Humanist ideals of universality of education, of social service and culture, toward individual selfishness, greedy corruption, and ever increasing superstition?

An ambitious plan grew rapidly in Erasmus' mind. Before he could present to the world his own humanistic plans on education, he must try to tear down some of the idols around him, must fight conceit and depravity in the most effective way open to him—with his pen.

This plan, so boldly and quickly conceived, was even more swiftly executed. Hardly had Erasmus crossed the continent and arrived in England than he sat down and completed, within a little more than a week, "one of the most effective pamphlets ever written." It was *Encomium Moriae* (The Praise of Folly).

The title of this work is already most intriguing. It is as if we had in our hands a work on the praise of wealth by St. Francis of Assisi or one by Rembrandt on the advantages of color blindness. It seems as if from the very beginning Erasmus must have been asking himself how he could criticize and yet be heard, how he could blame and yet be understood. Through its content and style, the work itself gives the answers. It shows Erasmus both as a master of his special field, written language, and as a most imaginative teacher.

Let us imagine for a moment that he could present to us the basic thoughts of this book in the form of a lecture and that we could hear directly, rather than merely read, what he has to say in behalf of his mysterious subject matter, folly. Let us hear the hush fall over the hall as the hour of the lecture approaches—then silence, the absolute stillness of complete surprise, as the great master enters. For there he is, the celebrated author of prose and poetry, the acknowledged master of Latin and Greek, the friend of princes, political and literary—there he is, dressed not in the robes of academic distinction but in the clothes of a fool. In the awesome silence, he begins to speak, giving his listeners an explanation, but no apology, for his strange appearance. He says, "I always appear in my natural colors, and in an unartificial dress, and I never let my face pretend one thing and my heart conceal another."

Look at me carefully, he exhorts, and learn about some of the strange attributes that so often accompany, like foolish attendants, my erudite profession of teacher. You will see one "who goes with a mincing gait and holds up her head so high: self-love; one that looks so spruce, and makes such a noise and bustle: flattery; that other which sits humdrum, as if half asleep, and is called forgetfulness; the one that leans on her elbows and sometimes yawningly stretches out her arms: laziness; this that wears a plaited garland of flowers and smells perfumed: pleasure;

the other which appears in so smooth a skin and pampered-up flesh: sensuality; the one that stares so wildly and rolls about her eyes: madness." And he adds, "As to those two gods whom you see playing among the lasses, the name of the one is intemperance, the other sound sleep."

For a second time the audience is stunned. First it was by the master's strange appearance, and now it is by his even stranger words. Does he really mean what he says, or is he "just fooling"? Is he expressing his own opinions or those of the bizarre clown whom he portrays? Throughout the entire lecture this basic question will remain unanswered while society passes in critical review before the audience.

The students themselves are second to the teachers who opened the procession. The master says, "Look at how your hard-plodding students, by a close sedentary confinement to their books, grow mopish, pale, and meagre, as if by a continual wrack of brains, and torture of inventions, their veins were pumped dry, and their whole body squeezed sapless." Both of us, the master implies, are really to blame for the deplorable conditions of education; and yet, strangely enough, both sides may perhaps survive only by what the listeners seem to see before them—folly. He continues, "There could be no right understanding between prince and people, master and servant, teacher and pupil, friend and friend, man and wife, buyer and seller, or any person however otherwise related, if they do not cowardly put up with small abuses, sneakingly cringe and submit, or after all fawningly caress and flatter each other."

Next in the parade are two extreme representatives of the business world. Of them, he says:

There is another sort of base scoundrel in gentility, such obsequious merchants who, although they lie, swear, cheat and practice all the intrigues of dishonesty, yet think themselves no way inferior to persons of the highest quality, only because they have raked together a plentiful estate . . . There are others so infected with the philosophical paradox of banishing property, and having all things in common, that they make no conscience of fastening on, and purloining what ever they can get, and converting it to their own use and possessions.

Teachers, once again, "these school tyrants," are singled out as follows:

I knew an old sophister . . . who after threescore years' experience in the world had spent the last twenty of them only in drudging to conquer the criticisms of grammar, and made it the chief part of his prayers that his life might be spared until he had learned how rightly to distinguish between the eight parts of speech—which no grammarian had yet accurately done.

Then, certain kinds of writers are discussed as "those scribbling fops who think to eternalize their memory by setting up for authors . . . who make additions, alterations, blot out, write anew, amend, interline, and yet can never please their fickle judgment, but that they shall dislike the next hour what they penned in the former." Among these so-called authors, literary thieves win this special mention:

They are yet the wisest who transcribe whole discourses from others, and then reprint them as their own. By doing so they make a cheap and easy seizure to themselves of that reputation which cost the first author so much time and trouble to procure. If, however, they are at any time pricked a little in their conscience for fear of discovery, they console themselves with this thought that if they are at last found guilty of plagiarism, yet at some time they have enjoyed the credit of passing for genuine authors.

Next in line are lawyers, who "of all men have the greatest conceit of their own ability," and philosophers, "who esteem themselves as the only favorites of wisdom and look upon the rest of mankind as the dirt and rubbish of creation."

Then come the astrologers, who believe in their pseudo-science as in revealed truth, and finally the theologians, who are perhaps the most difficult to discuss or criticize:

For they are a sort of men generally very hot and passionate; and should I provoke them, I doubt not would set upon me with a full cry and force me with shame to recant . . . They fence themselves in with so many . . . definitions, conclusions, corollaries, propositions implicit and explicit that there is no falling in with them.

In the face of these problems—and of the many others analyzed in *The Praise of Folly*—what can society and the individual do? The answer to this question is given toward the end of the book in the customary cryptic manner. First, concerning the whole of society:

In the first golden age of the world . . . what use could there have been of grammar when all men spoke the same mother tongue and aimed at no higher pitch of oratory than barely to be understood by each other? What need of logic when they were too wise to enter into any dispute, or what occasion for rhetoric, where no difference arose to require any laborious decision? . . . Thus was ignorance, in the infancy of the world, as much the parent of happiness as it has since been of devotion.

Equally ambiguous sounds the advice given to the individual. There are two kinds of madness, according to Erasmus, one that induces man to the excesses of haste, lust, and crime, and the other:

. . . that proceeds from folly, so far from being in any way injurious or distasteful that it is thoroughly good and desirable. And that happens when by a harmless mistake in the judgement of things the mind is freed from those cares which would otherwise gratingly afflict it, and smoothed over with a content and satisfaction it could under no other circumstances so happily enjoy.

Thus the strange lecture ends. The Master, still arrayed in the costume of his mysterious subject matter, departs slowly, probably exhausted by the knowledge that the cryptic answers to his many questions have pointed to almost as many new problems. Those students who have really tried to understand the lecturer remain behind in deep thought, as so many readers of *The Praise of Folly* have done after they have learned to grasp the real substance hidden under the fool's clothing. For the meaning of this work, which tries to uncover and answer some of the basic problems of all mankind, is ponderous as well as prophetic and it will not admit of quick and easy comprehension.

We can assume that Erasmus himself must also have felt a certain physical exhaustion during and after the ten days in which he completed this work. Yet, to the truly dedicated, life frequently offers strange, simultaneous compensations; and even while Erasmus was giving all the strength he possessed to the writing of *The Praise of Folly*, a work containing so many negative aspects, he was, simultaneously, making a most important positive discovery. He was discovering his ideal of a truly educated man—the crowning achievement, personified, of all that his future educational works might ever hope to represent. The person embodying this ideal was his host and close friend, Thomas More. Although we can well understand that Erasmus must have felt pleased and compelled to describe the life and character of this distinguished Englishman, it speaks well for the objectivity of the author's endeavor that he waited ten full years before finally writing the following detailed report to his fellow Humanist Ullrich von Hutten:

I shall try to sketch you an image rather than a full portrait of the whole man, so far as my observation or recollection from long observation with him in his home has made this possible . . . To begin with, that side of More of which you know nothing: in height and stature he is not tall, nor again noticeably short, but there is such symmetry in all his limbs as leaves nothing to be desired here. His eyes are bluish-grey, with flecks here and there: this usually denotes a happy nature . . . His expression corresponds to his character, always showing a pleasant and friendly gaiety, and rather set in a smiling look; and, to speak frankly, better suited to merriment than solemnity, though far removed from silliness and buffoonery. His right shoulder seems a little higher than the left, particularly when he is walking; this is not natural to him but due to the force of habit, like many of the little habits which we pick up. There is nothing to strike one in the rest of his body; only his hands are somewhat clumsy . . . His health is not so much robust as satisfactory, but equal to all tasks becoming an honorable citizen. . . .

Formerly he disliked court life and the company of princes, for he has always had a peculiar loathing for tyranny . . . Indeed, it was only with great difficulty that he could be dragged into the court of Henry VIII . . . He is by nature somewhat greedy of independence and leisure, but while he gladly takes advantage of leisure when it comes his way, none is more careful and patient whenever business demands it.

He seems to be born and created for friendship which he cultivates most sincerely. He is in no way fastidious in choosing friends, accommodating in maintaining them, constant in keeping them. If he chances on anyone whose defects he cannot mend, he dismisses him when the opportunity offers, not breaking but gradually dissolving the friendship. Whenever he finds any, sincere and suited to his disposition, he so delights in their company and conversation that he appears to make this his chief pleasure in life. He loathes cards, ballgames, gambling, and the other games with which the ordinary run of men are used to kill time . . .

He rules his whole household . . . agreeably. If any quarrel arises, he at once heals or settles the difference, and he has never let any one leave his home in anger . . . Recently his father gave him a third stepmother, and More swears his bible oath that he has never seen a better one. Moreover, he is so disposed toward his parents and children as to be neither tiresomely affectionate nor ever failing in any family duty.

But I must return to recounting his studies . . . In his youth he chiefly practiced verse composition, afterwards he worked hard and long to polish his prose, practicing his style in all kinds of composition. What this style is like, I need not describe, particularly to you who always have his books in your hands . . . His *Utopia* was published with the aim of showing the causes of the bad conditions of states, but was chiefly a portrait of the British State which he had thoroughly studied. He had written the second book first in his leisure hours, and he added the first book on the spur of the moment later when the occasion was offered. Some of the unevenness of the style is due to this.

One could hardly find a better ex tempore speaker: a happy talent has complete command of a happy turn of speech. He has a present wit, always flying ahead, and a ready memory; and having all this ready to hand, he can promptly and unhesitatingly produce whatever the occasion or subject requires. In arguments he is unimaginably acute, so that he often puzzles the best theologians on their own ground. John Colet, a man of keen and exact judgement, often observes in intimate conversation that Britain has only one genius, although this island is rich in so many fine talents.

He diligently cultivates true piety, while being remote from all superstitious observance. He has set hours in which he offers to God not the customary prayers but prayers from the heart. With his friends he talks of the life of the world to come so that one sees that he speaks sincerely and not without firm hope. Such is More, even in Court. And then there are those who think that Christians are to be found only in monasteries!

There you have a portrait not very well drawn by a very bad artist from a most excellent model.

What a striking contrast between this long discourse, an *Encomium Mori*, so to speak, and the *Encomium Moriae*, The Praise of Folly. In both writings, to be sure, the author's power of critical perception is clearly revealed, but in *Folly* this quality, flavored with wit and frequently approaching sarcasm, is used primarily for a negative purpose, whereas in the description of Thomas More the same quality appears entirely positive and almost overly idealistic. The description is a most fitting illustration of the author's own complex personality, revealing the deep gap between what he was and had and what he desired—his profound intellect, polished and perfected, on one side, and, on the other, his urgent desire for human qualities of a more material nature, many of which, he must have known, he would never be able to develop or possess.

Perhaps he blamed his obscure origins for this divergence in his character. His father was a wayward cleric whom he had never really known, and his mother, who entrusted him to a monastery at an early age, died when Erasmus was only twelve or thirteen. Perhaps he found his monastic training insufficient, too onesided, and his vows too stringent and binding. Whatever the reasons, we notice in his strictly educational writings, which began in the year 1511 with *De Ratione Studii* (On the Right Method of Instruction), a marked emphasis upon three factors: the importance of the development of practical skills; the necessity of expression; and, in general, the need for training the physical as well as the spiritual side of the human being.

"There are two kinds of knowledge: the knowledge of truths and the knowledge of words," Erasmus said at the beginning of *De Ratione Studii*, a short treatise written as a kind of educational guide for his friend and fellow Humanist John Colet, who had just founded a boys' school in England. "True education includes what is best in both kinds of knowledge, taught . . . under the best guidance."

He considered languages, especially Latin and Greek, the most important subjects to be studied, because "their literature contains all the knowledge which we recognize of vital importance to mankind." But he held that the study of these languages should not by any means become the traditional drill field for petulant grammarians. Mastery of grammar, Erasmus said, echoing the ideals of the Early Humanists, is secondary in importance to mastery of content and to the chief means of expression, conversation, and, above all, writing. "Whatever the form (of the work studied), whether prose or verse, or whatever the theme: write, write, and again write," Erasmus advised. "Supplement writing by learning by heart."

Memorization, a problem of special educational significance, was given further consideration. Erasmus believed that an effective memory depends upon three conditions: "thorough understanding of the subject; logical ordering of contents; repetition to ourselves." He added:

Without these we can neither retain securely nor reproduce promptly. Read, then, attentively; read over and over again; test your memory vigorously and minutely. Verbal memory may with advantage be aided by ocular impressions; thus, for instance, we can have charts of geographical facts, genealogical trees, large-type tables of the rules of syntax and prosody, which we can hang on the walls . . . I have known a proverb inscribed upon a ring or a cup, sentences worth remembering painted on a door or a window.

Conversation in a foreign language must be a matter of constant attention and concern for the language teacher, according to Erasmus. Games, plays, and contests of various kinds should be part of the regular program of instruction, and awards should be given to the most proficient students. Revision and repetition of the material studied must never be underestimated. "The master must not omit to set as an exercise the reproduction of what he has given to the class," Erasmus counseled. "It involves time and trouble to the teacher, I know well, but it is essential."

In order to supply the greatest possible stimulation for his students, the teacher must himself be well-read in his subject area. He must have "competent knowledge" not only of literature but also of philological details, especially the roots and derivations of words. In addition, he should be well acquainted with the subject matter of related fields of knowledge, such as archaeology, astronomy, history, and sacred history. In fact, "there is no discipline, no field of study, whether music, architecture, agriculture, or war, which may not prove of use to the teacher," Erasmus said.

When discussing literature with his students, the teacher must not take the work "as a text for irrelevant and universal commentary," Erasmus warned. "Respect the author and let it be your rule to rest content with explaining and illustrating his meaning."

Erasmus held that careful introduction to a work was almost as important as the discussion of it. He believed that the following introductory steps ought to be taken every time a new work of literature was to be studied: (1) presentation of the author's biography; (2) explanation of the type of work under consideration; (3) discussion of a story's basic plot; (4) analysis of details of the author's style; (5) mention of the moral applications of the story; and (6) explanation of the broader philosophical themes.

If the discussion of the work could proceed from such careful introduction, students would develop a more critical and objective attitude toward literature and would eventually learn to distinguish "good literature from mediocrity," according to Erasmus.

Unfortunately, many of the additional details given in *De Ratione Studii* are repetitive. The reader waits anxiously, but in vain, for explanations and ideas concerning subjects other than literature and in the end can only assume that the author did not feel qualified to speak with authority in any field but his own specialty.

From 1528 on, Erasmus continued his strictly educational writings with the short satirical dialogue *Ciceronianus*. Once again, as he had done in *The Praise of Folly* and in *De Ratione Studii*, he took to task the extreme grammarians of the Humanist School. He accused them of imitating the vocabulary and style of certain classical writers so closely that neither their students nor they themselves could possibly develop a style of their own. Instead of using the classical languages in an active and lively form, as Erasmus advised again and again, they made of them a kind of vise in which freedom and individual creativity were too tightly controlled, he said.

A year later Erasmus wrote what is sometimes called "his most mature educational work," *De Pueris Statim ac Liberaliter Instituendis*. Richard Sherry, in his sixteenth-century edition of this work, translated the elaborate title in the following interesting way: "That Children Ought To Be Taught and Brought Up Gently in Virtue and Learning—and That Even Forthwith From Their Nativity." The work was not meant to be a systematic discourse on child care—a fact obvious to the reader from the very first page—but rather an exhortation, a sermon in pamphlet form, emphasizing the importance of education.

We must start the educative process, Erasmus urged, as early as possible. We must "educate the child while his age is tender and tractable, and his mind flexible and ready to follow everything." Children are really never too young to learn, he said. Certain fables and poems are well understood in early childhood—and so is gentle instruction in good manners. *Gentle* instruction! For while it is important to start education early in life, it is equally mandatory not to expect too much from young children, nor to give them too many tasks. Erasmus advised that we proceed carefully at this stage.

Although most of the early training of children takes place at home, in their natural surroundings, it may sometimes be entrusted to a teacher, who must indeed be a person of special qualities. Not only must he know how to teach but also he must understand that for young children learning is more like playing. Erasmus was in agreement with the modern view that children are not simply small adults but have a distinct life of their own.

Lest his own contemporaries should misunderstand or perhaps even entirely reject him on this point, Erasmus added in a more traditional and severe manner, "It is not fitting that the age of infancy should slip away without all fruit of good instruction," and it would be a fallacy to say that "the first age is so rude that it can receive no discipline, and so tender that it is not made for the labor of studies."

Parents owe their children the rudiments of proper training at home, Erasmus emphasized. Mothers should give physical care, and fathers should give a reasonable amount of mental training. Animals, Erasmus argued, perform their tasks by instinct alone and are "taught by nature," but man "neither can eat nor go nor speak, lest he be taught."

Many fathers, he believed, do not draw this natural conclusion. He said, "They either take no care, or else care too late." Then there are others who take care admirably of their children's bodies, "but the mind by whose moderation all honest works do stand, they care not for . . ." He observed, "Often they have their land well tilled, but their sons are shamefully rude."

How can a father expect his son to become master of a ship if he does not prepare him for the difficult task of navigation? Erasmus noted that rich men, especially, often do not really care for the proper education of their sons. "Why should they be educated," they tend to ask, "if they will have enough to live on, anyway?"

Nor do mothers always take their educational duties as seriously as they should. "They be scant mothers which only bring forth, not up, their children . . ." Erasmus commented. "Men, trust me, are not born but fashioned . . . Reason maketh the man." There is no more shameful thing for parents than children who are brought up badly. "It is a weighty matter to bring up children well; but no man is born to himself, no man is born to be idle," he pointed out.

There are even some parents who go so far as to teach their children deliberately bad manners and "filthy words, and if the child repeats them, they kiss him for his labors," Erasmus charged. Animals that teach their young in accordance with the precepts of nature could indeed never fall so low.

At this point Erasmus must have felt that he had exhorted enough for a while. He therefore exchanged his assumed role of a preacher for that of a philosopher in order to explain his basic educational creed and give it the full weight of logical support, without the many *argumenta ad hominem* which he had used so frequently in this work. He wrote:

All the state of man's felicity stands especially in these three points: nature, good ordering, and exercise. I call nature an aptness to be taught, and a readiness that is grafted within us to honesty. Good ordering, or teaching, I call doctrine which stands in monitions and precepts. I call exercise the use of that perfectness which nature has grafted in us and that reason has furthered. Nature requires good order and fashioning. Exercise, except it be governed by reason, is in danger to many perils and errors. They be greatly deceived, therefore, who think it sufficient to be born, and no less do they err who believe that wisdom is obtained by handling matters and great affairs without the precepts of philosophy.

Erasmus' basic educational creed can, therefore, be summarized as the conviction that man's happiness, which is the most universally accepted aim of any educational system, depends upon three factors: nature, order, and exercise. The first of these, nature, deserves some special thoughts at this point, not only because it is so unusually well defined as "the aptness to be taught and the readiness for honesty" but because it reveals yet another side of the character and ideological position of the author himself.

Here is a man who dared to put nature, plain and simple, at the beginning of his scale of basic educational values. He did this in a time when most of his learned contemporaries would grant nature second place, at most, to the supernatural. He did this in an age when people most influential in educational planning, like Machiavelli, and in action, like Martin Luther, called this same nature so corrupt that they thought it could become useful only through the strictest educational controls, such as those outlined in Machiavelli's *Il Principe*, or through dedicated faith in the saving grace of God, as explained in Luther's *De Servo Arbitrio* (On Enslaved Will).

History, in its own complex way, seems to have made a point of upholding Erasmus in his conviction concerning human nature. Centuries after he wrote his educational creed, two hundred, three hundred, and four hundred years later, his rallying reference to nature and honesty sounded again from the lips and through the works of great educational planners, such as Rousseau and Pestalozzi, and flowed again from the pens of great writers, such as Goethe and Jean Paul Richter.

On the succeeding pages of *De Pueris* Erasmus continued with his philosophcial explanations. There exists, he asserted, in addition to the common nature possessed by all men, an individual nature that induces some people to be attracted to certain studies, others to be repelled by them. Educationally, this fact is of the greatest importance, he pointed out, for from it follows "that we learn the things most easily for which (our individual) nature has made us." Yet, again Erasmus added a conservative note of caution: "Albeit there is in my judgment scarcely any discipline which the mind of man is not apt to learn, if we continue teaching and practicing."

Returning then to a more practical level—and also to the more dogmatic style of writing—the author reasserted and enlarged his thoughts about the training of very young children. They should, of course, not be exposed to difficult literature and philosophy but should learn through fables and tales the basic principles of a virtuous life as well as the fundamental skills of reading. And above all, he insisted, "As soon as the child is born he is apt to learn manners." In this last process the good example of the parents is of the greatest importance and helps very much "to the good fashioning of children." Following his predilection for the classics, Erasmus cited the example of the Gracchi brothers of ancient Rome, who were brought up "not so much in their mother's lap as in her communication."

"Nobody can learn foreign languages more easily," he continued and reiterated, "than young children, if only they can listen to them often enough." The reason for this is that children have the desire as well as the capacity to imitate and generally follow directions well.

"Many fathers seek for their sons a wife with a good dowry," he wrote. "That done, they think they have done all they should." What a much greater advantage, however, can parents derive from providing spiritually for their children, that is, from teaching them! He took as an example Sir Thomas More, who, in spite of his many duties as lawyer and government official, found sufficient time "to be a teacher to his wife, daughters, and son, first in virtue and then in the knowledge of Greek and Latin." He urged the reader to consider carefully the advantages of such a life—and compare them with the habits of other people who take their children to banquets and fill them with all kinds of food "sometimes even until they vomit," and who also "load their bodies with unhandsome garments, as some trim apes . . . but when it comes to learning they are afraid that their children's minds might be overburdened."

Another interlude on methods follows at this point in De Pueris, this time on the question of how young children should be taught. Erasmus advised that it be in play rather than in labor and sometimes even "with sweet and flattering words which yet cannot tell what fruit, what honor, what pleasure learning shall bring to the children in time to come." He continued:

And this shall partly be done by the teacher's gentleness and courteous behavior, and partly by his wit and subtle practice whereby he shall choose diverse pretty means to make learning pleasant to a child and pull him away from the feeling of hard labor.

For there is nothing worse than when the waywardness of a teacher causes children to hate learning before they know why it should be loved . . . The teacher's first care, therefore, is to be loved, and this feeling should be followed, little by little not by fear but by a certain liberal and gentle reverence which is of greater value than fear.

Gentleness in teaching and consideration for the child—the basic law of good methods for teaching young children! Once again we hear Erasmus speak as a prophet whose vision has become reality only centuries later. And once again we see him as a person who, although primarily a man of theory, stood up firmly in protest against the abuses of his times. For how different from his ideals the teachers and schools of his days must have been, when he found reason to state that "there is none so vile, naughty, and wretched whom the common people do not consider sufficient enough to teach grammar school," and to say of schools in general that "you would say that they were not schools but tormenting places in which nothing is heard but howling, sobbing, and cruel threatening."

Going into some details of this subject, he complained bitterly about the frequent misuses of corporal punishment, which some teachers applied regularly and indiscriminately to all students, even the very new ones, just to impress them with their system of control and to get them properly "broken in."

"It is tyranny to oppress citizens by fear, but to keep them in good order by love, moderation, and prudence—that is princely," he wrote.

On the same degenerate level as unjust punishments were certain initiation rites during which new students were forced, among other things, to consume garbage and even excrement for the amusement of the older students. Such practices, Erasmus charged, were permitted by the authorities under the guise of "customs"—which was really nothing but a name for "old errors." He placed the blame for such excesses squarely upon the teachers who permitted them, and who claimed falsely "that liberal sciences should also have liberal sports."

Let us not tolerate such abuses, Erasmus urged toward the end of *De Pueris*. "Let gentle admonition be our rod, and sometimes chiding, but flavored with meekness, not bitterness," he said. Praise is such a better incentive than punishment, and even "if the punishment with a rod is required, it ought to be gentle and honest," he counseled.

As for the appointment of qualified teachers, he claimed, "it ought to be public care and charge . . . that those should be appointed who teach the citizen's children well and gently." He added:

It will help very much if he that takes it upon him to teach a child so sets his mind upon him that he bear a fatherly love unto him. By this it shall come to pass that both the child will learn more gladly, and that the teacher will feel less tedious about his labors. For in every business love taketh away the greatest part of hardship.

In such public instruction, he believed the rudiments of learning necessary for all children should include, first, that they should be able to speak readily. After this, he wrote, came:

. . . the care to read and write—which of itself is sometimes tedious, but the grief is taken away a great part by the cunning handling of the teacher, if it be sauced with pleasant allurements . . . Some have made the letters in sweet crusts and cakes which children love so well, that in this manner they might eat up their letters, and when they tell the letter's name get the letter itself for a reward.

Erasmus found it appropriate to relate, at this point, the story of a father who realized that his son preferred shooting to book learning and therefore had him shoot at targets made of Latin and Greek letters. Every time the boy hit the target and also pronounced the letter correctly, he would receive a special reward. Erasmus concluded:

By this device it was accomplished that the child within a few days had perfectly learned to know and say all the letters—which the ordinary sort of teacher will hardly accomplish in three whole years with beatings, threatenings, and brawlings.

Let such consideration be the main guide of all teaching! Erasmus added:

And sometimes we shall even suffer that the children should think they had gotten the better . . . By constantly changing praise and dispraise, we shall nourish in them a strife who shall do best.

After successful instruction in the rudiments of learning, he said that "there appears in children a certain readiness for some sciences, such as music, arithmetic, and cosmography." He believed that:

. . . they must then learn those higher things which can not be perceived without diligence and labor: the handling of themes, to turn Latin into Greek, or Greek into Latin, or to learn Cosmography without books. But most of all shall it be profitable if the child accustom himself to love and reverence his teacher, to love and make much of learning, to fear rebuke and delight in praise.

Although the sincere humaneness and basic honesty, which speak from every page of this book, can never be denied, several points of critical evaluation should be discussed, especially since this is Erasmus' most extensive systematic work on education.

There is, first of all, the matter of style—the constant and somewhat monotonous repetition of the same principle ideas that makes us feel that the book ought to be heard rather than read. To understand this point, one should remember that the book was written as a sermon for parents and that, therefore, its style met quite adequately its primary purpose. Also, Erasmus remained a cleric throughout his life. In spite of his travels and wide acquaintance with the world, he could never really discard the marks of his first profession, although he laid down, one by one, with permission of the Pope himself, the duties and outward insignia of his ecclesiastical status.

A second and educationally more significant point is that throughout the entire book very little mention is made of the one problem that is often crucial for the individual student and certainly most challenging for the teacher—how each student acts and learns as a member of a class, and how, in turn, the class influences his behavior. Once more, the basic purpose of the book serves as an adequate explanation of this deficiency. Erasmus, we can also assume, was more familiar with a tutoring situation than with a classroom situation and, furthermore, he wanted to make a specific point of the individual attention given to each student.

The strongest argument might be raised against Erasmus' single-minded defense of his own preferred subject matter, Latin and Greek; he not only advocated teaching grammar to relatively young students as a basis for future fluency in conversation and for understanding classical literature but also advocated their translating Latin into Greek and vice versa. He himself did not study Greek until he was more than thirty years old and then he had to confess frankly in a letter to his friend Battus, "This Greek language is almost killing me, but I have neither the time nor the money to buy books or hire a teacher." A significant confession from a man who had enough talent for this subject to become the foremost classical scholar of his time!

Yet, in order to view this point objectively, we must again take this very factor, the times of Erasmus, into careful consideration. In the almost complete absence of the natural sciences as reliable school subjects, the classical languages offered to both teachers and students a most useful area of knowledge and instruction. It was an area that combined logical thought with structural harmony; plain theory with a true challenge for daily work; rigid attention to detail with—eventually—the utmost in linguistic beauty; initial repression with the ultimate possibility of the freest expressions of thought and feeling. Here was indeed a field important enough to be defended in a somewhat single-minded manner. In fairness to Erasmus one should recall that this field, over the centuries, has served as a very competent mental training ground for a countless number of students, even though only the minority of these may have had the true talent to bring the preliminary training to its real application and full development.

Erasmus, moreover, had still deeper and more far-reaching educational aims. He wanted to promote the study of the Latin and Greek sources of the Christian religion in a truly scientific manner and thereby put theological research on a firm, rational basis. He wanted to combine, as best he could, reason and faith. This gigantic aim, still unattained and apparently becoming ever more difficult in our times, Erasmus pursued through constant and meticulous philological research on the Scriptures. It was a labor of love that extended over many years and finally resulted in a splendid critical edition of the New Testament in both Greek and Latin, published in 1516. "I have," he explained in a letter, "the fierce desire to get to the bottom of things and to transmit my discoveries to others, . . . especially to those ignorant theologians."

Finally, it was one of Erasmus' deepest desires to create among intelligent persons a common basis for discussion and understanding. He believed that the indispensable condition of this aim was the mastery of one common language, Latin, and the comprehension of one common culture, the classics. It is very significant that he won his first acclaim as author and editor of a fine collection of eight hundred Latin proverbs, which he compiled in Adagiorum Collectanea (1500) or simply Adagia, as the work became known later. Its publication and general appeal preceded his journey to Italy and paved the way for his acceptance and successes there as an accomplished scholar. It was indeed a special kind of compilation, selected not only for wisdom and ethical values but particularly for fine Latin prose. It was intended to be of special benefit for those, as Erasmus said in the dedication, who want to use these proverbs in their own writing and speaking and thereby improve their literary proficiency. The original selection of eight hundred quotations was increased in subsequent editions to several thousands and included many Greek sayings. In its final form this work, too, represents one of the several lifetime projects of its ingenious author.

In order to encourage the practical use of Latin in daily conversations, Erasmus began in 1526 the publication of his *Colloquies* (*Familiarium Colloquiorum Opus*), described by Johan Huizinga (*Erasmus*, Hamburg, Rowohlt, 1958) as "a rich and motley collection of dialogues, each a masterpiece of literary form, well-knit, spontaneous, convincing, unsurpassed in lightness, vivacity, and fluent Latin; each one a finished one-act play." This work, too, was augmented again and again in later editions and gradually became a most useful textbook for generations of Latin students.

Erasmus expressed his educational aspirations for the world he knew, in the following words:

Now that I see that the mightiest princes of the earth, King Francis of France, Charles the Catholic King, King Henry of England, and the Emperor Maximilian have drastically cut down all warlike preparations and concluded a firm and, I hope, unbreakable treaty of peace, I feel entitled to hope with confidence that not only the moral virtues and Christian piety but also true learning, purified of corruption, and the fine disciplines will revive and blossom forth . . ., when all the great scholars from different lands share out the work among themselves and set about this noble task, not only with enthusiasm but with a fair measure of success, so that we have an almost certain prospect of seeing all the disciplines emerge once more in the light of day in far purer and more genuine form . . .

Erasmus wrote these idealistic and tragically utopian sentiments in the year 1516, just about a century before a most horrible war between the powers he mentioned was to sack the goods and decimate the population of Europe as never before. He expressed with this statement what he had long believed to be the deepest aim of all educational endeavor: peace. This most desirable condition, he thought, would be attained when all rulers would be properly educated and thus would be able to understand and settle their problems.

In order to give practical support to the pursuit of this most important aim, Erasmus had already written in the year 1515 his *Institutio Principis Christiani* (On the Education of a Christian Prince). His specific—and also more material and practical—reason for writing this work was the fact that he wanted to give directions for the education of Charles V, then a young prince, as whose councilor he had recently been appointed at a salary of 200 Gulden (about $100) a year.

The main object of the prince's education should be to provide him with wisdom, that is, the capacity "to rule over free and willing subjects," according to Erasmus. He should, therefore, receive careful instruction in a special subject—philosophy. "By philosophy I do not mean that which disputes concerning the first beginnings of primordial matter, of motion and infinity, but rather that which frees the mind from the false opinions and predilections of the masses," Erasmus explained. After such instruction the prince might hope to achieve the best fruit of his reign, "to keep the kingdom bloodless and peaceful," he said.

Just as the mind of the prince should be led toward moderation, his character should be formed into that of a balanced person, "in no way rash and not excitable," yet also not so weak "as to be entirely out of sympathy with frivolity." He should learn that the ruler must be the ablest, not the wealthiest or handsomest.

His education should begin as early as possible, for "there is no better time to shape or improve a prince than when he does not yet realize himself as a prince," Erasmus said.

And how, in general, should the prince's teacher proceed with his difficult educational task? Erasmus declared, "In the education of anyone, but especially in the case of a prince, the teacher must adopt a mid-course; he should be stern enough to suppress the wild pranks of youth, and yet have a friendly understanding to lessen and temper the severity of his restraint. . ."

This basic theme is stated again and again throughout the entire work: the main concern with the education of a prince must be his morality, not—as in Machiavelli's *Prince*—his political skills; and the mid-course, Horace's *aurea mediocritas*, should be the guiding principles of the prince's instructor—as, in fact, they were the principles of Erasmus' personal life. Only if the prince would develop and follow these, Erasmus concluded, could he become a real ruler and avoid being a tyrant—in the same way, perhaps, that Erasmus strove to avoid the tyrannical excesses of life in order to pursue his cherished goal of "literary leisure."

The many objections to this kind of life and thought and the numerous criticisms of Erasmus' work and personality are all directed against the same principles and against the way in which he pursued them: his insistence on remaining aloof; his refusal to take definite sides; and his avoidance to the last possible moment of any serious conflict that would disturb the peace and balance upon which his life's work rested.

Any evaluation of the achievements of Erasmus must include consideration of a more objective question. What is Humanism? What is this large scholarly realm as whose prince Erasmus ruled, even during his lifetime?

John Dewey defined it briefly but adequately as "the conviction that spiritual and ideal values are of supreme rank in the make-up of reality, and that these values are most adequately expressed in the great and classic achievements of humanity in literature and art, particularly in literature."

A Humanist is, by this definition, both a scholar and a moralist; if he goes to extremes in either one of these two tasks, he may become a pedant or a preacher. Erasmus, as we have seen, fought determinedly against the pedantic scholarly tendencies of his Humanist colleagues, but could not always escape the second of the two extremes and its idealistic adjuncts, so that traces of these tendencies become obvious in many of his works, which, in turn, represent his life.

In his choice of material for scholarly research, the Humanist limits himself almost exclusively to the classics. His ideals are the educated Greek aristocrat of the classical period, who considered as the main purpose of his life the development of his individual talents to their fullest extent, and the well-educated Roman citizen of Cicero, who added to the ideal of individual development that of service to the state. These factors, too, together with the limitations they entail, we find well represented and developed in the works of Erasmus.

The true Humanist must, by virtue of the basic philosophy of his school, always hold or strive for a position above the spirit of his own time. He is basically a theorist who, in order to look ahead, must also constantly look back.

The look backward is, for the Humanist, the more important and essential one. If he can add to it a prophetic vision of future needs and realities, if he can successfully combine the conservative with the progressive—even though his kind of progress might have to be measured in terms of centuries rather than of years or decades—then, for this reason alone, his position, like that of Erasmus, will be secure among the ranks of the truly educated.

BIBLIOGRAPHICAL NOTE

Most of Erasmus' treatises on educational theory and practice must be read in translations, which, as a rule, are diligent but not numerous or sufficiently varied. To read the original Latin would require a mastery of this language on the level of Cicero and also ready access to the few libraries that are fortunate and proud possessors of original texts and transcripts.

Fortunately, Erasmus' most provocative and influential book, *The Praise of Folly*, has been translated frequently. Since it contains a fair sampling of the author's educational philosophy, and since it is relatively short and exciting, it provides good introductory reading.

The historical and philosophical background, especially the intimate relationship between Erasmus and the Humanist School, can be investigated in Louis Bouyer's *Erasmus and the Humanist Experiment*, a competent study published in London in 1959; in Stefan Zweig's *Triumph und Tragik des Erasmus von Rotterdam*, published in Frankfurt, a.M., in 1950; and above all in Johan Huizinga's *Erasmus of Rotterdam*, published in New York in 1962. The chapter on Erasmus, set within a comprehensive section on the Humanist evolution, in Robert Ulich's *History of Educational Thought*, published in New York in 1950, will provide additional, valuable insight.

For the study of Humanism as a whole, no source can be more adequate than the relevant sections of Werner Jaeger's *Paideia*, translated by Gilbert Highet and published in New York in 1939.

As to the specific study of Erasmus' educational theories, the research of W. H. Woodward is almost indispensable. His most comprehensive and interesting book, *Desiderius Erasmus Concerning the Aims and Methods of Education*, published by the Cambridge University Press in 1904, contains sufficient material and a clear analysis of all major educational concerns of Erasmus. Woodward's additional study on the Early Humanist School, *Vittorino da Feltre and Other Humanist Educators*, published by Cambridge University Press in 1921, provides more extensive information and deeper understanding.

Returning to primary sources, H. W. R. Hildebrandt's recent edition of one of the first English translations of any of Erasmus' works, *Sherry's Translation of the Education of Children by Desiderius Erasmus*, published in Gainesville, Florida, in 1961, is of special interest. Not only does this work give Erasmus' educational thoughts in great detail, but the sixteenth-century format of the work also comes close to simulating the effects of the original. If one has read selections from Cicero, one may well attempt to translate some of Erasmus' original texts beginning, appropriately, with his short satire *Ciceronianus*—if the text can be made available—and progressing, perhaps, to the *Colloquies*. Although the return to Latin may seem almost impossible, the attempt will be rewarding. For Erasmus can be fully appreciated only in and through Latin.

The educational theories of Erasmus, within the framework of the Humanist School, form only a small portion of his writings and accomplishments. History accords him a more eminent position in the fields of philology and religion. These fields surpass by far, in scope as well as available sources, the study presented here.

🏵 JOHN AMOS COMENIUS (1592–1671), the son of a miller who belonged to the Moravian Brethren, was born in the village of Nivmitz in Moravia. His early education at the village school consisted of instruction in reading, writing, catechism, hymn singing, and arithmetic. Not until he was sixteen—ten years later than most children of that time—did he enter a school that taught Latin to qualify for a scholarly career. In preparation for his ordination as a minister of the Moravian Church, Comenius studied at Herborn, Heidelberg, and Amsterdam before returning to his people. Comenius next became a rector of a school at Prenau and later of a school at Fulnek. In 1621 the Spanish invasion of Moravia drove him into Poland where he became rector of the gymnasium at Lissa. Here he wrote his *Great Didactic* and his *Gate of Tongues Unlocked (Janua Linguarum Reserata)*, an introduction to the Latin language. While in Poland, Comenius was made a bishop of the then exiled Moravian Brethren. In 1641 he was invited to England to join a commission about to be created by Parliament for the reform of education. The disturbed state of politics prevented the appointment of the commission, and Comenius left for Sweden where he contracted an agreement to write textbooks for that country's Latin schools. After six years of labor on textbooks, grammars, and lexicons, he accepted an invitation to establish a school at Sanospatak in Hungary. From 1654 to the end of his life he made his home in Amsterdam where he devoted his days to writing and to the care of his scattered fellow religionists. In 1658 he published his most famous book, the *Orbis Sensualium Pictus*, which was the first children's picture book.

7

THE PANSOPHIST: *Comenius*

BY JEROME K. CLAUSER

John Amos Comenius was a Renaissance Man living in the Age of Reason. Few scholars have ever attempted and, to a degree, succeeded in mastering as many diversified bodies of knowledge as did Comenius. In addition to being an internationally known teacher and educational reformer, he was also a theologian, an encyclopedist, a linguist, a scientist, a psychologist (before the science was created), a composer of religious music, an author of textbooks, a traveler, and an internationally known pacifist. In short, he was a model of the universal man (*uomo universale*) of the Renaissance living in the seventeenth century.

As no area of inquiry was large enough to satiate Comenius' intellectual appetite, neither was any country. Moving from his native Moravia to Germany, to Poland, to Sweden, to England, to Hungary, and finally to Holland, Comenius became a familiar international figure. In corresponding and conversing with the leading scholars and intellects of Europe, Comenius won high regard both on the Continent and in America.

As a student of the classics, Comenius devoted himself especially to the works that might somehow improve the lot of mankind. In this sense he qualified as a belated Humanist in an age that did not seem concerned with discovering new insights into human ideals.

To understand Comenius and to appreciate what often appears today as incredible naïveté, it is necessary to understand the period in which he lived. It encompassed the nebulous time when Copernicus' *Book of the Revolutions of the Heavenly Spheres* (1543) had not yet been digested, and Newton's *Principia* (1687) had not yet been inspected. It was the period when Francis Bacon gave most eloquent expression to induction as a mode of scientific inquiry, emphasizing the necessity of planned experimentation and proposing cooperative scientific research institutions. It was the period when Descartes advocated the systematic use of intelligent inquiry to reveal truths that had been previously kept secret by myth and superstition.

But periods do not abruptly sever themselves from the past. It was a period when religious intolerance reached its most devastating climax in the Thirty Years' War. And it was also a period of nascent nationalism when misguided patriots vied with religious bigots in fanaticism. In short, Europe reflected a kind of adolescence during the period from 1592 to 1670. It possessed the physical maturity to assert its strength, but sadly lacked the intellectual maturity to guide this energy toward positive ends.

Finally, this period was one of optimism when many scholars felt that the acquisition of universal knowledge and the establishment of world peace were attainable ideals. This, then, was the period in which John Amos Comenius attempted to provide the world with a methodology that would make available to all people the collected knowledge and wisdom of the world. This knowledge, Comenius believed, would enable man to live the good life here on earth and at the same time prepare him for eternal salvation. Few scholars of any age were as ambitious as this.

The paradoxical nature of Comenius' life may be most surprising to a student of educational history. For a scholar who exhorted others to be rigorous and systematic in educational matters, Comenius, in his own life, showed a considerable amount of inconsistency. For example, his major pedagogical work, the Great Didactic, was ostensibly influenced by Bacon. Yet, disregarding Bacon's admonition to employ induction as the more rewarding method for scientific discovery, Comenius gave to major portions of the Great Didactic a deductive organization. Specific methods were derived from first principles, which, in turn, were formulated presumptively (a priori).

Comenius saw himself in the role of a mediator and an arbitrator in international conflicts. In his book, The Angel of Peace (about 1660), which was submitted to the disputing statesmen of England and the Netherlands, he attempted to provide a method whereby international disputes could be permanently settled. Nominally he was a pacifist, yet, throughout his writings, bellicose statements advising the reader to "strap on the mighty armor of God," for example, seem incongruous. Furthermore, his covert political correspondence seems entirely out of place in the activities of a self-proclaimed pacifist.

Although he was an ardent ecumenicalist, Comenius expressed considerable vehemence against the Catholic forces that nearly exterminated the Bohemian Brethren (Unitas Fratrum) in his native Moravia. In fact, it was his vocal support for the Protestants during the Thirty Years' War that made him a special target for proponents of the Counter Reformation.

During his life he was recognized throughout Europe as the outstanding writer of Latin textbooks. Yet, of all of the tasks he undertook, he disliked most the "disgusting task of writing school books." (*Latinitatis studia mihi toties nauseata.*)

Although Comenius, the trained theologian, rose to be a bishop in his church, the *Unitas Fratrum*, it was as an educator, not as a theologian, that he gained recognition.

Comenius was strongly impressed with the potential power of science and was an ardent believer in sense realism and empiricism, yet he remained a believer in the mystical prophecies of Drabik, Kotter, and Poniatowski.

Finally, and perhaps most ironically, Comenius' didactical writings were an obvious attempt to create a science of pedagogy. Yet, despite the fact that he spelled out in most minute detail the specific steps for the teacher to follow in presenting a lesson, he referred to his works as revealing the true "art of teaching."

In a sense, Comenius was a set of contradictions. But a strong indictment on this account does not do justice to the great humanitarian. If Comenius occasionally lapsed from the rigors of logical consistency, it was not so much because of a lack of sophistication as it was because of a concern for mankind. When faced with the problem of deciding between logical consistency and the well-being of mankind, Comenius surrendered consistency every time.

Although perhaps oversimple and naïve by today's standards, Comenius' writings, especially his educational works, reflect his deep love and sympathy for his fellow man. Undoubtedly his own suffering and persecutions aroused within him an awareness of the plight of others. It was this concern that inspired Comenius' educational reforms, which are timeless by any standards.

The student of educational history may also be surprised at what appears to be a lack of originality in Comenius. While he is perhaps best known today for his *Great Didactic*, works of a similar nature were rather common in Comenius' day. Wolfgang Ratke, for instance, had devised a didactic method that he offered to princes throughout Europe. While Comenius was personally unable to get in touch with Ratke and examine his method firsthand, the tenets of Ratke's didactics were widely disseminated by Professors Helwig and Jung. It is very likely that the enthusiastic reception given this didactic method was made known to Comenius when he studied at Herborn. Comenius studied similar didactics by Rhenius, Glaum and Ritter. Even more immediate was the influence on Comenius of John Valentine Andreae and John Henry Alsted. It was Andreae who impressed upon him the significance of Christian ideals realized in a practical life, and it was the writings of Andreae that provided the basis for Comenius' strong reaction to Scholasticism. Comenius acknowledged this debt by devoting a section of his *Didactic* to listing the uses of the art of teaching as Andreae had stated them.

Perhaps the greatest influence on Comenius was John Henry Alsted, his teacher at Herborn. Alsted enjoyed an international reputation as one of the leading intellects of his time. It is interesting that his most significant work, *Encyclopaedia of all the Sciences* (1630), contains a section devoted to education very closely resembling Ratke's didactics. In short, while Comenius gave the most eloquent expression to a didactic scheme whereby all things could be taught to all children, the concept was neither unique nor original. In fact, as these few examples have shown, didactics were rather common in educational circles of the seventeenth century.

Another area in which Comenius excelled was methodology of language teaching. Here again it is not difficult to trace the influence of preceding and contemporary scholars on Comenius. For instance, Juan Vives, as early as 1531, proposed that Latin and the vernaculars be taught together through daily use. Alsted made a similar proposal, and J. Cecilius Frey in 1629 proposed that all languages be learned colloquially. Elias Bodinus and William Bateus had both compiled method books for teaching Latin before Comenius. In fact, the title of Bateus' work, *Janua linguarum* (1615), served as a model for Comenius' later work, *Janua linguarum reserata* (1631).

Finally, the emphasis that Comenius placed upon nature as the model for all educative processes was at least partially inspired by the teachings of the philosopher Tommaso Capanella.

The attribution of inspiration and influence to predecessors and peers is sometimes an unsound practice. Similarity of content does not necessarily imply "pirating" or even a mutual sharing. For example, Comenius had formulated the plan of his own *Janua* well before he had heard of the existence of the other *Janua*. But Comenius himself removed the burden of attributing influence, because in his own writings he generously pointed out his indebtedness to others.

It was not consistency of thought and action, nor was it originality in the strictest sense that gave Comenius the stature of a giant among educators. His genius lay elsewhere. It can be found in his eclecticism, for example. Few people could combine religious, scientific, encyclopedic, and Humanistic points of view into one comprehensive scheme. This attempt to encompass all of man's collective knowledge led to Comenius' most ambitious pansophic projects. He felt that his didactic method would make possible the most efficient transmission and expansion of this knowledge. And he believed that a sound method of language instruction, especially in Latin, would unlock the gates of knowledge. (*Janua linguarum reseratum* means The Gate of Languages Unlocked). One must remember that even in the seventeenth century the first requirement for learning was the acquisition of reading and writing skills in Latin.

As illustration of the scope of Comenius' contributions, his most significant writings will be discussed.

The works of a man like Francis Bacon, who took all knowledge for his province, do not lend themselves to precise categorization. How, then, does one attempt to classify the works of Comenius with their pansophic scope? Comenius' writings do not even fall into mutually exclusive classes. Under the all-inclusive heading of pansophy, the writings might be classified by subjects—historical, irenic, encyclopedic, theological, and pedagogical works. But even such a preliminary grouping would run counter to the canons of classification, because theology permeates every area of discourse. If Comenius aimed for any one ideal, it was a synthetic system that, instead of splitting up disciplines or bodies of knowledge, would bring together all knowledge into one consistent scheme. This was the desire that caused Comenius to reject the Copernican theory, not because of its lack of empirical validity but because it was inconsistent with Scriptural passages as he interpreted them. Again, his irenic contributions dealt as much with political situations as they did with religious reconciliation. Similarly, the historical writings of Comenius dealt primarily with church history or with biographical accounts of notable Moravian Brethren.

His theological writings, which included the usual catechisms and polemics, also embraced works devoted to revelation and prophecy. Comenius was strongly attracted to prophecy, especially to the predictions that foretold the renewed growth of the *Unitas Fratrum*. While this belief sustained him during those dark periods in which he watched his beloved church nearly dissolve, his eager acceptance of this prophecy also caused him much anguish when his church failed to regain its former prominence.

Closest to Comenius' pansophic ideals were his encyclopedic writings. Comenius' pedagogic works, especially his *Janua* and *Orbis pictus*, were produced as tools to enable students to comprehend encyclopedic knowledge. Ironically, his "tools" gained more fame than the pansophic knowledge they were to transmit. Today, encyclopedic attempts by one author in light of present standards would be greeted by incredulity or amusement. But in Comenius' day, it was still possible for one man to aim to be conversant with all the collected knowledge of the world.

That he failed in his pansophic ideal was not because of a lack of perspicacity so much as it was because of a bias for subordinating empirical proofs to theological proofs and for mistaking his nominalism for realism. That two different theories could be used to account for the same phenomenon was a notion Comenius could not accept. He believed that there was one unified, encompassing scheme of the universe, which, although its manifestation in nature was different from that in the Scriptures, still gave evidence of a hierarchy of truth. The ultimate truth, of course, was the word of God.

Although Comenius was invited to England to share his pansophic views with Samuel Hartlib, John Pell, Theodore Haak, John Wilkins, and John Milton, the Royal Society that later evolved from the efforts of this group followed Baconian rather than Comenian principles. Perhaps even in his own time some of Comenius' cherished ideals were held to be quaint and provincial.

But in pedagogy, Comenius was often centuries ahead of his contemporaries. His pedagogical writings fall generally into two groups: textbooks in specific subject matter such as languages, and in general encyclopedic knowledge; and works that were designed primarily for the teacher. Any choice of Comenius' most significant work would depend upon the reviewer's area of interest. However, it is generally accepted that the first work to bring Comenius international fame was his *Janua linguarum reserata*, first published in 1631.

His *Janua*, like many of his pedagogical works, was an attempt to start inculcating universal knowledge both quickly and effectively through a thorough grounding in Latin. Vladimir Jelinek, in his remarks preliminary to *The Analytical Didactic of Comenius*, translated the entire title of the Czech edition of the *Janua* as follows:

The Gate of Languages Unlocked, That Is, a Short and Easy Way of Understanding Any Language as Well as the Beginnings of All the Liberal Arts, Wherein under a Hundred Titles and in a Thousand Sentences All the Words of the Whole Language are Contained.

Unlike many contemporary educators of his day, Comenius did not limit himself to teaching Latin apart from specific content. In his *Janua* he displayed his concern for instruction in *things* as well as in *words*. (This emphasis on sense realism can be seen more clearly in his *Great Didactic*.)

The overall plan of the *Janua* was rather simple. It contained parallel passages, in Latin and in the vernacular, dealing with a specific topic. But the organization of the book was revolutionary. The grammar began with relatively short and simple statements and gradually progressed toward more complex and involved ones toward the end of the book. The subject matter was disposed according to classes of phenomena and ranged from diseases to angels. The chief criticism of the book was that in order to be comprehensive it permitted no repetition. One other minor criticism pertained to the quality of Comenius' Latin.

Comenius' method of teaching Latin departed from convention by approaching the study of a foreign language through the use of the mother tongue. But even in Comenius' time Milton questioned the validity of this approach, and Montaigne, who learned to speak Latin before he could speak French, argued for the direct approach to language instruction.

Far less controversial and perhaps more widely known was Comenius' *Orbis sensualium pictus*. This book, which was first published in Nürnberg in 1658, was intended as a supplement to Comenius' other Latin texts. The *Orbis pictus* consisted of a series of engravings, which had numbered features. The numbered illustrations were named both in Latin and in the vernacular. *Orbis pictus* was more than an illustrated schoolbook. It was one of the first attempts to motivate children's learning by appealing to the senses. Furthermore, it was the finest expression of Comenian (and Aristotelian) theory that "nothing exists in the intellect which does not exist first in the senses."

Whether or not it was the first illustrated textbook is less important than its success as by far the most popular book of its kind in its day. Translated into many languages, it was still being printed as late as the nineteenth century.

Traditionally, Friedrich Froebel has been given credit for originating the kindergarten idea. However, as early as 1630 Comenius had formulated certain basic concepts of rearing and training infants, which he set forth in his delightful book *The School of Infancy*. This book, originally published in Czech, then translated by Comenius into German and finally into Latin, was intended as a handbook to guide mothers in bringing up their infants in a Christian manner. In a typical Comenian style, the book starts with statements of basic principles and then proceeds to a description of methodology. Chapter I, for example, considers why "Children, God's most precious gift . . . claim our most vigilant attention," while Chapter IV points out "What children should learn . . . [and] In what things youth ought to be exercised gradually from Their very birth, so that They May Be Found Expert in Those Things in the Sixth Year of Their Age." Although this book was intended as the first in a series of handbooks for four different levels of school, it was popular as a separate work. Even today the reader finds the charm and warmth of the book most appealing.

Today the work that is almost synonymous with Comenius is the *Great Didactic*. This work, originally written in Czech between 1627 and 1632 and later translated into Latin in 1657, was Comenius' attempt to provide a methodology for teaching every branch of knowledge. In his introductory remarks he said:

> Let the main object of this our Didactic be . . . : To seek and to find a method of instruction, by which teachers may teach less, but learners may learn more; by which schools may be the scene of less noise, aversion, and useless labour, but of more leisure, enjoyment, and solid progress; and through which the Christian community may have less darkness, perplexity, and dissension, but on the other hand more light, orderliness, peace, and rest.

No area of pedagogy or knowledge was sacred to Comenius. He boldly plunged into the maelstrom of methodology, prescribing procedures for instilling piety and morality, inculcating scientific knowledge, and acquiring skills in languages and art.

Although a self-styled scientist, Comenius had no qualms about speculating in areas where empirical knowledge did not yet exist. For instance, he accounted for the differences of human character as being caused by:

> . . . a superfluity or a lack of some of the elements in the natural harmony, just as bodily diseases are nothing but abnormal states of wetness or dryness, of heat and cold.

"Stupidity," he said, was "but a clammy viscosity of the humours of the brain."

While Comenius may have sadly underestimated the complexity of many topics with which he dealt, and while he may have been considerably naïve by modern standards, the insights into the educative processes he revealed were centuries ahead of his time. In fact, many of his theories have only begun to be implemented today. That education should be made available to everyone regardless of social rank, while still not a completely achieved goal today, was a revolutionary proposal in Comenius' day. That language skills were not ends in themselves but merely means toward other ends was an opinion that rankled the Scholasticists of his day as much as the classical Humanists of today. That education is, perhaps, the best means for bringing about desirable social change was a theme as close to Comenius as it was to Dewey. Comenius was more than a teacher. He was a prophet.

Perhaps less familiar than the *Great Didactic* is Comenius' *Opera didactica omnia*, published in Amsterdam in 1657. The *Opera didactica omnia* represents the complete synthesis of all of Comenius' pedagogical writings. The four volumes deal with the educational theories formulated during different periods of Comenius' life. It includes the more imaginative and far-sighted works of his youth as well as some of the more labored writings of a man exposed to a barrage of caustic criticism in his old age.

The *Opera didactica omnia* is the source of the best known version of the *Great Didactic* as well as of the *Linguarum methodus novissima*. The *Linguarum* is significant because the tenth chapter contains still another didactic, the *Analytical Didactic*. While the themes of all of Comenius' didactics are essentially the same, the treatment of the methodology is considerably different. The *Great Didactic* is full of colorful analogies and allusions to nature while the *Analytical Didactic* is full of axioms and corollaries. The reader is treated with practical hints and advice in the *Great Didactic* but he is subjected to a bewildering set of definitions in the *Analytical Didactic*. In a sense, the *Great Didactic* represents the revolutionary Comenius—the *Analytical Didactic* represents the reactionary Comenius.

This brief discussion of the better known Comenian works is necessarily incomplete. A critical analysis of Comenius' writings would fill volumes. These seven examples were chosen as representations of the scope of Comenius' pedagogical theories. They also reveal a changing man—a man who, with the passing of years, no longer displayed the boldness of his youth but instead strove to prove the validity of his assertions through tedious analysis. In his last years he re-plowed his fields in ever more complex patterns without really planting any new seed.

To appreciate Comenian pedagogical theory fully, one must cast the theory in its historical perspective. Then it can be seen that as the Reformation was a product of the Renaissance, so was Comenius' pedagogy a product of the Reformation. But it was an earlier reformation, preceding Luther, from which Comenian pedagogy evolved. Jan Hus was a more influential force than Luther in Comenius' thinking. Although Hus was executed nearly two hundred years before Comenius was born, the two men had much in common. Hus stressed the Scriptures as the supreme authority in all matters of Christian faith and life, and Comenius derived his educational tenets from a literal interpretation of the Scriptures. Hus carried on the Czech language reforms originally begun by Cyrill and Methodius, and Comenius continued his efforts to establish etymological principles and to codify his native Czech. (As early as 1612 Comenius began writing a Czech dictionary.)

As Hus translated the Bible into the Czech vernacular in order to make the Scriptures more accessible to laymen, so did Comenius compose catechisms in the vernacular. As Hus composed church hymns in the vernacular, so did Comenius two hundred years later. Aside from their common religious background, perhaps the strongest similarity between the two men was their desire to resolve religious and political differences by peaceful means. Unfortunately, Hus failed to anticipate the internecine wars that were fought in Bohemia and Moravia as a consequence of his teachings, much as Luther did not anticipate that his doctrines would produce violence. The pugnacious Luther stands in sharp contrast to Hus and Comenius.

Luther did contribute to Comenius' educational reform, however, through his emphasis on the social aspects of the Reformation. Luther stressed education as an instrument for bringing about and maintaining civil order throughout the states of Germany. Aiming higher than national boundaries, Comenius a hundred years later proposed education as a means for ensuring world peace.

There are other, less important similarities between Luther and Comenius. Both men felt that harsh discipline contributed little to the educative process and both warned parents against letting certain "pernicious" books fall into the hands of their young. These admonitions were heard rather commonly throughout Europe, however.

The major emphasis of the Reformation was reliance on the Scriptures as the only guide to salvation. While the Scriptures were formerly restricted to the clergy, the Reformation placed the Bible in the hands of laymen. The Protestant clergy had to make sure that the common people could read it, and literacy, of course, required teachers and schools. It was natural for Comenius, a scholar and a theologian, to seek educational reforms, especially throughout the Protestant countries of Europe. Educators and theologians in America were keenly aware of Comenius and his proposed educational reforms, while many kings and princes feared certain possible results of such reforms.

Concern for the salvation of man's soul was by no means unusual for seventeenth-century theologians, but while the traditional theologian stressed the necessity of a pure heart (only) for spiritual salvation, Comenius felt intellectual enlightenment was a preliminary step toward this end.

Now a model was needed after which man could pattern his own life. Comenius chose Christ as the perfect model. He wrote:

. . . Since Christ has been given to the human race as the most learned teacher, as the most holy priest, and as the most powerful king, it is evident that Christians should be formed on his model and should be enlightened through their intellects. . . . Our schools, therefore, will then at length be Christians schools when they make us as like Christ as possible.

Departing from the more traditional Calvinistic version of Protestantism, Comenius felt that "... no matter how disorganized [man became] by his fall into sin, he can, through the grace of God and by certain methods, be restored again to harmony." The "certain methods" to which Comenius alluded referred to his methods of education.

Many of the unique features of Comenius' educational scheme now emerged. Since Christ made no distinction between rich and poor in his teaching, neither should education be restricted to a chosen few. Comenius advised:

... Not the children of the rich or of the powerful only, but of all alike, boys and girls, both noble and ignoble, rich and poor, in all cities and towns, villages and hamlets, should be sent to school.

Comenius advocated that children be educated in all areas of learning. Again the model exists in Christ. As God is omniscient, so should man attempt to emulate God and strive, at least, to acquire as much knowledge as possible. With so much knowledge to be gained and so short a period of learning, Comenius felt no time should be wasted by inefficient, nonproductive teaching methods. To help his fellow man to save time and accomplish more with less effort, he composed his didactic works. Here we find Comenius both ambitious and pathetic. There was something noble in his attempt to emulate God; yet there was something tragic about this finite intellect wrestling with an infinite universe.

In addition to Comenius' strictly religious aims for education, he had practical ends in mind. Reminiscent of Luther's *Letters to the Mayors and Aldermen of all the Cities of Germany in Behalf of Christian Schools* was his exhortation that education was the key to peace and prosperity. He wrote:

For those who are in any position of authority, for kings, princes, magistrates, pastors of churches, and doctors, it is as necessary to be imbued with wisdom as it is for a guide to have eyes, [and] an interpreter to have speech. ... Similarly, those in subordinate positions should be educated that they may know how to obey their superiors wisely and prudently, not under compulsion with the obedience of an ass, but of their own free will and from love of order. For a rational creature should be led, not by shouts, imprisonment, and blows, but by reason.

"It is to the interest of the whole Christian republic," he continued:

... that this Godly custom [of education] be not only retained but increased as well, and that in every well-ordered habitation of man (whether a city, a town, or a village) a school or place of education for the young be erected.

In Comenius' educational aims one finds an unusual mixture of Christian and classical Greek ethics, which is not surprising, considering his classical education and his theological training. Unique, however, are his synthesis of non-Christian ethics with Christian morality and his peculiar brand of realism that he somehow made consistent with his idealism. For instance, in *The School of Infancy* he said:

In short, the purpose for which youth ought to be educated is threefold: Faith and Reverence; Uprightness in Morals, Knowledge of Language and Arts. These are to be taken, however, in the precise order in which they appear, and not inversely. . . .

Elsewhere he said, "For all men the goal is the same, namely knowledge, virtue and piety."

Now this emphasis on virtue and knowledge closely resembles the ideas of Socrates and Plato. Socrates argued that no man sinned wittingly; only knowledge was required to make all men virtuous. Similarly, Comenius argued that regardless of how low man may have fallen, he could be restored through the correct educational methods and Christian guidance.

In matters of piety, Comenius again reflected his classical training. Throughout all of his didactic writings he stressed training for piety. In fact, the few offenses for which he strongly recommended the most rigorous punishment were those involving blasphemous behavior on the part of children. As the Greek gods of Olympus punished presumptuous behavior by man, so would Comenius' Judaic-Christian God punish impiety.

Comenius' classical heritage was further revealed in a number of aphorisms quoted by Keatinge. Examples follow.

Each object comes into existence in accordance with its "idea," "that is to say, in relation to a certain rational conception through which it can be what it is.

Therefore, all things that come into existence, whether they are the works of God, of nature, or of man, do so in accordance with their "ideas."

.   .   .   .

As all things share in the "ideas" of the Divine mind, they are also mutually connected and stand in a definite relation to one another.

It follows that the rational conceptions of things are identical, and only differ in the form of their manifestations, existing in God as an Archetype, in nature as an Ectype, and in art as an Antitype.

But before Comenius is labeled an idealist, it is important to notice that among these aphorisms he also pointed out that ". . . knowledge is true when things are apprehended as they exist in reality." Furthermore, he continued, ". . . the basis of producing as of apprehending all things is harmony." While Comenius' "idea" may be suggestive of Plato, his emphasis on rationality, reality, and harmony more strongly reflected Aristotle.

Perhaps even more revealing of Comenius' classical orientation are certain tenets of his didactic system. Again, his system reflects a fusion of idealistic and realistic themes. He stressed the necessity of imitating a perfect model, yet he patterned his methods of attaining perfection after laws of nature. He strongly oriented the content of his curriculum around religion, yet he was one of the first to bring the physical world into his classroom. He insisted on the importance of models as guides to behavior, yet he placed much emphasis on specific training in the rules of conduct.

This synthesis of Greek and Christian ideals is also manifest in Comenius' emphasis on pansophy. As Aristotle delved into every branch of knowledge in his day, so did Comenius in his time. (One should note, however, that while he strongly accepted Aristotle, he violently rejected Aristotelianism.) But there was a stronger motive for pansophy. Like the divine model that Comenius used for his educational scheme, pansophy was the counterpart of God's omniscience.

But the fame of Comenius rested upon his methodology, and it is his methodology that must be examined to see his farsightedness. The scope of his methodology is shown on the title page of his *Great Didactic*, which, according to its author, set forth:

. . . The Whole Art of Teaching
all Things to all Men

or

A certain Inducement to found such Schools in all
the Parishes, Towns, and Villages of every
Christian Kingdom, that the entire
Youth of both Sexes, none
being excepted, shall

QUICKLY, PLEASANTLY, & THOROUGHLY

Become learned in the Science, pure in Morals,
Trained to Piety, and in this manner
instructed in all things necessary
for the present and for
the future life,

in which, with respect to everything that is suggested,

> Its Fundamental Principles are set forth from the
> essential nature of the matter.
> Its TRUTH is proved by examples from the
> several mechanical arts,
> Its ORDER is clearly set forth in years, months, days,
> and hours, and finally,
>
> AN EASY AND SURE METHOD is shown, by which it
> can be pleasantly brought into existence.

This exhaustive title reveals more than just the scope of the book. It is a pithy statement of Comenius' educational principles and aims as well. Pansophy is suggested in the second line; the aim of universal education is declared; and the constituent elements of his overall didactic method are shown. Not only does his *Didactic* contain specific instructions to teachers, but also its outline of chapters suggests what should constitute an appropriate curriculum. Recalling, perhaps, that his own early schooling measured academic progress by the number of welts the student received from his teacher, Comenius emphasized the necessity of a pleasant environment as an inducement to rapid progress in learning.

Today most educators would be skeptical if someone should propose an over-all methodology for teaching all things to all people. Yet in Comenius' time these grand methods enjoyed a certain degree of popularity. Significant of their supposed value was the secrecy with which at least some early pedagogues, notably Wolfgang Ratke, guarded the specific content of their methods. These educators hoped to sell their plans to some prince who would establish and maintain the educational program throughout the state or country. Ironically, Comenius, who was most concerned with developing an educational method for purely altruistic purposes, was also most successful in literally selling his method to various rulers. Most educators in his day would have eagerly accepted such assignments for the rewards of fame and wealth, but Comenius reluctantly accepted his assignments as a means of sustaining himself and his family. Perhaps his lack of enthusiasm accounts for his long procrastination in producing his textbooks for Sweden; it at least partially accounts for his leaving Hungary before his plan for reorganizing the schools had been fully implemented. With his theologic, pansophic, and pedagogic irons in the fire simultaneously, Comenius had to spread his efforts thin at times.

The guide that Comenius followed in organizing his didactic works was the "book of nature." Comenius believed God revealed himself to man in three books—the book of nature, the book of the mind, and the Holy Word. Since man's mind was imperfectly developed and since so much diversity existed among men's minds, the mind alone was not a reliable guide. The Holy Word contained few specific hints for teaching, aside from the method of the parable used by Christ. The book of nature, however, seemed to reveal the greatest uniformity; Comenius therefore chose it as "the one and infallible guide." The concept of God revealed in the book of nature had existed since the Middle Ages. Because man lived intimately with nature, because his existence depended upon favorable growing seasons, and because his survival depended upon his successfully coping with the climate, man very early attributed supernatural significance to nature. Comenius carried over this medieval view to the post-Renaissance period.

Since all three "books," according to Comenius, had the same author, there existed no inconsistency among them. What was not made perfectly clear in one work would be better illustrated in one of the others. Comenius alluded both to Scriptural passages and examples in nature to substantiate his theories. The book of the mind was exemplified in the logical ordering and deduction from first principles. If any defect arose in the methods of instruction Comenius set forth, a remedy could be obtained from nature. It was certain, Comenius said, ". . . that art can do nothing unless it imitate nature."

Attempting to imitate nature, Comenius promulgated certain fundamental natural laws as applicable to the art of teaching. Since nature observed suitable times for growing, so should man's education commence in the "springtime of life." Since nature prepared the soil and provided sufficient warmth and moisture before the seeds could germinate, so should teachers "prepare the soil" by having their books and materials in readiness. Since nature ". . . is not confused in its operations, but in its forward progress advances distinctly from one point to another . . . ," so should a typical lesson be arranged in logical sequence and progress methodically from the simple to the complex, from the general to the specific, from the known to the unknown. (It was this last principle by which Comenius supported his notion of teaching in the vernacular rather than in Latin.)

"Nature makes no leaps, but proceeds step by step," he pointed out. It follows, Comenius believed, that all studies should be carefully organized in easily assimilable steps, progressing gradually and effortlessly.

Again in accordance with nature's time schedule, only learning material that is commensurate with the ability of the student should be presented. Furthermore, all learning materials should be arranged and scheduled so that specific studies could be assigned to specific hours of specific days. As nothing can arrest the changing seasons, so nothing should interrupt the division of time and studies.

While these instructions illustrate certain specific aspects of Comenius' didactic method, a better appreciation of Comenius can be gained by considering some over-all characteristics of his educational program.

Central to all of his pedagogical theories, perhaps, is the belief that a single method of teaching could be applied to all types of learning and to all subject areas. Since all men have in common the same human nature and essentially the same goals of education, it is only logical, Comenius reasoned, that a common method of teaching be employed. Furthermore, different methods of teaching only confuse the young, he said. The universal adoption of the "natural method" of instruction would be a boon to all scholars!

It seemed thoroughly consistent, after prescribing the common universal method of teaching, to advocate that all students be taught together. Now Comenius was not pleading merely for educational equality. He felt that a distinct educational advantage could be gained by having the faster students set examples for the slower ones. As an orchard keeper or forester cared for all of his trees at one time, so should the teacher attempt to care for all of the charges entrusted to him at the same time. The "brutish dullness and stupidity" of some would be all the more reason for teachers to employ the bright students as exemplars for the rest of the class.

Considering the times, one of the revolutionary features of Comenius' didactic method was its emphasis on teaching in the vernacular of the people. Ironically, the champion of vernacular teaching won wide recognition as a teacher of Latin. But regarding the role of Latin in the educative process, he carefully pointed out:

. . . my universal method has not as its sole object the Latin language, that nymph on whom such unbounded admiration is generally wasted, but seeks a way by which each modern language may be taught as well. . . .

Far better use of time could be made by teaching students those practical bits of knowledge so essential to their future well-being and transmitting this knowledge in the mother tongue, Comenius argued. When the essentials had been mastered, then the luxury of Latin could be permitted for those who would benefit by its use. Learning Latin before becoming proficient in the mother tongue was akin to learning to run before one could walk. In a time when education was synonymous with Latin proficiency this was indeed heresy.

It was natural that Comenius, champion of universal methodology, would cast his methods into a mold of rigorously organized classes. Not only were individual lessons highly structured and organized, but an entire educational program from infant training to college instruction was postulated.

"The whole period [of youth]," Comenius said, ". . . must be divided into four distinct grades, infancy, childhood, boyhood, and youth." ". . . To each grade," he continued, "six years and a special school should be assigned." The "schools" that Comenius had in mind included, first and perhaps most basic, the home ("the mother's knee"), for which *The School of Infancy* was composed. For early childhood he recommended the Vernacular-School. The Latin-School or *Gymnasium* was the appropriate school for boyhood age, while the university served the older youth. For each age-group, texts suited to the maturation level of the students were written.

Comenius never personally accomplished an actual large-scale organization of an entire educational program. Perhaps the closest he ever came to achieving this goal was during his stay in Saros-Patak, Hungary. He intended to create a miniature Latin state (*Latina civitatula*) in which the student body would be isolated from the outer world. The miniature state would have its own system of government, customs, and laws. In this carefully controlled situation he intended to create an ideal academic environment, free from distractions of the outside world. Unfortunately for Comenius, some of his innovations were too radical even for his teaching staff. Perhaps the most radical was his suggestion that plays be introduced into the curriculum in order to transmit grammatical and mathematical insights to the students. The manner in which the plays were composed, however, makes it doubtful if anything but boredom was achieved through their stilted, monotonous diatribes. By any standards, *Schola ludus* was abominable.

One of the more fruitful results of Comenius' emphasis upon graduated studies, however, was the attention it directed toward the education of very young children. Early youth was the most propitious time to inculcate habits of piety and virtue, Comenius felt. Furthermore, if educational progress were to be made, the groundwork must be established by proper training of early youth. He observed:

The tree remains as it grows, high or low, with straight or with crooked branches, and when it is full grown cannot be altered. . . . From this it follows that if the corruption of the human race is to be remedied, this must be done by means of the careful education of the young.

There was also a practical aspect to early education. This practical area, for which Comenius received much recognition, entailed sensory learning. Everything is learned through the senses, Comenius taught, and therefore education should be directed toward the objects that surround us. He advised teachers to place actual objects before their students, whenever possible. If the actual objects could not be procured, models should be constructed. If models could not be made, then pictures should be shown to the students. He said, "Surely . . . the beginning of wisdom should not consist in the mere learning the names of things but in the actual perception of the things themselves." Comenius recognized that very young children were especially impressed by sensory learning.

In another argument for starting the educative process as early as possible, Comenius amplified the *tabula rasa* concept as follows:

Wax, when soft, can be easily fashioned and shaped: when hard it cracks readily.

It is evident that this holds good with man himself. His brain, which we have already compared to wax, because it receives the images of external objects that present themselves to its organs of sense, is, in the years of childhood, quite wet and soft, and fit for receiving all images that come to it. Later on, as we find by experience, it grows hard and dry by degrees, so that things are less readily impressed or engraved upon it.

Another over-all characteristic of Comenius' educational program that represented a radical departure from the customs of the times was his advocacy of vocational training as part of the educative process. Since the universal method was designed to teach all things to all students, inclusion of vocational training in the curriculum was thoroughly consistent with Comenian theory. Furthermore, everything that was taught in the school should be designed for practical use. A great gap was left in the education of man when one element of his training for life was omitted, Comenius felt. A practical introduction to the world about them would enable students to discover for themselves, among other things, whatever inclinations they might have toward certain occupations.

Comenius realized, too, that some students would be neither financially nor intellectually capable of completing sixteen years of schooling. This made it even more important that students be able to make a smooth transition from schools to a profession or trade. Along with Comenius' emphasis on orderly and logical progression, sensory learning, and graduated schools and textbooks, an education oriented toward the practical life was a prominent theme in his didactic writings.

Finally, a further unique feature of Comenius' educational plan was his radical approach to discipline. Montaigne and Luther vividly described the brutality of schoolmasters in their day. Comenius described the schools he attended in his youth as "slaughterhouses of the mind." In place of the customary practice of "beating, carding and combing," Comenius urged throughout his didactic writings that ". . . education shall be conducted without blows, rigour, or compulsion, as gently and pleasantly as possible, and in the most natural manner. . . ." Teachers should be gentle and persuasive. They should commend excellence and treat their students kindly. Students treated in this manner, Comenius felt, would prefer attending school to staying home.

Now Comenius was not completely naïve in matters of discipline. He realized, as every teacher inevitably does, that certain kinds of student behavior required strong measures. Such conduct would be characterized by blasphemy, impiety, obscenity, or disobedience. But even then, the punishment, he said, "should . . . be free from personal elements such as anger or dislike, and should be exercised with such frankness and sincerity of purpose, that . . . the pupils may feel that the action is for their own good."

It is undeniable that Comenius was a revolutionary educator in his day. But merely departing from norms is not necessarily the same as making significant contributions. Regarding Comenius, the "great innovator," the question inevitably arises—how good were his pedagogical theories?

To answer this oversimplified question, certain portions of Comenius' writings must be examined again. His *Great Didactic* constantly emphasized the efficacy of one universal method for teaching all things to all students. Yet, there is little to support the notion that any one method can adequately encompass all the subtleties of, say, attitudinal, aesthetic, and factual learning. As much as Comenius attempted to depart from the strict memorization of factual data, a substantial amount of his pedagogical writing hints that this was the desired outcome of many learning experiences.

Now Comenius stressed the necessity of training in "virtue and piety." But the training method he proposed did not involve the students' critical examination of why they should be virtuous and pious. Instead, it involved their unquestioned obedience to prescribed canons.

That there may be a difference between teaching a student how to drive a nail and teaching a student how to solve a problem in plane geometry was never admitted by Comenius. Different kinds of learning suggest different kinds of teaching approaches to most educators. But although Comenius recognized different disciplines and different branches of knowledge, he believed that everything that could be taught was capable of being taught by one and the same method.

The proposal of one method for teaching all things to all students makes one ask whether Comenius meant that the same method of instruction would be used for teaching infants and for teaching adults. If so, the notion of graduated schools seems quite pointless except, perhaps, as a convenient device for distributing the school population among several teachers. Comenius never answered this adequately.

In the *Great Didactic*, Comenius used nature as the infallible model for his entire educational scheme. Now analogies are often quite useful in helping an author to clarify certain nebulous ideas. But when carried too far, reasoning from analogy may lead to confusion, absurdity, or both. In a sense, this happens with Comenius' allusions to nature. The comparisons of a growing child with a developing flower, of a teacher with a gardener, and of a school with a garden have a kind of charm that is endearing to parents and educators. Unfortunately, these comparisons are also somewhat unrealistic. To permit a seed to mature to its floral stage is simply to permit innate capabilities of the seed to manifest themselves. While the gardener may encourage the seed's development, he cannot cause the plant to produce anything that is not inherent in the seed.

As Dewey pointed out, the innate abilities of a child, like the innate capabilities of a seed, must be taken into account by the educator. But this is merely the start, not the end of the educative process. Comenius regarded the mind of an infant as a blank tablet upon which the knowledge and wisdom of society would be inscribed. Yet, he maintained that "development is from within." The question naturally arises—what *can* develop from a blank tablet? Comenius partially anticipated this question by telling how the gardener grafts strong shoots to weak stock. The teacher, similarly, "engrafts the graft of knowledge" to the tender "blank" minds of his students. But is this development from within or is it indoctrination from without? Furthermore, with all of his admonitions to follow nature and natural processes, Comenius advised the *unnatural* practice of grafting.

Throughout his didactical writings, Comenius observed that the period of early childhood is the most fruitful time to start the educative process. Among the many reasons he provided for starting the process early was the suggestion that the natural curiosity of young children could be exploited. But while children's natural curiosity was to be exploited, there is little suggestion in Comenius' writings that the *inquiring attitude* should be encouraged. In fact, one receives the impression that so long as the children cheerfully perform any task the teacher may set before them, the educational aims are being achieved. Along these lines, Comenius' suggestions on "The Method of the Arts" are especially depressing.

Although he emphasized practice and activity as opposed to verbalism, the kind of activity he proposed was imitative—not creative. In the *Great Didactic* he said, "The first attempt at imitation should be as accurate as possible, that not the smallest deviation from the model be made."

In all fairness to Comenius, one should note that "art" today has a broader connotation than it had in his time. Yet his point was quite clearly made. Imitation, not expression or creation, was the central goal to be attained.

Although his didactic writings had many faults and trivial inconsistencies, these weaknesses should not obscure the obvious strengths of his works. Theorizing long before the birth of modern psychology, Comenius accurately anticipated many educational practices that were later substantiated empirically. That students should progress methodically from the simple to the complex, from the general to the specific, sounds remarkably like modern educational psychology. That education should be publicly supported, open to all regardless of sex, age, or nationality, is a principle espoused by many nations in the world today. Graded schools with appropriately graded texts are almost as common now in Afghanistan as they are in Chicago. The abundance of training aids and teaching devices reflects Comenius' emphasis on sense realism. The gradual decline of the emphasis placed upon verbalism recalls Comenius' exhortation that education deal with things, not with words about things. Vocational education, physical education, and kindergarten training as integral parts of the curriculum were all suggested by Comenius at least two hundred years before they became fairly common practices in many school systems throughout the world. Although Pestalozzi, Froebel, and Herbart are widely recognized today as contributors of unique educational theories, it is impressive to see how much of their work had already been anticipated by the nearly forgotten Comenius.

Although most of Comenius' prophetic educational theories have now become commonplace practice, just how much of this achievement is attributable directly to Comenius' efforts is not very clear. Perhaps this is the saddest part of the Comenius story. In his day he was highly regarded by many. While there were critics who questioned the quality of his Latinity, or philosophers such as Descartes who scoffed at his pansophy, Comenius had as many loyal supporters who sought his aid and advice. Few men of any period have had as many of their works translated into as many languages as Comenius, in his day. Yet, the bitter part of the story is that he was virtually forgotten after his death. Ironically, he inadvertently contributed to his own anonymity.

Perhaps the main reason why Comenius was soon forgotten was that his most significant works were originally written in the difficult Czech language and remained untranslated until the middle of the nineteenth century. While much of his significant educational thought was included in his *Opera didactica omnia*, this Latin work was not published until 1657, twelve years before he died; further, it was lost for many years and nearly forgotten.

Then, too, Comenius' repetitive, cumbersome style of writing did not attract many readers. Few readers of his day were willing to thread their way through the detailed, almost painful derivations of principles. While today his writings may be appreciated for their quaintness and charm, these were hardly features which would attract readers in his own time.

Another reason why Comenius has not received the recognition his foresight would seem to demand is that, strictly speaking, he was not really original. Many of his significant theories were not his own innovations but instead reflected contemporaneous educational ideas of others. The artistry of Comenius lay more in his eclecticism than in his inventiveness.

Comenius' affiliation with the Moravian Brethren, a small and, at the time, widely despised religious group, further explains his failure to win universal acceptance. As a bishop of the group, Comenius became a prime target of Roman Catholic persecutions during and following the Thirty Years' War; it is not surprising that his works were similarly suspected of heresy.

Finally, the whole body of Comenius' suggested practices was simply too radical for his times. Since the practices were not widely accepted, they were quickly forgotten when Comenius died. Many of his suggestions seriously threatened the established governments of his day. For example, while an educated citizenry might tend to maintain civil peace and order, it is rather unlikely that this same enlightened citizenry would continue unquestioningly to accept the divine right of kings. In an age of monarchy, Comenius' democratic notions of education were potentially explosive.

In many respects Comenius earned his reception. He was not, after all, wholly discreet during the Thirty Years' War. Silence could have secured him the protection of anonymity, but his outspoken support of Gustavus Adolphus led to the destruction of his library when the Catholic forces re-entered Leszno after the sudden withdrawal of the Protestants.

Had he written all of his works in Latin, the universal language of the day, he probably would have won immediate world-wide recognition as an educator. Had he devoted his energies entirely to education rather than to his church, to international peace, to pansophy, and to dozens of other interests, his pedagogical works might conceivably have been more refined and polished for general acceptance. Had he been content with less than a complete educational scheme for teaching all things to all people, it is likely that he would have achieved more approval.

But had he done all these things, Comenius would have been an even greater failure to himself. While writing in Latin could and eventually did give him a greater audience, his first concern was for his Moravian and Bohemian countrymen. It was for these people that his first educational tracts were written, and for them the Czech language was most fitting. Acquiescence during the Thirty Years' War would have been tantamount to the surrender of everything he held sacred. It was his religion, after all, that was the cornerstone whereon his educational theories were built. Had he considered anything less than pansophy, he would have been a mere gadgeteer, dabbling in educational trivialities.

Comenius had alternatives. But he decided not to employ methods that would have required him to compromise his ideals for expediency. This was the trait of integrity that makes him monumental even in his personal failure. While anyone might realize less than he hoped for, only a giant could fail as nobly and as magnificently as Comenius.

Since it is generally conceded that Comenius personally brought about little or no permanent change in pedagogical practices, the question of his importance is moot. But it was not the soundness or unsoundnessness of his theories so much as the unreceptive political, religious, intellectual, and emotional climate of his times that prevented his work from being more fruitful. It remained for other educators to "discover" the very principles that he had laboriously spelled out in his didactics. Ironically, these educators, many of whom lived a century after Comenius, received recognition and fame for significant contributions to society. Among them were Pestalozzi, Herbart, and Froebel, for example. The fact remains that significant educational improvements have been made and, to Comenius, this would have been the ultimately important thing. For one whose concern for his fellow man was as great as Comenius', personal fame and recognition in the final analysis were expendable.

BIBLIOGRAPHICAL NOTE

It is disappointing to find so few works by the prolific Comenius readily available. Fortunately, those that are available generally reflect the range of his pedagogical writings, if not his political and theosophic ideas. Although his works were originally written in either Czech, German, or

Latin, there are a number of excellent English translations. Perhaps the best known of these is M. W. Keatinge's *The Great Didactic of John Amos Comenius* published by Adam and Charles Black, London, in 1896. For a contrast between the younger and the older Comenius, Vladimir Jelinek's translation, *The Analytical Didactic of Comenius*, published by the University of Chicago Press, Chicago, in 1953, is especially recommended.

Although there have been many editions and variations of the work, *The Orbis Pictus of John Amos Comenius*, edited and published by C. W. Bardeen, Syracuse, in 1887, remains an excellent source of one of the first illustrated textbooks for children. The student of Comenius can also find a version of *The School of Infancy*, translated and edited by Ernest M. Eller, and published by the University of North Carolina Press, Chapel Hill, in 1956.

For an insight into Comenius' pacifist and religious views, Milos Safranek's edition of *The Angel of Peace*, published by Pantheon Books, New York (no date available), and Mathew Spinka's translation of *The Labyrinth of the World*, published by the National Union of Czechoslovak Protestants in America, Chicago, in 1943, should be consulted. For the more serious students, there is *Opera didactica omnia*, published in Amsterdam in 1657, and reprinted by the Czechoslovak Academy of Sciences, Prague, in 1957. The four-volume work is in Latin.

For general information concerning the life and works of Comenius, Will S. Monroe's *Comenius and the Beginnings of Educational Reform*, published by Charles Scribner's Sons, New York, in 1912, and Mathew Spinka's *John Amos Comenius, That Incomparable Moravian*, published by the University of Chicago Press, Chicago, in 1943, should be considered. Keatinge's translation of *The Great Didactic* also contains an excellent biographical sketch of Comenius and a historical account of the development of Comenius' didactics.

Probably the most complete coverage of Comenius will be found in Dmitry Čyževśkyj's forthcoming biography. Čyževśkyj is also engaged in compiling a comprehensive bibliography of all of Comenius' extant works.

🌐 JOHN LOCKE (1632–1704) was born in Somersetshire of a middle-class Puritan family. He received his early education at home under his father's supervision. At the age of fourteen he obtained a place at Westminster School where he remained until, in his twentieth year, he was granted a scholarship to Christ Church College, Oxford. After taking his bachelor's degree in 1656, he remained at Oxford to obtain his master's degree and then became successively lecturer in Greek, reader in rhetoric, and finally, in 1664, censor of moral philosophy. At that time he began the study of medicine and by 1666 was engaged in occasional practice, although he never took a degree in medicine. In 1667 Locke abandoned the academic world for the political world of London. He became the personal physician, general adviser, and confidential secretary of Lord Ashley, the future Earl of Shaftesbury. In 1675 Shaftesbury fell from political power, and Locke spent the next four years in France mending his health, and resumed writing his *Essay on Human Understanding*—the book on which he worked for twenty years. He resumed his former duties in 1679 when Shaftesbury returned to power, but following the earl's death in 1683, Locke came under royal suspicion. This time he left for Holland and remained there until after the Glorious Revolution. The *Letter Concerning Toleration*, which had been written and published in Latin in Holland, appeared in English the year of his return to England. In 1690 the two *Treatises on Civil Government* and the *Essay* appeared. Three years later he published *Some Thoughts Concerning Education*. When he returned to England, Locke was offered several responsible positions in the new government but he took only a minor post and left that in 1691 in order to spend his last years quietly in retirement.

8

THE GENTLEMAN: Locke

BY KENNETH D. BENNE

John Locke was born in 1632, only ten years before the outbreak of open military struggle between Parliament and King Charles I, a struggle in which Locke's father fought for a time in the Parliamentary army. He was a student at Westminster School when the king was beheaded at nearby Whitehall. Cromwell was in control of a kingless England during Locke's student days at Christ Church, Oxford, an Oxford restive under newly forged Puritan controls. In 1660, near the time of the uneasy restoration of the Stuarts to the British throne, Locke commented on the turmoil that had environed his formative years—"I no sooner perceived myself in the world but I found myself in a storm which has lasted almost hitherto."

The storm was not yet blown out, as Locke was to discover during a period of political exile in Holland during the 1680s. Yet, in 1689 Locke returned triumphantly in the party of Queen Mary from his Dutch exile, following the Glorious Revolution of 1688. He wrote his treatises on government and published them at the age of 57 "to establish the throne of our great restorer, our present King William" and "to justify to the world the people of England whose love of their just and natural rights, with their resolution to preserve them, saved the nation when it was on the very brink of slavery and ruin." Locke lived out his remaining years, until 1704, in a stable England—where bourgeois and Parliamentary supremacy had been won and justified—as a writer, a respected civil servant, a governmental adviser, and an enlightened, though always modest, sage.

The manifest storm that beset Locke's life, and which as a participant observer he helped to quell, was political in nature. But the political revolution was symptomatic of more basic revolutions that were working themselves out in Locke's England as well as in the patterns of his thought.

THE SCIENTIFIC REVOLUTION

Locke read the works of René Descartes when he was a student under the influence of the chemist Robert Boyle at Oxford. And while he came to reject the Platonism of Descartes' theory of scientific method, the ideal of a rational explanation of a mechanically ordered universe as the goal of science never deserted him, even after empiricist doubts about the certainty of physical knowledge became prominent in his thinking. In this sense, Locke became and remained a Cartesian.

Cartesianism had made deep inroads upon the intellectual allegiances of men of learning throughout Europe by the end of the seventeenth century. With the successful efforts of Copernicus, Kepler, and Tycho Brahe to explain and predict astronomical happenings by a combination of observation and mathematical manipulation of the data of observation, understanding of the heavens surrendered residence in the province of revealed truth and became part of the province of natural knowledge. The work of Galileo, "the incomparable Mr. Newton," and others had successfully applied scientific methods to the explanation of movement and other physical phenomena. Scientific biological and medical investigations, in a few of which Locke participated, were also increasingly evident to the intellectuals of the time. While various theories of science had developed to explain this scientific conquest of nature, in many areas of knowledge a growing scientific certitude, which involved the overthrow of much that tradition or "supernatural" revelation had persuaded men to regard as ultimate, could not be denied.

Descartes was one of the first to assert clearly and boldly the claims of the new knowledge upon a rational and mechanical view of the world. His work was as much a claim for the free and vigorous application of a new methodology of human thought, as he understood it, as for the world view that physical discoveries to date seemed to make reasonable. His insistence on universal and unchanging mechanical laws of nature banished from the cosmos any necessity for a presiding Providence. To throw back upon man and his unaided reason responsibility for explaining the universe was to insist, in effect, that no bounds could properly be set to man's scientific investigations. And from this view, the extension of rational investigations into man's psychological, social, aesthetic, and religious life was inevitable, however repugnant to antiscientific traditions and institutions this extension might prove to be.

Both science and secularism were reflected in a new attitude toward religion. The balance and unity of the medieval period, which rested upon ecclesiastical and religious foundations, had been broken by the

Protestant revolt and by the development of national churches, as well as by growing discrepancies between economic practices and ecclesiastical controls. It was necessary to find a place for religion within an increasingly secular society, which affirmed man's efforts to control and exploit as well as to understand nature rather than expecting him to adjust passively to some preformulated and essentially traditional pattern of otherworldliness. Churches had to come to terms with the state in nations where more than one religious outlook flourished. Intellectual canons of reasonableness and of conformity with nature were jostling in the minds of men against canons of devout and obedient faith as the arbiters of religious conviction and conduct. Moreover, men of substance were anxious to put an end to religious struggles, which had threatened the social order and stability required by successful commerce and had levied costly tolls upon the fruits of commerce. While the English bourgeoisie of the seventeenth century was not generally ready for the "rational" religion of deism, which blossomed in the eighteenth, there was wide readiness for an antienthusiastic, that is, nonemotional, "natural" religion, for principles of religious toleration, and for a new ideal of the enlightened worldly gentleman; and Locke helped to formulate these.

THE BOURGEOIS REVOLUTION

The seventeenth century in which Locke acquired and expressed his wisdom has frequently been called the "century of genius." The term usually refers, in the spirit of the blossoming individualism of the period, to the proliferation of individual geniuses in this century in Europe— Descartes and Newton and Leibniz, Boyle and Sydenham, Pascal and Spinoza, Hobbes and Locke. To attain perspective on the social forces active in the same period, it is important to note a perhaps even greater genius at work in Locke's England, as Harold Laski pointed out when he wrote:

That collective genius of the English middle class which, in this age, wholly reshaped the framework of a kingdom to its purposes, does not suffer by comparison [with the individual geniuses of Newton, Locke and others]. For in its achievement it set the temper and guided the spirit of its contemporaries not merely in the next age, but for two hundred years longer. From the revolution it effected nothing escaped. In establishing its supremacy it changed both the substance and the manner of men's thinking (*The Rise of Liberalism*, page 93).

Cromwell may be seen as the great protagonist of the rising English middle class; his Puritanism was one of its most characteristic religious expressions. The political revolutions of the seventeenth century in England, already reviewed, grew out of a multiplicity of grievances against the old political order. But the focal result of the bourgeois revolution, confirmed in 1688, was a state fitted to the purposes and interests of men of property. This revolution established the civil and religious freedom required by men of property in order to make their way in an increasingly secularized society. It reduced the power of the Church over matters of economic practice and policy. It destroyed the medieval assumption of a close connection between poverty and personal salvation and worked to establish an opposite assumption that property is evidence of God's favor. It also freed men of property from restrictions by the state and its armies by elevating the conception of a state of strictly limited powers. In brief, the bourgeois revolution relaxed the disciplines, monarchical and religious, that had thwarted men of property in their unabashed exploitation of the economic resources available through new means of manufacture and commerce.

As men of the new property came to be confirmed in the ruling elite, an educational need of major proportions emerged. How could men of property acquire the symbols of the older gentlemanly ideal, the badges of the right to rule? The older ideal rested on the notion of birth into a gentlemanly family—newly created "gentlemen" could not depend primarily upon inherited gifts as the justification of their right and fitness to rule. They must acquire by tutelage both the badges and the means to empower them in their newly won estate. The older gentlemanly ideal, rooted in chivalry and the medieval establishment, required reconstruction in order to become apt to a new class of gentlemen. Locke's work on education was a contribution to this reconstruction.

THE SOCIAL REVOLUTION THAT FAILED

In order to place Locke accurately in his revolutionary background, one should remember that the Cromwellian revolt embodied two social revolutions, not one. The first successful revolution of middle-class men of property has been described. The revolution that failed is represented by men in more radical movements who joined Cromwell—the Levellers among the city artisans, the Diggers among men who worked the soil. Laski has described this second revolution in the following terms (*The Rise of Liberalism*, pages 123–125):

The other revolution, which failed, was a social revolution, more clear in the evils it attacked than the remedies it knew how to prescribe. It was the effort of men who suffered profoundly from the emergent social order, who fought on the side of Cromwell against tyranny in state or church. When they had enthroned Cromwell in power they found to their indignation, that the new dispensation brought them no more benefit than the old. There was still one law for the rich and one for the poor. There was still private property in land instead of "the ancient community of enjoying the fruits of the earth" to which they had looked forward. The "young men and apprentices of London" were still, as Lilburne knew so well, conscious that their masters looked no better than before to the interests of humble folk . . . The Levellers' plea for work or maintenance, for annual parliaments and universal suffrage, the abolition of taxes on food and imprisonment for debt, met with wide response in the army. The radicals felt that liberty is inherent in the fact of human existence as such, not merely in the men who can purchase it with property . . . Whatever their differences, the radicals shared the beliefs that the state must have a positive character and it could not be unified while it was divided into rich and poor. . . .

This social revolution failed because it was premature. Its protagonists lacked both the numbers and the organization necessary to give it coherence and strength. . . . The circumstances made for the rule by that body of property owners who constituted . . . an aristocracy by the very fact of their possession of economic power.

John Locke may profitably be seen as the creator of powerful rationalizations for the successful scientific and bourgeois revolutions of his time. The contours of Locke's mind were shaped by his own middle-class origins and by his identification with the causes of Whig gentlemen of property throughout his career. The aspirations of Levellers and Diggers, insofar as Locke took them into account, must have seemed to him impractical and irrational enthusiasms. Locke put strong negative weightings upon "impracticality," "irrationality," and "enthusiasm," as we shall see.

No doubt Locke was realistic in these judgments from the standpoint of what was politically possible within the pattern of historic forces in his time and place. As Laski remarked, "This social revolution failed because it was premature." But it is well to remember, as we explore Locke's educational ideals, that Locke accepted the idea of a class-stratified society while the radicals of his time envisioned a society without classes. Locke conceived of individual-social relations in atomistic terms, while the Diggers and Levellers tended to think of the ideal society in terms of an organic community. Locke developed and defended a state of narrowly limited powers; the revolutionaries who failed envisaged a state with positive programs of social welfare. And Locke's ideas about the education of propertied gentlemen diverged sharply from his suggestions for the education of the children of the poor.

In these ways Locke's rationalizations of the bourgeois revolution were far from universal in substance, whatever their form. This limitation is not characteristic in the same degree of his rationalization of the spirit and methods of the scientific revolution of his time. Some of the unresolved tensions in Locke's thought arose from his efforts to rationalize two revolutions, not one.

RECONCILIATION OF REVOLUTION WITH TRADITION

Locke's role in the historical drama of English thought was not alone that of a defender of the successful bourgeois and scientific revolutions of his period. He sought also to reconcile powerful traditions of English thought and practice with the newer outlooks that he espoused. In fact, Locke had little of the defense attorney in his character. He avoided controversy and abhorred disputation. He always sought a reasonable reconciliation between what he accepted as valid in the old and what he embraced in the new. Empirical investigation of the facts of any point at issue seemed to Locke the only proper foundation for a reasonable reconciliation of the differences involved.

Cranston, describing the roots of Locke's "scientific" empiricism in his experiences as an undergraduate at Oxford (*John Locke: A Biography*, page 40), wrote:

When he looked back on the troubled history of his country, Locke saw two particularly potent sources of human error. One was unreflective adhesion to tradition: the fault especially of Royalists in political and social life and of philosophers in academic life; the other was "enthusiasm" or the reliance on emotional conviction as a basis of truth, the fault especially of Puritans and dissenters. Reacting against both these attitudes, Locke embraced science gratefully: for here, instead of tradition, experience was the guide; and the constant appeal to reason precluded the dangers of "enthusiasm." Locke's links, as a mere Bachelor of Arts, with leading *virtuosi* of Wadham College were slight, and although he did later become one of their number [in the Royal Society], he was never to achieve much as a practical scientist. What exercised his mind most fruitfully was not the experiments themselves as such but rather the principles on which those experiments were based. . . .

No doubt other temperamental characteristics, laid down in Locke's character long before his days at Oxford, contributed to his favored pattern of reconciling the old and new in social experience. Locke dreaded chaos. He valued the amenities of civilized living and saw them endangered by aimless and unintelligent revolt against the forms of civilization. But his experience, his friends, and his intelligence all convinced him of the imperative necessity of transforming many of the patterns of traditional social arrangements and ideologies. The protest all around him was too strong to be repressed and too justifiable to be shunted aside. Political chaos and religious controversy convinced him that rapid changes in the body politic were inescapable as well as desirable. He saw the required adaptations as presenting two alternatives—violence and mutual persecution or rational adjustment and deliberate change on the basis of compromise. Both his temperament and his training led him to identify strongly with the latter alternative.

Locke's favorite method of reconciling differences and resolving conflicts is illustrated throughout his work. In the field of religion he sought to reconcile the minimum essentials of Christian faith and revelation with the claims of empirical science and the demands upon conduct of an increasingly secular society. In government his task was to reconcile parliamentary supremacy with the traditions of British monarchy. In education he sought to infuse the traditional gentlemanly ideal with the values of bourgeois morality and of an empirical philosophy of science, a project most pertinent, as we have seen, to the interests of Britain's new ruling elite.

Much of the immense influence of Locke and of his principles in lands beyond England during the century following his death grew out of the causes with which he was identified in his own time and country— the rights of property, constitutional government, and the spread and extension of the new science. As the bourgeois and scientific revolutions followed in other lands, the name and doctrines of Locke were prominent in both their prerevolutionary and postrevolutionary justifications. As we turn to the study of what Locke actually said about education, it is well to remember Merle Curti's description of him as "the philosopher of America." It is well to remember this as we study the elements in Locke's thought of "natural rights," "religious toleration," "bourgeois morality," "common-sense empiricism," and "utilitarian education." For these are still powerful elements in the thinking of American teachers and of other middle-class Americans as well.

LOCKE'S CLASS-BOUND EDUCATIONAL IDEAL

Locke's writings on education furnish a most convincing demonstration of his identification with the successful middle class. His educational ideals, with which this essay is mainly concerned, were developed most fully in *Some Thoughts Concerning Education*. These thoughts were originally formulated in familiar letters to his friend Edward Clarke of Chipley. Mr. Clarke, a bourgeois gentleman, sought advice about the bringing up of his son. Locke, in giving this advice, wrote, to use his own words, in "the style which is such as a man writes carelessly to his friends, when he seeks truth, not ornament, and studies only to be in the right and to be understood." Since many other bourgeois gentlemen were also seeking advice about the education of their sons, Locke acceded to the demand that these letters be prepared for publication. The first edition was printed in 1693.

In articulating his thoughts on the education of a gentleman, Locke drew on his experiences as tutor to the son of his early political patron and friend Lord Ashley, first Earl of Shaftesbury, and later as supervisor of the education of Ashley's grandson, the third Earl. Locke the physician is much in evidence in his thoughts on the physical education of a young man, and his wide experience in the public and private affairs of middle-class England is evident throughout his recommendations.

These educational ideas will be explored later in detail. For the present, the spirit in which Locke approached his task of advising is more to the point. He expressed throughout the *Thoughts* deep respect for the individuality of the young gentleman in the processes of his education. This respect was reflected in Locke's strong preference for individual tutorial instruction, in his concern for the selection of the right tutor, in his emphasis on following "the favourable Seasons of Aptitude and Inclination" of the child in instruction, in his appeal to reason whenever possible in discipline, and in countless other ways. The goal in the education of a gentleman is the development of a person committed to and skilled in processes of reasonable, individual choices. This educational goal is essential to a gentleman's calling, as Locke conceived it. And he emphasized this calling as central in his thoughts on education: "that most to be taken care of is the gentleman's calling; for if those of that rank are by their education once set right, they will quickly bring all the rest into order."

But Locke also advised concerning the education of children of the poor. As King's Commissioner of Trade and Plantations, he wrote a proposal for the establishment of working class schools (printed as Appendix A in R. H. Quick's edition of Locke's *Thoughts*, pages 189 to 191). Selections from this proposal, illustrating the contrasting spirit in which Locke formulated his advice concerning working-class education, follow:

The children of labouring people are an ordinary burden to the parish, and are usually maintained in idleness, so that their labour also is generally lost to the public till they are twelve or fourteen years old.

The most effectual remedy for this that we are able to conceive, and which we therefore humbly propose, is, that, in the forementioned new law to be enacted, it be further provided that working schools be set up in every parish, to which the children of all such as demand relief of the parish, above three and under fourteen years of age, whilst they live at home with their parents, and are not otherwise employed for their livelihood by the allowance of the overseers of the poor, shall be obliged to come. . . .

We do not suppose that children of three years old will be able at that age to get their livelihoods at the working school, but we are sure that what is necessary for their relief will more effectually have that use if it be distributed to them in bread at that school than if it be given to their fathers in money. What they have at home from their parents is seldom more than bread and water, and that, many of them, very scantily too. If therefore care be taken that they have each of them their belly-full of bread daily at school, they will be in no danger of famishing, but, on the contrary, they will be healthier and stronger than those who are bred otherwise. . . .

In order therefore to the more effectual carrying on of this work to the advantage of this kingdom, we further humbly propose that these schools be generally for spinning or knitting, or some other part of the woolen manufacture, unless in countries (that is, districts) where the place shall furnish some other materials fitter for the employment of such poor children. . . .

This, though at first setting up it may cost the parish a little, yet we humbly conceive (the earnings of the children abating the charge of their maintenance, and as much work being required of each of them as they are reasonably able to perform) it will quickly pay its own charges with an overplus.

The contrast between Locke's attitude toward the children of men of property and children of the poor could hardly be more sharply drawn than in his widely divergent recommendations for the "education" of each. However universal the form of Locke's statements about the indefeasible natural rights of men may be in his political theory, the concrete rights of men as these took shape in diverse recommended patterns for their education are far from universal. For these are conditioned basically by the accidents of the social status into which men happen to be born. Some of the almost morbid fears expressed by Locke concerning the possible contamination of young gentlemen by the "taint of servants" who wait upon them or by association with the "beggars' boys and the abhorred rascality" of the common people might have been allayed had he been able to envision a possible role for education in transforming the "taint" and the "rascality" of common men into the image of an ideal and common humanity. But to this possibility his strong class identification, as well as his empirical realism, blinded him.

LOCKE AND THE TRADITIONAL GENTLEMANLY IDEAL

Locke, then, in his major educational writings had the education of a gentleman centrally in mind. While new influences from the seventeenth-century social and intellectual revolutions were powerful in shaping his thought, Locke, true to his favored method of reconciling the old and the new, sought to integrate these new requirements and potentialities with certain strong traditions that commended themselves as valid to his experience and reason. How did Locke reconstruct the traditional gentlemanly ideal in English educational thought?

Probably the best source for a delineation of this traditional ideal is Sir Thomas Elyot's *The Boke Named the Governour*, first published in 1531. It was the first book on education written and printed in the English language. Elyot dedicated it to King Henry VIII; Locke was to dedicate his treatises on government to the cause of King William. There is no space here to deal in detail with Elyot's recommendations for the education of "governours" for a feudal England that was rapidly moving into its national renaissance. But a general comparison of Elyot's educational ideal with that of Locke may help to throw Locke's ideal of an enlightened, bourgeois gentleman into relief.

Both Elyot and Locke accepted the idea of rule by an aristocracy of gentlemen. Both believed that putting the gentlemen right through a proper education would tend to bring others into order. Both, thus, thought of education as an important dimension of statecraft.

Elyot lived in the presence or, perhaps more accurately, within the living memory of a hierarchical social system of graded rights and obligations that was continuous with the traditions of feudal England. The function of education, as he saw it, was to equip members of the ruling class with the motivations and abilities to discharge their responsibilities to those dependent upon them in the "natural" order of rank and rule as well as to the public weal. The obligations of the landed gentleman to those whom he ruled had already been reduced in Elyot's time by the disengagement of peasants from the land. The pool of free market labor in the cities was only beginning to develop in his time. The idea of personal rule of other persons—with both ruler and ruled bound in reciprocal, though unequal, obligations to each other—was not only an ideal to him but in part a social reality. And it was this ideal that he sought to restore to greater reality through education. In Locke's day, rule had become more impersonal, both economically in the rule that came through contractual employment of the labor of men for wages and politically in the rule of impersonal man-made laws with sanctions attached and enforced by magistrates like his father. His rulers had become more impersonal in their relations to the ruled; they were more dependent on reason in their judgments and less on personal charisma than were Elyot's rulers. Rule through status was rapidly yielding to rule through contract, in the terms of Sir Henry Maine. And the personal equipment of men of rule had to change accordingly.

A number of related contrasts stem from this central difference. One is the relative emphasis placed upon administration and upon legislation in the two systems of political thought. For Elyot, the primary function of government was wise and benevolent administration. Laws, he assumed, were already available in a body of legal thought that was continuous with the legal thought of Plato and Cicero. And these laws were for him formulations of *natural* law. The legislative function, therefore, was not a primary function of government. The just and wise administration of laws already established by "Providence" for men was the major function of political rule. The monarch and his counselors were central in the scheme of political stability and control.

For Locke, the legislative function was primary. Men had to make laws for the governance of men. And these laws were "positive" rules, forged out of compromise among conflicting interests, rather than derivations from natural laws decreed by powers above man. Personal administration of divine and natural laws by the monarch and his graded subordinates must, therefore, yield to a system of Parliamentary supremacy. And gentlemen must be trained to make the prudential judgments that Parliamentary processes require rather than personally to espouse, maintain, and enforce a pre-existing system of natural laws.

This does not mean that "nature" furnished no moral guidance for political processes in Locke's thinking. But the function of "nature" had shifted from a system of prescribed *obligations* for governors to a system of natural *rights* for the governed. And governors and governed had moved toward coalescence in a Parliamentary system. "Natural rights" operated to set boundaries to the legitimate province of government. The function of government was to maintain these natural rights for the governed, rather than to support the security and well-being, appropriate to their natural estate, of those who were subjects of governmental rule. Locke's "nature" thus supported the right of revolution against governments that overrode the natural rights of inherently independent men in the management of their private affairs. Elyot's "nature" and "Providence" prescribed the obligations of the governors in protecting and sustaining men inherently dependent on the governors for their maintenance and support.

The center of moral obligation for Elyot's gentleman was in his service to the public weal. The center of moral obligation for Locke's gentleman was in his wise and prudent management of his private property and affairs. Locke's gentleman was drawn into public and governmental affairs only as a secondary obligation—an obligation to maintain and conduct a government that would secure men in the independent management of their private businesses and properties. How much Locke contributed thus to a radical separation between individual morality and political and social morality will be evaluated later. Certainly, the political order had ceased to be primarily a moral order for Locke and the bourgeois gentlemen for whom he spoke.

When we turn to the form and content of the educational processes for producing gentlemen, we again find similarities and differences in Elyot's and Locke's prescriptions and points of view. Both saw education as including much more than intellectual learning. Both saw the purpose of education as the development of a character adequate to performance of the personal and social functions expected of a gentleman. Education, to both, began with the earliest socialization of the child, not with the period of his schooling. Both were concerned with purifying the early environment of the child from influences contrary to his ideal development. Both stressed the importance of proper physical as well as intellectual activity in the child's growth. While Elyot saw physical activity as providing a medium for learning personal graces, social skills, and desirable habits, Locke's criteria for choosing physical activities for the child were set *primarily* by the requirements of individual health.

At the age when intellectual development becomes important in education, both Elyot and Locke turned to a tutorial system as the principal method of education. Both stressed the importance of the tutor and urged greater social status and economic reward for tutors as more commensurate to their central function in the shaping of young gentlemen.

For Elyot, the Renaissance scholar, the ideal subject matter for education was to be found in the literatures of Greece and Rome. Mastery of the classical languages was the key to unlock the treasures of these literatures. (While Elyot was a modernist among Renaissance educators, along with Vives and Cardinal Bembo, in that he translated classics into the vernacular languages and stressed instruction in the vernacular tongues, he believed that the Latin and Greek languages were essentials within the repertoire of the educated man.) Locke de-emphasized the classics and languages in his scheme of education and turned more to science and mathematics as important instruments of thought and inquiry for the properly educated gentleman.

The differences between Elyot and Locke are actually deeper at this point than these variations in emphasis upon the preferred content of schooling may suggest. Language was the essential ingredient of education for Elyot. He believed that men's learning takes place through the imaginative and disciplined use of language in reading, writing, and discourse. And the poetic and rhetorical uses of language were, for Elyot, indispensable elements both in the process of educating a gentleman and in his mature functioning. Locke distrusted language, particularly in its poetic and rhetorical uses, as inimical to clear and rational thought. As he saw it, observation and direct experience and reflection upon these were the major avenues to knowledge for the scientists whom he revered and, by extension, for the gentlemen he sought to develop, at least partly, in their image. And reasoning, for Locke, was a private, individual process—communication with others was not an essential ingredient in rational processes of thought. For Elyot, reason grew and emerged in the processes of taking social counsel rather than in private thought.

It is important to note one last contrast between Elyot and Locke before turning to a more direct and detailed examination of Locke's educational ideas. For Elyot the major dynamic of socialization was a process of identification by the young gentleman with noble objects outside himself. These objects of identification were to be found in his direct associations—his tutor, his companions, and his friends—and in the examples of noble men—heroes, in fact—encountered in the study of history, literature, philosophy, and, in some measure, religion. Elyot was well aware of the possibility of identification with ignoble as well as noble objects. The arts and the wisdom of the tutor, and earlier of the nurses, became important at this point. But identification remained a major dynamic of personal growth in his scheme of education, as self-knowledge was its crowning aim. Locke, too, was aware of the powerful effects of identification in shaping character, as his frequent warnings about the dangers of early associates and associations make clear. But to him identification seemed always to be a danger to be avoided, rather than a dynamic to be used educationally. And his stress on the importance of reality orientation for his nascent enlightened gentleman led him to suspect as mischievous enthusiasms the identifications with ideal heroes, which might come through deep emotional experience of poetry, drama, philosophy, or religion. Valid learning for Locke was a private, an individual, and an unemotionally rational affair.

Locke, in these ways, reshaped the ideal of the gentleman to his educational and political purposes. His measure of the utility of various educational experiences is, in a sense, based on a job analysis of what an English gentleman with a sense of civic duty should know and be able to do in the society of his time. The prototype of English gentleman that Locke's utilitarian education sought to develop would have a healthy body, would be well equipped with pleasing social graces, and would be capable of engaging in harmless play and diversions. He would have the habits of honesty, frugality, and prudent judgment; he would have his impulses well controlled by habits of calmness, courage, rationality, and persistence in the face of adversity. He would be sensitive to the esteem of his worthy fellows but unwilling to sacrifice personal standards for popularity. He would be clear, accurate, and objective in his use of language; he would possess a body of useful, valid, and scientific information, seasoned by travel, about the contemporary world; and he would possess a mind trained in the critical and rational methods of logical analysis.

Locke deliberately put "Learning" last in his analysis of the four characteristics that every "Gentleman (that takes any care of his Education) desires for his son." Before it he placed "Virtue," "Wisdom," and "Breeding." Locke's own comment on the place of "Learning" in education communicates clearly the utilitarian spirit of his view of the gentlemanly estate.

Reading and Writing and Learning I allow to be necessary, but yet not the chief Business. I say this that when you consider of the Breeding of your Son, and are looking out for a School-Master or a Tutor, you would not have (as is usual) Latin and Logick only in your Thoughts. Learning must be had, but in the second Place, as subservient only to greater Qualities. Seek out somebody that may know how discreetly to frame his Manners: Place him in Hands where you may, as much as possible, secure his Innocence, cherish and nurse up the good, and gently correct and weed out any bad Inclinations, and settle in him good Habits. This is the main Point, and this being provided for, Learning may be had into the Bargain, and that, as I think, at a very easy rate, by Methods that may be thought on (Thoughts, Section 147).

Locke would thus have middle-class gentlemen maintain their strictly amateur status in the field of "Learning." In addition, he showed a bourgeois and Puritan distrust of the arts and their place in education. He firmly advised fathers to discourage any inclination their sons might show toward "making verses." Time spent on poetry is not merely wasted for Locke: interest in poetry leads a man into bad company and to a squandering rather than a husbanding of his patrimony. In Locke's mind, poetry and gambling were closely linked. Both were, to him, vices leading those addicted to them to a poor view of the importance of property. A major virtue in Locke's gentleman is the prudent management of his worldly estate. Devotion to the arts and to the values they embody is an inveterate enemy of the worldly asceticism required by devotion to property and its increase.

NONCOGNITIVE QUALITIES OF LOCKE'S GENTLEMAN

Locke placed the nurture of three noncognitive qualities—virtue, wisdom, and breeding—above the acquisition of knowledge in his scheme of education. It may be well to find what Locke meant by these before returning to his conceptions of cognition, knowledge, understanding, and their development.

As to virtue, he held it first among a gentleman's endowments. Virtue is required to make a man "valued and beloved by others" and "acceptable and tolerable to himself." It is a prime condition of happiness both in this and in the other world. In what does virtue consist?

It consists, first of all, in a simple faith in God as the author and maker of all things, the source of all good. Locke did not believe that such a faith could be induced by a study of theology or by attempts to image or define His nature, which is inescapably unknowable to man. In his *Essay*, Locke asserted that man could have certain, intuitive knowledge of God's existence but not of his attributes. For education, Locke prescribed religious observances—morning and evening prayers—rather than theological indoctrination or debate as conducive to the development of virtue.

A simple faith in God was, then, the cornerstone of virtue for Locke. Beyond this, he considered a commitment to speaking the truth as essential. The tutor would demonstrate to his pupil by his actions that twenty faults will sooner be forgiven than will straining the truth to cover any fault by an excuse. To falsify one's thoughts and acts is more reprehensible than to err and to make mistakes. And Locke would have the system of educational rewards and punishments geared to this maxim.

Finally, the pupil should be taught to love and to be "good-natured" to others. This is an element of virtue, since for Locke injustice is most likely to spring from too great love of ourselves and too little for others. Locke had little to say about how this element of "good nature" should be developed educationally. His rejection of identification as a trusted dynamic of education made it difficult to conceive how this quality could be developed except through precept, a method of education that Locke was inclined, with good reason, to consider ineffective.

Yet, there were proper limits to tolerance and "good nature," as Locke's pioneer writings on political toleration made clear. Here, as elsewhere, Locke tended to set cautious limits to his most basic principles in their practical application. One limit was a denial of toleration to atheists—Locke could not conceive of virtue apart from a faith in God. Another limit was fealty to one's nation—it was on the basis of allegiance to another state that Locke would deny full civil rights to Roman Catholics. And, finally, full "toleration" in respect to civic participation was denied to men with no property. Locke's version of "good nature" extended only partially beyond class, national, and denominational boundaries.

Concerning the second noncognitive quality, wisdom, Locke said, "Wisdom I take in the popular Acceptation, for a Man's managing his Business ably and with foresight in this World." This conception underlay the utilitarian focus of Locke's educational thought, a focus already emphasized. The center of a gentleman's moral preoccupation in this world should be the prudent management of his property and private affairs. Whatever diverted men from this preoccupation should be rooted out of education—we have noted this justification for extirpating poetry and gaming. Other pursuits, not morally unwise in diverting gentlemen from their calling, should be excluded from education because of the time they take from more important affairs. Music and painting were activities of this sort.

Operationally, wisdom for Locke is defined by those activities that promote a man's prudent management of his property. And valid recreation (defined as "not being idle . . . but easing the wearied part by Change of Business") should conform to this criterion. Locke believed that wisdom must be learned mainly through experience and observation of other men in young manhood, not in childhood. "All that can be done towards it, during this upripe Age, is, . . . to accustom them to Truth and Sincerity; to a submission to Reason; and as much as may be, to Reflection on their own Actions."

Breeding, the third noncognitive quality, rests for Locke on an inner attitude toward self and toward others. He expressed the proper attitude in negative terms—"not to think meanly of ourselves, and not to think meanly of others." Poor breeding manifests itself overtly in one of two extreme forms of conduct—"sheepish bashfulness" or unbecoming disrespect toward others' opinions and their right to these. Locke would teach his young gentleman to steer a course of life between the two. The goal was "a Disposition of the Mind that shows itself in the Carriage, whereby a Man avoids making any one uneasy in Conversation."

Locke condemned disputation both as a way to knowledge and as a way of social life. He was as eager as his illustrious predecessor Lord Bacon had been to root out this vestige of "medievalism" from the halls of learning. He extended his critique of disputation to everyday conversations among gentlemen and gentlewomen. To dispute is uncivil. Breeding manifests itself in polite exchange that is at once sincere and mutually respectful.

Locke focused on children's interruptions of others' conversations as advantageous opportunities for the learning of breeding. Locke did not wish to teach children ceremoniousness. He was aware that ceremony frequently can be a deceitful cloak to cover a lack of inner magnanimity, the quality on which true breeding rests. But he did wish to use the interchanges between children or between children and adults to teach the outer and inner habit of civil inquiry into their differences in place of the disputatious habit of destroying or degrading the opponent. Equally, he sought to develop ways of expressing dissent that would be heard and considered in place of the self-suppression of dissenting opinions in "sheepish bashfulness."

The test of breeding, as well as the occasion for its educational development, lay for Locke in human interchanges of opposing opinions. Civility in such interchanges was the goal. Whether Locke's viewpoint toward conflict tended to suppress the working out of the dialogue and dialectic that lead to creative synthesis in knowledge and opinion, in his concern for polite tolerance and compromise, is a question that must be faced later in evaluating his theory of knowledge.

KNOWLEDGE FOR THE ENLIGHTENED GENTLEMAN

As already noted, Locke subordinated "learning" to three noncognitive qualities as an educational objective, in *Some Thoughts Concerning Education*. This subordination of knowledge has been related to Locke's criterion of utility, which he based on his "job analysis" of a seventeenth-century English bourgeois gentleman. But Locke was also an ardent student of the scientific enterprise of his time. And his study of scientific ways of knowing led him to deal with the methods by which a man might improve the conduct of his understanding, in the image of the empirical scientists whom he admired. Locke's educational ideal envisioned an *enlightened* as well as a *bourgeois* gentleman. The *bourgeois* gentleman was in the ascendant in Locke's letters to Mr. Clarke about the education of his son. In *The Conduct of the Understanding*, the *enlightened* gentleman was at the forefront of Locke's attention. In order to understand his educational prescriptions in this latter work, it is necessary to review briefly Locke's theory of knowledge, which he developed in his philosophical masterpiece *Essay Concerning the Human Understanding*. Actually, *The Conduct of the Understanding*, an unfinished work, was prepared as a part of a projected revision of the *Essay*.

In the *Essay*, Locke attempted an analysis and "purification of knowledge." His declared purpose was "to inquire into the origin, certainty and extent of human knowledge, together with the grounds and degrees of belief, opinion, and assent." The actual organization of his *Essay* falls into three parts (not corresponding exactly to its four books): one devoted to the origin of a man's ideas and how they come into his understanding; a second to show the certainty, evidence, and extent of knowledge, and a third to inquire into the nature and grounds of faith or opinion. Locke believed that people, and not least men of learning, had tended to extend their inquiries into areas where the human mind could arrive at no knowledge having any degree of certainty. Consequently, questions have been posed which cannot be answered, disputes have been multiplied, and doubts have been raised about the importance, even the possibility, of knowledge. Locke hoped that his *Essay* might help men to employ their understandings more effectively by setting valid limits to the "origin, certainty and extent of human knowledge."

Locke began his *Essay* with a rejection of the doctrine of "innate ideas." In the Platonic and Augustinian tradition men were thought to be born with ideas already in the mind. The task of coming to know, on this view, is to "remember," to become aware of the true ideas with which the human mind has been equipped by its Maker. In the England of Locke's time Lord Herbert of Cherbury (1583–1648) and other Platonists, often called the "Cambridge Platonists," defended the doctrine of innate ideas in their war against "materialism and sensationalism" and in their attempt to establish a ground of certainty for the traditional logical and ethical principles they favored. Locke argued against innate ideas from the empirical evidence of individual, group, and cultural variations in moral principles and ideas. Whole peoples differ in their respect for human life, for truth-telling, and for property, and even in their beliefs as to the existence of a supreme deity. It is not that Locke rejected belief in the existence of God and the rightness of respecting human life, truth-telling, and property. He accepted all of these ideas. But he noted that there is no universal distribution of these ideas among men. Children, idiots, and savages show no knowledge of logical or ethical principles that are generally accepted as true by Christian Englishmen. If ideas were innate, could any of these variations exist among men?

Where, then, do a man's ideas originate? Locke defined an idea as whatever is "the object of the understanding when a man thinks . . . . whatever is meant by phantasm, notion, species, or whatever it is which the mind can be employed about in thinking." The sole sources of ideas, as Locke saw it, are a man's sensations and his reflections upon these sensations in thinking. Thinking processes are operations of the mind upon ideas. They are functions of the mind, so to speak, and not the subject matter upon which the mind works. Thus, all ideas arise from the external material objects that impinge, directly or indirectly, on our senses or they arise from the operations of the mind upon such sense data. Ideas may be simple or complex. Simple ideas are "uncompounded appearances," for example, whiteness or redness, softness or hardness. These are atomic ideas and only externally related one to another. The mind is passive in receiving simple ideas. They may come from one sense or another, as color does, or sound; or they may come from more than one sense, as do shape, motion, and extension. Other simple ideas come from reflection, for example, our volitions (wanting to do this or that); or they may come from both sensation and reflection, as does pleasantness.

Simple ideas, called qualities, correspond to properties of external objects or are attributed by us to such objects. Some qualities, named by Galileo "secondary qualities," are not objective but are the effects made in our minds by objects. Color, smell, and taste exemplify such qualities. Others, Locke agreed with Galileo, are "primary qualities," the ones that any material object must have in order to be a material object. Locke identified these primary qualities as extension, solidity, shape, motion, and number. A man's knowledge of the external world is true if his ideas of it correspond correctly to its primary qualities. The "real" external world, as Locke had learned from Descartes and Newton, is a mechanical world, consisting of extended bodies in motion. Yet, this world mysteriously produces in men secondary qualities that have no place in such a mechanical world. They exist only in the mind, no matter how one may project them upon the colorless, tasteless, odorless, external world of the new physics—the realm outside of man that is impervious to his feelings and volitions about it.

Complex ideas are made out of simple ideas by acts of the mind. These may be acts of *combining* ideas, or of putting two ideas side by side and *relating* them, or of *abstracting* ideas from their accompaniments in existence. In such ways a man forms and uses complex ideas of beauty, courage, gratitude, man, nation or universe.

Knowledge, for Locke, consists essentially in the agreement or disagreement of a man's ideas. The agreement may take the form of identity, relation, coexistence in the same object, or real existence. Some agreements and disagreements are intuitive—white is white, white is not black, four is more than three. Such intuitive knowledge is both the clearest and the most certain knowledge that man has. No other idea is needed to intervene between the ideas directly in question in order for one to establish certain knowledge. Moreover, all knowledge must eventually be based on certain intuitive knowledge. Demonstrative knowledge results from extended logical steps toward proof but it must be supported at each step by reference to what is known directly and intuitively. What, then, is the extent of man's knowledge? It certainly extends no further than ideas and perceived agreements and disagreements among ideas.

When can a man be certain of his knowledge? When knowledge deals only with his own ideas, he can have certain knowledge. But when ideas of substances, of nature, or of the external world are involved, such certainty is not forthcoming. For then the knower is attributing ideas to things that exist independently of his ideas. And such attributions must be tested by the correspondence of ideas to the properties of the things to which the ideas are attributed. Thus, Locke came to believe that "knowledge" of nature is only more or less probable. But, since he continued to hold to the ideal of *knowledge* as certain, natural "knowledge" is not really *knowledge* at all. Where is ideal certain knowledge to be found? In mathematics a man can know certainly that the sum of the angles of a triangle is 180 degrees, not because he can know actual triangular objects, but precisely because the mathematical triangle is an ideal triangle, a standard triangle. Measurements of the angles of triangular objects do not disprove certain knowledge about standard triangles because, in mathematics, "real" things are expected to live up to the ideal, rather than the reverse.

Locke also believed, "It is as certain that there is a God, as that the opposite angles, made by the intersection of two straight lines, are equal." Along with a man's certainty that he himself exists, this seems to have been man's only knowledge that Locke regarded as *both* certain and real. This certainty does not extend to the attribution of particular qualities to God. Locke believed that ethical principles, since they prescribe norms for conduct, can be known certainly. This certainty presumably does not extend to "real" knowledge about how men and societies actually do conduct themselves. In brief, Locke seems to have believed that men could have *certain* normative knowledge but could not have *certain* positive or, as he called it, "real" knowledge about substances, with the exceptions noted above.

. . Locke fell back on the pragmatism of "common sense," after throwing doubt upon the certainty of man's knowledge of the "real" world. Whatever difficulty man may have in knowing the nature of things as they are (apart from any relation to his mind), his observation and experience can give him enough "probable knowledge" or right opinion of things as they affect him so that he can go about his human jobs of caring for his affairs, gaining success in commerce, living at peace with other men, and learning to govern with decency and wisdom. Locke did not seem to see that in the analysis of such "probable knowledge" might lie a more just conception of mind, experience, and nature than that which he had accepted uncritically from the physicists of his time.

Even though Locke came to doubt the certainty of much contemporaneous learning, including the knowledge of empirical science, he did not forsake the ideal of rational-empirical method embodied in that science as the best guide for men in making the probable judgments on which their lives and livelihoods depend. Locke emphasized habituation in this rational method as the goal of cognitive development for his enlightened gentleman. It was in *The Conduct of the Understanding* that he developed most clearly his notions of how rationality operates in men and how it can be developed by them.

Locke was convinced that "most men come very short of what they might attain unto in their various degrees by a neglect of their understandings" and that there are "a great many natural defects in the understanding capable of amendment, which are overlooked and wholly neglected." It was to the identification and diagnosis of common pathologies in the use of the understanding and to prescriptions for the educational correction of these malfunctionings that Dr. Locke, turned physician of the mind, devoted his attention.

Locke found three major kinds of miscarriages in the actual reasoning of men. The first is rooted in a man's habit of doing and thinking according to the precept and example of others and, in effect, avoiding the pain and trouble of thinking for himself. The second results from the habit of putting passion in the place of reason. Men under the influence of this habit may not lack the ability to reason "where they have no secret inclination that hinders them from being tractable to it." But when they feel strongly on some issue, they do not use their own reason or listen to the reasons adduced by other people. The third failure is found in men who readily and sincerely follow reason but who lack "*large, sound, round-about sense*" and, therefore, base their reasoning on a partial and inadequate definition of the question being considered. All men, Locke believed, are in varying degree partial and biased in what they see as a basis for reasoning. The goal for man is to acquire a larger and sounder "round-about sense," not to achieve the completeness or detachment of an angel in his thinking.

Locke was optimistic about man's ability to cure the pathologies which beset his thinking. He wrote, "We are born with faculties and powers capable almost of any thing, such at least as would carry us farther than can easily be imagined: but it is only the exercise of those powers which gives us ability and skill in anything, and leads us toward perfection." Here Locke was emphasizing the major method of all his education—practice, reflection, followed by further practice. This emphasis has led many to attribute a faculty psychology and a related theory of "formal mental discipline" to Locke—the idea that a man possesses "mental muscles" of reasoning or of memory to be strengthened through sheer repeated exercise. This is a misinterpretation. It is a set of interrelated skills and orientations that Locke would have men acquire through practice. This set of skills and orientations taken together constitute a disciplined method of seeking truth in the midst of confusion and conflict. It is a "logic of discovery" that Locke assumes men may learn through thoughtful practice, not "mental muscles" or assumed formal psychological powers to be exercised without regard to the content of ideas to be analyzed or to the context of the inquiry.

The older methods of thought—dialectic and disputation and formal syllogistic reasoning—seemed to him designed to defend and justify what is already "known." The new method sought rather to find and verify new truth. He began the *Conduct* with an acknowledgment of his debt to Francis Bacon who had sought to formulate a new method for discovering new truth (a *novum organum*) in the early years of Locke's century.

It was in mathematical reasoning that Locke found his rational method of discovery most elegantly illustrated. And it was in the thoughtful study of mathematics that Locke believed men might find an image of potentiality for the release and use of their understandings. To study mathematics intelligently is to develop the habits necessary to carry out this method and to generalize the method as a way of thought in many fields. He wrote:

. . . but having got the way of reasoning, which that study necessarily brings the mind to, they might be able to transfer it to other parts of knowledge. For, in all sorts of reasoning, every single argument should be managed as a mathematical demonstration (*The Conduct of the Understanding,* Sections 6 and 7).

Transfer of learning by generalization of a method of thought practiced in one field of study and application of the method to problems of another field—this effort is far from the notion of training a psychological faculty.

We may quarrel with Locke's ideal of *the* method of reasoning as basically mathematical and insist that other kinds of method should be taken into account in teaching and in learning how to think. But, if we accept teaching "how to think" as an educational goal, we cannot avoid some notion of generalized method such as Locke held. And this certainly does not make us exponents of formal discipline. Actually, Locke did recognize that different types of subject matter require different methods of reasoning and that a well-educated man must be skilled in reasoning in different fields of knowledge, if he is to reason well outside his own area of specialization.

Locke believed that the effective conduct of the understanding required not only discipline in methods of valid reasoning but also a content of ideas and knowledge to apply to questions about which a man attempts to reason.

He that will enquire out the best books in every science, and inform himself of the most material authors of the several sects of philosophy and religion, will not find it an infinite work to acquaint himself with the sentiments of mankind concerning the most weighty and comprehensive subjects. Let him exercise the freedom of his reason and understanding in such a latitude as this, and his mind will be strengthened, his capacity enlarged, his faculties improved; and the light, which the remote and scattered parts of truth will give to one another will so assist his judgment, that he will seldom be widely out, or miss giving proof of a clear head and a comprehensive knowledge. At least, this is the only way I know to give the understanding its due improvement to the full extent of its capacity, and to distinguish the two most different things I know in this world, a logical chicaner from a man of reason (*The Conduct of the Understanding*, Section 3).

In his "enthusiasm" for releasing the rational powers of men, and in the security of his favored method of reasoning, Locke somewhat relaxed his fears both of personal commitment and of close association with and learning from others.

Only, he that would give the mind its flight, and send abroad his enquiries into all parts after truth, must be sure to settle in his head determined ideas of all that he employs his thoughts about and never fail to judge himself, and judge unbiasedly of all that he receives from others, either in their writings or discourses. Reverence or prejudice must not be suffered to give beauty or deformity to any of their opinions (*The Conduct of the Understanding*, Section 3).

This rather extensive examination of *The Conduct of the Understanding* serves two purposes in broadening our comprehension of Locke. It gives, first of all, his notions of how the objective of "Learning" may be pursued in processes of education. The ideal of "enlightenment" gains meaning in these writings. Enlightenment grows through release and discipline of a man's reasoning to become the chief arbiter of his judgments; it appears as a major force in men's understanding and management of human affairs. For Locke's bourgeois gentleman, the power of reasoning presumably works within the contours of his habituation in virtue, wisdom, and breeding. But Locke hinted here of a power in education that is universal in scope, that spills over the boundaries of existing classes, existing nations, existing sects and creeds, that takes the enlightenment of mankind as its proper province. The second purpose of this extensive examination is to remind us that Locke sought to rationalize two revolutions, not one. In the *Thoughts*, Locke, the rationalizer of the bourgeois revolution, was in the ascendant. He worked within the limits of what gentlemen of the bourgeois class wanted for their sons. The preoccupations, the prepossessions, the cautions, and the fears of the triumphant middle class operated as assumptions in shaping his prescriptions and recommendations for educating members of that class. True enough, "enlightenment" was present in both the goals and the methods of this education. But the enlightenment was circumscribed by the uses of it that gentlemen of property found important and practical for improving and consolidating their worldly estate.

In *The Conduct of the Understanding*, Locke, the interpreter of the scientific revolution, was in the ascendant. His prescriptions for the improvement of the understanding of men sought universality of the kind that scientists seek in their generalizations. The boundaries of possible application of the methods of the new science are extended beyond the practical concerns of members of a ruling class, without losing relevance to experience as the basic ground of knowing validly and of doing intelligently. Enthusiasm spoke unabashedly in the cause of reason rather than being proscribed as inherently and unavoidably the foe of reason.

There are unresolved tensions between the Locke who speaks prudently and cautiously of education in the *Thoughts* and the Locke who recommends enthusiastically a way of education in *The Conduct of the Understanding*. And, paradoxically on his own view, it is the enthusiastic Locke who attains the greater validity in his diagnoses and prescriptions.

DISTORTING EMPHASES IN LOCKE'S EDUCATIONAL METHODS

The Perils of Association

It has been noted that Locke leaned heavily upon his personal experience with schooling, as a student and as a tutor, in forming his viewpoints about education. (It is probable that he had studied no treatises on education apart from the essays of Montaigne.) Nowhere is this clearer than in his condemnation of early schooling in association with others. Locke, a timid and rather sickly boy, suffered in his school years at Westminster from the bullying and cruelty of the other boys. Moreover, he was appalled by the bad habits that boys teach each other. This experience probably strongly influenced his recommendation of tutorial education, which isolates the boy, insofar as possible, from associations with other boys as well as from contaminating associations with lower-class people.

This emphasis probably also reflects Locke's essentially individualistic view of the person and his learning experiences. While he seemed to recognize the powers of association and of identification in the learning of unhealthy habits, he seems not to have recognized their possible powers in establishing and reinforcing healthy and desirable habits as well.

Eventually, Locke believed, each man must see and reason by and for himself, if he is to be reasonable at all. And he seemed to have reasoned from this belief that if knowledge and reason are eventually private and individual matters, why should they not be developed as such? The following quotation from *The Conduct of the Understanding* (Section 24) illustrates this individualistic notion of knowledge and will be useful later in clarifying Locke's ideal of reason as thinking without the aid of language:

Knowledge is seeing; and if it be so, it is madness to persuade ourselves we do so by another man's eyes, let him use ever so many words to tell us that what he asserts is very visible. Till we ourselves see it with our own eyes and perceive it by our own understandings, we are as much in the dark and as void of knowledge as before, let us believe any learned author as much as we will.

Locke might thus have justified his own failure to learn from others concerning education. But the limiting effects of depending exclusively on one's own experience and private reflection as a basis of judgment are nowhere better illustrated than in Locke's blindness to the possible use of group association as an aid to desirable and autonomous learning by an individual, at least in his younger years.

Distrust of Language and of Humanistic Education

Locke's dictum—*"Truth is to be found and supported by a mature and due Consideration of Things, and not by artificial Terms and Ways of Arguing"*—illustrates his "sense realism" and his fundamental distrust of language. Locke apparently thought of reasoning as a kind of inner perception of ideas or of connections between ideas—a perception independent of language or linguistic proof.

We have seen that Locke rejected both dialectic and formal syllogistic reasoning as ways of reaching knowledge or forming valid opinions. In his rejection, Locke was, in effect, rejecting any integral place for language in processes of thought. Language was, for him, at best a way of translating what is already known (perceived, directly prehended) without the agency of language. This view not only separates "intellectual" processes from communication, which requires language integrally in its process. It also individualizes reason, subordinates it to private perceptions, and thus denies it a central place in maintaining and building common perceptions and perspectives among men. Further, it tends to limit thought to a dealing with "signs," to eliminate "symbolic" processes from thought, save as these stand as a shorthand for collections of "signs." In other words, the effect is to deny any integral place for hypotheses and theories, always mediated by the symbols of one language system or another, in the construction of knowledge. It actually involved a failure to describe or explain adequately the actual method of the new science that was supported by Locke against Scholasticism, which was resisting scientific advance in his day. For this science used the language system of mathematics, as well as supporting verbalization, within its very processes of discovery and verification. The proper foil to a metaphysics of rationalism, which neglects empirical tests for the adequacy of its symbolic constructions, is not an empiricism that rejects the propriety or necessity of making and using symbolic constructions. It is rather an empiricism that sees the creation of knowledge in the conjunction and adequation of symbolic constructions in relation to the signs of things and events that these constructions purport to order and control.

Locke was justified in attacking the verbalistic Humanism that dominated the schooling of his day and that obscured rather than illuminated important contemporary realities in students' lives. But the attack might better have been made in terms of the need for verbal formulations and disciplines that were more relevant to contemporary events, problems, and interests and more compatible with the requirements of the intellectual method then developing in the sciences, than in terms of a rejection, insofar as possible, of verbal formulations and disciplines in the processes of education.

CRITICISMS OF LOCKE'S THEORIES OF EDUCATION

A Framework for Organizing Criticisms of Locke

The previous exposition of Locke's theories has been supplemented by criticisms all along the line. The task here is primarily to summarize criticisms already stated or implied, and, secondarily, to introduce a few new considerations. It is important to remember a point already emphasized, as we criticize Locke's confusions and inconsistencies. He was a transition figure. He confronted a society in which the dominant moral and religious perspectives and, to some large degree, the political, psychological, and broadly intellectual perspectives were profoundly shaped by the traditions of medieval Christendom. Yet, two principal lines of challenge to these perspectives were powerfully at work in the England of Locke's time.

The first was the impact of the new science with doctrines and, more fundamentally, with revolutionary modes and methods of thought that had been taking shape for a long time in Europe but reached the stage of conscious formulation and synthesis in a profusion of fundamental works in Locke's own lifetime.

The second challenge was the rise of the middle class, the men of commerce and business enterprises, to a position of power within the social hierarchy of England. The aspirations of these men contrasted sharply at points with the feudal point of view, which the former aristocracy had tended to hold. This called for rationalization of new modes of social and political thought. And Locke, as we have seen, attempted this task of reconciliation.

How adequate were Locke's responses to these two major challenges to traditional modes of thinking about man and his education? One more qualification will be made before an answer to this question is attempted.

Criticisms of the adequacy of Locke's ideas in relation to the needs and conditions of his own time and in relation to the needs and conditions of our own age are two quite different enterprises. In general, the criticisms here focus on the former relationship.

Adequacy of Locke's Response to the New Science

Locke's uncritical acceptance of Galileo's radical separation of primary and secondary qualities in things—a separation "explained" in Descartes by a separation of physical from mental substances—has already been mentioned. The effects of this dualism in Locke, philosophically speaking, have been noted. Since, for Locke, mind can know directly only mental contents, the relationship between these and the physical objects they purport to explain and describe becomes an insoluble problem. The very possibility of "real" knowledge—positive knowledge of the physical world—is called into doubt. The sorts of fruitless discussion of the possibility or impossibility of knowledge that dogged Western philosophizing for two hundred years after Locke are rooted in this dualism and in the construction that Locke put upon it. The word "fruitless" may be justified in this context by contrasting this insoluble "problem" of knowledge, as formulated by Locke, to fully feasible inquiries into the character of cognitive processes in the sciences and also in the intellectual aspects of other human pursuits—inquiries that might have yielded fruitful results in terms of a more adequately grounded and understood "science" in its relationships with other human concerns and activities.

The individualism of Locke's conception of "reason" and of knowledge has also been stressed. This individualism was closely related to Locke's dismissal of the traditions of philosophy and his discounting of the place of the study of other men's works in developing one's own knowledge. In a real sense, "rationalism" stands for the claims of tradition and the cultural heritage upon the intellectual allegiances of men; one derives the meaning of individual and particular experiences by subsuming them under generalizations taken from this heritage. In Locke's sense, "empiricism," by contrast, stands for the primary claims of particular and individual experiences in the generation, construction, and validation of knowledge. It involves a distrust of, a discounting of the claims of "inherited" generalizations in the processes of coming to know anything validly.

The demerits of "rationalism" are imposition of the past upon the present, stagnation, lack of intellectual progress except by indirection, along with tendencies toward dogmatism. Of these demerits, "empiricists" have been fully aware, as Locke certainly was. But "empiricism" has demerits also. It tends to lead to uncritical glorification of the new and the contemporary, to the tyranny of the present over the minds of men, to unordered and uncommunicated variation, and to anarchy if it is not tinctured, as it was in Locke, by "common sense," which is actually a relatively uncritical borrowing from the heritage of traditional meanings. And it tends to lead to skepticism concerning the possibility of "objective" knowledge. Clearly, the ideal of method that avoids both sets of demerits is an "experimental" method, which implies also a "moderate realism." Knowledge as a process involves both acceptance and reconstruction of the tradition, with particular and individual variations from it providing both the occasion and the test of adequacy for the reconstruction. Within the logic of experimentalism there is a place for both universal and particular elements, but universals are not taken as self-evident in their adequacy, nor are perceived particulars taken as self-explanatory.

It has been observed that there is implicit in Locke a theory of "knowledge," which Locke himself developed as an "inferior" theory of opinion and judgment. In the practical affairs of men the aim of reason is not knowledge of the "essential" character of substances; the aspiration is not toward certain and self-evident truth. Rather, men seek out dependable relations among elements of experience by which they can predict the results of their actions and so attain some rational control over these. And their aspiration is toward a high degree of probability in their predictions and judgments, not toward certainty. Locke had the germs of what might have become an experimental theory of knowledge.

These demerits of Locke's position concerning knowledge apply with some force also to his educational theory. However, since Locke was mainly seeking to outline a theory for the development of an enlightened bourgeois gentleman, not a man of learning, he tended to stress the educational conditions for developing "judgment," rather than "certain knowledge." Thus, Locke's protoexperimentalism has fuller play in his educational prescriptions than in his theory of knowledge as such.

On the other hand, the demerits of his "individualistic" view of reason and of the learning process are fully evident in his theory of education, as already noted. These are evident in his rejection of "association" with others as desirable in learning, in his willful dismissal of the educational tradition—a dismissal that, as always, involved unconscious and uncritical acceptance of traditional modes of thought in the name of "common sense," and in his de-emphasis of language as a tool of thoughtful communication and of common thought. They are evident, too, in the incipient sense realism of his educational theory—the notion that individuals can learn by contact with "things" without the mediation of cultural and social meanings and generalizations.

Adequacy of Response to the Bourgeois Revolution

In this response, Locke may be seen as a formulator of classic liberalism in political and social theory. He sought to justify the freeing of individuals from the restraints of an arbitrary government and of a dominant religious tradition and church; he sought to substitute criteria of human utility in the judgments of right social policy for criteria of conformity to traditional morality. The tendency in Locke was thus to amoralize social and political judgments (as later economic liberalism was to amoralize economic judgments and processes). Rights were stressed and these have a moral connotation. But rights were seen as individual rights. They were guaranteed freedoms *from* social and political restraint. The restraints of government (or of custom and other institutions) were thus properly placed in opposition to the morality of natural rights, unless the restraints were seen and accepted merely as means to the safe-guarding of these rights. Valid government was viewed as a utility devoid of essentially moral significance. Any extension of government beyond this "nightwatchman" function was seen as immoral and so to be resisted on grounds of individual and natural morality.

Locke accepted the notion of the Christian God and the principal tenets of Christian morality. But he gave an individualistic interpretation to man's relationship to God and to the principles of Christian morality, as all Protestant thought has been inclined to do. Locke's tendency to individualize Christian morality and to amoralize the operations and controls of political and other institutions would seem to leave collective morality without institutional foundations, and institutions without moral sanctions and controls.

This is the central point that Alexander Meiklejohn made in his criticism (actually, his attempted demolition) of Locke in *Education Between Two Worlds*. As the Church has declined as the center of life in an increasingly secular society, men must find an alternative center in a secular and civic morality. The amoralization of secular society, which Locke's thought has supported, leaves men with no common moral bases of valuation and aspiration. This condition, as Meiklejohn sees it, tends toward social disintegration and toward the struggle of class against class, group against group, nation against nation, and all against all. Meiklejohn's criticisms are more cogent if viewed in terms of the needs of the twentieth century, that is, in terms of the inadequacy of Locke's ideas, of the ideas of classical liberalism, to guide men's efforts to stem Protestant-capitalist disintegration today, not in 1688.

They do not have the same force if taken as criticisms of Locke's influence in his own day. One may properly doubt if the great goods as well as the evils of capitalist development would have been possible in the West without the supplanting of ecclesiastical and monarchical controls. And Locke's ideas helped to power bourgeois revolutions and reforms directed against these controls throughout Western civilization. In brief, we can, without contradiction, see Locke's ideas both as aids to the democratization of life in his own period and as deterrents to the development of collective democracy in our own day.

The contradictions in Locke's assertion of the universal, natural rights of man stem from his class-centered, rather than classless or humanity-centered social perspective. The form of his statements about the rights of man was universal. But the concrete and operational meaning given to them, as in his two conceptions of education—one for working-class children and one for the children of gentlemen of means—was limited and particular. Whenever a particular masquerades as a universal, contradictions of this sort are bound to result, as they have through the whole modern history of middle-class hegemony. Yet, it was the universal form of Locke's theory of natural rights that helped Rousseau and Jefferson in different settings to achieve a more nearly adequate and universal rendering of the "operational" meaning of a "democratic" and "classless" society.

Locke's major contributions in launching the idea of constitutional and Parliamentary government upon its historic way should be praised. Yet, men must today find ways of replacing Locke's "policeman" state of rigidly limited and generally negative powers with a responsible welfare state having wide and positive powers. They must do this without losing the fundamental freedoms of speech, assembly, and conscience that he, too, sought to defend. And men must find ways to supplement Parliamentary representation and its related goal of compromise in public policy making with forms of popular participation aimed at consensus as a basis for public action. They must do this without losing their capacity to sublimate potentially violent intergroup conflict into verbal combat, which has been the central genius of the Parliamentary system where it has worked well.

Finally, insofar as we appreciate ourselves as Americans, we must look upon Locke also with appreciation. For his thinking about man and politics and nature has penetrated deeply into "American" middle-class ways of thinking about man and politics and nature. His ideas and viewpoints took concrete shape in his ideal of the enlightened, bourgeois gentleman as the goal of educational effort. This ideal, with whatever changes intervening experiences in the history of American and West European civilizations have wrought in it, is still pervasive and powerful in American middle-class modes of thinking about the goals of education—among professional educators and among laymen. A narrowly individual focus in education, a strong tendency to validate educational excellence primarily in terms of the secular achievement of "getting ahead," a verbal acceptance of Christian brotherhood with difficulty in extending the principle and practice to classes, races and nations other than one's own, an adulation of science with only limited understanding of its spirit and methodology—these were the mingled strengths and weaknesses of Locke and his enlightened bourgeois gentleman as they are of most middle-class Americans today as they prescribe for education.

We should recognize that illumination and criticism of Locke's educational ideas are, in many instances, illumination and criticism of our own educational ideas. It is for this reason that study and criticism of Locke's thought can contribute to our own intellectual and moral clarification and reconstruction.

BIBLIOGRAPHICAL NOTE

Locke's principal writings on education are to be found in *Some Thoughts Concerning Education* and *The Conduct of the Understanding*. The best edition of the former is Quick's revised edition published by Cambridge University Press, New York, in 1884. This edition contains, as Appendix A, Locke's scheme for working-class schools. A more recent edition of *Thoughts* has been edited by Peter Gay and published by the Bureau of Publications, Teachers College, Columbia University, New York, in 1964 under the title, *John Locke on Education*. Fowler's edition of *The Conduct of the Understanding*, published by the Clarendon Press, Oxford, in 1880, contains valuable editorial notes. For those who wish to read Locke's *Thoughts* in their original form of letters to Edward Clarke, a convenient source is *The Correspondence of John Locke and Edward Clarke*, edited by Benjamin Rand and published by Harvard University Press, Cambridge, Mass., in 1927.

Students of Locke's political thought should read the *Second Treatise on Government* and *A Letter Concerning Toleration*. A convenient source for these is *John Locke on Politics and Education*, edited by H. R. Penniman and published by D. Van Nostrand Co., Princeton, in 1947. J. W. Gough's *Locke's Political Philosophy* published at Oxford, in 1950, is perhaps the best single secondary source on his political thought.

The standard edition of Locke's *Essay Concerning Human Understanding* is the two-volume edition with an introduction and notes by A. C. Fraser, published at Oxford in 1894. Several abridged editions are available, including that edited by Raymond Wilburn and published by Dutton, New York, in 1947 as part of *Everyman's Library*.

Two critical studies of Locke's philosophical work are recommended: R. I. Aaron's *John Locke*, published at Oxford in 1937; and D. J. O'Connor's *John Locke*, published by Penguin Books at Harmondsworth, England in 1952. John Yolton's *John Locke and the Way of Ideas*, published at Oxford in 1956, places Locke's philosophical thought within the intellectual context of his time.

Henry Fox-Bourne's standard biography of Locke was published in two volumes by Harper, New York, in 1876. It is still well worth reading, though the author did not have access to the Lovelace collection of letters and manuscripts, which has recently been made available to students of Locke. Maurice Cranston's *John Locke: A Biography*, published by Macmillan, New York, in 1957, has taken full advantage of this resource.

Of the many critiques of Locke's viewpoints and influence, those by Alexander Meiklejohn in *Education Between Two Worlds*, published by Harper, New York, in 1942, and by F. S. C. Northrop in *The Meeting of East and West*, published by Macmillan, New York, in 1946, are perhaps most useful to contemporary students of education.

❧ JEAN-JACQUES ROUSSEAU (1712–1778) was born in Geneva. His mother died when he was a week old. His father, a watchmaker, taught him how to read when Rousseau was five or six years of age. When Rousseau was about ten his father abandoned him. The boy was put in the care of an uncle who entrusted his education to the Pastor of Boissy. At the age of twelve or thirteen, when Rousseau had completed his elementary studies, he was placed as an apprentice to a notary, and when that proved unsuccessful, to an engraver. In 1728 he forsook his master, left town, and set out on his own. During the next twenty years Rousseau tried many times to find a congenial vocation. He served as a lackey, studied for the priesthood (at one point he was converted to Catholicism but later gave it up), practiced music, and worked as a secretary. For a time he was employed as a tutor, but, like all his other efforts, this too ended in failure. Rousseau was thirty-seven years of age before he showed any sign of intellectual genius. In 1749 he won a contest held by the Academy of Dijon for the best essay on the subject "Has the Progress of the Arts and Sciences Contributed More to the Corruption or Purification of Morals?" Following this success Diderot asked him for an article on politics, and Rousseau wrote the *Discourse on Political Economy*, which first appeared in the *Encyclopédie* in 1755. In the same year he published the *Discourse on the Origin of Inequality*, which also had been written for a Dijon Academy contest. His most famous works both appeared in 1762: *The Social Contract* and *Émile*. The remainder of Rousseau's life was spent in the gloom of embittered quarrels and disputes— both public and private—generated by his writings as well as by his own paranoid behavior. During this time he traveled to Prussia and Switzerland and to England, where he was the guest of the philosopher David Hume. He finally returned to France in 1770 and there completed his *Confessions*.

9

THE NATURAL MAN: *Rousseau*

BY STANLEY E. BALLINGER

If it may be said that the modern world came into being in the eighteenth century, Jean-Jacques Rousseau may be considered its apostle, although a somewhat ambivalent one, as might be expected of a prophet of such a contradictory age. If contemporary culture in the West is characterized more by cleavages and contradictions than by uniformities and unities, Rousseau stands as an apt symbol of these paradoxical aspects of our modern world. It would be absurd, of course, to attribute the *creation* of this clash of polar tendencies to Rousseau. Nonetheless, his influence in this direction can hardly be called negligible, particularly as to the ways in which we moderns perceive and attempt to give order to the conditions and problems of our lives through the instrumentality of general ideas. This influence of Rousseau on the patterning of our thinking and on the problems we frame for ourselves and deem important has been no less evident in educational than in political and social domains.

The sixteenth and seventeenth centuries in Europe were periods of developments that were destined to reshape the course of Western civilization and the character of Western man. Among the particularly noteworthy of these developments were the fragmentation of Christendom by the Reformation; the rise of empirical science; the many variant forms of Humanism; the shift from feudal localism to political nationalism; and the emergence of the new middle class along with its capitalist institutions and ideology. Each of these movements placed a certain amount of strain upon existing ideas and practices in education as well as providing new foundation stones for reconstructed ideas and practices. It is generally agreed that the ruling groups in eighteenth-century France —monarchy, nobility, and clergy—found it to their interest to oppose vigorously most of the new currents of the day. Devices of despotism and tyranny worked for a time to keep the more restless elements of the populace quiet, but eventually the dam broke and the Old Regime was swept away in the Revolution of 1789.

Yet, in spite of the Old Regime's "obstructions to progress," a class of social critics appeared in eighteenth-century France who have come to be known as the *philosophes*: Voltaire, Diderot, La Chalotais, Helvétius, Rolland, Condorcet, and others. Perhaps just because eighteenth-century France afforded so little opportunity for the social actualization and institutional expression of the advanced ideas and forces of the time, the *philosophes* expressed themselves in writing, developing a body of literature of unusual theoretical and critical brilliance. Rousseau was much taken by the ideas of the *philosophes*, many of whom he knew personally, although he did not always find himself in agreement with them. Indeed, Rousseau contributed his own good share to the bitterness and dissatisfaction that paved the way for the Revolution, although he died some ten years before the event.

Such formal instruction as existed during the eighteenth century in France was controlled by the Roman Catholic Church. Schools and colleges were operated by monasteries, convents, or teaching orders like the Jesuits or the Ursuline Sisters. It was also customary for noble and other wealthy families to have their children educated by private tutors living within the household.

Dominating the educational scene in eighteenth-century France were the secondary schools and colleges of the teaching order of the Society of Jesus, spearhead of the Counter Reformation. The curriculum of the Jesuit secondary schools was essentially one of classical Latin studies, to which a little Greek was usually added. The Jesuit program was formulated as a Catholic expression of the classical revival that swept Europe in the fifteenth and sixteenth centuries. Permeated by an atmosphere of Humanism and orthodox religion, the Jesuit program was conspicuously lacking in any of the newer studies of the time such as geography, mathematics, bookkeeping, navigation, or such empirical sciences as astronomy, physics, or anatomy. On the other hand, Jesuit education enjoyed a high reputation for its well-ordered instruction.

The dominant instructional program at the dawn of modern Western civilization thus looked away from the new developments and discoveries of the period and gave its students a training in the rhetoric, grammar, and literature of a long-dead civilization. It was this total failure to consider as important any aspect of the modern world that excited the critical wrath of the Enlightenment thinkers. Rousseau especially found fault with the almost exclusive concern of eighteenth-century education with words—usually words to be memorized about matters remote from the experience or concern of the student.

Far more important to members of the aristocracy than the conventional program of school studies was the instruction provided their children by the dancing master. Good breeding for upper-class Frenchmen in the eighteenth century called for an elaborate education that had little to do with formal instruction in Latin rhetoric and grammar. The intricate network of social and ceremonial relations of polite society in pre-Revolutionary France meant that each person must know his place and must have learned his part. Such detailed and subtle learning had to begin early, and, indeed, children of the upper classes were subjected at a very young age to *salon* life in order to soak up thoroughly the outlook, speech, and manners of well-bred Frenchmen. As Taine wrote in *The Ancient Regime*:

. . . it may be said with truth that the fulcrum of education in this country is the dancing master. They could get along with him without any others; without him the others were of no use. For, without him, how could people go through easily, suitably, and gracefully the thousand and one actions of daily life, walking, sitting down, standing up, offering the arm, using the fan, listening and smiling, before eyes so experienced and before such a refined public? This is to be the great thing for them when they become men and women, and for this reason it is the thing of chief importance for them as children. . . . Scarcely is their tongue loosened when they speak the polished language of their parents.

As might be expected, Rousseau was no less critical of this type of education than he was of the verbalistic education of the formal schoolroom.

ROUSSEAU ON EDUCATION

It is not the intent here to explain Rousseau's educational ideas by referring to the details of his personal life or by psychologizing about his writings as an expression of his inner conflicts and frustrations, although these approaches might uncover ore that could be mined with profit. This section will set forth a portrait of Rousseau's thinking, more or less chronologically, with his educational ideas in the foreground against the background of his more general social and political theory. Connections among various writings of Rousseau will be pointed out, but no attempt will be made to present Rousseau's educational thought as a fully unified, interconsistent body of ideas. Even if such a unity were to be found in Rousseau's thought, as some scholars would contend, it would take a long and subtly argued presentation, out of place in this brief essay.

Jean-Jacques Rousseau was born in 1712 in the Swiss city of Geneva, the son of a Protestant watchmaker. His mother died soon after Jean-Jacques was born. For the next ten years it would seem that the young Rousseau was given affectionate, if not always wisely temperate, care by his father. He was taught to read by his father, and soon the two were plunged into what one commentator has called "a debauch of novel-reading." The boy had no other teacher until he was ten, when he was separated from his father. Later, in *Émile*, Rousseau went to no end of trouble to denounce books as miseducative; yet, at the end of his life, retrospecting in his *Confessions*, he did not seem to have viewed his own childhood preoccupation with books as having handicapped his own education in any way.

Rousseau's early life was troubled and hectic. The storminess of his inner life was manifested by restless wandering from place to place and from job to job for many years, achieving neither fortune nor fame. In his twenty-seventh or twenty-eighth year, about 1740, Rousseau accepted the position of tutor to the two sons of a M. de Mably, which he held for a little over a year. Largely on the basis of Rousseau's own assertions, it is generally agreed that this, his first teaching venture, was rather a failure. Insofar as it steered his thoughts toward education, however, the experience may have been well worth the anguish that Rousseau experienced. Of interest to us in this matter is that at the very end of his period in the employ of M. de Mably, he wrote the *Project for the Education of M. de Sainte-Marie*, which was in effect a plan for the education of M. de Mably's elder son. It was also Rousseau's first substantial pronouncement on the subject of education. As such, to the historian of Rousseau it is interesting but disappointing. It is for the most part a warmed-over version of the ideas of John Locke. It is only with careful scrutiny that the reader today can in any way recognize in the *Project* the future author of *Émile*.

In the year 1749 Rousseau was thirty-seven years of age. A couple of minor publications in the field of music, his *Project for the Education of M. de Sainte-Marie* in the field of education, and one or two other minor articles measured the length and breadth of his literary production. Nothing that had happened up to this point would in any way suggest that his life was to be notable in any respect. He was emotionally unstable, his habits were erratic, he constantly sinned deeply against his own sense of duty and right, he was quarrelsome and irritable, and he could not seem to stay at any one employment for more than a few months. In the light of what was to come by way of writing, no doubt the years up to 1749 must have been richly germinal, but no extant account, including Rousseau's own *Confessions*, gives any hint of his future greatness.

The year 1749 marked the turning point for Rousseau. That was the year Rousseau sought the prize offered by the academy at Dijon for the best essay on whether progress in the sciences and arts tended toward the purification or the corruption of morals. The essay itself was immature and full of weaknesses in logic and history. But in taking the general position that civilization had essentially been an evil thing for man,

Rousseau, with his wild impassioned rhetoric, won the Dijon prize and the acclaim of the intellectuals of Paris. Overnight he was famous. He had found his niche as a social critic. His *Discourse on the Arts and Sciences* had little to say directly on the subject of education, although if it had been more substantial than it actually was, its inferences for education would have been notably radical. If civilization were indeed as unmitigated an évil as he said, there would be little place for formal instruction in its sciences and arts. A hypothetical prayer, which Rousseau suggested that men in the future would utter, indicates well the general tenor of the essay as well as its characteristic rhetoric: "Almighty God! thou who holdest in Thy hand the minds of men, deliver us from the fatal arts and sciences of our forefathers; give us back ignorance, innocence and poverty, which alone can make us happy and precious in Thy sight." Perhaps the most unhappy consequence of this essay has been that so many of Rousseau's commentators right down to the present have taken it to be representative of his thought.

Rousseau's concern for the problem of what man was like in "a state of nature" is evidenced in his *Discourse on the Origin of Inequality*, written, like the *Discourse on the Arts and Sciences*, for a competition held by the Academy of Dijon, and published in 1755. The subject posed by the Dijon Academy was "What is the Origin of Inequality Among Men and Is It Authorized by Natural Law?" This second discourse did not win a prize but it is generally considered to be a better piece of writing and analysis than the first. In the *Discourse on the Origin of Inequality* Rousseau seems to be working through many of the same problems that appeared in the first *Discourse*, but at a higher level of analysis and with fewer logical and structural weaknesses. Rousseau identified two kinds of human inequality: individual inequalities, which men bring with them at birth; social inequalities, which are caused by the social conditions of men's environment. Inequalities originating in the individual natures of men would be those of ability, temperament, bodily form, and so on. Social inequality, while part of human nature in general as a matter of potentiality, does not manifest itself unless and until a certain stage of social development has occurred. This social inequality is founded upon artificial distinctions made possible and inevitable by the increasing sociality of man at a certain stage of history —distinctions as to property and other forms of wealth, differences in honor and prestige, and the like.

The *Discourse on the Origin of Inequality* did not, as many have asserted, exalt and glorify a presocial "state of nature" presumed to have occurred prior to the establishment of the first civil government among men. It is true that Rousseau found much to admire in an early stage of "social man"—man in a "savage society"—but this development had taken "natural man" (presocial) many centuries if not milleniums to attain. This was the level of the "noble savage," although that was not Rousseau's term. It was well above that of the brute animal, but still considerably short of the corruptions of actual civilization. This happy stage had no government beyond that of the patriarchal family unit, no property beyond personal possessions like weapons, tools, and a man's own shelter. But these nascent forms of government and property contained the seeds of all the evil to come in later civilization: property to produce inequalities among men; government to make these inequalities legitimate. As Rousseau saw it, man's potentiality for moral sensitivity and choice could also develop, at least feebly, along with human intelligence at this stage, but he viewed these aspects of natural goodness (la bonté naturelle) as largely submerged under the burgeoning expressions of man's natural wickedness (méchanceté naturelle) that grew out of man's illimitable capacity for self-love (amour-propre). Man in a state of society was doomed because the social organization provided the inevitable seed bed for man's "universal desire for reputation, honors, and preferment . . . which inspire men to all the evils which they inflict upon each other."

Although classical Athenian civilization formulated abstractly the problem of "the one and the many" or "the individual versus society," it was part of the genius of Rousseau—the quality that makes him rewarding reading even today—that within the compass of his own thought he gave passionate emphasis not only to man as a free individual but also to man as member of a cultural community. Most of his writings reveal both of these emphases, often in violent contrast and seldom in harmonious resolution, but usually with a dominant emphasis on one side or the other. Rousseau's article "Political Economy" appearing in the fifth volume of the Encyclopédie in 1755 is of interest here, not only because it contains several paragraphs devoted to a discussion of the role of education but because it clearly reveals Rousseau's advocacy of public education for the purpose of producing loyal citizens. The educated man, he stressed in this essay, is one who has been led to find his own transcendent interest in the welfare of others, particularly those others who, together with oneself, form the national political community. In its emphasis upon education by the state for the state, Rousseau's view here owes something to Plato's Republic and is reminiscent of the situation in ancient Sparta. Indeed, in this same article Rousseau spoke of how this type of education in ancient Sparta and Persia "met with very great success . . . and worked wonders." The date—1755—of Rousseau's "Political Economy" article shows that his emphasis upon education for national citizenship was not a mere aberration introduced into the posthumously published *Considerations on the Government of Poland*.

The decade following Rousseau's winning of the Dijon prize for his *Discourse on the Arts and Sciences* in 1749 was a period rich in mental productivity for him, although beyond the *Discourse on the Origin of Inequality* and the article on "Political Science" in the *Encyclopédie*, both in 1755, he published little of note. Rousseau seems to have responded to his reading and to his experience in and around Paris with a torrent of ideas. During the latter part of the decade, Rousseau worked on three manuscripts more or less concurrently: *The New Héloïse, The Social Contract*, and *Émile*. In view of his tendency to become passionately absorbed in ideas that were almost polar opposites of each other, it is hardly astonishing that these books, singly and collectively, lack logical consistency. Given an idea, Rousseau developed it and clothed it in an extreme and impassioned statement, viewed positively or negatively, as if there were no consideration which could conceivably cause him to accept any qualification. Yet, turning to another concept, apparently contradictory to the first, he would give it just as extreme a statement, ardently investing his penetrating insight with feelings of equal intensity. Whether there is a deeper, more unifying framework within which these violent contradictions can be placed is a much debated question, which can not be pursued in these pages.

Each of these three great books, *The New Héloïse, The Social Contract*, and *Émile*, had a profound impact on a different field of human concern, although for the proper understanding of any one of them there is much to be gained by reading the other two. The first of this trio to be published was *Julie: The New Héloïse*, a work which bears superficial resemblance to the tale of the thwarted love of Abélard and Héloïse in the Middle Ages. This book appeared in France in 1761. A long book written in the epistolary style, *The New Héloïse* is a novel of passion couched in sentimental language of the most extreme kind. Few readers of novels today would have the stomach for a story of such unrestrained sentiment. Yet, even though it is seldom read now as a novel for its own sake, it still constitutes an important element in the total range of Rousseau's writings. *The New Héloïse* is a complicated work, perhaps intended to be partly an allegory of eighteenth-century society. It is strongly autobiographical in many of its details, and can be read at any one of several different levels.

Julie is the central character of the book, and of special interest to us is the chapter on Julie's education of her children within the home. In long didactic conversations with Saint-Preux, her onetime lover, Julie explains the way she has brought up her children. Like the education in the first half of *Émile*, for which this is a kind of rehearsal, Julie's system of education is largely negative; it consists of letting the youngsters learn "naturally" from their own actions. It resembles *Émile*, also, in depicting an educational process that takes place in total isolation from the world at large. Julie's home is on a remote estate, and the children are brought up as though no occasion in the future would bring them into substantial contact with the world of men. Like *Émile*, again, the chapter on the education of Julie's children may be viewed as the logical educational consequence of Rousseau's position (stated in the two early discourses) that men's difficulties stem from civilization and from the social institutions that civilized man has created.

In addition, the chapter on the education of Julie's children in *The New Héloïse* is revealing in other ways. The only social unit of importance in the book is the family, which Rousseau had many times explicitly asserted to be the "natural" social unit. Although it leaves many questions unanswered, the book does afford us more than a glimpse of what Rousseau had in mind when he spoke of "natural man." Julie's life, threatened by corruptions of society at various points, realizes much of the potential of "natural man" in society, if one allows for Rousseau's views of the limited role proper to the female sex.

The Social Contract of Jean-Jacques Rousseau, perhaps his most controversial writing, begins:

Man is born free; and everywhere he is in chains. One thinks himself the master of others, and still remains a greater slave than they. How did this change come about? I do not know. What can make it legitimate? That question I think I can answer.

A little farther on in *The Social Contract*, Rousseau stated the problem in a slightly different way, as being ". . . to find a form of association which will defend and protect with the whole common force the person and goods of each associate, and in which each, while uniting himself with all, may still obey himself alone, and remain as free as before." The book is thus a treatise on the legitimate nature of the civil state, when it is as it ought to be.

The book is about much more than the "social contract," but this contract of association between men as they passed from a state of nature into a state of civil society and the associated concept of the "General Will" are the foundational ideas of the book. Rousseau did not here define "state of nature," but we may probably take it to mean the stage immediately prior to the stage of civil society, in which the family is the only social unit of consequence, and men are not yet constrained by any obligations to others, nor are some men the political subjects or political rulers of others. In such a state of nature Rousseau found much that was good, but it was a condition of man (perhaps only hypothetical) that could not last. Save for the social contract, this stage was doomed to degenerate into one of intolerable strife and social disorder much akin to Hobbes's conception of the condition of man that led him to accept an absolute monarch, with the life of man viewed as "solitary, poor, nasty, brutish, and short."

The social contract or compact was the implicit or explicit agreement undergirding the "act of association" of all men, each with the others. Each gave up everything to everyone else, that is, to the community of all within the society, and each agreed, in effect, to act in accordance with the "General Will" of all the people. There is no ethically defensible place, in Rousseau's thought, for the individual considered by himself. The individual can not deny the unitary character—viewed in moral perspective—of the community of which he is a part, the best interests of which he is bound to promote, and, in a rightly ordered situation, he *wants of his own free will* to promote. Thus, men, doomed to be activated by self-interest, can become moral only as their own fulfillment of self is identified with the common good.

There are some cherishable insights in this line of analysis, but Rousseau described a supposedly ideal society that lends itself readily to totalitarian interpretations, for all his championing of individual rights. The most striking contradiction to his concern for individual rights may, perhaps, be seen in his discussion of the civil religion to be decreed by the state. After asserting that the state has no right to determine the purely theological aspects of the religions of its citizens, when such dogma has no bearing on the civil duties of men, he went on to observe that:

... there is a purely civil profession of faith, the articles of which it behooves the Sovereign to fix, not with the precision of religious dogmas, but treating them as a body of social *sentiments* without which no man can be either a good citizen or a faithful subject. Though it has no power to compel anyone to believe them, it can banish from the State all who fail to do so, not on grounds of impiety, but as lacking in social sense. . . . Any man who, after acknowledging these articles of faith, proceeds to act as though he did not believe them, is deserving of the death penalty.

Rousseau's own footnote at this point reveals that he was willing to give the state unusual powers to coerce citizens, provided it could be said to be necessary from the point of view of citizenship. It is true that the articles of belief which Rousseau would have the state require are not numerous, centering in affirming "the existence of a powerful, intelligent, beneficent God [and] the reality of the life to come: the reward of the just, and the punishment of evildoers." But the small number of items of belief would probably not be happily regarded by those whose beliefs were coerced. Note that the truth of these items of belief is not at issue; it is, indeed, irrelevant. Truth, in this part of *The Social Contract*, is made subordinate to the principle of civic utility.

The Social Contract does not specifically address itself to education, but the problems of interpreting Rousseau's direct writings on education can not be approached adequately without reference to *The Social Contract*. Much of what is said in *Émile* leads one to believe that the educated man is to love truth. *The Social Contract* seems to be saying that, even in the ideal society, man may love only the portion of the truth that is left after the application of the principle of civic utility. *The Social Contract* is indispensable also for dealing with what Rousseau identified as the conflict between the education of man as an *individual* person and of man as a *citizen*. One might agree with the assertion of the noted Rousseau scholar William Boyd that a study of *The Social Contract* is indispensable to a critical appraisal of Rousseau as a major theorist on democratic education.

In approaching Rousseau's best-known and most substantial work on education, *Émile*, let us remember that *The Social Contract* and *The New Héloïse* were written more or less concurrently with *Émile*. *The Social Contract*, as a matter of fact, was published shortly after *Émile*, in the early part of 1762. It is reasonable to assume that Rousseau intended these three works to be consistent expressions of his thought, and at several places he says as much.

Émile is the story of the education of a boy from infancy through early manhood by a tutor whose sole responsibility in life is to provide for Émile's educational development—mental, moral, and physical—on a round-the-clock basis. It is unquestionably Rousseau's most significant piece of writing on education. It is a book rich with insights not only into the maladies of eighteenth-century society but into the enduring problems of man in general. It is difficult to be fully sure of what the book as a whole means or of how consistent it may be with any other thing that Rousseau wrote. Yet there is hardly a page of *Émile* that does not contain some trenchant comment on human nature and the ways of mankind and give a sharper focus to something only dimly discerned before. Above all, like most of Rousseau's writings, *Émile* can be profitably studied from the point of view of the problems with which Rousseau struggled and that he helps us to confront more clearly and honestly.

"Everything is good as it comes from the hands of the Maker of the world but degenerates once it gets into the hands of man"—this famous opening statement of *Émile* is more than faintly reminiscent of the opening statement of *The Social Contract*, that man is born free but everywhere is in chains. The root idea is the one expressed so extravagantly in Rousseau's *Discourse on the Arts and Sciences*, that civilization has corrupted the natural goodness of man through man's imprisonment within institutions, traditions, customs, and laws, which make it impossible for his moral nature to assert itself. Much of *Émile* is built on this same foundation and explores the problem of how, in the actual world of a corrupted civilization, children can receive an education that will permit the good side of their natures to develop. The essential answer that Rousseau offered to this particular way of putting the question is found in about the first half of the book; it consists in having Émile develop "naturally," apart from other children and away from the vanity and artifice of civilized society. Rousseau called for about twelve years of this "negative education," asserting that at least it avoids the debased, positive education in the home and school of the times. Since Rousseau believed the natural predispositions of the young child to be good, his problem was to block the evil influence of society and allow these natural predispositions to emerge and find expression and strength. It seems to have been Rousseau's hope that later on, when the child's natural predispositions had grown healthy and strong, he would be able to resist better the corrupting influence of society. It is well to keep in mind at this point the unusual degree of oppression, cupidity, brutality, deceit, hypocrisy, and the like that characterized "polite society" in eighteenth-century France. This "negative education" has been much misunderstood, having often been confused with the idea that one should let the child do what he wants (*laissez-faire*). Rousseau said clearly and emphatically that it was not his aim to produce "spoiled brats," headstrong children who play the role of master and in general tyrannize over their elders.

Émile is to have perfect freedom—what Rousseau called natural freedom—to do what he wants to do, but this freedom is to be exercised in a physical environment from which the tutor has carefully purged any elements that might cause the "free acts" of Émile to have bad consequences for his education. The tutor is seldom in the foreground, but never once is he to lose control over the experiences which Émile is to undergo. The tutor is the archcontriver, the scene setter, and scene manipulator. Rousseau advised, "Let him [the child] always be his own master in appearance, but do you take to be so in reality." The particular lesson that Rousseau's tutor is so anxious that Émile learn is the necessity to adjust to *things* and their ways. Thus, when Émile breaks a window in his bedroom, the tutor makes him live and sleep there in the cold drafts, which pour through the opening. In this way Émile will learn through the "natural" consequences of his acts. In contrast to the natural and simple life of Émile, middle-class and upper-class French children in the eighteenth century were generally learning the artificial intricacies of adult social life, learning to flatter and be flattered, to deceive, to pose, and to acquire the vanities of the dancing *salon* under the tutelage of the dancing master.

Part of Émile's negative education is that he be kept from books. "I hate books," wrote Rousseau. "They only teach us to talk about what we do not know." Things should be experienced directly and naturally; books are to be left to a later period of Émile's development. The important thing in life through the first twelve years is a strong, tough body and a knowledge of the physical world, achieved by direct experience. Also important for Émile is the shaping of his thinking and his behavior by things and not by the will of other people. It is essential that the tutor arrange matters so that Émile can understand that when he is thwarted, it is not because the will of the tutor is imposed on him but because of the way the natural world actually is. Émile can then learn to adjust his desires realistically to what is possible. It is the balance of desire with the opportunity to satisfy the desire that Rousseau makes central in happiness. Part of the evil of civilized society is its breeding of desires without attention to the corresponding opportunity for satisfaction of these desires.

An important feature of *Émile*, which has left a deep mark on subsequent thinking about education, is the notion of developmental stages by which the individual grows and matures: infancy, childhood (boyhood), preadolescence, adolescence, and young manhood. These five stages are quite sharply set off from each other; each has its own special possibilities and limitations. Part of what Rousseau means by "education according to nature" is that education ought to be appropriate to each stage; education should especially avoid the introduction of a phase of learning at a stage earlier than nature has provided for in the developmental scheme. Education for literacy, therefore, is not to be attempted until after the age of twelve, because the child's development before twelve is appropriate only for an "education of the senses"; the verbal and reasoning powers remain latent for the first twelve years.

In one form or another, education "developmentalism" is an ancient idea, but Rousseau gave it a special and unusually strong expression. For his advice about infants, Rousseau is usually credited with starting a craze throughout Europe for more "natural" patterns of child-rearing, such as breast-feeding by mothers. He treated the stage of boyhood, ending at the age of twelve, as especially suited to the "negative education" discussed above. In the third stage, from the age of twelve to the age of fifteen, the boy is considered to have developed physically into a tough, resourceful animal, and his powers of reasoning emerge and develop quickly. Self-reliance, in addition to usefulness, is a key objective of his education at this point. Rousseau seems to have resented bitterly his own perpetual dependence upon others and wanted Émile to be free of this debasing necessity. Small wonder that Rousseau's favorite book for Émile at this stage was *Robinson Crusoe!*

The fourth stage of Émile's development—adolescence—marks the beginning of direct instruction to prepare him for relating appropriately to others in human society. Sympathy and other cohesive sentiments arise in this stage, making it possible for Émile to learn to become a social being. In adolescence the sexual passions are aroused, but Émile is not to be given any help at this point. Sex education, in the usual sense of the term, goes unmentioned. It is the tutor's puritanical task to keep Émile from sexual adventures, so that he will bring to his eventual marriage a virginal innocence. While practicing premarital continence, Émile is to learn most of the other conventional virtues. Rousseau's discussion of this stage is not radical or even liberal. The revolutionary impact of *Émile* as educational doctrine has largely proceeded from the sections of the work dealing with the first three developmental stages, to about the age of fifteen.

At twenty Émile has become a young man; his education is at an end; it remains but to give him the finishing touches of the grand tour around the capitals of Europe. At this point a mate must be found for him, and Rousseau has a perfect mate ready in the person of Sophie, whose qualifications and education are the subject of the whole fifth book of *Émile*. Rousseau's treatment of Sophie leaves no doubt that his conception of the ideal educated *woman* was radically different from his ideal of the educated *man*. Girls have a different nature that leads them to play different roles in life from boys. The education of Sophie has but one aim: to create a being who will serve Émile and satisfy his every wish. The book ends with Émile married to Sophie, who has produced for him a son. Talking about his son to his tutor in the very last paragraph of the book, Émile states with considerable feeling that the education of *his* child will not be entrusted to a tutor, but that he, Émile, will himself undertake the precious duty of educating his own son. Thus Rousseau told us that while the tutor was a useful device for his theorizing, in real life the parents, especially the father, should play the role of tutor. No "outside" tutor could really be expected to have the single-minded, selfless concern for the welfare of another man's child that Rousseau's book described.

During the years from his publication of *Émile* until his death in 1778, Rousseau underwent a series of emotional crises that were intensified, no doubt, by the work of writing his autobiographical *Confessions*, a narrative of *feeling* as much as of *events* and intimately introspective as perhaps no book ever had been up to that time. The *Confessions* contain little of special interest for education, but Rousseau did produce an important work bearing on education, *Considerations on the Government of Poland*, written in 1772 but not published until after his death. He wrote it at the request of a Polish nobleman, concerned for his country in the period just prior to the first partition of Poland, when the people were harassed by aggressors without and disunified by cleavages within. Rousseau's answer to the problem was that the Polish people should deliberately set about creating Polish nationalism "to establish the Republic in the hearts of the Poles in such a way that it will subsist there in spite of all the efforts of its oppressors." How to do this? He said, "It is education which ought to give to minds the national form and to direct men's opinions and their tastes that they would be patriots by inclination, by passion, by necessity." The same Rousseau who had denounced the social institutions of civilized society as corruptive of man's original (good) nature in the two discourses, in *The New Héloïse*, and in *Émile*, wrote in *Considerations on the Government of Poland*:

It is the national institutions that form the genius, the character, the tastes, the morale of a people. By means of them is inspired that ardent love of country, based on ineradicable habits, that makes its citizens die of heart-weariness in foreign lands . . .

Rousseau urged that young Polish children be kept busy with exercises and other activities that gave them pleasure and served the needs of their growing bodies. He went so far as to say that children ought not to be allowed to play separately or privately, that their play ought always to be public and in groups so that they could be moved to rivalry and emulation—two things condemned in earlier works as being at the root of human evil. While Émile is to avoid doing anything because it is the will of others, young Poles should live as much as possible under the eyes of their fellow citizens so that the full force of public approbation and disapprobation might fall upon them.

Historians of educational thought have not often given emphasis to Rousseau's education for nationalism found in his *Considerations of the Government of Poland*. Yet, as we have seen, this point of view is put forward clearly in Rousseau's *Encyclopédie* article on "Political Economy." There is, furthermore, the romantic totalitarianism of *The Social Contract.* Indeed, even in *Émile* there are passages that foreshadow the nationalistic emphasis of the essay on Poland. It is an irony that the man who was to become the patron saint of the child-centered movement in modern education should have made his final statement on education to be an unqualified plea for an education that would be the chief instrument for producing blind and total loyalty to the state.

THE SIGNIFICANCE OF ROUSSEAU FOR EDUCATION

In a broad appraisal of Rousseau from the standpoint of the present, one thing may be said with certainty: he has been a difficult man to ignore. He wrote with high passion of a variety of matters basic to the condition of man. As might be expected, strong partisans have arisen on both sides of the question of the value of Rousseau's theory of education and ideal of the educated man. He has never lacked for either critics or disciples. Both appeared at the time of the publication of his books and in every generation since. Some of his supporters have turned out to be of less support than his critics, so widely have they missed his meaning. We might say that part of Rousseau's posthumous history has been a "literature of misinterpretation." One Rousseau scholar who must be granted at least a measure of the truth observed that the net result of five generations of critics had been to obscure rather than to clarify Rousseau, and that the people of Rousseau's day were better off, because the critics had hardly begun to explain him.

Much of what critics have said in a negative vein about Rousseau's educational writings would be readily granted today by anyone approaching the problem in a spirit of objective scholarship. His paradoxes and contradictions are frustrating. His language is extravagant, and feeling often runs wild at the expense of reflective judgment. He has little that can be called an intellectual method, and his ideas at times have to be treated one by one, apart from a unifying conceptual framework. His theory about how educational practice should be carried on is often couched in terms that almost defy translation to the world of practice. His most important ideas are frequently framed in undefined and ambiguous phrasing. All this and more would be admitted from the start, but these defects in Rousseau are to be seen as obstacles to getting at his positive value; they are not to be taken as a denial of this value.

Let it be briefly indicated *what kind* of contributions Rousseau may be said to have made. His worth to succeeding generations of educators lies mainly along two lines. First, he brought to our attention *problems* of special relevance to the modern world and provided unusual perspectives from which to view these problems. Often we may not want to accept his solutions but we are likely to have a much clearer idea of the nature of the problem for having seen how Rousseau dealt with it. Second, he opened up *lines of emphasis* that have paid rich dividends in later theory, research, and practice. He may have gone off on questionable tangents and he may have been naïve about many aspects of the problem, but the net effect of much of what he wrote has been to turn men's attention to matters that, but for him, they would have heeded much less, if, indeed, they would have noticed some of them at all. It is true that often these emphases had been made by others before Rousseau; sometimes his ideas go back to Comenius, Quintilian, Aristotle, or Plato. But Rousseau, typically, did two things with the ideas of others. He gave them a new twist, putting them into new combinations and adding new elements, so that what he offered was not merely a restatement of other people's wisdom. In addition to this, Rousseau *felt* deeply about what he wrote, and his writing conveyed these deep feelings to others. As Madame de Genlis once wrote, not entirely fairly:

"Wisdom is less persuasive than enthusiasm. Rousseau repeated what others had said; but he did not advise: he commanded and was obeyed."

Rousseau himself wrote in the preface to *Émile*, "If sometimes I take on a dogmatic tone it is not to force my views on the reader but just to talk to him as the thoughts come to me." Since the thoughts "came to him" charged with feeling, this is the way he wrote down his views.

Of central importance in Rousseau's writings on education has been his use of the idea of "nature" as a normative guide for education. He urged, "Follow nature!" Rousseau did not initiate this idea, but he gave the idea such thumping emphasis that thenceforth it was all but impossible to avoid considering the question from at least some point of view. It is true that Rousseau created a certain amount of confusion by using the idea of "nature" and "education according to nature" in many different ways, often without letting the reader know the sense in which he was using it. It is also true that he offered almost no criteria by which to distinguish "nature" from "art": the "natural" from the "artificial." There certainly is a danger that men may project their own prejudices onto the idea of nature and give these prejudices the guise of characteristics of human nature. Something of this sort seems to have happened with Rousseau himself, when he wrote on the education of women.

The positive value of Rousseau's emphasis upon nature as an educational norm lies in his having put the matter so that subsequent generations have not been able to ignore it; they have had to confront more directly the problem of identifying the educational bearings of man's enduring nature. Furthermore, Rousseau's idea of human nature was not merely a representation of what naturally exists, as a matter of fact. He viewed the natural as that which conforms to nature in its ideally potential form. He said, "The natural man is not our first brute follower, but the last man whom we are traveling on to be." Part of man's nature is to create ideals and moral norms for himself, in a process of realization of his ideal nature. Furthermore, ideals are *within* nature, not outside of it, as most who came before had maintained. The truly educated man is the "natural man" in the sense that he has achieved to the utmost the ideal potentialities of his nature. This is a far cry from the "noble savage," often imputed to Rousseau as his educational ideal. Often missed in discussions of Rousseau in this area is the belief by Rousseau that the ideal man—one who lives up to his natural potential—can develop only in society. Society is both the source for the problem of moral choice and the potential medium for man's moral growth. Putting it in the terms of the Garden of Eden, social man—man in society—is man after the Fall, suffering from the institutions he has created with his own hands. For Rousseau, man's redemption is possible, not through God as an act of beneficent intervention but through man's own efforts, through the upthrust of the better parts of his own nature.

Rousseau's conception of human nature was, as we have seen, partly centered in the developmental stages of human maturation. We no longer accept the unflexible educational meanings that Rousseau attached to overdiscretely construed stages of development. But there is no student of education today who does not feel that the developmental patterns of children are rich in educational bearings. In his general concept of developmental stages, Rousseau often spoke of the stage of childhood, past infancy and prior to adolescence. This stage had for Rousseau many particular features of great significance for education. Educators in Rousseau's day in effect assumed that the child as learner was more or less equivalent to an ignorant adult. That is, childhood had no special features that should be given particular consideration in the educational process as to subject matter or as to instructional procedures. In urging that children be treated and studied *as children*, Rousseau laid the basis for today's studies of child development and child psychology. Although he did not use the term "maturational readiness," no one reading the first two books of *Émile* would have any trouble understanding that general concept. The tendency of schools of his era to teach complicated matters far beyond a child's capacity for real comprehension became an obsessive concern for Rousseau, and *Émile* is full of warnings to educators to stay at the level of the child's understanding.

Perhaps we have learned this lesson a little too well in our contemporary school practices, which are sometimes so thoroughly within a bright child's understanding that he loses interest and stops learning. But the general principle involved is no less valid because of faulty application.

Rousseau's conviction that the developmental stage of childhood has special qualities relevant to education generated his concern for the rights of children. He exclaimed, "Let us speak less of the duties of children and more of their rights!" Because half the children in his day died before attaining adulthood, Rousseau was struck by the injustice of the viewpoint that adulthood is the only worthwhile stage of life. He attacked the notion that childhood is mere preparation. He saw child-hood, first and foremost, as a time for being a *child* with a child's nature to develop, without worrying how the future adult might be formed. Rousseau's "rights of children" left its mark on the theories of such American educators as Francis Parker, Caroline Pratt, and John Dewey.

It is probable that much of the sense realism of John Locke would have found its way into educational practice without Rousseau, but it was largely Rousseau's particular kind of overstatement of the case that gave such later movements as Pestalozzianism their forms. The subsequent history of education has revealed how firmly implanted were the ultra-verbalistic methods of traditional education and has indicated that efforts on the order of the exaggerations and distortions of Rousseau may well have been required for an effective assault upon entrenched methods. On the other side of the coin, it is worth noting here that neither Rousseau nor such disciples as Pestalozzi really helped the educational profession to see and grapple with the problem of vicarious learning.

The general problem of the "one and the many" or "the individual versus society" takes on radically different particular forms in different times and places. Rousseau raised the problem both in political and in educational terms. As to the educational aspect, he asked, in effect, whether it is possible to educate a person for his individuality and at the same to educate him for citizenship within his political community. This problem has by no means been resolved or lost its importance in twentieth-century society. As we have seen, he asked the problem in a very special way in *Émile*: given a corrupt society, how does an educa-tion for moral excellence (ideal human nature) proceed, granted that the source and ground of morality are in human experience within society and within culture? In other words, how can a corrupt society carry on public education to produce ethically adequate individuals? This is perhaps an extreme way to put the problem (for us, not for Rousseau), but one quick extrapolation to our current situation may carry the point. How can a government that almost continuously finds it necessary to make falsification and deceit (often toward its own citizens) principles of its activity conduct education in such a way that young people have a reasonable chance to develop commitments to principles of honesty and integrity? At the very least, *Émile* can be used as a way to raise serious questions about what "education for adjustment" may, in any acceptable terms, mean for modern society.

Compulsory education by the state would undoubtedly have made its appearance in the modern world, regardless of Rousseau. It is one thing to compel attendance at government-controlled or government-regulated schools; it is another to give a justification of it in moral terms. Rousseau provided such a justification when he said that the state, acting as the collective agent of everyone, can with justice force an individual against his will to be free, because the General Will (common good) can not be served when one's fellow citizens are not free. Each of us has a stake in the freedom of all the rest of us. Something like this has been the implicit, if not always explicit, moral grounding for compulsory school attendance. Free men in modern society can not be ignorant men. The decision must be made by the state (acting for all of us) in behalf of the child, so that he may not lose, through the community's inaction, this necessary condition to freedom: not only *his* freedom, of course, but the freedom of all of us. The argument is here put a bit oversimply, to be sure, but something very much like this is to be found in *The Social Contract*, supplemented by passages in several other writings of Rousseau. Whether this use of the principle of civic utility by Rousseau "to force men to be free" is morally adequate can not be settled here, of course.

An adequate evaluation of the bearing of Rousseau's writings for a theory of democracy *in* education and education *for* democracy is beyond the scope of this essay. Let us consider but two or three salient points. On the negative side, it must be admitted that it is hard to see how a democratically disposed and democratically oriented personality is likely to come from the situation within which Émile is brought up and given his education. It is unlikely that Émile will acquire the habits of critical intelligence demanded by the democratic process. It is also unlikely that he will acquire the behavioral skills of cooperative action with others that genuine forms of democracy necessitate. On the other hand, it can hardly be denied that Rousseau made definite contributions to a theory of "democratic selfhood." The ethically adequate self, for Rousseau, was a self that sought its own realization in the good of the whole.

Another positive contribution concerns the democratic value often described as the worth and dignity of the individual. Rousseau stated categorically that no one has a right to exploit children for his own benefit, that the only moral justification of control within the educational process is to be found in the extent to which the control is exercised for the actual benefit of the child. In Kantian terms (remembering that the writings of Kant in this connection did not appear until some three decades after Rousseau made the point), the pupil is always to be regarded as an *end* in himself, never simply or primarily as a *means* for the teacher, for the parent, or for some social group or agency. In considering the rights of children, Rousseau meant their right not to be regarded as steppingstones for the purposes of others and their right to be treated as intrinsically worthy for their own sakes rather than as plastic material to be molded for the benefit of traditions and institutions of doubtful value. Can it be said in the twentieth century that we have now fully identified the meaning of this ethical idea or that we have yet outgrown the need for it? Perhaps Rousseau's most valuable contribution to democratic morality was his concern for *people* as living, flesh-and-blood individuals who are not to be sacrificed to some abstract future adulthood or to any institution. There are, however, those who have felt that his concept of the General Will *in practice* would constitute just such a sacrifice of individuals to those who, in the name of the General Will, would exercise the actual power of the political state.

Jean-Jacques Rousseau died on the second day of July in the year 1778 in Ermenonville, France. He had helped to set in motion at least two revolutions, one political and one educational. The problems that premised these revolutions have by no means been solved. While at many points we can not agree on what Rousseau "really" meant, his writings continue to be read in most countries of the world and are still shaping men's notions of what it means to be educated and how the young may be guided in the process. That none who trouble to read him do so with indifference attests Rousseau's relevance for the modern world.

BIBLIOGRAPHICAL NOTE

Among the writings of Rousseau generally available in English translation are *Émile*, translated by Barbara Foxley, Everyman's Library edition, published by J. M. Dent & Sons, London, in 1911, and *The Émile of Jean-Jacques Rousseau: Selections*, translated and edited by William Boyd, published by the Bureau of Publications, Teachers College, Columbia University, New York, in 1962, and published under the title *Émile for Today* by William Heinemann, England, in 1956. Professor Boyd has included in the American edition editorial comments and a substantial epilogue that are useful supplements to his book-length analysis of Rousseau's educational theory noted below. *The Minor Educational Writings of Jean-Jacques Rousseau: Selections*, translated and edited by Professor Boyd, and published by the Bureau of Publications, Teachers College, Columbia University, New York, in 1962, originally published by Blackie and Son, Glasgow, in 1911, contains several smaller but quite important writings of Rousseau, such as the 1755 article on "Political Economy" and the educational section of *Considerations on the Government of Poland*. It also contains useful editorial comments by Professor Boyd.

Those who wish to read the writings by Rousseau on political and social theory that are most likely to shed light on his educational theory may consult *The Social Contract*, translation and introduction by G. D. H. Cole, published by J. M. Dent & Sons, London, in 1913, containing also the *Discourse on the Arts and Sciences* (1750) and the *Discourse on the Origin of Inequality* (1755); and *The Social Contract* with a long, useful Introduction by Ernest Barker, editor, in *The Social Contract: Essays by Locke, Hume, and Rousseau*, published by the Oxford University Press, London, in 1948. Also helpful for background purposes is *The Confessions of Jean-Jacques Rousseau*, Modern Library edition, published by Random House, New York (no date). C. E. Vaughan, editor, has prepared useful introductions in English to the two volumes of *The Political Writings of Jean-Jacques Rousseau*, published by the Cambridge University Press, Cambridge, in 1915 and generally regarded as the authentic text for the political writings, in French. By Louis J. Courtois, *Chronologie Critique de la Vie et des Oeuvres de Jean-Jacques Rousseau*, printed as *Annales de la Société Jean-Jacques Rousseau*, Vol. XV, published in Geneva in 1923, is a detailed chronology of Rousseau's life and works and is very valuable for checking such matters. It has not been translated into English.

The outstanding study of Rousseau's educational thought is by William Boyd, *The Educational Theory of Jean-Jacques Rousseau*, published by Longmans, Green & Co., London, in 1911.

Although somewhat dated in its approach, worth consulting still is Gabriel Compayré, *Jean-Jacques Rousseau and Education from Nature*, translated by R. P. Jago, published by Thomas Y. Crowell & Co., New York, in 1907. By Charles W. Hendel, *Jean-Jacques Rousseau: Moralist*, in two volumes published by the Oxford University Press, New York and London, in 1934, contains a chapter on Rousseau's educational ideas in the second volume. William Henry Hudson's *Rousseau and Naturalism in Life and Thought*, published by T. & T. Clark, Edinburgh, in 1903, has a good critical chapter on *The New Héloïse* and a useful chapter on *Émile*. By Mordecai Grossman, *The Philosophy of Helvétius*, published by the Bureau of Publications, Teachers College, Columbia University, New York, in 1926, has an interesting chapter on "Diderot, Rousseau, and Helvétius." Alexander Meiklejohn's *Education Between Two Worlds*, published by Harper & Brothers, in 1942, devotes substantial portions to an unusual interpretation of Rousseau. There are, of course, many other sources.

🏵 THOMAS H. HUXLEY (1825–1895) was born in Ealing, England. Although his father was a schoolmaster, young Huxley received almost no schooling. At the age of seventeen he began regular medical studies at Charing Cross Hospital. Soon after graduating in 1845 he published his first scientific paper, which demonstrated the existence of a hitherto unrecognized layer in the inner sheath of hairs, known since as Huxley's layer. After passing the necessary examination he became a member of the Royal College of Surgeons and spent five years as a physician on various Navy ships. He wrote several scientific papers on the marine life he observed on his voyages. At the age of twenty-five Huxley was made a fellow in the Royal Society. He soon resigned from the Royal College of Surgeons to devote full time to scientific research. In 1854 he became lecturer in natural history in the Royal School of Mines. Following publication of Darwin's *Origin of Species* in 1859, Huxley worked to defend and popularize the new theory. Many of his essays on evolution are collected in *Man's Place in Nature*. Public duties increasingly drew him away from scientific research. From 1862 to 1884 he served on ten royal commissions; from 1871 to 1880 he was secretary to the Royal Society and from 1881 to 1885 was its president; from 1870 to 1872 he served on the newly constituted London School Board. His interest in the role of science in education and in methods of biology instruction was always active. He was responsible for the opening of the first laboratory for biology teaching in Britain; his system of instruction by types—representative organisms of different groups—was universally adopted. Many of his papers on these subjects are collected in *Science and Education*.

10

THE SCIENTIFIC HUMANIST: *Huxley*

BY CYRIL BIBBY

"Posthumous fame is not particularly attractive to me," T. H. Huxley told George Howell, the old Chartist, "but, if I am to be remembered at all, I would rather it should be as 'a man who did his best to help the people' than by any other title." This was the most distinguished scientist of the age, one who had refused lucrative invitations to Oxford and Harvard, had been Governor of Eton and Rector of Aberdeen, was given honorary degrees from universities all over the world, refused a peerage on principle but became a member of Her Majesty's Most Honourable Privy Council—but it was of his pioneer work on the London School Board, in devising a decent elementary education for the teeming street urchins of the great metropolis, that he said, "I am glad to think that, after all these years, I can look back upon that period of my life as perhaps the part of it least wasted."

These two remarks provide the dual keys to an understanding of Huxley's work in education: his passionate concern for the cultural emancipation of the common man; and his recognition that, in the modern world, bright ideas are pretty useless unless accompanied by slow, slogging, patient work through the official organs of the community. And, of course, there is the master key—his extraordinary clarity of thought and effectiveness in action and modernity of outlook.

It is strange that, in the standard histories of education, Huxley usually receives but passing mention, and even this often implies that all he did was to press for more science teaching. Every prospective pedagogue in England is taught about Newman and is usually required to swallow *The Idea of a University* in one large gulp. Everyone learns about Thomas Arnold's reformation of Rugby and about Matthew Arnold's *Culture and Anarchy*, about Kay-Shuttleworth's foundation of the first teachers' college and Herbert Spencer's essays on education. But about the educational ideas and work of Huxley, whose thinking ranged through the whole field of pedagogy and whose actual achievements ranged almost as widely, there is often a strange silence. Perhaps it is partly because he never gathered together his educational writings into a single small volume, easily kept in print and as easily prescribed for examination purposes. Partly, perhaps, it is because so many historians of English education seem to suffer from a fixation on the schools and universities favored by the wealthy few. Or it may be that historians in general tend not to look among scientists for views on general culture. But, whatever the reason for this earlier neglect of Huxley, recent studies have marked him out clearly as one of the most significant figures in the history of English education.

On May 4, 1825 when Huxley was born above a butcher's shop in the sleepy old village of Ealing, the total electorate of Great Britain was but a quarter of a million, Australia was largely a convict settlement, and the U. S. A. was a not very important underdeveloped land. The first railway line had not yet been brought into service, Faraday had not yet produced his electromagnetic current, nor Fox Talbot his photographs. Wilberforce was still trying to abolish slavery in the British Empire, and an Englishman might be hanged for any one of more than a hundred different crimes. There was nothing in England that could be called an educational system. Most children did not go to school at all and, of those who did, the majority merely picked up a few scraps of lettering and figuring at some deplorable dame establishment. The more fortunate members of the poorer classes attended charity schools or those of the voluntary societies, usually run on mass-production principles prohibitive of proper education. The middle classes had a few endowed schools, but many of these were sadly shriveled relics that had become mere sinecures for their masters. For the upper classes there were "public" schools, institutions in many ways primitive and crude, whose pupils not infrequently engaged in open rebellion. And, of course, there were the two dormant universities, Oxford still under the statutes of 1636 and Cambridge under those of 1570. Yet, astonishingly, the educational views of Thomas Henry Huxley, who grew up in these conditions and himself had but two childhood years at school—from the ages of eight to ten—are most relevant to the cultural problems of the space age.

What are these problems? They are, most obviously, those of adaptation to the technological outcomes of scientific advance. Less obviously, but more fundamentally, they are those of ideological and emotional adaptation to modern science. They are those of an age in which it is essential to avoid an ultimately fatal cultural dichotomy, in which we must concern ourselves with the education not of an elite but of the common man (and the common woman), in which the non-pink majority of mankind must work out educational procedures benefiting from the long experience of Europe but not slavishly imitating it. It is an age in which we must ensure that a proper concern for educational assessment does not degenerate into a mania for minute labeling of the human mind, in which we must produce innumerable specialists who will be more than mere technocrats, in which we must educate not only for work but also for hitherto undreamed-of leisure. And, above all, it is an age in which most major problems are, at rock bottom, problems of morality—individual morality, social morality, international morality—an age that must establish moral standards and devise a moral education independent of all dogma and capable of flourishing without authoritarian indoctrination.

Huxley was intensely aware of the complexity of the universe and suspicious of any easy assumption of scientific omniscience. This is why, in a letter to Herbert Spencer he jokingly (but seriously) criticized their mutual friend John Tyndall, thus: "In fact, a favourite problem of his is—Given the molecular forces in a mutton chop, deduce Hamlet or Faust therefrom. He is confident that the Physics of the Future will solve this easily." Nevertheless, few have ever had a firmer faith than Huxley in the power of science, the frontiers of which, he believed, would "receive such a remarkable extension as to leave little but cloud-land for its rival." In consequence, he made claims for scientific and technical education that seemed to many of his contemporaries extreme. He told the 1884 Select Committee on Education in Science and Art "that the whole theory on which our present educational system is based, is wrong from top to bottom; that the subjects which are now put down as essential . . . are luxuries, so to speak; and that those which are regarded as comparatively unessential and as luxuries are essential." Thus, he wanted not some minor curriculum reform but a complete curricular *bouleversement,* so that it would no longer be necessary to say, as he had said to schoolteachers at South Kensington in 1861, "The modern world is full of artillery; and we turn out our children to do battle in it, equipped with the shield and sword of an ancient gladiator." In a series of articles and addresses, and by his actions at various educational levels, he specified some of the equipment that was needed.

Most obviously, there was need for scientific knowledge as a matter of utility. Speaking to the working men of South London in 1868, Huxley urged:

If anyone is concerned in knowing the ordinary laws of mechanics one would think it is the hand labourer, whose daily toil lies among levers and pulleys; or among the other implements of artisan work. And if any one is interested in the laws of health, it is the poor workman, whose strength is wasted by ill-prepared food, whose health is sapped by bad ventilation and bad drainage, and half whose children are massacred by disorders which might be prevented.

As for the commercial and professional classes, he told a comfortable audience in Liverpool twelve months later, "There are hardly any of our trades, except the merely huckstering ones, in which some knowledge of science may not be directly profitable." And, after reference to the more obvious professions in need of scientific knowledge, such as engineering and medicine, he went on to point out that theology rests on certain theories about the order of the universe and to ask, "Why do not the clergy as a body acquire, as a part of their preliminary education, some tincture of physical science?"[1] In the same way he urged the manufacturing magnates of Birmingham to learn something of the physics and chemistry upon which their arts and manufactures depended. And in 1877 he even expressed the hope that "in the remote future, there shall be no member of the legislature who does not know as much of science as an elementary schoolboy."

Unlike his friend Herbert Spencer, however, Huxley had none of the naïveté so noticeable in the essay "What Knowledge is of Most Worth?" and he was under no delusion that scientific knowledge would of itself necessarily improve standards of individual or social conduct. For him the cultural outcome of science depended entirely on the manner and spirit in which it was taught. In 1867 when Dean Farrar was a little despondent about the slow progress of the movement for scientific education, Huxley cheered him up—but added, "Do not despair . . . you may depend on it victory is on your side—We or our sons shall live to see all the stupidity in favour of Science, and I am not sure that that will not be harder to bear than the present state of things." Despite his intense conviction of the power of science and the futility of theology, Huxley never quite lost the feeling, expressed in his very first public lecture in 1856, that "living nature is not a mechanism but a poem." And the great educational virtue of science was that, unlike most other subjects, it depended not upon words or books but upon bringing the pupil into direct contact with nature itself.

Huxley believed that "the whole of modern thought is steeped in science; it has made its way into the work of our best poets, and even the mere man of letters, who affects to ignore and despise science, is unconsciously impregnated with the spirit, and indebted for his best products to her methods," and this was why he never wearied of urging that science be placed at the very center of the educational system. He

---

[1] "Physical science" had at this time the wider connotation of "natural science."

was careful, however, to make it clear that when he spoke of the utility of science he was using neither of these words in a narrow sense. "I judge of the value of human pursuits by their bearing upon human interests; in other words by their utility," he said, but went on to explain that "knowledge of every kind is useful in proportion as it tends to give people right ideas. . . . and remove wrong ideas. . ." He added, "It is not only in the coarser, practical sense of the word 'utility,' but in this higher and broader sense, that I measure the value of a study." As for science, he told Charles Kingsley that by that term he meant:

. . . not mere physical science but all the results of exact methods of thought whatever be the subject matter to which they are applied. . . . people fancy that mathematics or physics or biology are exclusively "Science"— and value the clothes of science more than the goddess herself. . . . our science teaching will be imperfect until . . . social science is made one of the great topics of instruction in the country.

All should learn, he said:

. . . the natural laws of conduct, or the laws which govern the organization of society . . . teaching a boy his relations to society; the conditions of stable social organization, the natural basis of morality.

As he told Lord Farrer, however, the so-called sociology of the time was riddled with supposedly self-evident assumptions, which were as much an anachronism in the study of social life as they would be in hydrostatics, and what was needed was an objective examination of how human beings would in fact behave under different circumstances. The political economists had traced out the effects of one great cause of human action, the desire for wealth, and he believed that the same sort of thing should be done in the wider field of ethics. He said, "Settle the question of what will be done under the unchecked action of certain motives, and leave the problem of 'ought' for later consideration." In the meantime, until this new science of "eubiotics" had been constructed, he would have all children taught the facts of social existence that had ethical implications and the ethical principles that appeared to lead to communal well-being.

Moral education, for Huxley, was most essentially education in intellectual honesty. "The longer I live," he told Charles Kingsley in 1860, "the more obvious it is to me that the most sacred act of a man's life is to say and to feel 'I believe such and such to be true,'" and he once spoke to St. George Mivart of "the sin of faith." It was because he believed that the religious attitudes of his day were responsible for much intellectual dishonesty that he attacked them so vehemently. He wrote to the editor of *The Nineteenth Century*: "Great is humbug, and it will prevail unless the people who do not like it will hit hard. The beast has no brains, but you can knock the heart out of him."

He did not wish to interfere with the individual's religious observance —and, since his wife wanted to, he agreed to her having their children baptized "as a kind of spiritual vaccination without which the youngsters might catch Sin in worse forms as they grow up." He even once told Mivart, "Children should be brought up in the mythology of their own time and country," but added that "as they grow up their questions should be answered frankly." And, although he told the London School Board that it would not enter his head to teach morality by means of the Bible if he were dealing with an untouched population, he agreed to Bible-reading in the London schools since, he said, "Any system, to gain the attention of these people to these matters . . . must be a system connected with or not too widely divorced from their own system and beliefs."

Huxley had, indeed, a high regard for the "vast residuum of moral beauty and grandeur" in the Bible and he asked," By the study of what other book could children be so much humanised?" He pointed out that "what we find in the Bible is a plain-spokenness . . . which in many cases I think ought to be imitated at the present day with very considerable advantage to morality," and he referred with approval to "the good old Biblical word 'harlot.'" But reading the Bible was one thing, and misleading or proselytizing pupils was another, and Huxley's vigorous opposition to such activities might well be copied more widely today. A proposal for the payment of fees for children at church schools he castigated as "one for the outdoor relief of denominational education" and warned that "if such a scheme were carried out," he would "undertake to raise a discussion on the case of every child." He did not believe, however, that, despite all precautions, religion could really be taught in the schools impartially, and eventually declared that "the principle of strict secularity in State education is sound, and must ultimately prevail."

Toward the end of his life, in writing the introduction to his *Collected Essays*, Huxley referred to "the conviction which has grown with my growth and strengthened with my strength, that there is no alleviation for the sufferings of mankind except veracity of thought and action, and the resolute facing of the world as it is when the garment of make-believe by which pious hands have hidden its uglier features is stripped off." The pious hands, however, were not always those of priests. Much make-believe was the handiwork of sociologists, scientists, and educators, and Huxley was as insistent on honesty in these fields as in that of religion. "I wonder if you are going to take the line of showing up the superstitions of men of science," he once asked Kingsley before a Royal Institution lecture. "Their name is legion and the exploit would be a telling one."

Unlike many famous educators who are content (and, indeed, competent only) to enunciate general principles, while leaving it to the poor classroom teacher to solve all the problems of practice, Huxley frequently showed exactly how his proposals could be made to work in the ordinary school. It seemed to him to be "plainly dictated by common sense, that the teacher . . . should commence with the familiar facts of the scholar's daily existence and . . . lead the beginner, step by step, to the remoter objects and to the less readily comprehensible relations of things." He told the Liverpool Philomathic Society:

If scientific education is to be dealt with as mere book work, it will be better not to attempt it, but to stick to the Latin Grammar which makes no pretence to be anything but book work. . . . if scientific training is to yield its most eminent results, it must, I repeat, be made practical. . . . [a child] must handle the plants and dissect the flowers for himself. . . . Don't be satisfied with telling him that a magnet attracts iron. Let him see that it does; let him feel the pull of the one upon the other for himself.

Admittedly, he told an 1876 class of elementary schoolteachers at South Kensington, "There are difficulties in the way of a lot of boys making messes with slugs and snails . . . but there is a very convenient and handy animal which everybody has at hand, and that is himself," and he would make human biology an important feature of elementary teaching. A year later at Birmingham he pointed out:

The principal constituents of the skeleton and the changes of form of contracting muscles, may be felt through one's own skin: The beating of one's heart, and its connection with the pulse, may be noted: the influence of the valves of one's own veins may be shown; the movements of respiration may be observed.

He went on to outline the possibilities of an elementary study of the phenomena of sensation, of the constitutents of the blood, and to say that even "a cold, with its concomitant coughing and sneezing, may prove the sweet uses of adversity by helping one to a clear conception of what is meant by 'reflex action.'"

Yet, although he anticipated John Dewey in his advocacy of "learning through doing," Huxley differed from some modern proponents of "progressive education" by his insistence on the importance of a thorough and accurate teaching of fundamentals. "I am sure," he told a Select Committee of the House of Lords in 1865, "that the great aim should be to teach only so much science as can be taught thoroughly; and to ground in principles and methods rather than attempt to cover a large surface of details." As early as 1861 he had told a London gathering of teachers that "what you teach, unless you wish to be impostors, that you must first know"; Aberdeen University was told in 1874 of "detestable [science textbooks] which ought to have been burned by the hands of the common hangman"; the new university of Johns Hopkins was advised in 1876 that "there should not be too many subjects in the curriculum and . . . the aim should be the attainment of a thorough and sound knowledge of each." And, despite his doubts on the whole question of written examinations, Huxley told Sir Michael Foster, functioning as an assistant examiner on one occasion:

You did quite right in plucking all those fellows. I let off a few that you were doubtful about—but the great majority are slain. . . . Sending up such papers as these is a mere swindle.

It was in 1863 that Kingsley had complained about "the Isle of Tomtoddies, all heads and no bodies," where the children sang morning and evening to the great idol Examination. Nobody looking around Britain, where examination success became the criterion for entry into the civil service, for earning school grants from the government, and for scholarships and fellowships at the ancient universities, would have had much difficulty in identifying the island. As the years went by, the disadvantages of the system became more obvious, and in his 1874 Rectorial Address at Aberdeen, Huxley spoke of students who "work to pass, not to know; and outraged science takes her revenge." He concluded, "They do pass, and they don't know." Three years later at the Royal Society of Arts he declared, "The educational abomination of desolation of the day is the excessive stimulation of young people to work at high pressure by incessant competitive examinations"; and he deplored the destruction of youthful freshness by "precocious mental debauchery . . . book gluttony and lesson bibbing." In the conditions of his time, however, he saw no alternative to examinations for certain purposes, especially as the only practicable check to the sham teaching encouraged by the pernicious system of "payment by results," so he tried to make the check an effective one by insisting on meticulous care by the examiners of the Science and Art Department.

"It is commonly supposed that any one who knows a subject is competent to teach it; and no one seems to doubt that any one who knows a subject is competent to examine it," Huxley pointed out at Aberdeen. "I believe both these opinions to be serious mistakes." Examining he held to be an art, and a difficult one, which, like any other art, had to be learned. He complained of the tendency to set questions that were too difficult, which was like trying to assess the relative physical strength of a group of young men by asking each to swing a hundredweight. "You must give them half a hundredweight, and see how they maneuver that," he insisted; examination questions should be easy enough to let reason, memory, and method have full play. "It is important," he advised Johns Hopkins University, "not so much to know a thing, as to have known it"; he therefore advocated the system practiced in his own college at South Kensington, which examined the student on the conclusion of each course and then allowed him to concentrate his attention on the next course. He was opposed to any rigid examination for the admission of students to institutions of higher learning, because although most of the candidates would reach the required standard as a matter of mere expediency, "very possibly the odd tenth may contain persons of defective education, but of a native vigour which makes them more worth having than all the other nine-tenths, and I would not lose them for any consideration."

Huxley believed that much mental talent lay undiscovered and unused among the common people of England and did his best to see that this state of things should not continue. When *Vanity Fair*, on January 28, 1871, printed a profile of Professor Huxley to accompany the cartoon by "Ape," it summarized its account with the comment, "Take him for intellect." The epithet "popular" was not one of which Huxley was afraid. He was, H. L. Mencken judged, "perhaps the greatest virtuoso of plain English who has ever lived," and this clarity of communication he gladly put at the service of his fellow citizens. In the five furious years following the publication of Darwin's *Origin of Species*, Huxley largely concentrated his extrascientific activities on the task of liberating the common man from the bonds of traditional beliefs about the origins of the world and its inhabitants. Then, as England engaged in the organization of a national system of education, over two decades he issued a stream of articles and lectures on the pedagogy of science, the planning of school curriculums and school systems, female education, liberal and technical education, the professional preparation of teachers and physicians, the nature of university education, and other topics on which he deemed it desirable to clarify public attitudes or arouse public opinion. Finally, in the last ten years of his life, he sought to satisfy the sharpening appetite of an increasingly literate population for guidance in matters of philosophy, theology, and public affairs.

For Huxley, popularization was not a matter merely of educating the workers—indeed, in many matters he regarded the artisan as less in need of instruction than the aristocrat. He also believed that the lower classes were more receptive to new knowledge than were their social superiors, which was why he once said to Hooker, "The English nation will not take science from above, so it must get it from below—We the doctors, who know what is good for it, if we cannot get it to take pills, must administer our remedies *par derrière*." For the popular education of the upper and middle classes, the Royal Institution in the West End and the Literary and Philosophical Societies of the provincial cities provided the force; for the office workers of the City, the London Institution; for other sections of the public, the lecture rooms of the Zoological Gardens or of the School of Science at Jermyn Street. As to the popular printed word, Huxley ranged from *The Quarterly Review* and *The Fortnightly* and *The Twentieth Century* for the comparatively sophisticated, through *Macmillan's* for the respectable family reader and *The Contemporary* for the liberal Christian, to obscure minority magazines like *Youth's Companion*. When one adds his popular little books—the thirty printings of Elementary Physiology in as many years, the 10,000 copies of *Coral and Coral Reefs* sold out on publication, the run on the shops for *Physiography*, the translations into Russian, French, German, Polish, Hungarian, and so on—one must conclude that in England there has never been another popularizer so potent.

The case for the universal provision of full educational facilities does not depend, as apparently supposed by some opponents of the testing of intelligence and temperament, upon any assumption that all men are mentally equal or that everyone is capable of the highest intellectual endeavor. Huxley perhaps exaggerated when he told a meeting of Working Men's Clubs, "The great mass of mankind have neither the liking, nor the aptitude, for either literary, or scientific, or artistic pursuits; nor, indeed, for excellence of any sort"; but such a statement at least has the advantage of clearing a great deal of sentimental nonsense out of the way of rational discussion. Nevertheless, to recognize individual variation, and to cater to it fully, is quite different from supposing that whole categories of people are capable or incapable of this or that particular excellence. It was his complete recognition of this fact that marked Huxley off from his many contemporaries who pressed only for adequate educational facilities for the emerging middle classes (and, usually, for the male members of those classes).

A newborn infant, he once remarked, does not come into the world labeled scavenger or shopkeeper or bishop or duke, but comes as a mass of red pulp much like another, and it is only by giving each child a decent education that we can discover its capabilities. And, as he told a Marylebone meeting, he did not believe that "if 100 men were picked out of the highest aristocracy in the land and 100 out of the lowest

class there would be any difference of capacity among them," nor was
he at all worried by the prospect that the workers might emerge into
positions of power. "Compare your average artisan and your average
country squire," he suggested in 1868, "and I don't believe you will find
a pin to choose between the two in point of ignorance, class feeling, or
prejudice. . . . Why should we be worse off under one régime than
under the other?"

It was this belief in a vast reservoir of untapped ability which led
Huxley to devote so much of his time and energy to the promotion
of working class education. "I believe in the fustian, and can talk better
to it than to any amount of gauze and Saxony," he told a friend. So,
while sometimes rejecting invitations from comfortable dilettante clubs
like that of Leamington, he traveled up and down the land to speak to
artisan audiences in South Wales and the industrial areas of the Mid-
lands and Lancashire and Yorkshire. In a life of incredible busyness, he
was not always able to accept invitations to honorific lectures but he
could find time to help F. D. Maurice by speaking occasionally at the
Working Men's College. And, south of the Thames, he found time to
act as principal of his own South London Working Men's College.
William Rossiter, a self-educated portmanteau worker, did most of the
donkey work, but for twelve years Huxley gave important help and
advice, especially in securing the services of distinguished lecturers like
Palgrave and Morley and Moncure Conway. It was here that Huxley
delivered his famous address on "A Liberal Education and Where to
Find It," and it is to this workingmen's college that we can trace the
origin of the South London Art Gallery, the Camberwell School of Arts
and Crafts, and several of the free libraries of South London.

Although never in any doubt about the educational potential of the
workers, Huxley did doubt whether in most fields women were likely, on
the average, to match the attainments of men. For this he has sometimes been considered as halfhearted in the battle for sexual equality,
but it may rather be that he was more capable than most of recognizing
unwelcome facts even when engaged in partisan combat. Certainly, he
considered that some of the pioneers of female education were blinding
themselves to the distinctions of biological function between men and
women, and he once told Benjamin Jowett that "no witness is so dishonest as a really good woman with a cause to serve." But such reserva-
tions could not warrant the blatant injustices to which women were subjected, and we find Huxley supporting Emily Davies in the foundation
of Girton College, helping Maria Grey to promote the National Society
for the Improvement of Women's Education, taking the chair at a
public meeting that led to the establishment of the South Hampstead

High School for Girls, serving on the education committee of the Princess Helena College for Girls at Ealing, and petitioning Cambridge University to open its degrees to women. When Elizabeth Garrett (Anderson) found the doors of all medical schools closed against her, Huxley gave her admission to his classes at South Kensington, and much later he acted for many years as a Governor of the London Medical School for Women.

In 1860 Huxley told Sir Charles Lyell that nine-tenths of the women at that time were sunk in ignorant parsonese superstition, and that no permanent advancement could come until the female half of the human race had been emancipated. This was the great theme of his 1865 essay "Emancipation—Black and White" in which he declared:

With few insignificant exceptions, girls have been educated either to be drudges, or toys, beneath man; or a sort of angels above him . . . The possibility that the ideal of woman-kind lies neither in the fair saint, nor in the fair sinner . . . that women are meant neither to be man's guides nor their playthings, but their comrades, their fellows, and their equals, so far as Nature puts no bar on that equality, does not seem to have entered into the minds of those who have had the conduct of the education of girls.

So far as his own daughters were concerned, he told Lyell, "They at any rate shall not be got up as mantraps for the matrimonial market," and he gave a very clear answer to those who asked what should be the nation's policy:

We reply, emancipate girls. Recognise the fact that they share the senses, perceptions, feelings, reasoning powers, emotions, of boys, and that the mind of the average girl is less different from that of the average boy, than the mind of one boy is from that of another . . . Let us have "sweet girl graduates" by all means. They will be none the less sweet for a little wisdom; and the "golden hair" will not curl less gracefully outside the head by reason of there being brains within.

This recognition of the distinction between the mean measures of the capabilities of two groups and the variance within the groups, combined with a full appreciation of the power of the material and social environment to promote or stultify mental development, helped Huxley also to a rational view of the cultural potential of non-European peoples. As a young man he had shared the common prejudice against the Negroid peoples, at least to the extent of believing them in general to have lower intellectual potential than the Caucasoids. However, while supporting the cause of the American North in the Civil War and serving on the committee which sought the prosecution of Governor Eyre of Jamaica for the pseudojudicial murder of a colored agitator, he examined the ethnological evidence for himself and became satisfied that there was no biological basis for prejudices of this kind. So, when he spoke in Birmingham in 1867 on "The Character, Distribution, and Origin of the Principal Modifications of Mankind," he pointed out that he was "very careful not to use races, species, varieties, or any such phrases; for all those words were simply theories and hypotheses." The English, he reminded his audience, would have seemed to the Romans two thousand years ago as uncivilized as the natives of New Zealand appeared in the nineteenth century to Englishmen, and one could not assume that such primitive peoples were incapable of advancement. Miscegenation, he remarked, depended as to its results on its social setting, and need not be damaging. As for physical characteristics, he informed the Mayor and other civic dignitaries present in that respectable assemblage that in some respects the European peoples were more similar to the apes than the Negroes were. Such views no doubt helped Huxley in his work as one of the Governors of that fascinating educational experiment, the International College at Isleworth, which after its opening in 1867 included among its students Germans, Spaniards, Portuguese, French, Indians, North Americans, Brazilians, Chileans, Nicaraguans, and a Negro from Bermuda, "a giant of a fellow."

This same suspicion of neat categories and of problem-begging terminology stopped Huxley from swallowing the "faculty psychology," which still survived until quite recently in certain educational circles. In 1878 he wrote:

In the language of common life, the "mind" is spoken of as an entity, independent of the body, though resident in and closely connected with it, and endowed with numerous "faculties" . . . Very little attention to what passes in the mind is sufficient to show, that these conceptions involve assumptions of an extremely hypothetical character. And the first business of the student of psychology is to get rid of such prepossessions.

For Huxley the word "mind" was merely a convenient expression denoting the aspects of human functioning commonly called "mental," and he knew of no evidence that it was in itself an entity. He was in no doubt that the minds of some individuals were superior to those of others, but was suspicious of easy assumptions about lack of educability. "Stupidity," he believed, "in nine cases out of ten, *fit non nascitur,* and is developed by a long process of parental and pedagogic repression of the natural intellectual appetites, accompanied by a persistent attempt to create artificial ones for food which is not only tasteless, but essentially indigestible."

It was the belief that ordinary children were quite capable of considerable cultural advance that fortified Huxley in his brief but immensely important work on the first London School Board. During the first half of the nineteenth century, England had fallen badly behind Germany and France in the provision of elementary schools, and as late as 1861 the Newcastle Commission had been able to report that "none are too old, too poor, too ignorant, too feeble, too sickly, too unqualified in one or every way" to take up teaching. Dissension between the churches had long delayed any effective national action to educate the nation's children, and even Forster's Education Act of 1870 was but a patched-up compromise. Nevertheless, it held out the possibility of providing schools for those who had none, and Huxley was determined to make it work effectively. His *Contemporary Review* essay, "The School Boards: What They Can Do and What They May Do," was judiciously leaked just before the election of the School Board for London and made a great public impression. Not surprisingly, he advocated the teaching of science, but first he put physical education (for the Board schools were to cater to the dirty and undisciplined street arabs of the sprawling metropolis) and domestic science (for both girls and boys) and training in the elementary laws of conduct and social responsibility.

The various sects, each determined to secure as many seats as possible, put enormous effort into the London School Board elections, and the chances for Huxley, whose name was already anathema to the orthodox, could not have seemed very high. Nor did he improve things by choosing as fellow candidate a radical carpenter who had signed a manifesto calling on the French workers to join with the English in united action against "the cajolery and brute force of the so-called rulers"; nor perhaps by telling a comfortable audience that "no breeder would bring up his pigs under such conditions as those to which the poorer classes of England were now subjected." Only those who paid rates had the vote and, as Huxley commented in his printed election address, "It seems to be the fashion for Candidates to assure you that they will do their best to spare the poverty of the Ratepayers." But, he went on, "It is proper, therefore, for me to add that I can give you no such assurance . . . my vote will be given for that expenditure which can be shown to be just and necessary, without any reference to the question whether it may raise the rate a halfpenny." Elected despite all this, he then proceeded at the first Board meeting to oppose one suggestion to pay the chairman a salary and another to open Board meetings with a brief prayer. It is an astonishing tribute to the power and charm of his personality that, at its second meeting, a Board consisting predominantly of denominational representatives appointed him Chairman of its all-important Scheme of Education Committee.

Starting from scratch, Huxley's Committee devised the administrative scheme of Infant Schools, Junior Schools, and Senior Schools that was to be copied the country over and provide the pattern of English elementary education for three-quarters of a century to come. It was a speech of his which provided the figure, soon to pass into common parlance, of "a great educational ladder, the bottom of which shall be the gutter, and the top of which shall be [the] Universities." His protests that "that which was originally the birthright of the poor has been converted into a mess of pottage for distribution among the dependents of the rich" led to an inquiry aimed at the better use of the great educational endowments of London. When there were objections to the teaching of music to the little ragamuffins of London, he got his way by insisting that this was "one of the most civilising and enlightening influences which a child can be brought under"; the frequent use of corporal punishment he castigated as a mark of incompetence, and rules were adopted to limit it; and it was on his proposal that the Board started inquiries into the best method of teaching and the training of teachers.

It seems incredible that all this was accomplished in little more than a year, after which Huxley's health broke down from overwork. The manifold accomplishments do honor not only to Huxley but also to his clerical fellow members, who were men big enough to collaborate with this agnostic tornado of energy that had appeared among them. The achievement can also be an encouragement to all who wish to believe in the power of sheer goodness. Benjamin Waugh was not the only clergyman who, despite initial hostility to Huxley:

. . . was drawn to him most, and was influenced by him most, because of his attitude to a child. He was on the Board to establish schools for children. His motive in every argument, in all the fun and ridicule he indulged in, and in his occasional anger, was the child. He resented the idea that schools were to train either congregations for churches or hands for factories. He was on the Board as a friend of children.

By temperament the most independent of men, Huxley yet recognized that a considerable measure of governmental intervention would be necessary if the nation were to have the educational system it needed. The extreme individualism of the age he regarded as "merely reasoned savagery, utter and unmitigated selfishness incompatible with social existence," and he declared that he would be ashamed to accept all the benefits of society and then object to paying a contribution toward the education of other people's children. Nor, with his intimate knowledge of the workings of the Science and Art Department, would he accept the idea that governmental undertakings were necessarily inefficient. He pointed out:

The State lives in a glass house. We see what it tries to do, and all its failures, partial or total, are made the most of. But private enterprise is sheltered under good opaque bricks and mortar. The public rarely knows what it tries to do, and only hears of failures when they are gross and patent to all the world.

By its 1944 Education Act, Britain adopted almost precisely the balance of power between a central Ministry of Education and local educational bodies that Huxley had advocated exactly sixty years earlier, in presenting evidence to a Select Committee of the House of Commons. There should be, he testified, "a sagacious and influential Minister, with a seat in the Cabinet, enabling him to give the greatest force to his views which a Minister can give." This minister's business would be "not to interfere and reduce the whole educational system of the country to one dead level, but to correct abuses"; he would be "very unwise if he attempted to meddle with the special regulations of each school because they very often depend upon all sorts of local conditions." Nevertheless, he knew that freedom might be interpreted by some local educational bodies as freedom to do nothing, so the Minister should "by distinct regulation occasionally, if necessary, force upon these bodies, if they would not initiate it voluntarily, a modification of their educational system in the desired direction." In the meantime, until there should be such a ministry, he was prepared to exercise pressure through any other channel that might present itself. A few months after he became a governor of Eton, he secured agreement to the building of a new science block there. After beating the "Cock o' the North" (the Marquis of Huntly) at his own gates in an election in which the atmosphere was thick with *odium theologicum*, he managed as Lord Rector of Aberdeen University to let in great gusts of fresh air that eventually swept the cobwebs right out of the window. As a member of various royal and other commissions he exercised gentle (and not always so gentle) compression on all sorts of resistant bodies. By placing his protégés in influential posts in Britain and abroad he started many an educational institution along new paths. In a speech in Manchester he commented:

There is a well-worn adage that those who set out on a great enterprise would do well to count the cost. I am not sure that this is always true. I think that some of the very greatest enterprises in this world have been carried out successfully simply because the people who undertook them did not count the cost.

It was not, however, with intentions of great enterprise that Huxley had gone in 1854 as half-time lecturer in paleontology to the new School of Mines in Jermyn Street. The simple fact was that, having been struck off the Navy List for repeated refusal to accept a posting until the Admiralty should provide some money to publish his researches, he was glad of £100 a year to provide his daily bread. But, once there, and before long given a full-time post, he moved into a position of power with quite mystifying speed. In his second session he was already regarded as indispensable by Sir Roderick Murchison, the director, who lamented Huxley's departure on a field trip to Scotland. "How we are to get the whole machine in the right working order is not yet quite clear to me," he wrote to Huxley. "If you were present all would go right." By 1858 Huxley felt able to say to a friend, "To speak nautically, I have been there long enough to 'know the ropes'—and I shall take pleasure in working the place into what I think it ought to be." A year later he was arranging for the Chair of Physics to be offered to his educational ally John Tyndall; a year after that he was recasting the School's entire prospectus; one more year and he was deputed to join with two of the senior professors to consider the type of certificate to be awarded to successful students.

In 1861, when a Commission was set up under Lord Granville to recommend what the future of the School should be, Huxley and Sir W. W. Smyth were asked to report on the Commission's proposals— but one may doubt whether Smyth was aware that Huxley had already given Granville his own personal views in a long personal letter of seven foolscap pages. Seven years later, when a second Commission made inquiry, Huxley not only gave evidence recommending a vast improvement in staffing and facilities, but—presumably by a well-timed piece of string-pulling—a complaint about the inadequacy of his own laboratory was aired in Parliament at just the right moment. When the third inquiry, by the Duke of Devonshire's Commission, took place in 1870, Huxley (although still junior to several members of the teaching staff) found himself in the comfortable position of serving as a commissioner and questioning his superiors. The Director and most of the senior professors combined in a memorial recommending that the school remain specifically one of mining, but by this time no one was much surprised when the Commission reported in favor of what *The Times* called "Professor Huxley's plan for founding an imposing National College of Science" at South Kensington. In 1872 the great move got under way, and by 1880 Huxley was Dean of the Normal School of Science, shortly to become the Royal College of Science, and eventually the great Imperial College of Science and Technology.

Nothing in the way of wealth, family influence, or formal position exists to explain how Huxley did it. Why a very junior member of staff became immediately so influential, how he succeeded in the face of opposition from men of high academic and social standing, must be a mystery to any one who has not studied the details of his methods. And any modern educator who wishes to learn the art of overcoming official inertia might do worse than make such a study. When one follows the ways in which, sometimes by private lobbying and sometimes by public campaigning, now by dull plodding committee work and now by the exercise of personal charm, he succeeded so often in moving matters in the direction he desired, one is forced to agree with William Irving that as a political operative Huxley was devastatingly efficient. He had, indeed, "more talents than two lifetimes could have developed." Irving said, "He could think, draw, speak, write, inspire, lead, negotiate and wage multifarious war against earth and heaven with the cool professional ease of an acrobat supporting nine people on his shoulders at once." These talents brought him several invitations to important posts at ancient universities at home and wealthy ones abroad, but he refused them all. One suspects that he not only hated the humbug and cant of academic snobbery but positively enjoyed being outside the educational "establishment." It must, indeed, have been gratifying for a man who had received no schooling worth speaking of and had no university degree (apart from all the honorary ones that came his way) to be able to sit tight in his own South Kensington College and simply let the world of learning come to him. Certainly he seems never to have been bothered because his college was without university status or because a technical college was (as it still is in England) widely regarded as a somewhat inferior type of institution. Indeed, he often made it clear that he had little regard for the commonly accepted sharp distinction between technical education and professional education or even for the distinction between these and a "liberal" education.

The nineteenth-century debate about the nature of technical education was not an abstract one of terminology, but rather a real cleavage between those who wanted merely to train the workers' children to be more efficient workmen and those who wanted to develop their full potentialities as individual human beings. As Huxley put it to his South London Working Men's College in 1868:

The politicians tell us "You must educate the masses because they are going to be masters." The clergy join in the cry for education, for they affirm that the people are drifting away from church and chapel into the broadest infidelity. The manufacturers and the capitalists swell the chorus lustily. They declare that ignorance makes bad workmen; that England will soon be unable to turn out cotton goods, or steam engines, cheaper than other people; and then, Ichabod! Ichabod! the glory will be departed from us.

And a few voices are lifted up in favour of the doctrine that the masses should be educated because they are men and women with unlimited capacity of being, doing, and suffering, and that it is as true now, as ever it was, that the people perish for lack of knowledge.

Of these few voices, perhaps none was more influential than that of Huxley.

He was not willing for the worker's child to be fobbed off by narrowly vocational instruction, nor did he believe that even from a purely commercial point of view this would be successful. "It was a great thing to make good workmen," he remarked, "yet it was much more important to make intelligent men." He considered it a profound and mischievous mistake to believe that vocational instruction alone could lead to even the material flourishing of society, for "the savage of civilisation is a more dangerous animal than any other wild beast; and . . . sooner or later every social organization in which these *ferae* accumulate unduly, will be torn to pieces by them." A comprehensive scheme of technical education, therefore, should cover all those means by which the productive capacity of a population may be fully and permanently developed, so "that our people will not only have the knowledge and the skill which are required, but that they shall have the will and the energy and the honesty, without which neither knowledge nor skill can be of any permanent avail."

It was this high view of technical education, combined with his innocence of academic snobbery, that led Huxley to describe medicine, law, and theology as "technical specialities." For him there was no fundamental distinction between the function of a physician and that of a factory worker; each was a worthy occupation if well done and each unworthy if neglected or botched. Whether their futures lay in the surgery or the sewingroom or the steelworks, people needed, first of all, an education for their whole persons; and, that priority well provided, they needed to be really expert at whatever they claimed as their special skills. It is this specification of dual fundamentals that explains what might otherwise appear to be a contradiction in Huxley's views on technical and professional education: on the one hand he insisted on liberality of learning; on the other he urged the ruthless excision of curricular deadwood. "Practice can be learned only by practice," he told the Easingwold Agricultural Club. "The farmer must be made by and through farm work." Similarly he told University College Medical School that he would remove most of the botany and zoology and comparative anatomy from the medical curriculum, would retain physics and chemistry only in their relation to medicine—and, as for *materia medica*, he said: "I cannot understand the arguments for obliging a medical man to know all about drugs and where they come from. Why not make him belong to the Iron and Steel Institute, and learn something about cutlery, because he uses knives?"

It was a similar concern for professional competence, as much as his dislike of clerical control, that led Huxley to write to Sir Henry Roscoe so harshly about the sectarian training colleges for teachers: "Half the time of their students is occupied with grinding into their minds their tweedle-dum and tweedle-dee theological idiocies, and the other half in cramming them with boluses of other things to be duly spat out on examination day." Himself a teacher to his finger tips, Huxley was vividly aware of the difficulties of the educational process. "Teaching in England," he complained to the 1868 Select Committee on Scientific Instruction, "is pretty much a matter of chance, and the mass of the people are ignorant of the fact that there is such a thing as a scientific method in teaching." Fifteen years later he was still pressing the same point in Liverpool:

There are a great many people who imagine that elementary teaching might be properly carried out by teachers provided with only elementary knowledge. Let me assure you that that is the profoundest mistake in the world. There is nothing so difficult to do as to write a good elementary book, and there is nobody so hard to teach properly and well as people who know nothing about a subject.

It is sad to reflect that, if he were alive today, he would still find it necessary to press this fundamental point.

Naturally enough, Huxley encouraged teachers to take a properly professional view of their calling, and he found time to support the recently founded College of Preceptors, to pay visits to training colleges, to speak on behalf of the Teachers' Training and Registration Society, to serve as President of the National Association of Science Teachers, to advise on syllabuses in domestic science, and to promote a scheme for teaching teachers the laws of health. At his own South Kensington College (named "The Normal School of Science" on the model of the French *Ecole Normale*) he taught prospective teachers during the term and practicing teachers during vacations—and, when doubts were expressed about the practicability of some of his suggestions, the great professor was not too great to take up the challenge by giving a series of lessons, himself, to a class of children from the slums of London's East End.

Over the country as a whole, a great influence was exerted by the conferences and examinations on technical education conducted by the

Royal Society of Arts, and it is not surprising to find Huxley's name cropping up fairly frequently in this connection. Nor is it surprising that during the 1870s he did a good deal to persuade the City Companies to devote some of their great wealth to this cause; nor that, having obtained agreement to the principle, he provided detailed plans and memoranda indicating how the money could be most effectively spent. Huxley allowed the sluggards no rest. He wrote to a friend: "You may depend upon it, I shall lose no chance of striking a blow for the cause. The animal is moving and by a judicious exhibition of carrots in front and kicks behind, we shall get him into a fine trot presently." The trot produced both the Finsbury Technical College and the City and Guilds College at South Kensington, and one of its leading members later declared that Huxley had been "really the engineer of the City and Guilds Institute; for without his advice we should not have known what to have done." When Huxley came to deliver his Presidential Address to the Royal Society in 1885, he was able to announce that the Institute had already affiliated some 250 technical classes scattered throughout the kingdom.

Two years later, the Prince of Wales suggested that Queen Victoria's Jubilee might be worthily marked by the foundation of an imperial industrial institution in London, and soon the air was filled with the cannonades of a rip-roaring controversy about the form the foundation should take. At the request of the Prince, Huxley agreed to be one of the speakers at a great inaugural city meeting of which *The Pall Mall Gazette* wrote, "With the exception of Professor Huxley, whose interesting speech we give in full elsewhere, everybody was dull, stale, and unprofitable." But, although Huxley caught the general imagination with his vision of "a place in which the fullest stores of industrial knowledge would be made accessible to the public; in which the higher questions of commerce and industry would be systematically studied and elucidated; and where, as in an industrial university, the whole technical education of the country might find its centre and crown," the vision faded when it was decided to place the Imperial Institute out at South Kensington instead of, as Huxley urged, at the very hub of the nation's commerce in the City of London. The Institute, and its successor the Commonwealth Institute, have done valuable work, but Britain is still without anything corresponding to the great industrial academy for which Huxley had hoped.

He wrote to Ray Lankester: "The modern university looks forward, and is a factory of new knowledge: its professors have to be at the top of the wave of progress. Research and criticism must be the breath of their nostrils." Yet, devoted as he was to the advancement of knowledge,

Huxley had little sympathy with those university lecturers who wished to be concerned only with research or who regarded their teaching duties as an unfortunate distraction from more important things. "I do not think that it is any impediment to an original investigator to have to devote a moderate portion of his time to lecturing, or superintending practical instruction," he told Aberdeen University. "On the contrary, I think it may be, and often is, a benefit to be obliged to take a comprehensive survey of your subject; or to bring your results to a point." His own teaching he took most seriously, and many of his students have left testimony of his effectiveness. One wrote: "As a class lecturer, Huxley was *facile princeps*, and only those who were privileged to sit under him can form a conception of their delivery. Clear, deliberate, never hesitant or unduly emphatic, never repetitional, always logical, his every word told." Another remembers "that rich fund of humour ever ready to swell forth when occasion permitted." And H. G. Wells has testified: "That year I spent in Huxley's class was, beyond all question, the most educational year in my life. It left me under that urgency for coherence and consistency, that repugnance from haphazard assumptions and arbitrary statements, which is the essential distinction of the educated from the uneducated mind." Others have related how, in the laboratory, Huxley urged his students to independence of observation and delightedly encouraged each sign of initiative; he would have little patience with those professors today who seem to consider it below their dignity to teach elementary classes.

The Oxford and Cambridge of his younger days Huxley once described as "half clerical seminaries, half racecourses, where men are trained to win a senior wranglership, or a double first, as horses are trained to win a cup," and he spoke ironically of "the host of pleasant, moneyed, well-bred young gentlemen, who do a little learning and much boating by Cam and Isis." But after the middle of the century things began to change, and it seemed worthwhile to support good men like Michael Foster at Cambridge and Ray Lankester at Oxford. Huxley advised Jowett in the promotion of scientific and medical education at Oxford, and at both universities he was in repeated demand as an assessor for the award of fellowships or the appointment of professors. He was one of those who managed to secure the establishment of a Final Honours School of English and a new chair of English Literature at Oxford, and it is interesting that he was a much more vigorous advocate of this reform than his literary friend Matthew Arnold. In 1874 he had told John Tyndall, "It is as well for me that I expect nothing from Oxford and Cambridge, having burned my ships as far as they were concerned long ago," but in fact each recognized him by an honorary doctorate and by invitation to an honorific lectureship. Oxford went further and tried to entice him first to a professorship and then to the headship of a college. But, as he explained to his son Leonard, "I do not think I am cut out for a Don nor your mother for a Donness," and at South Kensington he stayed for the rest of his working life.

As a young man, he had naturally been tempted by suggestions that he might allow his name to go forward for the Regius Chair of Natural History at Edinburgh, which promised £1,000 a year against the meagre £200 he was earning. But, as he told a friend, "I dread leaving London and its freedom—its Bedouin sort of life—for Edinburgh and no whistling on Sundays." His refusal did not prevent the University from making him an honorary Doctor of Laws, and later the Home Secretary asked his advice about the best nomination for the professorship from which he had himself recoiled. Later, as Visiting Professor at Edinburgh, as Rector of Aberdeen, and as a member of the Royal Commission on the Universities of Scotland, Huxley was able to do a good deal to bring the universities of the Northern Kingdom into the modern world. Similarly, as a Governor of London's secular University College, by lectures at the Birkbeck Institution, which grew into Birkbeck College, by helping to found the People's Palace, which was the parent of Queen Mary College in the East End, and by so unifying the discordant desires of the capital's many institutions of higher learning as to permit the emergence of the great federal University of London, he did much to promote the university life of the metropolis. As a member of two Commissions of Education in Ireland he had his influence on University development in the Western Kingdom; as a Governor of Owens College in Manchester he influenced provincial university development; Johns Hopkins and Princeton and the University of Minnesota in the United States benefited from his ideas—and, of course, Harvard tried to get him in person. He was asked: "Now is it any use to make any kind of proposition to you? . . . We could offer you say $10,000 a year for the benefit of your presence and influence."

Huxley's idea of a university was in some respects far different from that of many of his contemporaries, for he had no background of Eton or Winchester and Oxford or Cambridge to blinker his vision. While others sought to open the universities to the middle classes, he was concerned with entrance for "the sons of the masses of the people whose daily labour just suffices to meet their daily wants." While Newman at his Catholic university was thankful for the style of youths he had got— the French Vicomte, the Irish Baronet, and the English Lord—Huxley congratulated Aberdeen on not becoming "a school of manners for the rich; of sports for the athletic; or a hot-bed of high-fed, hypercritical refinement." Yet, in more important ways Huxley and Newman had much in common. Each had a passionate regard for truth and each was contemptuous of all merely human authority. They were similar, too, in the universality of their respect for learning and in the somewhat puritanical tinge of their morality. Of the two, it is not immediately obvious from internal evidence that it was Huxley who described a university in these terms:

In an ideal university, as I conceive it, a man should be able to obtain instruction in all forms of knowledge, and discipline in the use of all methods by which knowledge is obtained. In such a University, the force of living example should fire the students with a noble ambition to emulate the learning of learned men, and to follow in the footsteps of the explorers of new fields of knowledge. And the very air he breathes should be charged with that enthusiasm for truth, that fanaticism of veracity, which is a greater possession than much learning; a nobler gift than the power of increasing knowledge; by so much greater and nobler than these, as the moral nature of men is greater than the intellectual; for veracity is the heart of morality.

Both men, too, took the traditional view of the university as a place for teaching universal knowledge, a view well expressed by Huxley at the opening of Baltimore's new foundation in 1876:

University education should not be something distinct from elementary education, but should be the natural outgrowth and development of the latter . . . the university need cover no ground foreign to that occupied by the elementary school. Indeed, it cannot; for the elementary instruction which I have referred to embraces all the kinds of real knowledge and mental activity possible to man. The university can add no new departments of knowledge, can offer no new fields of mental activity; but what it can do is to intensify and specialize the instruction in each department . . . The primary school and the university are the alpha and the omega of education.

Everyone knows that Huxley did much to secure the full recognition and development of science teaching in the universities, but he was vividly aware of the dangers of narrow specialization in that as in other directions. "An exclusively scientific training will bring about a mental twist as surely as an exclusively literary training," he commented at the opening of Mason College in Birmingham. "The value of the cargo does not compensate for a ship's being out of trim." Similarly, at the opening of the new medical school of Owens College in Manchester, he urged that the importance of the arts faculty should never be diminished. He added, "Unless we are led to see that we are citizens and men before anything else, I say it will go very badly with men of science in future generations, and they will run the risk of becoming scientific pedants when they should be men, philosophers, and good citizens." But he considered that there was a good deal of cant in much of the current one-sided talk of culture, and he argued that "a man who knows no language but his own, but has had a thorough training in medicine and its ancillary branches of knowledge, has had a more truly liberal education than the high classic who is devoid of any tincture of scientific culture." Nearly a century before C. P. Snow hit the headlines with his talk of "the two cultures," Huxley had made much the same point to the Senate of London University:

The possessor of a Scientific degree ought not I think to be ignorant of the existence of Cromwell and of his general significance in English History— though I think it would be most unreasonable to require him to have read Mr. Carlyle's edition of Cromwell's letters and speeches . . . It would be as great scandal that any person possessing a University degree in Arts should be ignorant of the law of gravitation, or of the chemical fact that air is not an element . . . or of the circulation of blood in his own body.

He thought, however, not in terms of two cultures, but of a many-sided culture. At Aberdeen he declared: "The man who is all morality and intellect, although he may be good and even great, is, after all, only half a man. There is beauty in the moral world and in the intellectual world; but there is also a beauty which is neither moral nor intellectual—the beauty of the world of Art." And he asked: "If there are doctors of music, why should there be no masters of painting, of sculpture, of architecture? I should like to see professors of fine arts in every university."

Huxley was not content to enunciate generalities without indicating how they could become reality. First, he suggested that in the organization of a university great care be taken to avoid placing some professors in positions of permanent power, for, he warned: "The besetting sin of able men is impatience of contradiction and criticism. Even those who do their best to resist the temptation, yield to it almost unconsciously and become the tools of toadies and flatterers." Second, he considered that the governing body of a university should include representatives of independent learned societies. Third, he believed that there should also be on the governing body a number of "common-sense members of recognised weight and authority in the conduct of affairs," to deal with that sprinkling of professors who were likely to be "one-idea'd fanatics, ignorant of the commonest conventions of official relations, and content with nothing if they cannot get everything their own way." When, toward the end of his life, it seemed that a great federal University of London might emerge, Huxley put down on nine foolscap sheets his plans for its organization. There would have been teaching institutions for general education in the arts and sciences; others for the various professions relating to law, medicine, industry, teaching, music, painting, sculpture, and architecture (and theology if the churches could agree on common ground); and others paying special attention to instruction in research. These teaching institutions or "Colleges" might themselves be federal in nature, and he envisaged that this would particularly apply to the medical schools and teacher-training colleges of the area. The students of the "College of General Education," which was also to be responsible for Extension work, were to be examined by the University as such, while the "Professional Colleges" were to be semiautonomous, each arranging its own scheme of instruction and examination and presenting its students for degrees *ad eundem*. Cutting right across the organization into teaching "Colleges," there were to be "Schools" consisting of the teachers of the various disciplines, irrespective of the institutions in which they taught—so that, for example, there would be regular meetings of philosophers (irrespective of whether they were in a general college or training teachers or preparing parsons and priests) and of scientists (similarly irrespective of whether they were teaching future research workers or future teachers or future technicians). These plans were unfortunately not adopted—Huxley was dead before the University took final shape—but today, as universities become larger and the risks of departmental isolation become greater, and as the problem of making proper provision for professional education becomes more urgent, our planners might do worse than look up Huxley's proposals of some seventy years ago.

Widely spread through the world today there is once again that sense of weariness with old organizations which Matthew Arnold had detected in England in 1869 and once more that vague and obscure desire for a general transformation. We are no longer ruled by such a Parliament as the one in Huxley's childhood that reluctantly voted £20,000 for education after willingly providing £50,000 to improve the Royal stables, but the nuclear powers squander on missiles and satellites more than would provide a decent education for most of mankind. And, unfortunately, too many of the seats of power are still occupied by men whose pedagogic preconceptions are those of the comfortable minority. Such men may intellectually discern the educational demands of the age, as Arnold and others did a century ago, and yet like him keep casting lingering glances over their shoulders to their youthful days at Oxbridge or Ivy League. It is a valuable corrective, in studying the history of education, to pay more attention to the thoughts and works of men like Huxley, who found his century pregnant with exciting possibilities, who was optimistic about the cultural potentialities both of his own uneducated fellow citizens and of the inhabitants of undeveloped lands, who not merely acknowledged the *Zeitgeist* but was himself in harmony with it, and who was courageously aware that "those who elect to be free in thought and deed must not hanker after the rewards . . . which the world offers to those who put up with its fetters."

BIBLIOGRAPHICAL NOTE

The major early sources for any study of T. H. Huxley follow.

T. H. Huxley, *Collected Essays*, nine volumes. Macmillan, London, 1893–94.

M. Foster and E. R. Lankester, eds., *Scientific Memoirs of Thomas Henry Huxley*, five volumes. Macmillan, London, 1898–1903.

Leonard Huxley, *The Life and Letters of Thomas Henry Huxley*, two volumes. Macmillan, London, 1900.

The Huxley Papers (unpublished), in the Muniments Room of Imperial College of Science and Technology, London.

The major recent published work is that of the author of this chapter, largely in a series of papers published during the 1950s. Nearly all the quotations and important facts contained in the chapter may be found in, and the original sources easily traced by reference to, this work:

Cyril Bibby, *T. H. Huxley: Scientist, Humanist and Educator*. Macmillan, London, and Horizon Press, New York, 1959.

🌼 KARL MARX (1818–1883), the son of a prosperous lawyer in the service of the Prussian government, was born in the city of Trier in the Rhineland. After completing his early schooling in Trier, he continued his studies at the Universities of Bonn and Berlin. He turned from the study of law to history and philosophy and received his doctor's degree in 1841. Marx became a journalist. Suppression of the liberal paper that he was editing led him to socialism. He married, went to Paris, and became acquainted with leading French and German socialists, including Friedrich Engels. In 1845 the entire staff of the magazine for which Marx was working was ousted from France at the request of the Prussian government. Marx went to Brussels where Engels joined him, and together they acquired a German-language weekly. They joined "The League of the Just," a secret communist society with branches in all the leading cities of Europe. It was for this league that Marx and Engels wrote *The Communist Manifesto* in 1847. When the Revolution of 1848 broke out in France, Marx and Engels were expelled from Belgium. After a short visit to France, they went to Cologne to aid the revolution there by starting a newspaper they called "An Organ of Democracy." It was suppressed within a year. Banished from both Prussia and France, Marx went to London where he lived with his family for his last thirty-four years. His only sources of income were small donations from Engels and small stipends from the *New York Tribune* for commissioned articles. He spent most of his time studying and writing at home or in the British Museum. During these years Marx produced the *Critique of Political Economy* and the first volume of *Capital*. The second and third volumes were brought out by Engels after the death of Marx.

11

THE COMMUNAL MAN: *Marx*

BY PAUL NYBERG

Comprehension of the importance of Marx for the education and development of modern man requires an understanding of certain features in his doctrine of man.

A salient characteristic of the Marxist concept of man is the conviction that man fails to be what he ought to be—his existence and education in modern industrial society do not correspond to his true humanity. Existent man, in other words, contradicts the essence of man. It is in this concept of a dialectical tension between existence and essence that the meaning of the educational message of Marx may be found.

Man in a technological society is not his true self because he is alienated; he is alienated from his work, from other men, and from himself. The relationships of modern industrialism engender a type of mind that views the world in terms of manipulation. According to Marx, man is not merely exploited by the capitalist—he is reduced to a commodity, a thing, a dehumanized factor that can be calculated. In such a situation man dons a "character mask" that hinders and finally prevents his development as a person; he no longer engages and grasps reality as a "whole man." He is separated, cut up, and cut off from himself, that is, from his true being. Man is self-estranged because he lives in a historical situation that is humanly insane. This theme of alienation, dehumanization, and estrangement in an age of industrialism is at the core of Marx's whole philosophical position: his analysis of political economy; his theory of knowledge; and his interpretation of history and society. For him, the capitalist society does not deal with men as men but as functions performing roles. In this light, relationships between man and man, between man and his work, and between man and his world are seen as artificial and humanly deformed. The worker lives at a stage of history in which his development and education are dramatically impaired. But it is not only the worker's human personality that is threatened; the nonworker, too, is caught in the trap of industrialism. Marx declared:

The bourgeoisie has stripped of its halo every occupation hitherto honoured and looked up to with reverent awe. It has converted the physician, the lawyer, the priest, the poet, the man of science into its paid wage-labourers.

Modern industrial society has:

. . . left no other bound between man and man than naked self-interest, than callous cash payment; . . . it has drowned the most heavenly ecstasies of religious fervour, of enthusiasm, of philistine sentimentalism in the icy water of ego-tistical calculation; . . . it has reduced the family relation to a mere money relation.

It is a society that reduces "labourers, who must sell themselves piece-meal," to a "commodity, like every other article of commerce," and consequently exposes them "to all the vicissitudes of competition," he wrote; in short, the nature of work in modern society "has lost all individual character."

Man is no longer confronted with the situations and problems that require the full use of his creative talents and the exercise of mature and considered judgments. According to Marx, the highly specialized and differentiated character of work reduces each man to a "partial operation," and society becomes atomistic in character. Marx stated that the division of labor as distributed in an industrial society makes "man's own deed . . . an alien power opposed to him, which enslaves him instead of being controlled by him." In this way the demands of an industrial society contradict the interests of the individual as a total human being. "The sub-division of labour is the assassination of the people," said Marx.

A society that forces the mind to contend solely with technical and isolated issues can not hope to achieve a general and global outlook that could translate itself into an enterprising social unity. "Thinking itself, in this age of separations, may become a peculiar craft," Marx said. The fragmented character of life and work in a technological society threatens the human mind and life and, in doing so, threatens the very foundations of society and government as a democratic process. The self-perpetuating nature of the technological system tends to outdistance man's intelligent and enlightened control of it. Men do things because they *can* do them, not because they *should* do them. A society that reduces man to a means in the service of more means is a directionless body politic; and a body politic that downgrades morality to taking orders or following a mundane route without invoking a human question is a society that loses all sense of morality, fair play, and justice.

The Marxist philosophy, therefore, is a critical assessment of the threatening power of a purely technological industrial existence. Marx belongs to that group of thinkers who have portrayed and protested the dehumanizing character of modern life in which man becomes a means and a thing to be manipulated. He stands with Kierkegaard who cried out for "That Individual" because "the crowd is untruth"; he belongs with Nietzsche who cried out for "new values" because of the "advent of nihilism"; he stands with Dilthey who cried out for the "whole man" because our age is an age of narrow positivism; he belongs with John Stuart Mill who cried out for the "eccentric" because of the "increasing inclination to stretch unduly the powers of society over the individual"; he belongs with Karl Mannheim who cried out for the "integrated personality" because of the dangers of specialization; he stands with Jaspers who cries out for "self-hood" because modern man has been "deracinated and reduced to the level of a thing;" he stands with Tillich who cries out for the "courage to be" because the "self is more and more lost in its world"; he belongs with social scientists like David Riesman who cry out for the "autonomous character" because of the conformity of the "lonely crowd"; he stands with Ernest Hocking who cries out for a movement of thought beyond modernity in realizing the "imputed possibility in what a man is."

To relate this heterogeneous group of thinkers is not to suggest they all profess an identical philosophy; it is merely one way of identifying a theme of thought that was sounded by Marx and has been developed with variations by other important thinkers in a crescendo that has reached a climactic volume in our own time.

The crisis of human society about which Marx philosophized is essentially the critical station of the human person in the modern world. Crisis, however, signifies not only danger but opportunity. This doubly charged meaning averts complacency because danger is recognized; it circumvents despair because opportunity is entertained. And so it was with Marx. Philosophy was not enough; for him, theory must yield to practice, and interpretation must be coupled with the will to transform history. Marx challenged any philosophy that could not at some point translate itself into action.

The Marxist transformation of society is embedded in the dialectical theory of historical change. According to this theory, every thesis contains its antithesis. And in the struggle between the thesis and antithesis, a synthesis is gained that unites the conflict by preserving both within a wider and higher sphere of generalization. Marx inherited the vocabulary of the dialectical approach from Hegel, but Marx changed it. Marx's alteration of Hegel's dialectic reveals the special character of the Marxist interpretation of history and of his theories relevant to the development and education of man. The controversy Marx had with Hegel provides the point of departure for unraveling the decisive nature of the Marxist dialectic.

Hegel's dialectical science of history is encompassed by the "actuality of reason," with history seen as a rational sequence of events patterned on the metaphysical process of being, nonbeing, becoming. Marx, on the other hand, removed the dialectic from its idealistic sphere and used it to interpret social and economic forces. Marx, like Kierkegaard, sought to put the Hegelian system into the realm of actual life.

Marx wrote:

In direct contrast to German philosophy which descends from heaven to earth, here we ascend from earth to heaven. That is to say, we do not set out from what men imagine, conceive, nor from men as narrated, thought of, or imagined, conceived, in order to arrive at men in the flesh. We set out from real, active men and on the basis of their real life process we demonstrate the development of the ideological reflexes and echoes of this life process.

Hegel visualized the problems of history and man (alienations) only "in their thought-form"; Marx comprehended them always in terms of the contradictions and antagonisms of the class society. The dialectical development of Hegel's spirit of reason toward the absolute idea found its concrete expression in the development of the nation state in history; Marx's dialectic materialized itself within the structure of production that shaped the basic economic and social character of life. Marx understood the dialectical process, not in terms of spiritual and rational development but in terms of the improvement of the economic and human conditions of social life. He held that the nature of man could not be determined apart from the social world in which he lives. Man is not only an individual but a social being. The education of man is rooted in the character of his social existence.

It is in this context that the Marxist meaning of materialism must be understood. Historically and philosophically, materialism has had a variety of meanings. One meaning is derived from the speculations of the pre-Socratic Greeks who interpreted the universe as a whole in terms of materials. They were primarily interested in the nature of the physical world, a necessary preliminary for the development of the science of nature. This meaning of materialism recurred in the Renaissance period, which rediscovered in a variety of ways the learning of the ancient world.

A second meaning points to a moral attitude, affirming the acquisition of material goods as a way of satisfying personal desires. This hedonistic doctrine of self-indulgence has its counterpart in the everyday saying, "He is a materialist."

It would be misleading to equate Marxist materialism with either of these two meanings. Marx explicitly attacked the metaphysical materialism of Feuerbach and the hedonistic materialism of capitalism. Historical materialism, to Marx, meant that the act of production for physical existence is the basis for all other activities and expressions in the world. Because Marx was a child of the industrial revolution, he was particularly sensitive to the importance of economic and technical factors in history and tended to overdramatize them. A critical assessment of materialism will give the Marxist interpretation a deeper perspective.

It is an error of the materialist conception of history to attribute everything to the economic sphere. Max Weber, in his studies dealing with the impact of Protestantism on the spirit of capitalism, did much to correct the one-sidedness of historical materialism. Historical materialism is correct, however, to the extent that it negates the self-contained character of idealism. The one-sidedness of idealism is as wrong as the one-sidedness of materialism. The stimulus for historical development is to be found, not in the sphere of the ideal alone nor in the sphere of matter alone but in the continuous interdependence of both spheres. As soon as the mechanical distinction between the substructure and the superstructure is eliminated, the historical process may be viewed as a living Gestalt (integrated configuration). When history is viewed as a unified process, the propelling stimulus that determines social development and human images is to be found, not in some preordained sphere of reality but in the meaningful experiences that man as an existent and interpretative being lives and understands most radically. Marx stressed the material factor in history, because he lived in a special period that experienced most intensively the economic side of a changing culture. Marx did not live in academic seclusion, reconstructing partial problems out of a partial existence. The philosophy of Marx is, as Hegel would have said, a reflection of his own time. It is an accident of history that Marx, as a thinker in terms of existent reality, emphasized the economic factor. In another age Marx might well have been not a social philosopher but a religious poet. He lived in the middle of events where he combined interests of a theoretical kind with the moving questions of a distorted world. The lack of restriction and specialization in Marx accounts for the encyclopedic and dynamic quality of his work. This breadth of scope also permits Marx to be considered, along with thinkers like Nietzsche and Dilthey, as a member of the movement concerned with the philosophy of life. When one understands Marx in terms of this analysis, one recognizes that the traditional interpretation of Marxism as material-ism is only partially correct. The classification of Marx as a pure mate-rialist will be suspended but not discarded; it will be preserved within a larger categorization of Marx as a concerned thinker about actual exist-ence, disturbed not simply about economic inequalities but about the human predicament in general. The determining force of history for Marx was the activity of real men aware of economic conditions and functioning to change the social process. The concern with changing the course of history represents a second major difference between the dialec-tic of Marx and the dialectic of Hegel.

While Hegel used dialectic to develop a conservative world view, Marx used the dialectic as an analytical tool in the service of revolution. Hegel's synthesis stopped in his own time for as Hegel said, "The owl of Minerva begins its flight when the dusk is falling." Philosophy can only paint grey upon gray. But Marx said, "Philosophers have interpreted history, our job is to change it." Marx's synthesis was a projection of history into the future; Hegel's synthesis was a summary in which the antinomies of history and the world were finally resolved. The Marxist synthesis was one yet to be realized, reflecting the irreconcilability of the class struggle and voicing proletarian aspirations not yet attained; Hegel mirrored a processs of accomplishment already achieved. Hegel's nega-tivism ends in a kind of moral historical positivism; the negativism of Marx is translated into a moral historical utopianism. Hegel was satisfied with interpreting history. History, for Marx, had to be changed and revolutionized.

According to Marx, man lives in a stage between "prior history" and "real history," between the primitive realization of the "savage in his cave" who "feels as much at home as the fish in water" and the full conscious realization of a new social order. He believed this transition stage to be a historically alienated society that could be transformed into a new order in which man could wholly participate. Marx sought a world in which man might live free from alienation and exploitation, a world in which the dignity of man and social justice might be realized. The Marxist goal, as it is clarified within the revolutionary dialectic, finds its echo in the Kantian ethic: "Act so as to treat man, in your own person as well as in that of anyone else, always as an end, never merely as a means."

The struggles and education of man in social history had a meaning for Marx; the goal of history was a body politic free from the fetters of manipulation and class conflict so that man might develop as a man. Marx's aim was emancipation and liberation from the depersonalizing structures of economic life under capitalism. Marx, like Rousseau before him, hated the gross inequalities that characterized their aristocrat-dominated or bourgeois-dominated societies; and Marx, like Rousseau, developed an ideal of freedom from the inequalities and corruptions of society. This ideal animates the educational philosophy of both men. But there were differences in their appoaches to actuation. Rousseau believed that the perfectibility of man could only be realized by, first, withdrawing the individual from the oppressions of society and, secondly, instructing him to ask the right questions (such as, "What is the best interest of the community?") in order to actualize the "general will." Marx stressed, first, the recognition of social forces in the development of man's consciousness and, secondly, the utilization and organization of such forces in order to actualize the collective will. The Marxist vision of the new order where "nobody has one exclusive sphere of activity, but each can become accomplished in any branch he wishes (because) society regulates the general production," finds its counterpart in Rousseau's philosophy of the social contract in which "man does not surrender completely to the sovereign ruler, but each man gives himself to all, and therefore gives himself to nobody in particular." If it is possible to say that Rousseau united the absolute sovereignty of Hobbes with the popular consent of Locke to create the doctrine of popular sovereignty, is would not be entirely incorrect to state that Marx combined the collectivism of Hegel with the anarchism of Proudhon to institute the doctrine of socialistic democracy. Because of the efforts of both Rousseau and Marx to combine apparently contradictory elements into a single philosophy, many conflicting interpretations have subsequently arisen. This problem is compounded by the generality of Rousseau's philosophy and by the prophetic character of aims in the revolutionary thinking of Marx.

Some thinkers (such as Aiken) have suggested, for instance, that the Marxist "vision of the good society is virtually anarchistic"; others (such as Nisbet) have indicated that "Marx's goal is the political community, centralized and absolute." Such interpretations are not based on an understanding of the reconciliatory character of Marx's prophetic vision. Marx sought a society that would overcome the "contradiction between the interest of the separate individual or the individual family and the communal interest of all individuals who have intercourse with one other." Marx envisioned a society that would educate man to be neither a servant to the state nor an economic partial operation and would encourage man to grow whole, reconciled, and real. The new environment that Marx visualized would create a society of whole and real human beings.

The vision Marx illuminates is of a society that:

. . . is the definitive resolution of the antagonism between man and nature, and between man and man. It is the true solution of the conflict between existence and essence, between objectification and self-affirmation, between freedom and necessity, between individual and species. It is a solution of the riddle of history and knows itself to be this solution.

This Marxist vision is, in other words, the end of history; it is the vision of the classless society. Its prophetic character links Marxist thought with all those philosophical and theological movements of thought that expect and know of a new reality and a new order of being. In this way Marx stands in the tradition of the great religious prophets who knew of a "new creation," of Renaissance men like Giordano Bruno who knew of a "new light which dawns after a long darkness—and rises apace until it will become the sun at noon"; of Enlightenment and post-Enlightenment philosophers like Kant who knew that "children ought to be educated, not for the present, but for a possibly improved condition of man in the future."

Marx, therefore, did not develop a philosophy of adjustment by conforming to the pragmatic demands of modern society; his thought developed a philosophy of adjustment by resisting the pragmatic requirements of contemporary society. The difference is fundamental in our time, for it introduces an ethic that goes far beyond assessing the primary aim of education as accommodation of man to the behavior requirements of a given historical group. A nation that holds to an educational standard of accommodation cannot hope to create the evaluative and critical spirit that is always a necessary preliminary for developing the good society.

No pattern of behavior can be justified solely in terms of its pragmatic efficiency; such a philosophy would lead nowhere because it leads everywhere. The pragmatic behavior and existent condition of man have to be confronted with a mediating ideal that mirrors man's essential nature. This tension between existence and essence, between something old and something new, between the inadequacy of present society and the something better of future society, is a decisive feature of the Marxist dialectic of history. The Marxist dialectic is at once critical and prophetical: it gives a negative account of the depersonalized state of existence and at the same time offers a utopian image of a new society to be attained sometime in the future. For Marx, therefore, the dialectic is not simply a scientific law of social development, and history does not simply follow a predetermined path to a predetermined goal. The dialectical view of society and its possible transformation does not see history as a series of events that can be calculated mathematically. Human action to change human events is not officious meddling in the determinable course of history because history is not that predictable. The dialectical making of history involves not only necessity but freedom.

The Marxist dialectic is characterized by a conscious, active, and deliberate understanding of the normative dimension of history. The social philosophy of Marx explicitly develops a strategy for intervening in the process of historical development. This normative strategy in Marxism is a basic challenge to the philosophy of liberalism. Nineteenth-century liberalism held to a radical separation of the social process from moral standards. The primary assumption of liberalism was that the common good could be achieved without anyone's being concerned about the common good. The "invisible hand" of Adam Smith's invention would achieve the desired end automatically and unintentionally. The welfare of society and economic progress were considered by-products of the competitive game, a game in which private vices, to use Mandeville's phrase, would produce public virtues. Selfishness, in other words, would unintentionally promote the public welfare. A generation educated in the belief that individual selfishness would produce the good society, could have little understanding of the meaning of public responsibility. A people educated in the belief that the "invisible hand" would translate individual selfishness into social and human betterment could do little, in the end, but allow and justify antihuman behavior. A society that will not reach beyond the limits of an extreme individualism, cannot produce that vision and spirit out of which the general welfare may be developed. Ernest Hocking wrote, "If a dour critic were to say that liberalism as a dominant note in American education has produced a nation of spoiled and juvenile minds, unable to think, devoid of the power of self-criticism and therefore incapable of mature political responsibility, we might consider his picture unduly savage, a mere half-truth; yet as a half-truth, hardly to be denied."

Liberalism had a theory of individualism and individual rights but it had no theory of public (conscious) responsibility and political obligation. Marx, on the other hand, understood the limitations of an atomistic society which exploited the alienated man. In such a society "the only force that brings (men) together is the selfishness, the gain and the private interests of each," Marx wrote. "Each looks to himself only, and no one troubles himself about the rest, and just because they do so, do they all, in accordance with the preestablished harmony of things . . . work together to their mutual advantage . . . in the interest of all."

The taunting criticism of Marx exposed the central weakness of nineteenth-century liberalism. The laissez-faire theory of organization did not create a social condition for the dignified education of free individuals but perpetuated an ideology which camouflaged the exploitation of man in the concrete world. For Marx, therefore, social progress and human welfare could not be fashioned out of an ideology which equated freedom with indifference. Social progress and freedom could not be guaranteed through automatic adjustments based on a preordained harmony but required deliberate and collective activity. Industrial capitalism was not a history of human harmony, but a story of social conflicts and a picture of broken ideals and promises. Not the values but the techniques of liberalism were bankrupt.

The appeal of Marxism arises from its call for conscious social action by groups composing the great majority, the proletariat. These groups, acting in freedom, are the vehicles of the historical struggle. Human effort is a prerequisite for turning the tide of history. History, as such, is not a mechanical process, nor are events determined solely by chance. The educator is not simply conditioned by circumstances; circumstances are changed by men. This means that the educator himself must be educated—to create and change circumstances. In order for the educator to know history, he must *make* history. Knowledge of the world lies in a radical union of theory and practice; the truth of society is opened up only to those who are truly alive, to those who participate with passionate awareness and with the intensity of their full existence in the course of history. And in knowing the truth of what *is*, one knows what ought and must be done. The dialectical thinking of Marx overcomes the subject–object split of previous philosophy (connects subject and object with the existential *is*), and unites within a single science the factual and evaluative insights of man. Marx was not inhibited by the obsolete separation of fact and value, so easily taken for granted in the social sciences today. Without values, there cannot be an adequate critique and profound analysis of history. Without an existential understanding of history values remain abstract. The Marxist theory of knowledge unites concrete observation with a conscious desire to transform society according to the "revolutionary ideal." The ideal is not detachable from the positive movement of history, as it is in Kant's philosophy. Marx wrote: "Communism is for us not a stable state which is established, an ideal to which reality will have to adjust itself. We call communism the real movement which abolishes the present state of things." The revolutionary process, which abolishes the alienated character of present conditions, also clarifies man's true needs, man's true humanity, man's true being. In this way Marxist thought repudiates the absolute separation of fact and value by acknowledging all human facts as essentially part of the process of development—a historical-educational development—the truth of which can only be grasped through the participatory union of the knower and that which is to be known. To use a

Marxist phrase, "real, active men" constitute the epistemological basis for the "ideological reflexes" of life and history. He said, "Life is not determined by consciousness, but consciousness by life." This method of approach premises men, "not in any fantastic isolation or abstract definition, but in their actual, empirically perceptible process of development under definite conditions." With this approach, the study of history and education "ceases to be a collection of dead facts," as it is with the empiricists and the idealists; it becomes "the representation of . . . the practical process of the development of man," Marx wrote.

Marxist thought is, therefore, a direct challenge on two fronts. It opposes a trend in philosophy running from Descartes through Comenius to the modern Positivists—a philosophy that splits "the world" off from the "knowing mind" and that establishes mathematical reason as the yardstick for true knowledge.

Such an epistemology generates an ontology reducing the reality of the world to things that can be manipulated. Marx was as critical of epistemological dehumanization as he was of social depersonalization. This split between the scientific and human world is eradicated in the existential character of Marxist thought, that is, thought rooted in existence. Marx was not an abstract and artificial philosopher but, first of all, a man; he did not think as a thinker but as a real being living in existence. Marx was more than a scholar registrating the facts. He was a passionate and creative thinker vitally concerned with the changes and human course of history. The active element in contradistinction to the ascetic element in knowledge is predominant in the Marxist philosophy.

Knowledge by participation in the world of history and society is a distinctive quality of Marx's epistemology. It opposes those empirical and theoretical programs that eliminate from their agenda those human meanings that can only be grasped existentially, by living them. In this regard Karl Mannheim and Paul Tillich may be singled out as thinkers indebted to Marx, who have repeatedly emphasized the participatory character of knowledge. They constitute a healthy opposition to men like Max Weber and Talcott Parsons whose ascetic orientation tends to produce an academic estrangement from human life.

Academic estrangement is the second front on which Marxist thought is a direct challenge. Marx was not curtailed by the artificial boundary lines that are prevalent in contemporary academic work. Marx employed all of the social science specialties—politics, economics, history, psychology, sociology, education, and anthropology—in such a way as to offer, not a segmented and abstracted view of men in society but an imaginative master picture of the structure of society and the dynamics of historical change.

The labyrinthine character of modern social science is directly analogous to the directionless quality of a culture in which labor is highly differentiated. Without a "regulative total image" the "individual sciences" are but "strings," wrote Nietzsche, "that reach no end anywhere and merely make our lives still more confused and labyrinthine . . ." He pointed out, "Only a man who has a firm grasp of the over-all picture of life and existence can use the individual sciences without harming himself." Marx had such an image that manifested itself in a human way.

For instance, in his method of analyzing economic phenomena, Marx always considered the social and human factors. His scope transcended that of a purely formal economics, which eliminates the human dimension from analysis. When one studies Marx the political economist, one encounters Marx the human and existential educator. Marx did not drain language of its meaningful and evaluative character for the sake of formal description. Unlike Marx's terminology, the formal, mechanical, and dehumanized categories used in contemporary social sciences fail to penetrate social reality. They are incapable of dealing with life and historical processes, because thè terms—often jargon—are not rooted in human situations.

The mediating character of Marxist thought, when stripped of its dogmatism, provides a method of verifiable exploration that goes beyond the partial procedures and observations of positivistic science by enabling the mind to grasp the structure of society as a whole. The legacy of the Marxist theory of knowledge in our time is its challenge to a restricted empiricism and to the fragmented social sciences. For neither a restricted philosophical empiricism nor the specialization of the social sciences can develop an understanding awareness of the critical condition of the human individual in a technical society. Such an awareness of man's true being and its historical distortion is most adequately achieved by people who participate in the struggles of the alienated and the exploited against the vested interests and special privileges of those in power. When human life is most radically threatened, a true human consciousness is most likely to occur.

The development of full consciousness meant for Marx, as it meant for Freud, breaking the bonds of illusion. The ruling social, political, educational, and religious thoughts of a period are determined by the particular structure and functioning of the economic order. Such thoughts do not reflect, therefore, the conscious concerns of the human person as a human person; they reflect the special interests of the ruling classes of society. Because selfish economic motivations are hidden within such patterns of thought, Marx continuously made critical appraisals of their validity. Just as Freud strove to make conscious the unconscious within the individual, so Marx strove to make conscious the unconscious in the collective, and to uncover the concealed identity of the social-economic structure with man's mental productions. In uncovering this concealed identity, the truth would be known and the truth would set man free.

The camouflage of thought covering up social injustices and human degradation with ideological deceptions must be shattered. Out of this shattering, an awareness of the human world, as it really is, can emerge; the false consciousness of the ruling classes can be voided, and the ideologies that narcotize man's awareness of himself can be eradicated; man's humanity and the historical distortion of man's humanity can be revealed; the revolutionary building of a new society can begin.

These aspirations were what Marx had in mind when he said that "the communists have not invented the intervention of society in education; they do but seek to alter the character of that intervention, and to rescue education from the influence of the ruling class." In the new society education would be free "for all children in public schools," and "child factory labour in its present form" would be abolished. In the Marxist view, historical change and man's education are generated by dialectical understanding of the intimate relationship between the sphere of knowledge and the realm of society.

The sociology of knowledge initiated by Marx and developed by Karl Mannheim carries the philosophical import that a true consciousness of being (historical being as well as man's essential being) can only be grasped existentially, that is, by thinking that is grounded in actual existence. Existential thinking and the sociology of knowledge do not, in the final analysis, lead to a complete and skeptical relativism. The skeptical relativism that this kind of thinking reveals is only the antithesis to the thesis that man's being in history can not be totally grasped with a one-sided doctrine of life (materialism or idealism, for instance) or with a restricted methodology (narrow empiricism or formal logic, for instance). The relativism of the sociology of knowledge, in other words, is only a preliminary relativism. It is part of the dialectical approach that drives beyond both the false thesis of a one-sided absolutism and the false antithesis of a complete skeptical relativism. And in moving beyond both alternatives, the truth of man's being in historical existence and as a whole is revealed. The existential-dialectical character of the sociology of knowledge recovers the image of man as a man by pushing aside partial, abstract, and ideological images and coming in contact with the concrete, living reality of the present. It opens up a life orientation that seeks to redress the alienation and disruption accompanying the exaggerated claims made by artificial doctrines and individualistic (nominalistic) approaches.

The Marxist sociological understanding of the dialectical relationship between the substructure and the superstructure of life not only resembles aspects of Freudian psychology but parallels in a remarkable way the "hymn of the dialectic" in Plato's thought. For Plato, the philosophical aim of education was to banish the shadowy illusions of the dark cave of existence and to enable the light of truth to shine upon life. As Plato moved to undercut the "previous sciences" and limited perspectives that dim man's vision, so Marx moved to destroy the previous illusions and social ideologies that keep man in bondage. The decisive power of dialectical thought, whether employed by Plato or by Marx, is its critical and negative capacity to expose the deficiencies in man's interpretations of reality. Dialectical thought reveals that what appear to be the facts about life are only the facts of a distorted conception of man and his world, hiding the real nature, essence, and true being of man. Dialectical thought attempts to drive beyond factual appearances, the shadows of the cave, and man's ideological world. It seeks that level of reality from which the "philosopher" can compare the "light of the sun" with the "darkness of the shadows," as Plato expressed it, or from which the "sociologist" can unscramble the "phantoms formed in the human brain" as sublimated echoes of the "material life process," in Marx's terms. Dialectical thought in its very critical-evaluative negativity begins to comprehend the reality of the world, man's essential nature, man as he is, and as he ought to be. The "higher vision" of Plato's education and the "fuller consciousness" of Marx's education are both fashioned out of a dialectical methodology, the aim of which is to develop awareness of life as a whole in terms of what is best. However, despite their dialectical similarities, there were philosophic attitudes peculiar to the thought of Plato and to the thought of Marx that led, as has already been suggested, to some fundamental differences. Plato contrasted the realm of essence with the realm of existence; he found an abyss between existential knowledge and essential knowledge, between the cave and the light. Marx held that the essence of being is clarified within the existential movement of history, and that this clarification of man's essence (ideals) emerges from an existent understanding of the dynamic facts of life. Unlike Plato, Marx did not view the two realms as absolutely divided. But like Plato, he saw the two kinds of knowledge corresponding to the two realms of reality as qualitatively different. This qualitative difference is rooted in the "dialectical nature" of "man in history," whose existence contradicts his essence, according to Marx; it manifests itself in the basic opposition between the "new society" and the "old society." While the Platonic ideal is, in a sense, a super-imposition on society because the "philosopher–king" alone can see the light and can know what is best, the Marxist ideal grows out of the historical-utopian aspirations of the disinherited and alienated classes of society, is clarified by those who participate in society and in the moving course of historical reality, and emerges from an enlarged aware-ness of the world in which men live.

In our age this aim of an enlarged awareness is continuously threat-ened. It is threatened by the overriding considerations given to training technical and vocational personnel, by a teaching process that retails knowledge in standard packages (textbooks and teaching machines, for instance), by an acute overspecialization that neutralizes interest in the open interpretation of real problems, and by administrative practices that twist the learning effort into an academic ritual. The enlargement of awareness is not merely quantitative, nor does it depend upon artificial attempts to balance scientific and humanistic types of education. Aware-ness is more than the accumulation of bits and pieces of information. Enlargement of mind is qualitative. It must be understood dialectically as a decisive way of thinking and being. A dialectical awareness strives to comprehend the nature of the social situation in any given historical period as a whole and in depth critically, and to base necessary policy, not upon narrow and technical considerations but upon a total vision that recognizes the higher ideals by which man may organize his life, his education, and his society. The dialectical mind is able to penetrate the specific happenings of a changing society in order to discover new possi-bilities and strategies for achieving a world worthy of man's essence.

The dialectical mind, therefore, is driven by its very nature to con-template qualitative change and to move beyond the established order of life and thought in the direction of an ideal implicit in what man really is. Dialectical thought is inevitably caught up with questions that concern man deeply, such as, for instance, the meaning of life, the goal of conduct, and the end of history. Dialectical thinking, in one form or another, mediates between existence and essence, between good and evil, and between inadequacy and something better. It is, in other words, an evaluative enterprise. As an evaluative endeavor it interprets the forces of history and the themes of social effort in reference always to a meaningful goal. It is a type of thinking, therefore, that is fundamental to the making of decisions and to the determination of conduct.

Unless the leaders of society, including those who teach, are given an education that helps to develop this quality of mind, the guidance of man in society could be reduced to small and arbitrary considerations.

In such a situation no generation could regenerate itself. The concept of dialectical awareness, only partially elaborated in the class-conscious writings of Marx but inherent in his philosophy, is a contribution of primary importance to our times.

Dialectical interpretations are essentially opposed to functional and positivistic theories of man in society, precisely because such inquiries say nothing evaluatively; they do not relate their findings to a meaningful and human goal of conduct nor do they give any indication as to the real nature of man. While such theories may be highly useful in the sphere of abstract scientific research, they prove largely inadequate within the context of real live human situations. It is one thing to describe man in society in terms of functions, mathematical equations, roles, and abstracted positions; it is another thing entirely to understand the inner meaning, values, and aspirations of the lives of people as they struggle to maintain themselves in a changing world. To eliminate the perspective of the ideal from social analysis and interpretation is ultimately to destroy all meaning; to eradicate the utopian aspirations of man for the sake of a sterile factuality is to produce a state of mind that reduces man to a thing; to undercut man's evaluations is to lose sight of the possibilities within society that make history and life humanly significant. A purposeful perspective, in other words, is not only a condition necessary for understanding man in history but is also the prerequisite for shaping, transforming, or revolutionizing the world. The impulse to change the world is clearly visible in all dialectical interpretations of life and history—in the thinking of Plato who required the philosopher to return to the cave, in the thinking of Hegel who made supreme the principle of negation. In Marx the desire for change was primary.

An understanding of the events that have revolutionized the modern world requires an understanding of the philosophy of Marx. The revolutionary character of modern life can only be comprehended by people who have at some point received a Marxist education and know of Marxism's power and its limitations. Marx's philosophy should not be rejected or accepted dogmatically, but approached with an open mind. A critical appraisal of Marx requires a flexible turn of mind as an approach to reality. Such an appraisal may proceed philosophically, by essaying the basic deficiencies of the Marxist view of man and education; or it may proceed historically, by noting the invalidity of Marx's generalizations from the perspective of the present time. These approaches should not be considered as entirely separate; each inevitably meets the other, if it proceeds very far.

The way to historical change and the development of man depended, for Marx, upon the practice of revolution, which was made necessary by the conflict between capitalists and workers. Revolutionizing the social order required, not gradual reform and compromise through parliamentary procedure but active struggle and, if necessary, force.

A society "in which the free development of each man is the condition for the free development of all" can only be achieved by the social revolution of the proletariat, Marx declared. "Estrangement" can only be abolished when it becomes an "intolerable power"—a power, that is, "against which men make a revolution." For estrangement to become an intolerable power it must necessarily have rendered "propertyless" the great mass of humanity and must have produced at the same time "the contradiction of an existing world of wealth and culture," according to Marx. In such a situation the free actions of the proletariat become the instruments of history and through force achieve the absolute utopia of a classless society. "Force," Marx said, "is the midwife of every old society pregnant with a new one." Violent struggle is the travail accomplishing the birth of the new society. While Marx indicated that there may be exceptions to violent revolution as the means to this end, the general tone of the argument is that the new society "can be attained only by the forcible overthrow of all existing conditions."

A closer look should be taken at two related issues in the revolutionary doctrines of Marxist philosophy. One is the problem of force and violence. The other is the question of social class and class consciousness.

Marx pictured society as composed of two powerful groups, the capitalists and the workers. Marx considered the middle class as crushed in the conflict between them. In the actual historical development, modern society has witnessed the formation of an elaborate middle-class group: the technicians, the professional people, the managerial operators, and the small entrepreneurs. This group, especially in America, has created a kind of Aristotelian social balance in which the social extremes required for the Marxist revolution have largely been eliminated. (Incidentally, affluence so widespread brings forth peculiar problems of its own, for instance, complacency.) When a large middle class dominates the character of society, when a society shows a high degree of upward mobility, and when ethnic and religious differences cut across socio-economic differences, the formation of class consciousness can be only a spasmodic phenomenon. When class consciousness is a spasmodic occurrence within society, the class struggle as conceived by Marx tends to remain dormant. Nevertheless, modern society has at times exhibited profound tensions between social and economic groups, between the owners of production on the one hand and workers on other.

The resolution of these tensions, however, has not always been of the forceful kind advocated by Karl Marx. The gradual evolution of the Labour Party to political power in Great Britain and the economic and social legislation of the New Deal in the United States show what democratic political processes can do. The development of such policies in the Western democracies demonstrates that capitalism can be modified and changed through constitutional means. Marx failed to see that just political action could be a powerful influence in the life and education of man. The historical life of man has been revolutionized without the war of forced conflict.

To state that violent conflict is the only way to transform the old society removes from consideration at the very outset the possibility of creating a new society through gradual processes, through reform. If reform is capable of rescuing man in society from practices that hamper his development toward an ideal, change by violent revolution becomes unnecessary.

Marx entangled himself in two self-contradictory concepts for which he may be justly criticized. One concerned the achievement of a free and relatively equal society through undemocratic procedures. Marx never fully faced the problem of the transition. To suspend democratic procedures during the transitional period allows for the possibility of avoiding responsibility for democratic ideals altogether. In periods of vast social changes the need to preserve democratic ideals is especially acute. Those who substitute dictatorial government for constitutional procedures, supposedly temporarily, can be expected to affirm values that are essentially undemocratic and to prolong such so-called transitional arrangements indefinitely. While the political officers of such "provisional states" may talk about democracy, they invariably fail to institute the substance of democratic life. For the very object of democratic political life is to realize a community in which the participants learn how to govern themselves, and this requires the institution of means whereby such an educational enterprise may effectively take place. When social arrangements develop that curtail the human dialogue and prevent effective communication, the very foundations of constitutional life are threatened. Forceful revolutionary tactics undercut the rationality of the participatory dialogue that is essential for the preservation of democratic institutions. Only the casuistical mind can justify use of violent procedures for the purpose of overcoming the injustices of a prevailing society and establishing a genuine democratic order.

Advocacy of force was a Marxian error that contributed to the development of Stalinism and to the organization of a ruthless centralized state in Russia. For, paralleling the Marxist philosophy of revolutionary force as a necessary preliminary to achieving a society of free and peaceful men, is the thinking that the dictatorial supremacy of the proletariat is a necessary political and educational condition for achieving the "withering away of the state," and, thus, the classless society.

Marx wrote: "Between capitalist and communist society lies the period of the revolutionary transformation of the one into the other. There corresponds to this also a political transition period in which the state be nothing but the revolutionary dictatorship of the proletariat." How this "contradictory transition" would take place Marx never explained, although the rationale behind the use of dictatorial force may be understood. Marx was blinded by his passion to kill the bourgeois capitalist order, on the one hand, and on the other hand he was blinded by his belief that the right moment was near at hand for actualizing his vision. For the combined objective of the total overthrow of the old order and the immediate realization of a totally new order, there was devised a combined revolutionary and dictatorial method that was bound to vitiate the exercise of wisdom and practical judgment.

The extreme activism inherent in Marx has had various critical consequences. It prevented Marx and the socialist movements generally from undertaking the kind of sustained self-criticism that is essential if original intentions are not to be distorted. Marx did not sufficiently utilize the Socratic element of dialectical theory, that is, the continuous testing of ideas and assumptions by a radical form of questioning. Marx did not turn against his own position the antiideological criticism that he directed against his opponents. This kind of self-scrutiny awaited the arrival of sociologists like Mannheim and theologians like Tillich, in our time. The failure of Marx to temper his activism with sufficient critical scrutiny resulted in a variety of theoretical errors and in historical catastrophes that ultimately negated his humanitarian aspirations. Marx never entertained the possibility of a prolonged ruthless barbarism such as was developed under the communistic dictatorship, nor did he imagine the possibility of the destructiveness of war as witnessed in the twentieth century. The activistic-utopian-uncritical element of Marxism was, in part, responsible for the forces unleashed in our age, which in many places helped to destroy the "domains of liberty" designated by John Stuart Mill as essential for human creativeness. The ideals that truly inspired Marx were ultimately lost in his own dogmatism. This irrational dogmatism prevented Marx from grasping the critical and normative principle that is at the center of Immanuel Kant's philosophy—that war and violence do not pay. A world community of peaceful and free cooperative men, an ideal that was basic to Kant as well as to Marx, requires that the transforming procedures used to achieve and maintain it be reasonable and just. Marx failed to grasp and Kant understood well the importance of reasonable and just procedures in establishing a peaceful world community under law. This principle is acutely meaningful to our own time. In theory, policies can be, and in actuality ought to be formed and executed in a gradual and just way. Within this perspective the Marxist doctrine of unavoidable forceful revolution is untenable. This doctrine is a tragic disfigurement of the Marxist philosophy of history.

Closely related to the question of procedures is the problem of the validity of the Marxist vision. The changes and upheavals of the present world both affirm and negate the insights of Marx. Bourgeois liberalism and pure capitalism have been transformed, even though the direction and the spirit of the transformation were not entirely anticipated by Marx. The Marxist analysis of the contradictions of capitalist society has largely written off the liberal idea of a preordained harmony and the liberal belief in automatic progress. State interventionism has increasingly restricted the sphere of free economic competition. The great depression was no routine occurrence within the structure of economic life but a crisis of the liberal capitalist tradition itself. In pointing out the factors that would produce such a crisis, Marx the analyst was largely correct. However, the growth of governmental power and the increasingly bureaucratic character of the middle classes (clerks, technicians, managerial operators, and professional groups), deny the "withering away of the state" anticipated by Marx the prophet. The coming of the classless society remains a prophecy; as an ideal it stands as an indictment against gross inequality.

The exploitative character of capitalist industrialism has, at least on the surface of man's life, been mitigated largely through the union of workers. However, on a deeper level, the alienation and depersonalization of life continue as ever-present problems not only among the workers but in every group, not only in capitalist countries but in every technical-industrial society. Marx's prophecy of a future when the ideal of a nonalienated and just life would prevail remains a prophecy. It is precisely this progressive element in the Marxist dialectic interpretation of society, envisioning a final stage as immanent and possible within history, that points to a basic inadequacy in the philosophy of Marx. The Marxist final and absolute classless society precludes a new contradiction. The classless society is, by definition, undialectic. A final stage of history in which the dialectic process would come to an end is a contradiction of the dialectic principle itself. This is the second self-contradictory concept in the philosophy of Marx. In this contradiction the limits of the Marxist dialectic interpretation of history become apparent. The deification of history either in terms of the present (Hegel) or in terms of the future (Marx) requires reconsideration.

The upheavals of the contemporary world have resulted in a reappraisal of the nineteenth-century belief in human perfectibility and the inevitability of historical progress. The idea that man is perfectible has had to recoil before the catastrophes that have overtaken modern man. The Marxist "guarantee of future history" has been torn to bits in the convulsions of the present age. It is only in our time when the upheavals of the world agitate all mankind and when the "edge of history" is ultimately comprehended that the failure of Marx and his generation can be fully grasped. Our age is painfully aware that science and technology do not necessarily lead to a better world; it realizes that education does not inevitably make men virtuous and rational; it begins to understand the limits of historical achievement itself. The distantiation (or condition of being at variance) of present history in terms of future history is only a partial and inconclusive form of distantiation. The social and historical transformation of man is always a fragmentary and incomplete transformation; man's fulfillment within history is always an incomplete fulfillment.

In the dialectic of social effort new problems arise out of the solutions to old difficulties. The achievements of one epoch may be lost in the next. The incongruities of life and history are infinite, and man's social and political triumphs over particular evils do not overcome the fragmented and distorted nature of human existence as a whole. The forces that contradict man's true humanity will never be fully and ultimately eradicated within the context of history. The regeneration of man through history and social education is peculiarly ambiguous. The prophetic hope that the ultimate realization of man's essence may be achieved within the "kingdom of history" fails to take into account the distorted meanings of life that appear in every historical period. A final stage when the conflicts, tensions, and human problems of men would be absolutely resolved and man's essence would override his distorted existence has not and cannot be achieved within the context of history. Marxist utopianism fails to grasp the universality of man's estrangement in existence.

The security of history has vanished, and in its place stands the question that concerns man most, the question about the meaning and ultimate fulfillment of life. An answer to the question of personal and historical fulfillment in a world that is universally estranged cannot, therefore, be extrapolated from the confines of Marxist thought. The answer cannot be found in the security of past history nor even in future history;

it will be hammered out in the very insecurity of our times and in the anxiety that threatens everyman's being in every moment of time.

This does not suggest that man should disengage himself from the refractory character of historical and educational effort, nor does it counsel a philosophy of despair. What it does indicate is that the full meaning of life and history appears, not in the historic dialectic between present time and future time but in the inward dialectic between man in history and the depth of reality beyond history that is eternal. The frontier of eternity is approached whenever man reaches the edge of history; face to face with the finiteness of his existence, he apprehends the infinite mystery of the universe. Marx never grasped this form of distantiation (or standing apart); his philosophy distrusts and attacks it.

Marx considered religion, as he did all structures of thought except his own, as ideology; religion for Marx was a product of economic forces, an instrument invented by the dominant class to justify the misery and exploitation of workers and thereby hold in check their impulse to change the established order of society. Religion renders insensible the feeling of the oppressed by promising salvation in the life hereafter. For this reason Marx called religion the "opiate of the people." His criticism of the uses of religion by the Christian church was not without foundation. Christianity during the industrial revolution was used to blunt the social unrest of the alienated classes. In aligning itself with the *status quo* and with the vested interests, the church failed to voice an effective judgment upon the exploitations and human injustices of the period. From one viewpoint Marx was more Christian than many of the religious leaders of the nineteenth century; he carried on a secularized debate of protest and promise that in former times would have been undertaken in theological circles. The secularized theology of Marx was the primary substitute of the last century for an often impotent religion and a frequently forgetful church. The way religion manifested itself in the history of the generations that passed through the industrial revolution was as wrong as the historical messianism of Marx.

When a religion becomes the weapon for one party as against another party, when it absolutely supports one institution as against another institution, when it arbitrarily justifies one epoch as against another epoch, it becomes as idolatrous as Marxism and it fails in its essential religious task. One of the fundamental contributions of Christian theology to Western social thought is the idea that no historical reality and moral social standard can be accepted as final. The quality and standard of life in all historical periods have been inadequate. The dialectical tension between the accepted actual morality of society and the demand for a higher approximation of perfectibility generates a permanent challenge.

Every moment of history is an eternal moment open to evaluation and subject to criticism. Not even the utopianism of Marxism can escape this challenge. Its implications for a philosophy of life, history, and education are decisive.

Religion may be regarded as the supreme drive of the human person to move beyond the relativity of historical occurrences and stand within the vantage ground of eternity. It is the ultimate form of distantiation that man can make. Distancing the immediate historical world is the way to that realm of being that cannot be manipulated; it is the way along which the tragedies of human time are excluded and therefore overcome; it is the way to that ground of reality from which an eternal judgment can be rendered upon the distorted character of historical existence; it is the way along which man is transformed; and it is the way to ultimate historical and human fulfillment. A view of life and history is here opened beyond the restrictions inherent in the Marxist philosophy. Man's development and re-education are realized not only through altering the institutional and social arrangement of life (as Marx would do) but through changing the personal and human attitudes of man in his approach toward the world. Institutional change unaccompanied by a human change within man is incapable of achieving a better and more just society.

When Marx guaranteed that a more humane, free, and just life would emerge simply from an alteration of the conditions of ownership, he failed to understand the deeper conditions in which these human values are embedded. The socialization of the instruments of production is not a final remedy for the irresponsibility of private ownership; it is only a surface and, therefore, a false and quite possibly disastrous remedy. The totalitarian character of collectivism is clearly an inadequate substitute for the possible tyranny of an unrestrained capitalism guided only by Adam Smith's "invisible hand." Collectivism as such does not guarantee the conditions for a humane education.

The collectivist can be as irresponsible as the selfish individualist. The rejuvenation of man in society must come from a source deeper, richer, and more integrated than the individualistic-collectivistic dichotomy of current political and educational thought.

The invigorant for history and man's education is not the powerful ascendancy of one group within society, as Marx held, but the realization of self-distantiation within the personal life of every human being.

To indoctrinate a mutually related group with an intransigent philosophy, claiming that the victory of the proletariat will of necessity be a victory for everyone, violates that quality of restraint and compassion necessary for wise statesmanship and wise followership. Self-distantiation undercuts the pride and demonic arrogance that readily develop when the limited and finite endeavors of man are taken as absolute and final. Man's essence is not to be realized in future history, as Marx believed, but rather in the return that reveals eternity in the ultimate depth of man's being.

This eternal return is not fostered within the collective drama of history nor can it be nurtured through organizational or individual busyness. It matures in those moments of private inwardness that cannot be regimented by the world outside or by officialdom. This eternal return develops a reservation that cannot be conquered by the tragedies of history and the anxieties that disintegrate the human soul. This return is the process by which man outgrows the worldly flatness and sameness that result from institutional pressures and from too much adjusted socializing. This return creates the power that enables man ultimately to resist the "fathoms of change" and break the image of himself as nothing but a bundle of reflexes and a pawn in the drama of history. It is the way in which man discovers himself as truly a human being, because he becomes aware of the eternal mystery within him. For man to forfeit distancing his world through the eternal return, whether in the name of science, realism, revolution, or future history, would be to destroy a basic quality of man as man. Belief that the message of the social manipulator and the historical revolutionary contains the total truth would suppress man's essential humanity in his encounter with reality. Human life and meaning are not fulfilled on the surface of history but in that order of reality away from the surface in the depth of history. The great task of modern education is to open up that distant but near world in the depth of every human being that cannot be revolutionized and manipulated by practical science. This task is primary and reduces the technical problems of a scientific pedagogy to a secondary level of importance.

This does not mean that the inwardness of the eternal return should make man an absentee from the historical process. Nothing would be worse than for man to withdraw so completely into his own soul as to lose sight of the concerns of the everyday world. Such a departure from life would be self-defeating. The significant and necessary act is to focus the vision gained in moments of inwardness upon the changing issues and difficulties of history. Within this dialectic, the immediate concerns of history and life are not forgotten, nor are they able to overpower and destroy the human person as a person.

There are, therefore, two interrelated dialogues. The first dialogue is the dialogue of the eternal return that moves beyond all surfaces of life to the ultimate depth of man's being. The second dialogue is the dialogue of the eternal meeting, as Martin Buber has put it, between man and man. The inwardness of the first dialogue is essential to the mutuality of the second dialogue. An education that does not ground itself upon a dimension of eternal depth cannot hope to create the sense of mutual trust between teacher and taught, leader and follower, employer and employee, that is necessary to engender a spirit of human responsibility and social justice. In these everlasting dialogues of interpretation within each man and between man and man, man and his alienated world are always but never quite transfigured.

Within the circle of these two dialogues the fate of Marx the historical prophet is sealed; the fanatic fury of his revolutionary sociology is dissipated; the individualistic-collectivism of his philosophy is smashed by concerns of deeper import; and the enlarged awareness Marx made available through his social analysis of ideas is able to reach beyond itself and receive the final fruit of consciousness, the mystery that encompasses it.

BIBLIOGRAPHICAL NOTE

The study of Marx and his relation to modern life and education may be continued in a number of different directions. A wise beginning would be to read what Marx wrote himself. The following books and edited anthologies, many now available in paperbacks, are recommended.

Karl Marx and Friedrich Engels, *Basic Writings on Politics and Philosophy*, edited by Lewis S. Feuer. Anchor Books, New York, 1959.
Karl Marx, *Capital and Other Writings*, edited by Max Eastman. The Modern Library, New York, 1932.
Karl Marx, *Capital: A Critique of Political Economy*, edited by Friedrich Engels. The Modern Library, New York, 1906.
Karl Marx and Friedrich Engels, *Manifesto of the Communist Party*. International Publishers, New York, 1948.
Karl Marx, *Selected Writings in Sociology and Social Philosophy*, edited by T. B. Bottomore and M. Rubel. Humanities, New York, 1960.
Karl Marx and Friedrich Engels, *German Ideology*. International Publishers, New York, 1960.

Erich Fromm's *Marx's Concept of Man*, published by Frederick Ungar, New York, in 1961, contains the "economic and philosophical manuscripts" of Karl Marx, translated by T. B. Bottomore.

A range of reading in Marx's productions is required if one is to grasp the humanistic and educational value of his thought. For some general interpretations that link Marx with other thinkers and the course of

302   THE EDUCATED MAN

Western history, the reader may like to pursue some of the works listed below.

Henry Aiken, *The Age of Ideology: The 19th Century Philosophers*. The New American Library, New York, 1956.

R. C. Collingwood, *The Idea of History*. Oxford University Press, New York, 1946.

Jorn. Dillenberger and Claude Welch, *Protestant Christianity Interpreted Through its Development*. Charles Scribner's, New York, 1954.

C. J. Friedrich, *Inevitable Peace*. Harvard University Press, Cambridge, 1948.

C. J. Friedrich, *The Philosophy of Law in Historical Perspective*. The University of Chicago Press, Chicago, 1958.

Erich Fromm, *Beyond the Chains of Illusion: My Encounter with Marx and Freud*. Simon and Schuster, New York, 1962.

Herbert Marcuse, *Reason and Revolution. Hegel and the Rise of Social Theory*. Beacon Press, Boston, 1960.

Karl R. Popper, *The Open Society and its Enemies*. Princeton University Press, Princeton, N. J., 1950.

Robert A. Nisbet, *The Quest for Community: A Study in the Ethics of Order and Freedom*. Oxford University Press, New York, 1953.

G. H. Sabine, *A History of Political Theory*. Henry Holt, New York, 1950.

The comprehension of Marx requires some understanding of Hegel, and Hegel cannot be grasped without an appreciation of Kant. The Modern Library volumes edited by Carl J. Friedrich, *The Philosophy of Hegel*, New York, 1954, and *The Philosophy of Kant*, New York, 1949, are valuable introductions for this purpose. Kant's little essay on *Education*, published by the University of Michigan Press, Ann Arbor, in 1960 captures his general philosophy and is highly valuable.

For penetrating comments on and criticism of Marx one may profitably turn to works by some social, philosophical, and theological thinkers. An interesting biography leads off a suggested list.

Isaiah Berlin, *Karl Marx: His Life and Environment*. Oxford University Press, New York, 1959.

Martin Buber, *Between Man and Man*. Beacon Press, Boston, 1947.

Erich Fromm, *The Sane Society*. Rinehart and Company, New York, 1955.

Ernest Hocking, *The Lasting Elements of Individualism*. Yale University Press, New Haven, 1937.

Edward Heimann, *Reason and Faith in Modern Society: Liberalism, Marxism and Democracy*. Wesleyan University Press, Middletown, 1961.

Karl Mannheim, *Essays on the Sociology of Knowledge*. Routledge and Kegan Paul Ltd., London, 1952.

Karl Mannheim, *Ideology and Utopia*. Harcourt, Brace and Company, New York, 1953.

Karl Mannheim, *Diagnosis of Our Time*. Routledge and Kegan Paul Ltd., London, 1943.

Reinhold Niebuhr, *Faith and History: A Comparison of Views of History*. Charles Scribner's Sons, New York, 1949.

Joseph A. Schumpeter, *Capitalism, Socialism and Democracy.* Harper Torchbooks, New York, 1962.
Paul Tillich, *The Protestant Era.* University of Chicago Press, Chicago, 1948.
Paul Tillich, *Systematic Theology.* Vol. 1, Nisbet and Co., London, 1951.

No bibliography can be complete. Many valuable writings have been omitted. Perhaps the only way to correct the limitations of this sketch is to browse in the library and the bookstore. The craft of studentship is made more exciting by finding the unexpected and is developed through an imaginative resourcefulness. This foray into additional readings requires an imagination.

Should the reader be interested in the problem of knowledge, for instance, it may be more useful to turn to the volume on *German Ideology* before entertaining *Das Capital* and to delve into Mannheim's *Ideology and Utopia* rather than pursue Fromm's *The Sane Society.* Such discriminations will increase as one reads the titles of recommended volumes carefully and gains enlightenment as to what the books are all about.

🌸 JOHN DEWEY (1859–1952) was born in Burlington, Vermont, where his father was proprietor of a general store. After receiving his bachelor's degree from the University of Vermont, Dewey taught school in Oil City, Pennsylvania, and later in a rural school in Vermont. He left school teaching to pursue graduate studies at Johns Hopkins University where he received his doctorate in 1884. That year he became instructor of philosophy at the University of Michigan. In 1888 he became professor of philosophy at the University of Minnesota but returned to occupy the university chair of philosophy at Michigan from 1889 until 1894. Thereafter for ten years he headed the department of philosophy, psychology, and education at the University of Chicago and from 1902 to 1904 served as director of the School of Education. From 1904 until his retirement in 1930 he was professor of philosophy at Columbia University. While at the University of Chicago, Dewey organized the Laboratory School to test his educational ideas. He first expressed these views on education in a series of lectures, published as *The School and Society* in 1899. This book was translated into almost every European language as well as into Arabic and Japanese. After becoming professor of philosophy at Columbia University, Dewey continued his interest in education by lecturing at Teachers College and by the publication of further books on education, *How We Think, Experience and Education,* and *Democracy and Education,* his most comprehensive work on education. During his years at Columbia University, Dewey was invited to lecture in Japan, in China where he stayed two years, and in Mexico. He also made inspection tours of the schools in Turkey and in the Soviet Union at the request of these governments. Dewey's published books and articles include over 1,000 titles.

12

THE REFLECTIVE MAN: *Dewey*

BY BRIAN HOLMES

Any Englishman who has the temerity to write about John Dewey—
a famous American institution—should offer an explanation. There are
three reasons why, as a comparative educationist, I felt that I might
throw some light upon some aspects of an educational theory that is now
very much part of the climate of opinion in the United States. First of
all, any European reading Dewey will find debated many of the assumptions and theories on which traditional European (including English)
systems of education rest. Dewey's forthright attack on many sacred
cows is refreshing, particularly for those Europeans who wish to improve
their own systems of education. Few such readers can fail to have been
influenced not only by his criticisms of classical educational theories but
by his positive proposals for reform. Secondly, his writings can provide
for the European a rationale for American education—a pattern of assumptions and beliefs against which it is possible to make sense of a
highly complex system and what goes on within it. In particular, *How
We Think* seems to offer in a single volume as *useful* a picture of American educational assumptions as Plato's *Republic* provides for European
education. No better example of this assertion can be found than the
title of a recent book by H. Gordon Hullfish and Philip G. Smith—
Reflective Thinking: the Method of Education.

I mention this book for another reason too. It enables me to acknowledge the debt I owe to the late Gordon Hullfish personally and to the
writings of Dewey and Boyd H. Bode and other progressive educators
in the evolution of my thinking about education. Undoubtedly I have
accepted many aspects of pragmatism, and throughout the fabric of this
essay will be interwoven opinions that I have accepted as my own. This
acceptance of the central ideas of American educational theory provides
my chief justification for writing about Dewey's concept of an educated
man. I trust that in my interpretation I have not ascribed to Dewey
views that he would have rejected. The danger is all too obvious in view
of his voluminous writings; the warning to readers is, I hope, equally
clear.

On the first point, it is not possible to appreciate Dewey's proposals without understanding and considering the views against which he was arguing. These fall essentially into two main schools. First of all, he was opposed to many of the assumptions of one of the European traditions represented by the works of Plato and Aristotle, while the views of the Sophists were much nearer to his own. From the philosophy of the second group of thinkers whom he opposed, the eighteenth-century laissez-faire liberals, he selected certain items for rigorous criticism. He found in the Jeffersonian concept of the American dream features of such permanent value that today his contribution may be seen as a reinterpretation of them in the light of twentieth-century conditions. Reinterpretation is necessary. One reason, for example, why Dewey rejected some of the major premises of both groups seems to be that he regarded philosophers as reporters on social life. The conclusions Plato and Aristotle reached after studying Greek life cannot then be regarded as appropriate to the organization of twentieth-century living. By the same token, not all Jefferson's views can be successfully applied today.

The theoretical key to Dewey's almost total dislike for Plato's theories of knowledge, society, and the individual seems to lie in his attitude toward change. He observed, "Plato took comparatively speaking a pessimistic view of change as mere lapse."[1] Plato viewed the just society as the stable static society in which each person finds personal happiness by knowing his place and being content to remain in it. As for individuals, he considered that each is born possessing innate immutable qualities of character and ability, a view that justifies a social class structure based upon the ability of individuals within each group to perform the functions appropriate to it. These tasks would be performed in the light of special knowledge, whether of the statesman or the carpenter, in Plato's ideal society. The belief held by most Greeks (other than the Sophists of the Protagorean school) that behind the ceaseless flow of experiences there is something permanent, and that this and only this is knowable, was anathema to Dewey. This belief leads inevitably to an absolutism that Dewey abhorred, whether based upon intellectual rationalism or, indeed, upon empiricism. No less harsh was Dewey's criticism of Aristotle whose complacent view of change "as tendency to realization" nevertheless left him as sure as Plato "that the fully realized reality, the divine and the ultimate, is changeless."[2] True knowledge is possible only of what does not change. Individual members of any species or class of objects show such variations and are so liable to

---

[1] John Dewey, *Reconstruction in Philosophy*. Mentor Book, p. 97.
[2] *Ibid.*, p. 97.

change that nothing can be *known* about them except their essence or nature, which, embodied in each of them, is yet the distinguishing feature or characteristic of them all. Knowledge of essences was for Aristotle as important as knowledge of ideas was for Plato. Both distinguished between the realms of reason and experience and, in the last analysis, regarded reason as a reliable approach to the acquisition of knowledge and experience as not. With this dichotomy Aristotle associated two others. First, according to Dewey, there was the dichotomy between theory, which "had to do with things which were supreme because divine and eternal," and practice, which "had to do with things that were merely mundane, things at worst menial and at best earth-bound and transient."[3] At this level, support is found for the downgrading of applied science as compared with pure science. More significantly, the second dichotomy between manual work and intellectual activity, between the liberal arts and the useful arts has helped to perpetuate sharp contrasts between what is considered to be liberal education and vocational training and inevitably between the cultured or educated man and the artisan. Dewey regarded these particular dualisms as among those most damaging to the progress of modern education—a point that has been increasingly brought home to educators throughout the world today.

Absolutism, refusal to accept change, and the dichotomy between liberal education and vocational training were perhaps the aspects of Europeanism most emphatically rejected by Dewey. As for the American dream to which Dewey in many ways was committed, Ralph Barton Perry wrote: "Thomas Jefferson remains the most complete exponent of the Enlightenment—both in its general tone and its diverse doctrine."[4] Quite central to this thesis was the idea of progress through the "indefinite perfectibility of man."[5] This justified belief in a theory of government in which an aristocracy by birth would be replaced by an aristocracy of talent. Even so, the best government would be one that simply protects the inalienable rights of individuals—life, liberty, property, and the pursuit of happiness—and interferes least in their personal affairs. According to Jefferson an ideal society would need no government, but he was driven to the conclusion that such an ideal was unattainable in the larger American society. Nevertheless, a modified form of agrarianism would give scope for self-government in communities smaller in size than a state or even a county. Dewey, in fact, did not accept the view that Jefferson was merely the champion of state against federal govern-

[3] Dewey, *Philosophy of Education.* Littlefield, New York, 1956, p. 162.
[4] Ralph Barton Perry, *Puritanism and Democracy.* Vanguard Press, 1944, p. 177.
[5] Dewey, *Democracy and Education.* Macmillan, New York, 1916, p. 106.

ment or that he thought of government simply as a necessary evil. On the contrary, Dewey's opinion was that "the heart of his philosophy of politics is found in his efforts to institute these small administrative and legislative units as the keystone of the arch."[6]

Political and economic theories of society depend for their successful implementation on the quality of individuals within it, according to Jefferson, who recognized that "it is the manners and spirit of a people which preserve a republic in vigor."[7] He regarded the mass of people with a certain suspicion. "The mass of citizens may be divided into two classes—the labouring and the learned," he said.[8] The learned citizens were to form the aristocracy of talent. As for the laboring classes, since conditions affected man's virtues, substantial virtue had been deposited in the agricultural workers—"the chosen people of God."[9] But the industrial workers—the class of artificers—were, to Jefferson, "the panders of vice, and the instrument by which the liberties of a country are generally overturned. . ."[10] A nation could remain virtuous and the will of the majority prevail only "as long as agriculture is our principal object."

Under these conditions two principles should, according to Jefferson, govern the behavior of individuals—reason and self-interest. Natural liberty and economic necessity implied that every man should be free within limits to pursue his own interests. Economic progress was possible because men were powerfully motivated by it. Reason, argued Jefferson, would enable men to see that certain actions were in their own self-interest. A little education, for example, would ensure that the common people appreciated the need to "preserve peace and order." What remains somewhat obscure in Jefferson's writings is what exactly constitutes "reason." Undoubtedly he shared the faith of the encyclopedists and Protagoras that each man possesses an element of civic virtue. Educate men and develop this virtue, and democracy would be secure. Not all men, however, possessed virtue in equal amounts. Jefferson agreed with Rousseau who wrote, "I conceive that there are two kinds of inequality among the human species; one which I call natural or physical, because it is established by nature, and consists in a difference of age, health and bodily strength, and the qualities of mind or of the soul; and another which may be called moral or political inequality, because it depends on a kind of convention, and is established, or at least authorised by the consent of men."[11] Moral and political inequali-

---

[6] Dewey, *The Living Thoughts of Thomas Jefferson*. Cassell, London, 1946, p. 22.
[7] S. K. Padover, *The Complete Jefferson*. Tudor, New York, 1943, p. 679.
[8] *Ibid.*, p. 1099.   [9] *Ibid.*, p. 678.
[10] Padover, *Thomas Jefferson on Democracy*. Mentor, p. 69.
[11] J. J. Rousseau, *Social Contract*. Everyman, London, p. 174.

ties were unjust and should be removed. Intellectual differences could not be removed, but each man through education could be improved.

Evidently Dewey accepted many features of this Jeffersonian faith. His most serious disagreement with the laissez-faire liberals seems to be on two points. First, he found their concept of individualism that isolates the individual from his social context relevant only to the period of history in which it was proposed. Moreover, self-interest was no longer an appropriate regulator of human affairs. He pointed out that in nineteenth-century America when the individuals were pioneering a wilderness "the demands of the practical situation called for the initiative, enterprise and vigor of individuals in all immediate work that urgently asked for doing, and their operation furthered the national life."[12] This was no longer the case. Dewey's second serious point of disagreement concerned the characteristics of "reason," and on this question Dewey was almost as much opposed to uncritical empiricism as he was to the rationalism of the Greeks and Descartes. The reservation is important because he approved Bacon's concept of knowledge as power and forgave him much on the grounds that he advocated a "State organized for collective inquiry."[13] These two points—individualism and reason—are so central to the whole of Dewey's theory of what constitutes an educated man that they need to be considered in greater detail.

But first, two difficulties should be mentioned. In the preparation of an essay such as this, selection of material from a large number of books and periodical articles is a serious enough problem; but when the subject's writings stretch well over fifty years of active work, the difficulty is considerably increased. Fortunately, after he disposed in large measure of Hegelianism and accepted pragmatism, Dewey constantly returned to the same major themes. Running through his writings there is a consistency, and for this reason no attempt is made in what follows to arrange references to his writings in the order in which they appeared, nor is any attempt made to trace the evolution of his thinking.

The second difficulty is inherent in the writings themselves. A description of the educated man would be tidy at least if offered in terms of the categories established by philosophers of the kind Dewey attacked. It would, for example, be useful to say what skills an educated man should possess, what knowledge he should acquire, what attitudes and qualities of character should distinguish him from the uneducated man. But the weight of Dewey's attack is, in fact, just upon those dualisms that traditional philosophers have established. He rejected the *either-or*

---

[12] Dewey, "Toward a New Individualism (Individualism, Old and New III)," *New Republic*, Vol. 62, Feb. 19, 1930.
[13] Dewey, *Reconstruction in Philosophy*, p. 52.

implications of dualisms like "labor and leisure, practical and intellectual activity, man and nature, individuality and association, culture and vocation."[14] And at another level dualisms like "mind (or spirit) and matter, body and mind, the mind and the world, the individual and his relationships to others"[15] have been set up. In proposing to synthesize what were previously antitheses, Dewey applied the principle of continuity to such an extent that Paul Crosser maintains it leads to complete nihilism.[16] Perhaps he states his case rather too strongly, but there is no doubt that any attempt to give precision to key terms used by Dewey involves some recognition of the constant and intimate interactions between ends and means, individuals and environments, thinking and behavior, etc. In attempting to separate out from Dewey's writings his major concepts of the individual, society, and knowledge as they bear upon his view of the educated man, I am aware of failure to abide by Dewey's own method. Yet it should soon be apparent from what follows how close are the links between the various concepts to which he constantly returned.

Consequently, it is impossible to talk about an educated man in isolation. In Dewey's thinking, the individual has no separate existence except in a limited physical sense, and even biologically he is to be seen as an organism continuously interacting with a natural environment. Individuality is neither originally given nor is it "complete in itself, like a closet in a house or a secret drawer in a desk, filled with treasures that are waiting to be bestowed on the world."[17] On the contrary, individuality "in a social and moral sense is something to be wrought out,"[18] or, in other words, "created under the influences of associated life."[19] The individual and the social should not be set against each other as separate entities, for without one the other has no existence. Therefore, under changing circumstances individuality takes on new forms and, in doing so, further modifies the circumstances. The antisocial concept of the individual, expounded particularly by Rousseau, linked him not with his immediate social environment but with nature. This was appropriate enough, as has been said, to the nineteenth century, but individualism in the twentieth century has to be given new meanings, because the social environment is so different and is more significant than it formerly was in the growth of individuality. "Our problems," Dewey wrote, in an

[14] Dewey, *Democracy and Education*, p. 377. [15] *Ibid.*, p. 377.
[16] P. K. Crosser, *The Nihilism of John Dewey*. Philosophical Library, New York, 1955.
[17] Joseph Ratner, Ed., *Intelligence in the Modern World*. Modern Library, New York, 1939, p. 415.
[18] Dewey, *Reconstruction in Philosophy*, p. 152. [19] *Ibid.*, p. 155.

analysis of individualism, "grow out of social conditions: they concern human relations rather than man's direct relationship to physical nature."[20] His refusal to accept individuality as something in itself apart from these conditions is perfectly compatible with his warning against the dangers of a certain kind of child-centered education.[21]

Man must, therefore, be educated for a particular kind of society. The society in which Dewey found himself in the twentieth century was very different from that of the pioneering period of American history. The early pragmatists were, of course, products of the age of transition between two eras—the watershed of which was the last decade of the nineteenth century. Just as Dewey suggested that William James "gave intellectual expression to the life of the pioneer who made the country. . . ,"[22] so Dewey himself has been described as an apologist of American commercialism and materialism. Bertrand Russell's claim that he found "love of truth in America obscured by commercialism of which pragmatism is the philosophical expression; and love of our neighbour kept in fetters by Puritan morality,"[23] was sharply challenged by Dewey. Dewey seems to have been equally resentful when Lewis Mumford implied that he had willingly surrendered "to industrial utilitarianism."[24] In this quite acrimonious debate it is important to distinguish between statements of what is and of what ought to be. As we have noted, Jefferson believed in a laissez-faire economic society founded on property-owning agarianism, yet he foresaw, according to Dewey, the development of industry and commerce. Except perhaps in his reply to Russell, Dewey neither accepted nor rejected the desirability of the kind of society envisaged by Jefferson, but he appreciated that it had largely disappeared under the forces of industrialization and urbanization. The changes, whether desired or not, had occurred and created a new type of society in which the old individual found himself submerged both economically and politically. Old techniques could not be used in this kind of society, and a new individuality, not just more of the same rugged self-interestedness, had to develop if the obnoxious features of commercial and industrial life—the most dominating of which he saw as "corporateness," analyzed in his "Individualism, Old and New," a

---

[20] Dewey, "Toward a New Individualism (Individualism, Old and New III)," *New Republic*, Vol. 62, Feb. 19, 1930.

[21] Dewey, "How Much Freedom in New Schools?" *New Republic*, Vol. 63, July 9, 1930.

[22] Dewey, "William James in 1926," *New Republic*, Vol. 47, May 26, June 30, Aug. 18, 1926.

[23] Dewey, "Pragmatic America," *New Republic*, Vol. 30, Apr. 12, 1922.

[24] Dewey, "The Pragmatic Acquiescence," *New Republic*, Vol. 49, Jan. 5, 1927.

series of articles in the *New Republic*—were to be ameliorated. Because such conditions create problems for the individual and help to mold him, Dewey believed it important that he be aware of the forces of change around him, so that instead of being a helpless pawn he could, with his fellow men, control events.

Politically, too, Dewey was prepared for change. For example, he did not even accept without question that American society should be based on a constitution drawn up over 150 years ago.[25] Moreover, he appreciated that fine Lockian ideals about government—such as that the best is the one that interferes least with the individual's everyday activities— do not prevent individual freedom from being seriously limited under modern conditions. Political liberalism in its extreme form, indeed, does not protect the freedom of individuals from "further subjection to the owners of the agencies of material production and distribution."[26] That is to say, the authority of economic forces has meant that "economic freedom has been either non-existent or precarious for the large mass of the population."[27]

Of course Dewey was committed to a republican form of democracy. But he did not see democracy as a set of institutions, political forms, and devices, nor yet as a "final end and a final value."[28] These are but means through which "ends that lie in the wide domain of human relationships"[29] can be realized, and human personality developed. Democracy is a way of life made possible by the willingness of individuals to cooperate with one another, in Dewey's view. He declared, "A democracy is more than a form of government; it is primarily a mode of associated living, of conjoint communicated experience."[30] Dewey's criterion for a form of government was the extent to which it makes possible the kind of free and open inquiry that encourages change. Thus he was unable to accept the restrictions placed on individuality by the institutions established in the nineteenth century against a background of idealistic philosophies, particularly those prevailing in Germany. Certainly, authoritarian governments set up institutions that are designed to prevent change and to retain the *status quo*. Such attempts are bound to fail. Change is one of the most important facts of life. Since it is pointless to try to stop it and foolish to close one's eyes to it, the object

[25] Dewey, "Education for a Changing Social Order," NEA *Addresses and Proceedings,* 1934, pp. 744–752.
[26] Ratner, *op. cit.,* p. 354.
[27] Dewey, "Can Education Share in Social Reconstruction?" *Social Frontier,* I, Oct., 1934.
[28] Ratner, *op. cit.,* p. 401.   [29] *Ibid.,* p. 400.
[30] Dewey, *Democracy and Education,* p. 101.

of education should be to help individuals cope with changes in society, according to Dewey.

The willing acceptance of the idea that society is bound to change has major implications. In the first place it represents a most revolutionary and generous view of society. Dewey gave James credit for stating some of its main characteristics. He wrote that "the fundamental idea of an open universe in which uncertainty, choice, hypotheses, novelties and possibilities are naturalized will remain associated with the name of James."[31] Such a view has within it no preconceived notion that change implies only decay and loss, as Plato thought. Nor, on the other hand, is progress assured as the encyclopedists seemed to hold. Nor is change quite the mechanical process implied by social Darwinism. Certainly it offers tremendous opportunities. Dewey put it this way: "Change becomes significant of new possibilities and ends to be attained; it becomes prophetic of a better future."[32] But at the same time, change implies at least three closely related difficulties of adjustment. First, change inevitably brings with it more or less serious social problems that have to be faced and, if possible, solved. Second, the question of social control is raised when individuals seek to direct social change rather than allowing it to dominate them. Third, in the process of problem solving, individuals will change and should be prepared to do so.

Problems, of course, cannot exist in a vacuum. They are, in one sense, states of mind. For example, when an individual's normal course of action is blocked, the difficulty he faces gives rise to a perplexity that constitutes the problem. There are collective problems in which not only one individual is perplexed, but groups—either large or small—face difficulties. Quite simply, there are perplexing situations in the affairs of individuals, communities, nations, and the world of nations. Individuals acting either alone or, more often, collectively have to face them. But how are they created? In any society a number of forces are at work to bring about change. The directness and power of their impact are not distributed equally over all aspects of a society; thus asynchronous changes are set up within it. The most significant illustration of this phenomenon, to which Dewey constantly referred, is found by comparing the changes that scientific applications have wrought in man's material environment with the lack of adjustment in man's beliefs, attitudes, customs, and social institutions—the instruments he needs for coping with this changed world. Subsequently, further analysis will show some specific features of this general hypothesis.

[31] Dewey, "The Pragmatic Acquiescence," *op. cit.*
[32] Dewey, *Reconstruction in Philosophy*, p. 102.

Control of change raises the issue of planning; the problem is to find a balance between stability and change and to adjust authority and freedom. Dewey believed that if social planning is to take place, it is important to ensure it the freest possible play of intelligence.[33] Thus planning was not automatically rejected as undesirable by Dewey. Indeed he appreciated that it takes place very successfully in limited fields, such as the realms of economics and the control of many aspects of the physical environment. But he was not prepared to accept "social control by means of collective planned economy."[34] And he realized that total planning is at best an uncertain operation. He wrote: "Judging, planning, choice, no matter how thoroughly conducted, and action no matter how prudently executed, never are the sole determinants of any outcome. Alien and indifferent natural forces, unforeseeable conditions, enter in and have a decisive voice."[35]

Dewey suggested that the solution lies, at least in part, in bringing about changes in the equipment of educated men. Too often when an individual is tackling problems, habit determines his course of action. Dewey explained, "When tradition and social custom are incorporated in the working constitution of an individual, they have authority as a matter of course over his beliefs and his activities."[36] Action undertaken on the basis of this kind of authority is unlikely to be very effective in a changing society. Men have to change too; and if they are to become true individuals, Dewey held that "the grip of the authority of custom and tradition as standards of belief"[37] must be relaxed. Associated with this emancipation should be a *"willingness to re-examine and if necessary to revise current convictions, even if that course entails the effort to change by concerted effort existing institutions, and to direct existing tendencies to new ends."*[38] Evidently educated men should be aware of change and its implications—a situation not yet reached, in Dewey's opinion; he wrote that a revolution would have occurred "if we were to recognize that we live in a changing social order and proceed to act upon that recognition in our schools."[39] Again the educational task is to prepare individuals not only to meet problems but to anticipate them. Dewey advised, "A nation habituated to *think* in terms of problems and of the struggle to remedy them before it is actually in the grip of the forces

---

[33] Ratner, *op. cit.*, p. 432.
[34] Dewey, "Authority and Resistance to Social Change," *School and Society*, Vol. 44, Oct. 10, 1936, p. 464.
[35] Dewey, *Quest for Certainty*. Minton, Balch and Co., New York, 1929, p. 11.
[36] Dewey, "Authority and Resistance to Social Change," *op. cit.*, p. 459.
[37] Dewey, *Democracy and Education*, p. 356.   [38] Ratner, *op. cit.*, p. 777.
[39] Dewey, "Education for a Changing Social Order," *op. cit.*

which create the problems, would have an equipment for public life such as has not characterized any people."[40] The problem-solving, problem-anticipating individual cannot rely on procedures appropriate to a relatively static social order. Effective participation in a changing social order demands that individuals, singly and collectively, shall not simply obey some external authority but shall be capable of discrimination and able to make choices between one course of action and another. The component of individuality that enables them to perform these functions is intelligence. The extent to which choices in problematic situations are based upon the exercise of "organized intelligence" is a measure of an educated man. It is, according to Dewey, the prime office of intelligence to help individuals or a community to meet problems by effecting a "working connection between old habits, customs, institutions, beliefs and new conditions."[41]

As may be expected, intelligence is not something innate, in the accepted sense of the word, and possessed once and for all. Rather, declared Dewey, "it is in constant process of framing, and its retention requires constant alertness in observing consequences and open-minded will to learn and courage in re-adjustment."[42] Evidently it cannot be defined as the ability to perform any one operation unless it be to think reflectively. Intelligence seems to encompass intellectual ability, power to observe, but also certain attitudes of mind and qualities of character. Unless certain dispositions are present within the individual, the release of his intelligence would appear to be unlikely, according to Dewey, although sometimes Dewey seems to distinguish more sharply between intelligence and character. Be this as it may, he regarded the relationship between them as intimate. Furthermore, organized intelligence is observed through ways of acting. Since no intelligent action can precede thought, it follows that intelligent behavior is either a consequence of intelligent thinking or an integral part of it. The latter seems to be more likely. Certainly, if a measure of high intelligence is the extent to which all phases of reflective thinking are performed, then intelligence reflects an ability to perform intellectual operations and observe data, and also the presence of certain attitudes, dispositions, and a willingness to act. Clarity of meaning can be obtained only through considering two activities, science and reflective thinking, which seem so similar as to be indistinguishable.

Before moving on to an analysis of these terms, it should be noted that in Dewey's view intelligence can grow as an individual grows,

---

[40] Dewey, "Schools and Social Preparedness," *New Republic*, Vol. 7, July 1, 1916.
[41] Ratner, *op. cit.*, p. 452.
[42] Dewey, *Reconstruction in Philosophy*, p. 89.

through interaction with an environment and through education. To be sure, it can do so only under certain conditions, and Dewey virtually defined freedom in terms of intelligence. He stated that "the basic freedom is freedom of *mind* and of whatever degree of freedom of action and experience is necessary to produce freedom of intelligence."[43] One should also note Dewey's attitude concerning the extent to which all individuals might attain the same level of intelligence. Dewey, like Jefferson, did not regard equality as a psychological fact but rather as a legal, political, and moral concept that is part of democratic ideology. Certainly, his arguments in favor of equality of opportunity should not be taken to imply "belief in equality of natural endowments."[44] Dewey considered that equality of opportunity is established by law to protect the less gifted from the competitive opposition of the more gifted. It is difficult to escape the conclusion that Dewey had a more traditional conception of intelligence than seems apparent from disclaimers.

One might compare his view with what Protagoras called "civic virtue"—the uniquely human characteristic that enables men to compete successfully with other animals and to live together in societies. All men possess "civic virtue" but in unequal amounts. How then can democracy work? According to Dewey, through cooperation and the pooling of intelligence. He said that, although "intelligence may be distributed in unequal amounts, it is the democratic faith that it is sufficiently general so that each individual has something to contribute, and the value of each contribution can be assessed only as it enters into the final pooled intelligence constituted by the contributions of all."[45] Here there is a suggestion that there is something like a group intelligence— or, as Dewey termed it, a "collective organic intelligence." The development of intelligence—both individual and collective—so that maximum reliance can be placed upon it is absolutely necessary to the successful working of a liberal democracy. Dewey's conclusion seems to be that the degree to which such forms of government operate successfully will provide a measure of the release of intelligence. Conversely, were it possible to develop intelligence in societies other than democracies (and this seems to have happened in history) then the result would be the establishment of a democracy.

Looked at in another way, organized intelligence is synonymous with science—the initiator of change and at the same time the emancipator offering above all, like intelligence, "freedom from the limitations of habit." Thus, through the applications of science, the conditions under

---

[43] Dewey, *Reconstruction in Philosophy*, p. 61.
[44] Dewey, *Philosophy of Education*, p. 60.   [45] Ratner, *op. cit.*, p. 403.

which people associate with one another have been revolutionized. At the same time, science has successfully challenged the right of religion or theology to exercise social authority. The conflict, Dewey said, was not carried out simply at the theoretical level; rather it was between "two alignments of forces."[46] Institutional power remained in the hands of the theologians until the forces of science were able to gain recognition. These forces did so, not by stifling individual initiative and intelligence but by fostering the spirit of free inquiry. The greatest advance in the authority of science has been in the physical field. Dewey wished to see the methods of science applied as widely as possible to human affairs. So far, their success has been too restricted simply because they have been applied in too narrow a field.

Before science is accepted as the emancipator, Dewey wished to make clear that only a certain view of what constitutes science can provide organized intelligence with appropriate tools of inquiry. Science, for example, should not mean that one kind of dogmatism is replaced by another. He quoted James as protesting rightly "against science when it sets fixed bounds and restricts freedom."[47] In *Reconstruction in Philosophy* he presented a critique of traditional and even of some aspects of Baconian science. He challenged the details of Bacon's method rather than the spirit of experimentation and inquiry. He agreed with Bacon that "knowledge is power" and that knowledge can finally be acquired only by an "invasion of the unknown, rather than repetition in logical form of the already known."[48] And as the prophet of the cooperative inquiries that constitute science in our own day and of a "State organized for collective inquiry,"[49] Dewey was prepared to forgive Bacon a great deal. It was, indeed, this cooperative aspect of scientific work that was so important to Dewey. The authority of science, he maintained, "issues from and is based upon collective activity, cooperatively organized."[50] This statement, among many, illustrates why Dewey held that science is the method of organized intelligence and the kind of inquiry on which democracy should rest.

Evidently it was not science as an organized body of knowledge that was important to Dewey but the methods appropriate to its pursuit. If these are used correctly, they will lead to knowledge in its most characteristic and perfected form. In other words, knowledge is not of something fixed, immutable, and outside human experience but is always the outcome of inquiry. Because a quite fundamental aspect of scientific

46 Dewey, *Philosophy of Education*, p. 106.
47 Dewey, "William James," *Independent*, Vol. 69, Sept. 8, 1910.
48 Dewey, *Reconstruction in Philosophy*, p. 49.   49 *Ibid.*, p. 52.
50 Dewey, *Philosophy of Education*, p. 107.

inquiry is experimental testing, the knowledge to which it leads can never be certain or absolute, merely probable. The tests applied to scientific statements or hypotheses merely increase or lessen their probability. The same tests give meaning to the statements of propositions. That is to say, if the predictions made from the propositions are confirmed by actual events, then the propositions can be said to have "warranted assertability." The usefulness of testing should be abundantly apparent. Dewey substituted "warranted assertability" for the word "knowledge," perhaps because the words "knowledge "and "truth" held so many philosophical implications that he rejected. One of these implications was that scientific laws have a universal validity, that is, that they correspond to reality irrespective of the context. For Dewey, reference to the circumstances in which hypotheses are formulated and tested is essential if the meaning of the hypothetical statements is to be understood and the "warranted assertability" of them established.

Stated in yet another way, there can be no such thing as objective knowledge or truth. The so-called objectivity of the scientist arises not because of his personal insights (or intuition) or because his material consists of hard facts or "things-in-themselves" but rather because his procedures of testing are public. Objectivity depends, then, upon the possibility of agreement by individuals with conclusions reached on the basis of the tests that were carried out and the instruments of measurement that were used in these processes of verification and refutation. There are, of course, associated with this view a number of sociological and psychological assumptions and even, as Russell says,[51] prophecy. This kind of objectivity means that there are some conclusions (knowledge) on which, finally, consensus among men can be reached. Consensus may easily be reached, for example, on the relative speed at which aircraft are traveling or on the temperature of things; but it is not so easily reached on whether things are "hot" or "cold" or, even if wavelength measurements were accepted, on color. Obviously, there is even less likelihood of agreement concerning conclusions like "this is pleasant" or "this is nasty" or "this is good." Because agreement has been reached so much more readily in the spheres of physics and chemistry (and to some extent in biology) than in the social sciences and morals, the argument has arisen that there are different ways of knowing and different kinds of knowledge. Scientific methods, according to this argument, are appropriate in some fields but not in others. This claim Dewey could not accept. Inquiry is primary; knowledge, truth, and even war-

---

[51] P. A. Schilpp, Ed., The Philosophy of John Dewey, Northwestern University Press, Evanston, Ill., 1939, p. 145.

ranted assertability are derivative. Central to Dewey's philosophy is his concept that the processes of inquiry are applicable not only in the realm that has traditionally been regarded as the province of the natural scientist but in every other realm, too. "The general adoption of the scientific attitude in human affairs," he wrote, "would mean nothing less than a revolutionary change in morals, religion, politics and industry."[52] This revolution depends for its success on the use by all men, to the maximum of their ability, of the method of organized intelligence and science, that is reflective thinking. It is this, above all, toward which one must direct attention when seeking to understand Dewey's concept of an educated man.

While the theme of reflective thinking recurs often both in Dewey's articles and in his major writings, an orderly analysis of the process is presented in *How We Think*. According to William H. Kilpatrick, this analysis had a tonic effect on American teachers and enabled them to discover the "problem approach" as a teaching device.[53] The process represents both an educational aim and a method, and the analysis is such that specific aspects of the complete act of thinking can be isolated (however improper Dewey may have regarded such a procedure) and amplified. Reflective thinking can appropriately be used to identify a pattern of attitudes and the qualities of mind and character that should constitute the equipment of any educated man; it cannot, one must realize, be used to indicate what knowledge the educated man should possess or the hierarchy of values by which he should live. But it will become clear that reflective thinking can hardly take place unless an individual accepts the assumptions on which its processes are based. An act of faith is necessary, albeit one that may not be as difficult to make as the suppositions asked of students who would follow other paths to knowledge. Moreover, there are certain presuppositions about how thinking is initiated and what its purpose is.

First of all, Dewey assumed, "Thinking is not a case of spontaneous combustion; it does not occur just on general principles!" but originates in some "perplexity, confusion, or doubt"[54] within the experience of the individual. Exhortations to think are bound to be ineffective unless this condition is fulfilled. Parenthetically, it should be asked whether the range of life situations in which individuals will experience this kind of perplexity is as limited as Dewey, or perhaps some of his followers, implied. If the condition is fulfilled, however, reflective thinking can proceed, with the intent "*to transform a situation in which there is ex-*

---

52 Ratner, *op. cit.*, p. 459.   53 Schilpp, *op. cit.*, p. 469.
54 Dewey, *How We Think*. Heath, New York, 1933, p. 115.

perienced obscurity, doubt, conflict, disturbance of some sort, into a situation that is clear, coherent, settled, harmonious."[55] Between the pre-reflective and postreflective situations, occur the five states, or phases, of thinking. Dewey presented them in the following form:

In between, as states of thinking, are (1) *suggestions* in which the mind leaps forward to a possible solution; (2) an intellectualization of the difficulty or perplexity that has been *felt* (directly experienced) into a *problem* to be solved, a question for which the answer must be sought; (3) the use of one suggestion after another as a leading idea, or hypothesis, to initiate and guide observation and other operations in collection of factual material; (4) the mental elaboration of the idea or supposition as an idea or supposition (*reasoning* in the sense in which reasoning is a part, not the whole, or inference); and (5) testing the hypothesis by overt or imaginative action.[56]

Without enlarging on each of these phases in turn, it should be emphasized in a general way, first that they do not necessarily follow each other in the stated order. In fact, there is likely to be fairly continuous interaction among the different aspects. Any improvement in the quality of thinking in any phase does something to refine each of the other processes. A second general point is that any one of the phases might be expanded very considerably, depending on the problem and the circumstances. For example, the formulation of a problem involving the proposal of questions to which answers are sought may be extremely complicated. The central problem may have many facets, and the search for solutions may require careful distinction of these various elements. With another kind of problem, the analysis of the circumstances or context, of problem may demand most attention. Furthermore, in each of the phases, judgments have to be made that "are so related as to support one another in leading to a final judgment—the conclusion."[57]

The quality of reflective thought depends in general upon the quality of the thinker's judgment throughout the various phases. His judgments, to be sound, must be pertinent and discriminating. The greater the number of persons of sound judgment, the higher will be the quality of any inquiry, and, therefore, of the operation of democracy. Very significantly, Dewey wrote, "A man of sound judgment in any set of affairs is an *educated* man as respects those affairs, whatever his schooling or academic standing."[58]

It is difficult to enumerate criteria on the basis of which sound judgments are made. Past experience certainly makes some contribution, and they are evidently easier to make in the physical sciences than in the human sciences and in morals. An appeal to an unconditionally valid

---

[55] *Ibid.*, pp. 100–101.   [56] *Ibid.*, p. 107.   [57] *Ibid.*, p. 119.   [58] *Ibid.*, p. 120.

prior principle cannot, however, provide an adequate basis of sound judgment. Its quality will depend to some extent, but not entirely, on the manner in which the various phases of thinking are performed. Judging consists of selecting and weighting contextual data, hypotheses, ideas, and so on. If the analysis on the basis of which judgment has to be passed is incomplete, the judgment itself is bound to be less than sound. In order to perform adequately in the phases of thinking, one needs a number of qualities, abilities, and attitudes. They will be classified under these headings, although it is impossible to give them full meaning in isolation. Their meanings are essentially to be sought in the interrelationships existing among them.

The foremost necessary quality might be termed emotional awareness or sensitivity. Without this, the reaction of an individual to a total situation may well be dulled. This awareness represents something more than a general recognition by the individual that his world of change will constantly develop new problems. It is a sensitivity that perhaps precedes reflective thought but is essential to it by making the individual alert to the presence of an obscurity, doubt, conflict, or confusion. It is also something rather different from the first of Dewey's three levels of curiosity—"a vital overflow, an expression of an abundant organic energy" or (and this comes nearer to sensitivity) "a physiological uneasiness." Even the next stage, developed under the influence of social stimuli, is only the "germ of *intellectual* curiosity."[59] Only on the basis of this curiosity, which education must above all keep alive and foster, is the process of intellectualization possible.

Another important human quality is imagination. This, like judgment, enters into all phases of thinking and influences its quality. Its base may be past experience or a natural endowment of which Dewey spoke. It enters into the process particularly at the level of suggestions, hypotheses, or ideas. These are creative if knowledge, as defined by Dewey, is to issue from inquiry. For knowledge is not of "things as they are" but the outcome of discovery, which always involves a "leap beyond what is given and already established."[60] The novel or imaginative idea or hypothesis often leads to radically new conclusions and implications. The innovation often runs counter to the hypotheses used in the past to seek solutions. The hypothesis most useful to the problem-solving enterprise does not necessarily arise simply from procedures (particularly concerning observation, as the J. S. Mill school of empiricists often implies) carried out carefully and in accordance with certain rules. Certainly Dewey claimed that the process of problem formulation is very closely con-

---

[59] *Ibid.*, p. 38.   [60] *Ibid.*, p. 96.

nected with the emergence of hypotheses as solutions. But there may be a number of possible solutions, and each has to be tested before the most satisfactory one, that is, the one leading to the resolution of the confused situation, is identified. The testing process takes place in a person's imagination, too, although the techniques of testing are often fairly clearly prescribed. Imagination, then, may be taken to imply a mental quality that makes possible the leap from sense experience or empirical data to ideas, and from ideas back to concrete, singular, experienced events.

The quality of imagination is supported by abilities that should perhaps be regarded as most closely associated with mental activity. Traditionally, these abilities would have been regarded as belonging to man's rational capacity, independent of sense impressions. This view is, of course, not Dewey's, but it might be safe to say these are the abilities that enable an individual to intellectualize a confused situation by analyzing the conditions producing it and by breaking it down (though Dewey did not like this term) into its constituent parts so that specific features significant to an understanding of the problem can be empha- sized. Synthesis places each such feature into its context, that is, into its relationship with other selected parts and with the whole. The processes of analysis and synthesis are complementary, one enriching the other. It should be noted that judgment takes place as a result of analysis, insofar as discrimination between the important and the trivial is involved. These processes are essential to selection and description of the circum- stances or context in which the problem is located and in which the solution is proposed. An illustration carried to absurd lengths may serve to make the point. Any human problem occurs within the universe. Can the context in which the problem occurs be described, and would the problem become more meaningful if it were? Evidently not, although such an attempt might have to be made to solve certain problems. Simi- larly, an analysis of the solar system is not relevant to all problems, only to some. By the same token, there are world problems, but the context is so enormous that selection of material relevant to understanding and solving a particular problem has to be undertaken. This selection is a highly intellectual activity, often carried out in terms of concepts and vicarious experience.

Another important ability associated with intellectual activity is that of reasoning, in the limited sense of deductively inferring conclusions or consequences from given premises. In the physical sciences this type of reasoning is mathematical, but in all kinds of reasoning, the logical in- tention takes similar form: "if p then q." Pragmatists place an important reservation on the application of this process. Deduced inferences can be made only in the framework of the context in which the premises are advanced as hypotheses or solutions. The absolute dependence of successful prediction on an accurate analysis (by one's identifying and giving relative weight to the factors bearing on the problem) is of paramount importance. This means that no principle is unconditionally valid or appropriate as a solution. Judgment enters into this process, too, because the consequences deduced from any hypothesis may occur in a number of areas. If a social problem and its solution be considered, the hypothesis offered may lead to economic, political, and educational consequences. Which of these sequences is selected for deductive elaboration will depend upon the investigator.

In contrast to procedures that are basically rational, there are those that depend upon sense impressions and thus constitute the empirical side of reflective thinking. The fallacy of assuming that observation will furnish "crude masses of raw material, to which, later on, reflective processes may be applied"[61] is implicit in Dewey's whole development in *How We Think*. Observation is not simply a matter of sense data flowing into an individual; it has to be initiated either by a natural desire to learn or by the demands of the problem under consideration. The observation of data through ears, eyes, nose, and touch is part of intelligent action. The problem itself directs attention towards observable data; this and the hypothesis do rather more—they direct attention to data of a certain kind. Judgment, therefore, precedes observation for whatever reasons the observation is undertaken—whether to find out what sort of perplexity confronts the observer; for the sake of revealing features that may give rise to hypothetical explanations; in order to make the context clear; or for the sake of testing the ideas that are being used as possible solutions. Testing involves the comparison of consequences that were predicted from the hypothesis with actual events. The extent to which agreement among individuals on the outcome of a problem is possible depends on the kind of consequences predicted. In the physical sciences the predictions are usually reduced to the level of meter readings; in economics and commerce the predicted consequences are often quantifiable in terms of profit or loss; in politics the predictions may be expressed in terms of the retention of loss of power. Again they lead back to singular events in experience, as do predictions suggesting that the acceptance of this or that solution will lead to "happiness." The establishment of observable events signifying happiness on which agreement can be reached is obviously more difficult, though not, perhaps, impossible. In spite of this difficulty, Dewey wrote, "It is folly rather than wisdom

---

[61] *Ibid.*, p. 248.

to include in the concept of success only tangible material goods and to exclude those of culture, art, science, sympathetic relations with others."[62] The criteria of success should, however, be firmly based in experience so that the tests can be repeated by all and thus be public.

It is the public nature of testing that gives to the scientific method its objective character. Acceptance of this, the method of organized intelligence, depends upon the adoption by an individual of certain attitudes. First of all, there must be a desire to apply this method to problems. Then, and among the most important of the attitudes required, there must be a willingness on the part of an individual to act. Dewey wrote:

Even in moral and other practical matters, therefore, a thoughtful person treats his overt deeds as experimental so far as possible; that is to say while he cannot call them back and must stand by their consequences, he gives alert attention to what they teach him about his conduct as well as to the non-intellectual consequences.[63]

Inevitably when he embarks upon the processes of reflective thinking, the individual is committed to act or to experiment and thus to reconstruct to some degree his environment. Willingness to act is, however, associated with restraint. To engage in these activities no doubt commits a person to experimental action but at the same time defers commitment to irretrievable action of the kind that may occur if based upon the first immediate suggestion leaping to mind as a solution. Two attitudes essential to reflective thinking are open-mindedness and responsibility. Open-mindedness implies that the individual is free from prejudice and willing to entertain new ideas and examine them by the process of experimental testing. Responsibility means, not that an individual is cautious in proposing new ideas or novel solutions or that he avoids change and the problems it brings but that he is prepared to put them to the test of experience and is prepared in the light of evidence to abandon such ideas as are unable to stand the tests applied to them. Out of these attitudes, which Dewey said are essentially moral in nature, there may grow a habit of reflective thinking. But moral attitudes, he insisted, are traits that have to be cultivated.[64]

Habits of reflective thinking are, of course, more likely to develop in areas of professional interest. The scientist, for example, using these processes in his own work, may fail to do so in his political thinking, either because he lacks desire or lacks information and experience in this field. What is important, according to Dewey, is that individuals possess

---

[62] Ratner, *op. cit.*, p. 772.   [63] *Ibid.*, p. 856.
[64] Dewey, *How We Think*, p. 33.

an attitude of readiness to consider problems by the method of reflective thinking, in whatever sphere of human endeavor they occur.

The application of reflective thinking in the physical sciences represents the greatest achievement of this process. Compared with social scientists, physical scientists have an important advantage—they can identify all the factors relevant to a problem, give relative weight to the factors, and then, when testing hypotheses, control and alter at will these relevant conditions. Social scientists experience difficulties of experimental control and of identification of all the relevant factors in a problematic situation. There is, nevertheless, Dewey maintained, a unity of method. He wrote: "Every step forward in the social sciences—the studies termed history, economics, politics, sociology—shows that social questions are capable of being intelligently coped with only in the degree in which we employ the method of collecting data, forming hypotheses, and testing them in action which is characteristic of natural science, and in the degree in which we utilize in behalf of the promotion of social welfare the technical knowledge ascertained by physics and chemistry."[65] He explained how methods of dealing with some of the many social problems—insanity, intemperance, poverty, city planning, the conservation of natural resources and so on—depend upon the application of the methods and the results of the natural sciences. It has already been noted that in fields where the criteria of success in the solution of a problem are relatively simple and quantifiable, the difficulty is not insurmountable. In such fields as business operations and military planning, the method can readily be applied. In other areas it is more difficult. And perhaps the greatest difficulties lie in the sphere of moral conduct or behavior. Nevertheless, Dewey chose reflective morality as a better way of reaching moral decisions than mere appeal to authority.

Moral judgments, in his opinion, should be reached only after working out (predicting) the consequences of alternative (or several) moral injunctions. "Thou shalt not kill," for example, should not be used as an absolute standard by which to make a judgment. First, it is necessary to consider the consequences of accepting this solution and the consequences of accepting the exact opposite. The alternative consequences should be deduced within a given context because no moral statement can, it seems, be valid under all circumstances. A choice of consequences now remains, and moral judgment is still required: it is still necessary to select and give additional weight to one consequence, or a pattern of consequences, rather than to another (or another pattern). Evidently it is necessary to have standards or a value system in accordance with

---

[65] Dewey, *Democracy and Education*, p. 333.

which a moral judgment can be made even in the light of predicted consequences. Dewey pointed out, "The development of inclusive and enduring aims is the necessary condition of the application of reflection in conduct; indeed, they are two names for the same fact."[66] Unfortunately, reflective thinking, or scientific method, cannot itself form the basis of a normative science. Historical traditions, of course, provide not only a pattern of norms or values but suggest by what authority they were established. These precedents are valuable insofar as they are used instrumentally, but there should always be a willingness on the part of an individual to reexamine and revise his value system if it seems necessary. It appears that Dewey means men have to use the accepted norms of their society as long as they find them applicable and appropriate. These norms should be used, too, in the making of moral judgments, but they should not be regarded as sacrosanct: they should be re-examined in the light of new situations. K. R. Popper argues that men, and men alone, are responsible for the norms by which they live, not so much for the norms that they already find operating as for those that they are willing to accept when they realize it is within their power either to accept or reject them.

Nevertheless, the difficulty of finding values to which, under given circumstances, all men will subscribe is apparent. Few of these are quantifiable, that is to say, reducible to numbers or, as it were, meter readings. The difficulty would be reduced if a less sharp distinction than is usual were drawn between "ideal" values and "material" values. The answer seems to lie in consensus, a conclusion that must rest on an assumption that in the long run the majority of educated, intelligent individuals thinking reflectively will accept certain consequences as morally right and others as morally wrong. Thus a basis for moral judgment would be provided by the community itself.

A scientific assessment of the consequences that may flow from a proposed solution to a moral problem is difficult, because the psychological characteristics of the individual enter as important features of the context in which the elaboration of ideas is to take place. Successful prediction depends upon a knowledge of these, since a person's attitudes find expression in the very act of judging. Psychological knowledge and insight are required if another person's moral judgments are to be anticipated. Introspection will provide for any individual information that is necessary if one is to predict the nature of his own moral judgment. Controlled judgment requires, therefore, not only a sociological analysis of

[66] Ratner, *op. cit.*, p. 767. Also see Dewey, *Human Nature and Conduct*, Part 3, Sec. 6, "The Nature of Aims." Holt, New York, 1935.

the social environment in which judgment is to be made but also a description of the associated attitudes and dispositions of the person who is to take the decision. There are, of course, many spheres of activity where judgment is needed.

Two examples of the need for discrimination, as a result of the application of science in the modern world, may now be cited. Mass media of communication have placed in the hands of the demagogues a power previously unknown. Dewey was aware that the new media have transformed the means of influencing public opinion upon which political action depends.[67] In an address summarized in *School and Society*,[68] Dewey pointed out that while radio could tremendously improve the quality of a democracy and hasten its progress, it yet "lends itself to propaganda in behalf of special interests." He said, "It can be used to distort and mislead the public mind." The problem of educating the public to detect "subtle propaganda and the motives which inspire it" is one of the most important in an age of mass media of communication.

Another aspect of modern life affected by the application of science is represented by automation, which has brought to many more people than previously a great deal more leisure. Mass media fill part of the gap with entertainment. How to solve the problem of more leisure and how to develop discrimination among people are questions education should attempt to answer. Stated simply, under conditions of unaccustomed leisure, individuals must learn to discriminate between "the enjoyments that enrich and enlarge their lives and those which degrade and dissipate." As in the case of moral judgments, criteria of enrichment are difficult to establish without danger of contradiction. Since the links between leisure time and aesthetic experiences are (or should be) close, it is of interest to note that S. C. Pepper in his essay on Dewey's aesthetics wondered whether Dewey, in *Art as Experience*,[69] had, in fact, abandoned his pragmatism. But Pepper's concluding remarks gave, perhaps, some indication of the main themes of Dewey's interest in aesthetics—his desire to see a breakdown in the artificial separation between art and life and his wish to encourage people to realize that "there is beauty in the commonest and meanest things and on Tuesdays and Wednesdays as well as on Sundays."[70] This opinion is perfectly consistent with Dewey's general aim to make the educated man appreciate that the old dichotomy between culture and the sordid materialism of every-

---

[67] Dewey, "The Relation of Science and Philosophy as the Basis of Education," *School and Society*, Vol. 47, No. 1215, Apr. 9, 1938.
[68] "Radio's Influence on the Mind, Summary," *School and Society*, Vol. 40, No. 1042, Dec. 15, 1934.
[69] Schilpp, *op. cit.*, p .384.   [70] Pepper in Schilpp, *op. cit.*, p. 388.

day living is false, and that rather than reject the world he should attempt to improve it.

From all this we can derive a picture of an educated man who is able to make sound judgments, to discriminate, to make choices, to take decisions, and to act upon them, not on impulse or from habit, custom, or tradition but through controlled thinking. This method of problem solving is appropriate to all aspects of his life—the economic, the political, the moral, and the aesthetic. Nothing has yet been said about the body of knowledge with which he should be familiar. More conventional spokesmen for education, while frequently maintaining that its purpose is to train individuals to think, have also maintained that such an objective could only, or could best, be achieved through certain types of subject matter. The liberal-arts tradition of the medieval educational system typifies these beliefs in the efficacy of a certain type of subject matter as promoting thinking, and, indeed, sometimes character, too.

Dewey, however, gave primacy to method in education and not to content. But more than this he maintained that knowledge is the outcome of inquiry and, therefore, until inquiry has taken place, no knowledge will have been acquired. Information and data are relevant only to the degree to which they contribute to the process of inquiry. The first thing, then, to be said about Dewey's proposals is that they suggest, quite explicitly, the dissolution of traditional subject matter as such. If subjects are to be retained, then ideally every one of them in the curriculum should be taught "in connection with its bearing upon creation and growth of the kind of power of observation, inquiry, reflection, and testing that are the heart of scientific intelligence."[71] But in fact, history, geography, science, modern languages, and other such subjects have no place in the store of knowledge that Dewey's educated man should possess, except to the extent that certain data from each of the disciplines might contribute to problem solving or reflective thinking. Evidently a selection of data on this basis is desirable. For example, history should not be treated chronologically but should be used pragmatically. Dewey declared, "The true starting point of history is always some present situation with its problems,"[72] and for this reason economic, industrial, or intellectual history would be more appropriate than political history, because more likely to enlarge young people's sense of the significance of direct personal experience.

In order to make any generalizations about what subject matter an

[71] Dewey, "The Relation of Science and Philosophy as the Basis of Education," *School and Society*, Vol. 47, No. 1215, Apr. 9, 1938.
[72] Dewey, *Democracy and Education*, p. 251.

educated man should possess, it is necessary to ask not what traditional subjects he should study but what problems he should be trained to tackle or, in fact, be given to tackle. Effective learning will, of course, take place only if the student feels himself in a state of doubt or perplexity and is working on a problem he feels to be real and not a sham problem invented by a teacher. Certain assumptions have to be made about the kinds of problems children of particular ages are likely to meet. For those about to leave school and enter the adult world, problems of the kind already indicated in economic life, in politics, in the family, in the use of leisure, in aesthetics, and in morals are soon bound to arise. Herbert Spencer's reply to his own question, "What knowledge is of most worth?" gave a clue to the organization of likely problems. These suggestions have been embodied in the Seven Cardinal Principles of Curriculum Development issued in 1918. On the basis of these suggestions, the reorganization of subject matter could theoretically be undertaken. What is needed, said Dewey, is the development of "new subject matter, as well organized as was the old . . . but having an intimate and developing relation to the experience of those in school."[73]

Whatever youth's problems are, they largely reflect applications of scientific information to society. Young people will have to take up work in a technological age; many of them will need to become specialists or technologists in scientific fields. At the same time they will have to live in large conurbations whether they like it or not, with all the social and human complications associated with aggregate living. They will have to cope with complex machinery and devices—the products of science. In an observation typical of many he made on science and society, Dewey said, "The stationary and traction steam engine, gasoline engine, automobile, telegraph and telephone, the electric motor enter directly into the lives of most individuals."[74] Today we may add that H-bomb warfare enters and threatens the lives of everyone. Few aspects of living are untouched by modern scientific developments. Judgments about the applications in society of scientific techniques cannot be made on the basis of reflective thinking unless their physical and biological consequences in given situations can be predicted and weighed carefully. In short, the educated man's store of scientific information that through reflective thinking can be turned into real and human knowledge is today enormous. Any education designed to meet today's needs must take full account of this fact.

---

73 Dewey, "How Much Freedom in New Schools?" *New Republic*, Vol. 63, July 9, 1930.
74 Dewey, *Democracy and Education*, p. 335.

The content of a science course can hardly be determined, as in the past, by the inclusion in the syllabus of data arranged in the order of their historical discovery. Nor can it be designed simply to meet the interests of the future science specialist. It must be arranged to provide the very core of a sound liberal education. The difficulty here is twofold: there are the prejudices of generations to be overcome; there is the important and real, practical problem of teaching science in a way that it is truly liberalizing.

Dewey was always concerned about the false (as he thought) dichotomy between scientific and vocational studies and the humanizing liberal arts. This dichotomy is part of the Aristotelian heritage, mentioned previously. It was related economically and socially to the distinctions drawn between the gentleman and the artisan or laborer. Brutish conditions of labor undoubtedly reinforced in a practical way the dislike an "educated" man had for vocational courses designed to prepare their recipients for depleting work. Conditions have changed. Automated factories reduce hard manual work to a bare minimum. At the same time, prejudices still need to be overcome. Dewey declared, "We must surrender that superstitious tradition which identifies humanism with the interests of literary training, and which in our country, whatever it may have accomplished elsewhere, produces only a feebly pretentious snobbishness of culture."[75]

Convinced as Dewey was that vocational studies and science should form the core of a general education, he had to face the question of how this would be done. First, he considered how it should not be done. Industrial education must not emphasize technical trade efficiency but rather should contribute to the efficiency of industrial intelligence.[76] Similarly, science should not be regarded as an organized body of knowledge, nor yet a technique or system of skills learned in the laboratory (however valuable these experiences may be). In the positive approach, he believed that vocational education, correctly used, would "react upon intelligence and interest so as to modify, in connection with legislation and administration, the socially obnoxious features of the present industrial and commercial order."[77] The object of teaching science, he said, is to encourage individuals to become acquainted with the scientific way of "treating the familiar material of ordinary experience."[78]

Science should be taught not only for the methods inherent in it. Most modern social problems have their scientific aspects, and to understand and help solve these problems data from the sciences must be

[75] Dewey, "Our Educational Ideal in Wartime," New Republic, Apr. 15, 1916.
[76] Dewey, "A Policy of Industrial Education," New Republic, Vol. 1, Dec. 19, 1914.
[77] Dewey, Democracy and Education, p. 374.   [78] Ibid., p. 257.

selected. In short, science teaching should fundamentally concentrate on the social implications of science. A practical approach would be to organize courses around major social problems and select scientific data and theories in terms of the bearing they have on the solution to these problems. By the extent to which science education would help individuals to solve their problems alone or collectively, it would become truly liberal. But, if these are the main aims and methods of science education, less time will have to be spent on stuffing future specialists with hard facts and little understanding. Without some change in the quality of science education itself, the traditional approach may be justified. Moreover, at least two dangers of concentrating on the production of future specialists are apparent. In the first place, the division of the world into scientists and arts men, finding communication increasingly difficult, would be assured. Secondly, scientists would be turned out in increasing numbers who are apolitical, amoral, lacking in aesthetic sensibility, and bereft of a sense of social responsibility. Dewey offered as a practical solution to this very real dilemma a reorientation of the liberal arts colleges. He counseled, *"The problem of securing to the liberal arts college its due function in democratic society is that of seeing to it that the technical subjects which are now socially necessary acquire humane direction."*[79] Science is a human activity; Dewey envisioned making it a humane, liberating study.

Thus equipped with a method of inquiry and a desire to apply it to the problems of society, the educated man has a major task to perform. It is to study the changing world as he finds it and to improve it. He identifies the competing forces that are inducing change, creating problems, and tending to give social development direction; one complex of forces is operating to make change take one course, while another complex is moving it in another direction. The individual's responsibility is to decide which forces he will support. Since he is bound to make a choice, he should do so intelligently. The central question is the moral one: by what standards can this major decision be taken? Dewey said that his social objectives will be framed on the "basis of knowing the forces and the causes which produce the evils from which we suffer."[80] The social reconstructionist's lack of fixed ends toward which to work and the dangers of complete relativism are all too obvious in these statements of Dewey. Perhaps, contrary to his intentions, he presented an either–or choice that is too sharp: absolutism or complete relativism.

[79] Dewey, *Philosophy of Education*, p. 86.
[80] Dewey, "Education and our Present Social Problems," *School and Society*, Vol. 37, Apr. 15, 1933.

Yet, if this is in fact the choice that has to be made, then I have no hesitation in accepting the open society of Dewey with all its possibilities and dangers. The choice may not be between the absolutism of the Puritan fathers and complete moral and social relativism. But if it is, the consequences of accepting relativism seem to be no more serious than those associated with the acceptance of any form of social absolutism. Man has lived by faith in the past. Dewey offered a new faith: a faith in the authority of a method of inquiry and in the ability of all men singly and collectively to use it and finally to reach agreement.

However serious the logical difficulties of Dewey's position and however uncertain the answer to the problem of conduct, his concept of the educated man is fully in accord with modern conditions. Increasingly, modern man is subjected to the pressures of industrialization and urbanization. More and more frequently he finds himself living in societies that offer wider opportunities of choice. And the power of many of his traditional authorities is in process of being broken. Consumer goods flood the markets of the world; democratic institutions are being established in many countries; and the authority of traditional institutions is declining. Even though in some places the *status quo* is being maintained by arbitrary force, nearly everywhere the *ideal* of democracy is being proclaimed. This is the age of the common man and the industrial worker. Whether we like it or not, Dewey's assessment of the social situation is proving itself broadly correct. It seems fairly evident, too, that new forms of social authority are needed in a postwar world where changes brought about or accelerated by the war have been so traumatic that larger problems exist and touch more people than ever before. Acceptance of Dewey's solutions is a matter of personal judgment. His faith in our ability to educate individuals to recognize the problems around them and then to tackle them by the method of organized intelligence placed great trust in education. While his solutions were based upon faith, they are rich in possibilities and they are of the kind to which the peoples of most countries in the Western world are, in a sense, committed. Dewey offered no more than extremely illuminating clues to the way in which we may grapple with problems. The educators of the world have yet to find completely adequate ways of translating his theories into actuality. His theories have thus not yet been put to the practical test. Until workable actuations of theory are found, and men not only learn how to use the method of organized intelligence but also desire to use it at all levels, including the international level, the fate of the world hangs in the balance. Yet, even before the task of putting Dewey's theories into practice has been completed, there are signs that much of what Dewey was striving to teach educators has been forgotten under the stress of national pride, international competition, and the constant threat of nuclear war (which, if it came, would effectively end discussions of how men should be educated). The present tensions in the world seem to offer the strongest reason why Dewey's thoughts should be used, not neglected—used, in the way he would have them used, as tools for the reconstruction of a world where fear, prejudice, poverty, ignorance, disease, and injustice will be reduced to the final minimum, leaving as mankind's important and significant task the heightening of aesthetic appreciation and the improvement in quality of work and leisure.

BIBLIOGRAPHICAL NOTE

A short but useful biographical essay on John Dewey appears in *The Philosophy of John Dewey*, edited by P. A. Schilpp, and published by Northwestern University Press, Evanston, Ill., in 1939.

It was when Dewey went to Chicago in the 1890s that his flow of books and articles on education began. Two quite short books, *The School and Society*, published by the University of Chicago Press in 1899, and *The Child and the Curriculum*, published by the University of Chicago Press in 1902, bear witness to his interest in the Laboratory School and soon became very influential. Of his numerous other books, perhaps *How We Think*, published by Heath, New York, in 1910, and *Democracy and Education*, published by Macmillan, New York, in 1916, draw together Dewey's thoughts on education best. The former presents a concept of reflective thinking on which the problem-solving approach in education is based. *Democracy and Education* is a statement of the democratic ideal in education but also makes explicit for education the implications of social, economic, and political changes in American life.

During World War I another side of Dewey's widely ranging interests became apparent. In the *New Republic* and other periodicals he began to comment on public affairs. Few issues of topical concern escaped his pen thereafter. In the late 1920s and through the next decade he wrote about the Soviet Union, the economic situation, the teachers' union, and his own proposals on the need for a third party. Many of these articles were published in *New Republic*, *School and Society*, *Progressive Education*, and *Social Frontier*. They are well worth reading because they show how passionately Dewey was concerned with the practical affairs of men.

At the same time a definite pattern can be discerned in Dewey's more directly philosophical writings. *Reconstruction in Philosophy*, published by Henry Holt, New York, in 1920, initiated a new trend. In comparing traditional philosophies with the new scientific outlook, Dewey covered the whole field of philosophy and sought to reconstruct philosophical thinking so that the world, or some part of it, might be changed through changes in the minds and ideas of men. Dewey's major works of the 1930s show how, having surveyed the philosophical field, he then examined problems within it from his own general pragmatic position. Since experience was for him the source of knowledge, he considered the logic of selected forms of it. *Art as Experience*, published by Minton, Balch, New York, in 1934, deals with aesthetic experiences; *A Common Faith*, published by Yale University Press in 1934, deals with religious ones; *Human Nature and Conduct*, published by Henry Holt, New York, in 1922, deals with the logic of ethics; *The Quest for Certainty*, published by Minton, Balch, New York, in 1929, and *Logic: The Theory of Inquiry*, published by Henry Holt, New York, in 1938, deal with the philosophy and logic of those scientific experiences to which Dewey gave so much importance. Since Dewey wished to stress the interconnected character of experience, the analyses are not as sharply differentiated as the titles suggest. Moreover, several of these volumes grew out of lecture series, and Dewey constantly returned to the same themes seen in different contexts. *Experience and Nature*, published by Open Court Publishing Co., Chicago and London, in 1925, represents a most general review of Dewey's position as an empirical philosopher and deals with the problems of gaining knowledge through experience.

Apart from these major works, not all of which are easy to read, several collected works are of considerable interest. Of these, *Characters and Events*, edited by Joseph Ratner and published by Henry Holt, New York, in 1929, *The Public and its Problems*, published by Henry Holt, New York, in 1927, *The Problems of Men*, published by Philosophical Library, New York, in 1946, and *Intelligence in the Modern World*, edited by Joseph Ratner and published by Modern Library, New York, in 1939, may be mentioned as among the most important. The last book edited by Mr. Ratner includes a great many articles and gives some idea of the wealth and range of Dewey's writings over a long period.

A full bibliography, *John Dewey, A Centennial Bibliography*, published by the University of Chicago Press in 1962, has been prepared by M. H. Thomas. With some modifications this is also presented in Mr. Schilpp's book, mentioned earlier, which provides a good introduction to the philosophy of John Dewey, through essays written by different philosophers. Educationists would do well, however, to start with *The School and Society, How We Think*, and *Democracy and Education*—these are still relevant today.

🏵 т. s. eliot (1888–1965), the youngest of seven children of a prosperous brick manufacturer, was born in St. Louis, Missouri. His grandfather, the Reverend William Greenleaf Eliot, was a founder of Washington University in St. Louis. Eliot attended Smith Academy (attached to Washington University) before going to Harvard University where he received his B.A. in 1909 and his M.A. in philosophy in 1910. He continued his studies in philosophy at Harvard, the University of Paris, Marburg University, and Oxford University. He became a schoolmaster in England during World War I, first at a grammar school in High Wycombe, Buckinghamshire, and then at Highgate School in London where he taught "French, Latin, lower mathematics, drawing, swimming, geography, history, and baseball." In 1922 he published his most famous poem, *The Waste Land*, in which he summed up the disillusion and disgust of the postwar generation with the barrenness of a standardized civilization. In 1927 he became a British subject and a member of the Church of England. He had apparently found his way out of the waste land, for he now described himself as "an Anglo-Catholic in religion, a classicist in literature, and a royalist in politics." Eliot's views on the relationship between religion, politics, and culture are found in *The Idea of a Christian Society* and *Notes Towards the Definition of Culture*. He claimed that "the only hopeful course for the world today is in a 'truly' Christian society." He championed a national church to serve as the final authority on dogma, faith, and morals— for a "positive culture must have a positive set of values."

13

THE CULTURED MAN: *Eliot*

BY G. H. BANTOCK

T. S. Eliot believed that we live in an age of cultural decline. Indeed one of his main concerns, as a social theorist, was with definition of the conditions under which greater cultural vitality could exist, with definition, in fact, of the nature of the "educative society." For culture was, to him, "that which makes life worth living"; a concern for cultural health was central in his view of a good society. And it is for a *good* society that Eliot believed man should be educated; he repudiated those views of education that interpret its function as the adaptation of man to his present environment. Furthermore, he drew extensively on his own experience as a poet and critic to define, in particular, that education in the traditional learning of Europe necessary for the purveyors and consumers of the more self-conscious aspects of this culture, often referred to as "minority" culture. For this reason, what he said about education comes to us with the greater relevance, assurance, and worth. His views on education were not abstractions derived from some socio-political theory remote from the pressures of actual conduct; they sprang from a specific creative effort and a self-conscious understanding of the conditions under which such an effort could best be made. Thus, the experience implicit in the poetry, drama, and criticism and the particular consciousness he displays there, with all its intense historical awareness, are very relevant in considering his educational ideas; and the more explicitly formulated conception of society discursively adumbrated in his books of social theory have behind them the living experience of the poetic creative effort.

Central to this poetic experience, and implicit, therefore, in any evocation of a truly "educative society," is the inevitability of man's being involved in a variety of states of tension. One of these unavoidable tensions arises from the need to act anew on the basis of past experience:

> Time present and time past
> Are both perhaps present in time future,
> And time future contained in time past.
>   (*Burnt Norton.*)

And this notion that man is the product of his past as well as of his present environment gives the lie to a great deal of current theorizing, stemming from the eighteenth-century Enlightenment, which ascribes disharmony to an avoidable conflict between man and his contemporary social conditions. According to these theories, some form of adaptation between man and society would make possible an "uncomplicated adjustment to an uncomplicated world," as though both man and society existed solely in the present, independent of memory and the past, both of which make adaptation on either side a matter of immense difficulty.

The notion of adjustment has, indeed, been a key concept in the view of the social order that has accepted only two factors in the social equation—the "individual" and the "environment." As Philip Rieff put it in his recent book on Freud, "In liberal psychology as it has evolved from Bentham to Dewey, social organisation . . . has become the source of and the limitation upon the perfectibility of human nature." Increased knowledge and wise legislation can, it is thought, gradually bring about the evolution of an earthly paradise, and "perfectibility" has thus seemed just around the corner. Eliot's analysis of the human situation was derived from a quite different set of premises. *His* central assumption was that contained in the Christian world view. At the heart of all human experience he saw yet another tension—that between man's unredeemed state and his apprehension of a supernatural Grace in which abide his hope and his despair, for man needs to appreciate both his own inherent sinfulness and the redemptive possibilities of the divine. As an inhabitant of both the natural and the transcendental worlds, man finds no resting place in the possibilities of any human perfectibility but remains perpetually aware of the tensions inherent in his position. Holding, as he did, this view of the inherent nature of human activity, Eliot saw so many features of the human scene in terms of the antinomies that betoken the paradoxical nature of human behavior and thought. And this notion of paradox, of the assimilation, yet the incompatibility, of opposites, lies at the heart of his great, postconversion poetry:

> Only by the form, the pattern,
> Can words or music reach
> The stillness, as a Chinese jar still
> Moves perpetually in its stillness.
> Not the stillness of the violin, while the note lasts,

Not that only, but the co-existence,
Or say that the end precedes the beginning,
And the end and the beginning were always there
Before the beginning and after the end.
And all is always now.

(*Burnt Norton.*)

Throughout the *Quartets* recur the antinomies implicit in the juxtaposition of words like "end" and "beginning," "movement" and "stillness," "past," "present," and "future":

Only through time time is conquered.

Naturally, a mind so aware of the paradoxes and tensions in human experience saw man's life in society, not as leading to unilateral adjustment and reconciliation but as composed of ultimately incompatible elements in which the most favorable condition is that where opposing forces achieve a temporary and unstable balance, the still point, as it were, in a turning world. Such a world can be described, at its best, not in terms of an attainable harmony but of an equilibrium between opposing forces of disintegration:

The danger of freedom is deliquescence; the
danger of strict order is petrifaction.

Whether he was speaking at the most general or at the most intimately human level, Eliot always conceived the essentially ambiguous nature of the human condition in terms of the antagonism and yet reconciliation of opposites; he saw that disharmony is as necessary as harmony for the creative spirit. In *Notes Towards the Definition of Culture* he wrote, "Fortunate the man who, at the right moment, meets the right friend; fortunate also the man who at the right moment meets the right enemy." It is not to be wondered at, then, that Eliot's image of the educative society was one allowing for the necessity, in any true cultural creativity, of conflict and irritation as well as of collaboration and harmony. In contradistinction to modern egalitarian views, he urged the necessity of a class structure—but a class structure of sufficient fluidity to preserve social continuity without degenerating into the petrifaction of a caste system on the one hand or the deliquescence of excessive social mobility on the other. Also, he sensed the need for a regionalism that would encourage just the right amount of provincial independence without involving a disintegration into a number of distinct local cultures. And he desired a "church capable of conflict with the state as well as of co-operation with it," he declared in a lecture series on "The Aims of Education." He elaborated these suggestions:

At this point I introduce a new notion: that of the vital importance for a society of *friction* between its parts. Accustomed as we are to think in figures of speech taken from machinery, we assume that a society, like a machine, should be as well-oiled as possible, provided with ball bearings of the best steel. We think of friction as waste of energy. I shall not attempt to substitute any other imagery: perhaps at this point the less we think in analogies the better. In the last chapter I suggested that in any society which became permanently established in either a caste or a classless system, the culture would decay: one might even put it that a classless society should always be emerging into class, and a class society should be tending towards obliteration of its class distinctions. I now suggest that both class and region, by dividing the inhabitants of a country into two different kinds of groups, lead to a conflict favourable to creativeness and progress. And (to remind the reader of what I said in my introduction) these are only two of an indefinite number of conflicts and jealousies which should be profitable to society. Indeed, the more the better: so that everyone should be an ally of everyone else in some respects, and an opponent in several others, and no one conflict, envy or fear will dominate (*Notes Towards the Definition of Culture*).

He concluded with a characteristic paradox: "The universality of irritation is the best assurance of peace."

But it is not only within the various geographical, social, and institutional aspects of society that there is a need for tension, implying both reconciliation and disharmony; there is a need for a similar tension within the mind of the individual, also, as he apprehends the nature of the world by which he is beset. And though Christendom ought to be one, such unity, to be healthy, should allow a certain degree of diversity and some conflict in ideology, ". . . for it is only by the struggle against constantly appearing false ideas that the truth is enlarged and clarified, and in the conflict with heresy that orthodoxy is developed to meet the needs of the time" (*Notes Towards the Definition of Culture*).

It is significant that Eliot's poetry is essentially dramatic in nature and that he took such an interest in revivifying poetic drama. For, of course, the essence of drama is conflict. His relative failure as a stage dramatist compared with his overwhelming success in his essentially dramatic poetry serves to indicate the superior histrionic potency of the personal monologue in a disintegrating social order. The essence of the Eliotic experience is a personal agony; when this is projected into a series of external incidents necessary for successful stage action (to find an "objective correlative," to use Eliot's own phrase), it seems to lack the sustained social awareness and contact that could translate it into convincing situations and characters in the separate and distinct social world that the dramatist must create. Eliot's development, that is, was an intensely *personal* development, for it could find no adequate and *sustained* set of objectively dramatic symbols by which it could be projected in the modern world; this is perhaps because his poetic experience depended to a considerable extent on the reassertion of a world largely past, a world of tradition. His outlook was historically oriented, whereas the drama needs the living present and its sense of time is essentially one that looks to the future.[1] Eliot, indeed, was the most historically conscious of writers; his density of experience was derived not so much from the life around him—he was contemptuous of much of the modern world—as from an appreciation of the richness of the consciousness he had inherited. This is in no way intended as an adverse criticism of him; a poet of his stature must be allowed to make what sense he can of his experience and in what terms he can.[2] In his total poetic experience, the unsatisfactory nature of the world he inhabited was balanced by the positive affirmations implicit in his realization of the eternal struggle for salvation characteristic of the consciousness of Europe, particularly in its Protestant phase—a consciousness that is, of course, explicitly Christian; and in the "neutral era" that he inhabited, when Christianity largely ceased to court socially, he could find very deep significance only in the Christian philosophy (he was, of course, in some degree, a convert, and thus came to Anglo-Catholic Christianity self-consciously).

Because of these elements, one may find in his social thinking a curious reality and, at the same time, a curious sense of unreality. The sense of unreality springs from the unlikelihood that the conditions for the educative society he desiderated will be realized; in the face of contemporary events and pressures these conditions represent only an idealized abstraction, partly historical, partly Christian, and therefore residual. But the reality and the relief one gains in appreciating it stem from a realization that his view of experience represents something more permanent in the human condition, more profound about human beings, than that

---

[1] In *Feeling and Form*, Susanne K. Langer wrote: "Literature projects the image of life in the mode of virtual memory; language is its essential material; the sound and meaning of words, their familiar or unusual use and order, even their presentation on the printed page, create the illusion of life as a realm of events—completed, lived, as words formulate them—events that compose a Past. But drama presents the poetic illusion in a different light: not finished realities or 'events,' but immediate, visible responses of human beings, make its semblance of life. Its basic abstraction is the act, which springs from the past, but is directed toward the future, and is always great with things to come."

[2] I am assuming here that my critical judgment concerning Eliot's comparative failure as a dramatist is acceptable. Furthermore, I find no incompatibility in my emphasis on the *personal* nature of Eliot's achievement here with my remarks about his concern for "impersonality" below.

implicit in so much of the vapid social theorizing of our times. Eliot assisted, indeed, in that long process of *un*learning that is an essential element in any true education today—an unlearning that implies a true recognition of the false idols we worship. In Eliot's view of society memory plays an essential part in the definition of sanity and wisdom. We regard education as an unqualified good; but Eliot saw that an older freedom offered its creative possibilities. He was acutedly aware that the value of modern education is essentially ambivalent. In speaking of Blake, for instance, he noted as favorable for Blake's genius the conditions that he "was not compelled to acquire any other education in literature than he wanted, or to acquire it for any other reason than that he wanted it"; he commented:

It is important that the artist should be highly educated in his own art; but his education is one that is hindered rather than helped by the ordinary processes of society which constitute education for the ordinary man. For these processes consist largely in the acquisition of impersonal ideas which obscure what we really are and feel, what we really want, and what really excites our interest. It is of course not the actual information acquired, but the conformity which the accumulation of knowledge is apt to impose, that is harmful (*Selected Essays*).

Yet, again paradoxically, if, by education, we imply an induction into a heritage, Eliot was himself essentially a learned poet and believed in the importance of an intense assimilation as part of the very process of creation. He was highly conscious of the part to be played by tradition, of the creative artist's place in an orthodoxy that has been defined over the centuries and that the writer ignores at his peril. This awareness led him to develop a notion of the function of personality in creativity that is very much at odds with popular notions of the importance of the individual talent in the writing of works of literature. His notion of tradition and of the place within it of the individual creative mind, indeed, represents so fundamental a feature of his attempt to define the educative society that it must be examined.

His best-known analysis of tradition appears in the famous essay entitled "Tradition and the Individual Talent." A full appreciation of his account probably requires some awareness of the things against which Eliot was reacting when he wrote it. He declared:

Tradition . . . cannot be inherited, and if you want it you must obtain it by great labour. It involves, in the first place, the historical sense, which we may call nearly indispensable to anyone who would continue to be a poet beyond his twenty-fifth year; and the historical sense involves a perception, not only of the pastness of the past, but of its presence; the historical sense compels a man to write not merely with his own generation in his bones, but with a feeling that the whole of the literature of his own country has a simultaneous existence and composes a simultaneous order. This historical sense, which is a sense of the timeless as well as of the temporal and of the timeless and of the temporal together, is what makes a writer traditional. And it is at the same time what makes a writer most acutely conscious of his place in time, of his own contemporaneity (*Selected Essays*).

Thus the present adjusts to the past and, at the same time, serves to reorient the very nature of that past; the new work of art, by the very fact of its novelty, enables us to look at the past in a slightly different way. What forms the mind of the poet, then, is very much derived from the inherited wisdom of the race; at the same time, such a mind is representative of more than the past. Eliot said:

He [the poet] must be aware that the mind of Europe—the mind of his own country—a mind which he learns in time to be very much more important than his own private mind—is a mind which changes, and that this change is a development which abandons nothing *en route*, which does not superannuate either Shakespeare, or Homer, or the rock drawing of the Magdalenian draughtsmen.

An essential element in Eliot's concept of tradition is the notion that "tradition cannot mean standing still." Eliot devoted some space in *After Strange Gods* to the "danger" of associating "tradition with the immovable"; he warned categorically against indulging a "sentimental attitude towards the past." He wrote, "What we can do is to use our minds, remembering that a tradition without intelligence is not worth having, to discover what is the best life for us not as a political abstraction, but as a particular people in a particular place."

In this later book, indeed, Eliot tended to define the notion of tradition in terms of the more unconscious elements in our make-up; he used the word "to cover much in our lives that is accounted for by habit, breeding and environment" (and, of these unconscious elements, especially of habit, I shall have more to say later). He assigned the notion of orthodoxy to the more conscious intellectual effort that preserves the writer from the disastrous effects of too great an eccentricity. It is necessary, indeed, to lay emphasis on that "too great," for Eliot insisted in *After Strange Gods*: ". . . perfect orthodoxy in the individual artist is not always necessary, or even desirable. In many instances it is possible that an indulgence of eccentricities is the condition of the man's saying anything at all."

What is disastrous to creativity, indeed, is not the mere venting of an individuality, without which no work of any significance is likely to be produced at all, but the deliberate exploitation of eccentricity in the romantic mode, the deliberate assertion of personality, and the cultivation of deviation. The counterbalancing of such deliberate idiosyncracy requires the application of critical standards that Eliot considered to be "almost in desuetude." And, to illustrate his point, he examined a story by D. H. Lawrence from a critical standpoint stressing the centrality of the concept of Original Sin and of that moral struggle in which is to be found the reality of human beings. In *After Strange Gods*, he summed it up thus: "It is in fact in moments of moral and spiritual struggle depending upon spiritual sanctions, rather than in those 'bewildering minutes' in which we are all very much alike, that men and women come nearest to being real."

Eliot's practice as a poet admirably reveals this tension between acceptance and novelty—his enunciation in so novel a form (for English poetry) of a peculiarly individual appreciation of very particular experiences and yet his fostering of an awareness of the essential continuity of the individual predicament in a strange and mysterious world. Thus, Eliot's use of quotation from earlier poets was an essential part of his poetic method and of the means by which he sought to display the uniqueness of his vision, a uniqueness consisting in part of the very stress to be laid on a *common* obligation and a *common* experience implicit in the poetry of the past. Characteristic, too, in his animadversions on the nature of individual creativity, was his emphasis on the *making* more than the *experience*, his total rejection of the element of autobiography. He wrote:

What happens [to the poet in the act of creation] is a continual surrender of himself as he is at the moment to something which is more valuable. The progress of an artist is a continual self-sacrifice, a continual extinction of personality (*Selected Essays*).

Here, indeed, we encounter the famous notion of impersonality as that which characterizes the mind in its most intense work of creation. If we take the nature of the poet as the prototype of a particularly valuable sort of educated mind—a not unreasonable assumption—the conception of impersonality deserves some further definition, for it appears to be the main characteristic of this type of mind and is thus relevant to any consideration of the truly educated man. And central in the notion of impersonality is the particular role assigned to the will.

Eliot was very much concerned with deprecating direct action as a means of improving cultural conditions. When attempting to state the circumstances under which the truly educative society—the cultured society—could best function, he continually stressed the impossibility of bringing about such a set of conditions by conscious will and deliberate act. He wrote:

For if any definite conclusions emerge from this study, one of them is surely this, that culture is the one thing that we cannot deliberately aim at. It is the product of a variety of more or less harmonious activities, each pursued for its own sake: the artist must concentrate upon his canvas, the poet upon his typewriter, the civil servant upon the just settlement of particular problems as they present themselves upon his desk, each according to the situation in which he finds himself. Even if these conditions with which I am concerned, seem to the reader to represent desirable social aims, he must not leap to the conclusion that these aims can be fulfilled solely by deliberate organisation (*Notes Towards the Definition of Culture*).

Thus, the "pursuit of perfection, or of comprehensive culture, is not enough, because it is a by-product of our desire to *do* something."

Here, writ large in a macrocosm of society, we sense something of the role of impersonality: it contains qualities analogous to those implicit in Keats's idea of negative capability—when a man is capable of being in mysteries, doubts, and fears, without any irritable reaching after fact and reason. Similarly, in the microcosm of the poet's mind, Eliot excluded the element of will, the purely personal pressure of emotion and experience in the process of poetic creation. For one thing, the poet has not a " 'personality' to express, but a particular medium, which is only a medium and not a personality." Therefore, Eliot said: "Impressions and experiences which are important for the man may take no place in the poetry, and those which become important in the poetry may play quite a negligible part in the man, the personality." Also, in the very process of creation, considerable weight must be assigned to "passivity," to awaiting the event, as Eliot pointed out in making the following comment on an earlier description of poetry writing:

Consequently, we must believe that "emotion recollected in tranquility" is an inexact formula. For it is neither emotion, nor recollection, nor, without distortion of meaning, tranquility. It is a concentration, and a new thing resulting from the concentration, of a very great number of experiences which to the practical and active person would not seem to be experiences at all; it is a concentration which does not happen consciously or of deliberation. These experiences are not "recollected," and they finally unite in an atmosphere which is "tranquil" only in that it is a passive attending upon the event (*Selected Essays*).

He noted, of course, that there is necessarily an aspect of poetry writing which is "conscious and deliberate"; but the concentration on the medium, on the extinction of personality necessary in the act of creation, led him to the conclusion that "the emotion of art is impersonal." He insisted that "the poet cannot reach this impersonality without surrendering himself wholly to the work to be done." In both the creation of a favorable cultural climate, then, and in the creation of a particular work of art, Eliot stressed the function of impersonality in which unconscious elements play a vital part—stressed what, in fact, comes as a by-product of an activity that is concentrated on something other than itself. One of the reasons for the failure of most poetry writing, he said, is that it all too consciously seeks for "new emotions to express; and in this search for novelty in the wrong place it discovers the perverse." In a similar way, the attempt consciously to create "culture" fails because this would assume that culture could be planned; but Eliot declared in *Notes Towards the Definition of Culture*: "Culture can never be wholly conscious—there is always more to it than we are conscious of; and it cannot be planned because it is also the unconscious background of all our planning."

This emphasis on unconscious factors in our cultural life—whether in the creation of poetry or in any other cultural activity—and this deprecation of the assertive will are of great interest at a time when it is widely agreed that, as a necessary concomitant of the movement toward universal literacy, we are "committed to more consciousness." Two features of such "consciousness" are usually implied. First, there is the development of an increasing self-consciousness. A characteristic of this is the skepticism that has accompanied the increasing complexity of civilization and that Eliot has described as the "habit of examining evidence and the capacity for delayed decision." An essential element in the capacity for delay is the ability to step outside the immediate concerns of the self and its desires and to see such a self and its activities within a larger context requiring consideration and elucidation. In such a context, action results only from ratiocination—or is inhibited by it, as when:

> . . . the native hue of resolution
> Is sicklied o'er with the pale cast of thought.

The general tendency of this has been, for some, to inhibit action, to load behavior with a weight of forethought turning the activity of living into a careworn apprehension of life as an endless series of "problems," each a burden to the self in its range of complexity.[3] Eliot's answer is

---

[3] In "Aims of Education" (*Measure*), Eliot wrote: "In the world to-day we find ourselves more and more trying consciously to manipulate what had been left to take its own course—that is, our area of conscious manipulation becomes bigger and bigger. A problem comes into existence through our ability to become aware of it; the awareness shapes the problem; and once we are conscious of a problem, we cannot dismiss it from consciousness; we find ourselves under obligation to try to find an answer."

that we must learn to "care and not to care"; he said that "we need not only the strength to defer a decision, but the strength to make one."

The second feature implicit in the notion of the extension of consciousness concerns the area and range within which decision making[4] is thought to be possible for most people. Here the important factor is the level of abstraction and generality with which the individual can cope. Where, for instance, there were once narrow traditional pieties and loyalties, unconscious assimilations and acceptances, the spread of education and the breakdown of the traditional authoritarian hierarchy have widened, for most people, the area within which decisions have to be made, particularly in the moral sphere; thus unconscious habit has tended to be increasingly replaced by self-directive action based on conscious decision. And this raises the profoundest personal and social problems of which, in some degree, education has needed to take cognizance. "We must remember," Eliot pointed out, "that being more conscious about everything is a very great strain."

It is interesting, then, to appreciate how deeply Eliot was wedded to the necessity of unconsciousness for certain aspects of behavior and for certain intellectual levels of the community. One of the crucial elements in any culture he found to be the unconscious level at which certain cultural manifestations may be said to "work." For instance, understanding a culture he considered to be well-nigh impossible for anyone who does not belong to it; yet even for those who do, involvement with it may well deprive them of the point of view from which *conscious* "understanding" can have any significance; for, Eliot said, "Understanding involves an area more extensive than that of which one can be conscious; one cannot be outside and inside at the same time." The appreciation of the need for unconscious factors is relevant to his views on Liberalism. Indeed, Eliot has been regarded as a notorious—and, in some quarters, as a scandalous—critic of Liberalism. This imputation is not altogether fair[5]—he has, in fact, upheld the Liberal ideal as a

---

4 A frequent desideratum of democratic educationists.

5 Nor would it be fair to regard him as an enemy of democracy; he disliked certain features of it, but he refused to deride the idea. He wrote:

"It is one thing to say, which is sadly certain, that democratic government has been watered down to nothing. It is one thing to say, what is equally sad and certain, that from the moment when the suffrage is conceived as a *right* instead of as a privilege and a duty and a responsibility, we are on the way merely to government by an invisible oligarchy instead of government by a visible one. But it is another thing to ridicule the *idea* of democracy. A real democracy is always a restricted democracy, and can flourish with some limitation by hereditary rights and responsibilities . . ."

He was certainly no believer in equality; he once said to me, "You can have equality; you can have culture: but you cannot have both."

"necessary negative element"; but his well-known description of our society as "worm-eaten with Liberalism" has had the wider currency. And, indeed, his definition of the effects of Liberalism does seem to contain more criticism than is common among the political philosophers of our period. He diagnosed Liberalism as a "movement not so much defined by its end, as by its starting point; away from, rather than towards something definite," in *The Idea of a Christian Society*. Furthermore, he blamed Liberalism for "destroying traditional social habits of the people" and for "dissolving their natural collective consciousness into individual constituents."

Let us examine first this aspect of the Liberal state. As Eliot correctly alleged in *Notes Toward the Definition of Culture*, Liberalism leads rapidly to the "atomic view of society" that produces what Michael Young recently called a "Meritocracy," having as its main feature what Karl Mannheim implied in his notion of an "elite." Such an "elite" exists *per se*, in some measure of isolation from the community at large, and not as one traditionally attached to the highest class in the community from which it gained its cultural coloring, as was characteristic of elites in the past. Thus an elite in Mannheim's sense will be marked by its cultural hetereogeneity. Eliot pointed out in *Notes Towards the Definition of Culture*: "In an elite composed of individuals who find their way into it solely for their individual pre-eminence, the differences of background will be so great, that they will be united only by their common interests, and separated by everything else." The effect of this will be a breach of the fundamental continuity of cultural life that should form an essential element in the educative society and that is assured by a *class* structure. Too much emphasis in an elite society will be placed on the formal educative agencies, and too little on that primary agency of cultural continuity, the family. As a result of current policies of selection according to "brains," Eliot wrote:

The elites . . . will consist solely of individuals whose only common bond will be their professional interests: with no social cohesion, no social continuity. They will be united only a part, and that the most conscious part, of their personalities; they will meet like committees.

Such a society, too, will suffer from the faults of the increasing specialization that characterizes it, the lack of those contacts and mutual influences at the highest reaches "at a less conscious level, which are perhaps even more important than ideas."

Eliot stressed, indeed, the importance of unconscious influences at a number of levels. Such influences are needed in the *transmission* of culture, which, at any level, depends in large measure on the family (including its ancestors). I say "at any level" because it is important to realize that "culture" is not to be equated with the culture of a single class. Eliot said, "What is important is a structure of society in which there will be, from 'top' to 'bottom,' a continuous gradation of cultural levels." The culture of the highest level will be the most conscious and the most specialized, but it, too, will need to feed on the unconscious elements fostered by class continuity and social contacts within the class so that the specialism of the specialist is modified by the broader contact. The culture of the other levels is again in part transmitted by contact—indeed, in a larger part. Where the crafts are concerned, for instance, Eliot explained:

. . . the apprentice (ideally, at least) did not merely serve his master, and did not merely learn from his as one would learn at a technical school—he became assimilated into a way of life which went with that particular trade or craft; and perhaps the lost secret of the craft is this, that not merely a skill but an entire way of life was transmitted (*Notes Towards the Definition of Culture*).

In general, Eliot placed a greater emphasis on the importance of unconscious factors insofar as the lower classes are concerned. He found the regulative sources of their behavior to be ideally not in self-conscious decisions but in the force of *habit*. The importance of habit, then, as an educative factor deserves some consideration.

In analyzing what he meant by a political philosophy, Eliot stated that it was not:

. . . merely even the conscious formulation of the ideal aims of a people, but the substratum of collective temperaments, ways of behaviour and unconscious values which provides the material for the formulation. What we are seeking is not a programme for a party, but a way of life for a people (*The Idea of a Christian Society*).

tion, and the Community of Christians, involving the more intellectual, self-conscious elements, in these terms:
between the Christian Community, comprising the bulk of the popula-
In describing the Christian society that he desired, he distinguished

In the Christian Community . . . the Christian faith would be ingrained, but it requires, as a minimum, only a largely unconscious behaviour; and it is only from the much smaller number of conscious human beings, the Community of Christians, that one would expect a conscious Christian life on its highest social level.

Eliot emphasized the role of unconscious behavior for the larger group, because, he said, "their capacity for *thinking* about the objects of faith is small, their Christianity may be almost wholly realised in behaviour: both in their customary and periodic religious observances, and in a traditional code of behavior towards their neighbours." He recognized the importance of conduct in the preservation of beliefs, for behavior affects the nature of beliefs as much as beliefs can be said to affect behavior. He said:

. . . to be conscious, without remission, of a Christian and a non-Christian alternative at moments of choice, imposes a very great strain. The mass of the population, in a Christian society, should not be exposed to a way of life in which there is too sharp and frequent a conflict between what is easy for them or what their circumstances dictate and what is Christian (*The Idea of a Christian Society*).

He concluded that for the majority of people "religion must be primarily a matter of behaviour and habit" and that the religious life of the people would be largely a matter of behavior and conformity." The emphasis on "habit," indeed, has interesting Platonic overtones. In depicting the ethical society in *The Laws*, Plato stressed the process of habituation by which the ordinary man is able to achieve right conduct through the relevant manipulation of pleasure and pain. For the average member of society what can be achieved is not Socratic understanding, fit, according to both Plato and Eliot (I quote from Eliot), only for those of "intellectual and spiritual superiority"; attainable, rather, is right habit through the correct canalizing of the emotions. In Plato's view, average people can only attain excellence (*arete*) by the process of developing tastes and character through habit. Eliot, indeed, believed that "behaviour is also belief," and that even the most highly conscious among us "live also at the level on which belief and behaviour cannot be distinguished." How much more, then, are the unconscious elements important where the less sophisticated are concerned. Eliot saw, for instance, that the industrial worker needs to be engaged in the industrial process at a deeper level than that represented by the purely conscious level. He agreed with Miss Majorie Reeves when she urged that the worker take an active intellectual interest in the nature of the industry by which he is employed; further, in *Notes Towards the Definition of Culture*, he advised that "an industry, if it is to engage the interest of more than the conscious mind of the worker, should also have a way of life somewhat peculiar to its initiates, with its own forms of festivity and observances." He saw, too, that part of the strength of regionalism comes from the presence of people who have lived in the same part of the country for some generations and have attained a loyalty that is largely unconscious. In *Notes*, he wrote, "I think we should agree there would be something artificial, something a little too conscious, about a community people with strong local feeling, all of whom had come from somewhere else." And the link between this emphasis on unconscious factors and Eliot's conception of tradition became clear when he asserted:

Tradition may be conceived as a by-product of right living, not to be aimed at directly. It is of the blood, so to speak, rather than of the brain: it is the means by which the vitality of the past enriches the life of the present. In the co-operation of both is the reconciliation of thought and feeling (*After Strange Gods*).

The keystone binding the arch of the educative society is, of course, religion—and specifically, as I have made clear, the Christian religion. In such a society, it is paradoxically true, Eliot wrote in *Notes Towards the Definition of Culture*, that "religion and culture are aspects of one unity, and that they are two different and contrasted things." This unity can be understood by realizing that the identity of religion and culture "remains on the unconscious level, upon which we have superimposed a conscious structure wherein religion and culture are contrasted and can be opposed." It is doubtful whether any culture could come into being without a religious basis; but the identity of the two only exists at the level at which people are unconscious of both their culture and their religion. If the identification of religion and culture persists to the conscious level, it leads to both an inferior religion and an inferior culture; at the same time, the conscious connection between the two is greater than would be implied by the use of the word "relation." In his attempt to define the nature of the connection, Eliot finally spoke of the "culture of a people as an *incarnation* of its religion."

He analyzed the present state of our society—which, in ultimate values, he found to be a "neutral" one—and was led to the belief that the only possible alternative, on the one hand, to an "apathetic decline . . . without a philosophy of life, either Christian or pagan; and without art," or, on the other, to a totalitarian democracy, is religion. He stated in *The Idea of a Christian Society*: "The only possibility of control and balance is a religious control and balance; . . . the only hopeful course for a society which would thrive and continue its creative activity in the arts of civilisation, is to become Christian." This is not a matter simply of toleration of worship, he continued:

. . . the Christian can be satisfied with nothing less than a Christian organization of society—which is not the same thing as a society consisting exclusively of devout Christians. It would be a society in which the natural end of man—virtue and well-being in community—is acknowledged for all, and the supernatural end—beatitude—for those who have eyes to see it (*The Idea of a Christian Society*).

The main aim of education, which would form this society in its religious aspect, would be to enable people to think in Christian categories, though not to compel belief. Indeed, the beliefs of the rulers would be less important than the categories of behavior within which they would be obliged to act.

Members of the Christian State, then, would belong to the "Christian Society under the aspect of legislation, public administration, legal tradition, and form," which would be confined to a "Christian framework within which to realise their ambitions";[6] to the Community of Christians, composed of the more intellectual and self-conscious elements in the state; and to the Christian Community, comprising those who would realize Christianity largely unconsciously in their behavior. There would be a Church, which in England would have to be the Church of England, and which would have some relationship to all three elements in the community. The possibility of nonbelievers is allowed for on the grounds that some such admixture or dissent would be beneficial to the intellectual vitality of the state. But, of course, the basis of such a state is the dogmatic truth of Christianity—not the mere need for a morality or an enthusiasm. "It is not enthusiasm, but dogma, that differentiates a Christian from a pagan society," Eliot declared in *The Idea of A Christian Society*. A fundamental belief of Christians, to which Eliot made a number of references in his work, is the doctrine of Original Sin. He praised Baudelaire, for instance, for his appreciation of the possibilities of damnation, because "the possibility of damnation is so immense a relief in a world of electoral reform, plebiscites, sex reform and dress reform, that damnation itself is an immediate form of salvation—of salvation from the ennui of modern life, because it at last gives some significance to living." Emphasizing the notions of sin and redemption as basic to the human situation, Eliot wrote in *After Strange Gods* that "with the disappearance of the idea of Original Sin, with the disappearance of the idea of intense moral struggle, the human beings presented to us both in poetry and in prose fiction to-day, and more patently among the serious writers than in the underworld of letters, tend to become less and less real."

The "Unreal City" of the modern world is characterized by a frightening lack of a sense of fundamental realities; in this failure of all firm

---

[6] "The State is Christian only negatively; its Christianity is a reflection of the Christianity of the society which it governs."

conviction Eliot found the most terrifying feature of modern life. The "neutral" society in which we live—one essentially of the lower middle classes—may well find its highest ideal in material efficiency. In *The Idea of a Christian Society,* Eliot warned: ". . . the tendency of unlimited industrialism is to create bodies of men and women—of all classes— detached from tradition, alienated from religion, and susceptible to mass suggestion: in other words, a mob. And a mob will be no less a mob if it is well fed, well clothed, and well disciplined." The bitterness of Munich drew forth from Eliot the query as to whether our society was "assembled round anything more permanent than a congeries of banks, insurance companies and industries and had it any beliefs more essential than a belief in compound interest and the maintenance of dividends?" The drive for "educated manpower" characterizing the 1960s in Britain forced a reluctant "no" to Eliot's question. Such a drive, the most pressing reason for educational expansion, confirmed Eliot in the belief expressed in his essay entitled "Modern Education and the Classics" that contemporary education is associated only with "technical efficiency on the one hand, and with rising in society on the other." The danger of such a society lies in the boredom and apathy it induces. In an essay on the music-hall artist Marie Lloyd, Eliot deprecated the passing of the old audience-participation music-hall shows in which, when the spectator joined in the chorus, "he was engaged in that collaboration of the audience with the artist which is necessary in all art and most obviously in dramatic art." Eliot concluded his remarks with a pessimistic assessment of the progress of mechanization—and particularly of mechanical entertainment—in England:

In an interesting essay in the volume of *Essays on the Depopulation of Melanesia,* the psychologist W. H. R. Rivers adduced evidence which has led him to believe that the natives of that unfortunate archipelago are dying out principally for the reason that the "Civilisation" forced upon them has deprived them of all interest in life. They are dying from pure boredom. When every theatre has been replaced by 100 cinemas, when every musical instrument has been replaced by 100 gramophones, when every horse has been replaced by 100 cheap motor-cars, when electrical ingenuity has made it possible for every child to hear its bedtime stories from a loudspeaker, when applied science has done everything possible with the materials on this earth to make life as interesting as possible, it will not be surprising if the population of the entire civilised world rapidly follows the fate of the Melanesians (*Selected Essays*).

In his reaction, Eliot showed some respect, at least, for the "primitive" mind by observing that "without sentimentalising the life of the savage, we might practice the humility to observe, in some of the societies upon which we look down as primitive or backward, the operation of a social-religious-artistic complex which we should operate on a higher plane."

In effect, the nature of the educative society that I have been trying to analyze in Eliot's work amounts to just such a social-religious-artistic complex; and it is one of the marks of Eliot's perceptiveness and one of the virtues of his profoundly historical sense that he was prepared to learn certain restricted lessons from more primitive eras, to see something of an essential continuity in human affairs, emotions, and dilemmas. In this way he showed a profound respect for the people of the past, which was entirely lacking in the peculiar arrogance of the twentieth century with its conceit as to the nature of its "progress," and its assumption of superiority toward its ancestors. He saw the futility of perfectionist schemes and of any "apocalyptic vision of a golden age of virtue"; whatever reforms may be carried out, he believed that the "result will always be a sordid travesty of what a human society should be." It may, indeed, be argued that, on occasions, he failed to appreciate certain very real achievements of the twentieth century.

My own view is that only two twentieth-century writers have had anything of fundamental importance to say about education in their times— D. H. Lawrence and T. S. Eliot—and that what they said was important precisely because they both challenged the very assumptions in terms of which our society operates in the name of a profoundly *human* set of priorities and values. The positive views of both show marked dissimilarities, as is only to be expected; but they join in an unexpected condemnation of the major tenet of educational policy in the West for the last hundred years and more—the cry to expand the provision of formal education more and more extensively. Lawrence expressed his doubts in the more dramatic fashion. He said that *"the vast majority of people should never learn to read and write, never."* Eliot conveyed his criticisms more allusively, through the tone of his remarks and through such side comments as, "We insist upon 'educating' too many people; and Heaven knows what for." Or again, as he wrote in "The Aims of Education":

What I wish to maintain is a point of view from which it appears more important—if we have to choose, and perhaps we do have to choose—that a small number of people should be educated well, and others left with only a rudimentary education, than that everybody should receive a share of an inferior quality of education, whereby we delude ourselves into thinking that whatever there can be the most of, must be the best.

It is natural, then, that Eliot's main interest was in the education of the minority—that minority to whom he looked for the preservation of "high culture." He considered, he said in *Notes*, that "it is an essential condition of the preservation of the quality of the culture of the minority, that it should continue to be a minority culture."

But it is necessary to preface any discussion of remarks he made on this or on any other aspect of education by a brief comment on his view of the role of formal education and of the extent of its possible influence. The place he assigned education is, indeed, a high one. In *The Idea of a Christian Society*, he stated, "A nation's system of education is much more important than its system of government; only a proper system of education can unify the active and contemplative life, action and speculation, politics and the arts." Yet he was aware that the role of formal education is necessarily restricted. We need, he urged, to make a distinction between the education that can be transmitted by the educative society and that diffused by the Ministry of Education:

For the schools can transmit only a part, and they can only transmit this part effectively, if the outside influences, not only of family and environment, but of work and play, of newsprint and spectacles and entertainment and sport, are in harmony with them (*Notes Towards the Definition of Culture*).

Formal education cannot by itself create a culture because it is itself one of the instruments through which a culture realizes itself:

Culture cannot altogether be brought to consciousness; and the culture of which we are wholly conscious is never the whole of culture: the effective culture is that which is directing the activities of those who are manipulating that which they *call* culture (*Notes Towards the Definition of Culture*).

Furthermore, the education we transmit through the formal agencies of the Ministry is essentially an abstract one, as demonstrated by the way in which we speak of the "half-educated." Such a way of speaking seems to assume that there is one standard of "whole" education for everyone, whereas the whole point of the educative society lies in its recognition of different classes that would permit, on Platonic lines, everyone to receive the education necessary for the function he was to perform. Eliot emphasized:

Education in the modern sense implies a disintegrated society, in which it has come to be assumed that there must be one measure of education according to which everyone is educated simply more or less. Hence *Education* has become an abstraction (*Notes Towards the Definition of Culture*).

Our society, then, has evolved a quite false view of both the nature and the power of education. It has substituted instruction for education and it has desired the indefinite extension of such instruction. Eliot had no confidence that this desire would continue, if education were widely spread; he suggested that the wish for it may persist longer when there are some difficulties in the way of obtaining it, and commented:

If this is so, we may conjecture that facility of education will lead to indifference to it; and that the universal imposition of education up to the years of maturity will lead to hostility towards it. A high average of general education is perhaps less necessary for a civil society than is a respect for learning (*Notes Towards the Definition of Culture*).

Education, he added, "deteriorate it as you may . . . is still going to demand a good deal of drudgery." To attempt to induct a whole population into the more conscious part of culture, he said, is to "adulterate and cheapen what you give." He elaborated:

To treat the "uneducated" mass of the population as we might treat some innocent tribe of savages to whom we are impelled to deliver the true faith, is to encourage them to neglect or despise that culture which they should possess and from which the more conscious part of culture draws vitality (*Notes Towards the Definition of Culture*).

The whole emphasis on a common culture—a notion that has had some currency on both sides of the Atlantic—is illumined by this comment:

The culture of an artist or a philosopher is distinct from that of a mine worker or field labourer; the culture of a poet will be somewhat different from that of a politician; but in a healthy society these are all parts of the same culture; and the artist, the poet, the philosopher, the politician, the labourer will have a culture in common, which they do not share with other people of the same occupations in other countries (*Notes Towards the Definition of Culture*).

He considered at some length the concept of equality of opportunity. The attempt to sort out the entire population on the basis of intellectual merit he regarded as unattainable in practice and, of pressed to the exclusion of other aims, it "would disorganise society, by substituting for classes, élites of brains, or perhaps only of sharp wits." He wrote:

Any educational system aiming at a complete adjustment between education and society will tend both to restrict education to what will lead to success in the world and to restrict success in the world to those who have been good pupils of the system. The prospect of a society ruled and directed only by those who have passed certain examinations or satisfied tests devised by psychologists is not reassuring; while it might give scope to talents hitherto obscured, it would probably obscure others, and reduce to impotence some who should have rendered high service (*Notes Towards the Definition of Culture*).

Such a system offers, indeed, the possibility of increased state control. And Eliot questioned the "Mute Inglorious Milton dogma," which suggests that a great deal of first-rate ability is being wasted for lack of opportunity. Although he asserted that such a notion could be neither proved nor disproved, the irony of his reference would seem to imply a considerable skepticism on his part. Indeed, he considered that our real motive in extending education in length and breadth is not that everyone will benefit from extended schooling, but simply that:

. . . the conditions of life in modern industrial society are so deplorable, and the moral restraints so weak, that we must prolong the schooling of young people simply because we are at our wit's end to know what to do to save them (*Notes Towards the Definition of Culture*).

Eliot admitted the force of the three positive aims of education set forth by C. E. M. Joad in his book *On Education*—learning for vocation, for good citizenship, and for individual self-development. A good part of the four lectures he delivered at the University of Chicago in 1950 was devoted to an analysis of the interrelations of these aims and of the extent to which any one of them reacts on and modifies the others. He urged, too, the importance of the attainment of wisdom, the acquisition of knowledge for the satisfaction of disinterested curiosity, the development of a respect for learning, and the preservation of cultural continuity as desirable aims for education. Other educational desiderata developed out of his antipathy for D. H. Lawrence. In view of his ideas about orthodoxy and the need to avoid intellectual eccentricity, it is not surprising that Eliot was unsympathetic to much of Lawrence's work—though he did once inform me that he found many of Lawrence's views on education very sound. In a review of *Son of Woman*, a life of Lawrence by Middleton Murry, Eliot contrasted Lawrence's "ignorance" to what true education should accomplish:

What true education should do—and true education should include the suitable education for every class of society—is to develop a wise and large capacity for orthodoxy, to preserve the individual from the solely centrifugal impulse to heresy, to make him capable of judging for himself and at the same time capable of judging and understanding the judgments of the race (*Criterion*).

Much more palatable than the iconoclasm of Lawrence, to Eliot's mind, was the humanism of Irving Babbit who "to the end of his life . . . opposed the heresies of the school of John Dewey"—though Eliot said it must be remembered that "humanism as a way of life, and in particular as a way of education, is not enough."

Eliot, indeed, rightly appreciated that questions about the aims of education ultimately involve questions about the nature of man, that questions about good citizenship involve the political philosopher, and that questions about the development of the individual involve the theologian. To these last questions, as we have seen, he propounded the Christian answer. He held that in a Christian society it would be important to have some "settled, though not rigid agreement as to what everyone should know." He advised:

Even with a smaller amount of total information, it might have been better if they had read fewer, but the same books. In a negative liberal society you have no agreement as to there being any body of knowledge which any educated person should have acquired at any particular stage: the idea of wisdom disappears, and you get sporadic and unrelated experimentation (*The Idea of a Christian Society*).

The search, he said, is for "permanent principles of what should be the goal of education, and permanent standards of quality in relation to which we ought to try to direct the ways in which this changing world should change." He noted the proliferation of subject matter that followed the development of the natural sciences and condemned the failure to discover "dominant principles" in terms of which patterns of education could be "co-ordinated." In the jargon of our times, he stood for a subject-centered rather than a student-centered curriculum and repudiated the belief that a "youth of eighteen" be thought competent to "decide for himself what subject or combination of subjects could best provide him with a liberal education." The "democratic" approach to subject matter introduced to America by President Charles William Eliot of Harvard was objectionable to his British namesake; T. S. Eliot deplored the notion that the "only criterion of whether a subject was necessary for your education, was whether you happened at that time to be interested in it."

Concerning the details of the desired curriculum, Eliot naturally was not very explicit—he was much more concerned with general principles. His most nearly specific interest lay, as I have suggested, in the training necessary for a man of letters. He urged the maintenance of a classical education as "essential to the maintenance of the continuity of English literature," for the classics provide a common background of instruction, helping to counterbalance any centrifugal tendencies that may appear in the process of literary creation. The classics, indeed, form part of that orthodoxy on which social communication depends. Eliot wrote in "The Classics and the Man of Letters" that on them "depends the possibility of general audience, the possibility both of the author's being able to communicate with people in all walks of life, and of their being able to understand each other." In general, the writer needs whatever will help him to acquire precision in the use of language. He will, therefore, need to investigate various modes of communication in language. For instance, Eliot said, he will need to study "logic, for that is an investigation of the anatomy of thought in language; . . . philosophy, for that is the attempt to use language in the most abstract way possible." He will also require, in addition to his knowledge of Latin and Greek, proficiency in "one modern language besides his own" and "a reading knowledge of several others." And he must be able to take an interest in subjects in which he has not been trained—so that, for instance, he can understand the general meaning of some scientific discovery, though his interest here will be analogous to that of a Shelley or a Lucretius who informed their "scientific knowledge with an emotional life with which the scientist, as such, has no concern."

The value of Eliot's conception of education lies in the shock it administers to received opinion and current assumption. In America some of the policies he condemned seem to have brought about their own nemesis; in England we still have a little time to heed his warnings. The rationalizing tendencies and the educative demands of the modern industrial-bureaucratic state have induced a concern for education that seems to accord well with the current emphasis on social justice; but, in effect, this concern often produces a peculiarly thin sort of educative experience. The apparent injustice of Mr. Eliot's regard for depth rather than expansiveness could, paradoxically, produce the richer social reward; at the very least he has forced upon his opponents the immense stimulus involved in rebuttal: "Fortunate the man who, at the right moment, meets the right friend; fortunate also the man who at the right moment meets the right enemy."

BIBLIOGRAPHICAL NOTE

The main sources for Mr. Eliot's educational ideas may be found in his sociocultural writings: *The Idea of a Christian Society*, published in London in 1939; *After Strange Gods*, published in London in 1934; and *Notes Towards the Definition of Culture*, published in London in 1948. He also published a short series of lectures delivered at the University of Chicago, "The Aims of Education," in the periodical *Measure* (Vol. 2, No. 1, December, 1950, No. 2, Spring, 1951, No. 3, Summer, 1951, No. 4, Fall, 1951). In addition, he wrote a number of essays on education, including "Modern Education and the Classics," which appears, in *Selected Essays*, third edition, published in London in 1951; his presidential address to the Classical Association in 1942, "The Classics and the Man of Letters," which appeared as a pamphlet published at Oxford in 1942; "Cultural Forces in the Human Order," appearing in a series of essays edited by M. B. Reckitt entitled *Prospect for Christendom*, published in London in 1945. "The Christian Conception of Education," in *The Life of the Church and the Order of Society*, the Proceedings of the Archbishop of York's Conference held at Malvern in 1941, was published in London in 1942. There are additional references to education in Eliot's *Selected Essays*, third edition, published in London in 1951, in his *On Poetry and Poets*, published in London in 1951, and in his uncollected "Notes," "Commentaries," and reviews published in the *Criterion* and the *New Criterion* (between 1922 and 1939) of which he was the editor.

🌱 MARTIN BUBER (1878–   ) was born in Vienna. He studied philosophy and history of art from 1896 to 1899 at the Universities of Vienna, Berlin, and Zurich. In 1900 at the University of Leipzig he was converted to Zionism, which offered him not only a political movement but also a religious idea that he said resolved his former spiritual confusion. Zionism led him to an interest in Hasidism, a mystical movement in which he found the essence of Jewish national character. He retired to study the Hasidic literature, which at that time was regarded as occult and disreputable by most enlightened thinkers. His studies resulted in the publication of 100 Hasidic tales and parables retold in his own words. Buber spent several years in Florence, Berlin, and Vienna, studying the philosophy of religion. He was awarded the doctor's degree from the University of Vienna for a dissertation on German mysticism. In 1916 Buber became the editor of Der Jude, the leading periodical of German-speaking Jewry. From 1923 to 1933 he occupied the chair of Jewish religion and ethics at Frankfurt; this was the only chair of its kind in a German university. When Jewish students were excluded by the Nazis from all educational institutions in 1933, Buber became director of the Central Office for Jewish Adult Education in Germany. In 1938 the philosopher fled to Palestine where he became professor of social philosophy at the Hebrew University; in 1951 he became professor emeritus. In 1949 he founded and became the director of the Institute for Adult Education, an Israeli institution that trains teachers in the instruction of newly arrived immigrants. Dr. Buber is the author of a large number of books and essays. His most important works translated into English include I and Thou, Between Man and Man, and Good and Evil.

14

THE EXISTENTIAL MAN: *Buber*

BY MAURICE FRIEDMAN

Martin Buber's great contribution to the life and thought of our time, as to the philosophy of education, is his sixty years of work pointing to "the life of dialogue." Buber's philosophy of dialogue is best known through its classic presentation in his little book *I and Thou*. In this book Buber made his now famous distinction between the two relationships or basic attitudes that constitute human existence: the "I-Thou" and the "I-It." What distinguishes these relationships is not the object of the relation but the nature of the relationship itself and the difference between the "I" that enters into the one relationship and the "I" that enters into the other. The "I-Thou" relation is direct, mutual, present. In it the "I" relates to the other person in his uniqueness and for himself and not in terms of his relations to other things. In an "I-Thou" relation my partner reveals himself to me directly as just the person he is. I do not seek for his meaning by enregistering him in one or another general category. In the "I-It" relationship, on the other hand, the other is my object and not my partner. I observe him and use him; I establish his relation to this or that general category. I know him with the same detachment with which I know any object or I see him in purely emotional terms but, in either case, not as a really independent person standing over against me. Hence this relationship is never really direct or mutual or truly present. In the "I-Thou" relation the whole person enters. Here emotion and reason, intuition and sensation are included in the wholeness of the person responding to what he meets. The "I" of the "I-It" relationship, in contrast, is always partial, and it is just as much "I-It" when it is emotional as when it is rational, when it is subjective as when it is objective.

Both I-Thou and I-It are necessary for human existence. I-It again and again provides the base for ordered civilization, for technical accomplishment, for scientific advance. Yet I-It is not sufficient for human existence even on the barest terms. Without the I-Thou relation, the biological human individual would not become a person, a self, an I at

all. He begins with the I–Thou in his relation to his mother and family
and only later develops the separating relationship of I–It. As long as
the I–Thou and the I–It remain in healthy alternation, ever new material from the realms of the physical, the biological, the psychological,
and the social is brought into the I–Thou relation and given new, present meaning. When I–It becomes predominant and prevents the return
to the Thou, however, man loses authentic existence and ultimately falls
into pathological self-contradiction. Thus, Buber's I–Thou philosophy
is both descriptive *and* normative, offering both fact and value. The
normative element appears in the difference between mere existence and
authentic existence, between being human at all and being more fully
human, between holding the fragments of the self together sufficiently
to get by and bringing the conflicting parts of oneself into an active
unity, between having partial, disparate relations with others and having
fuller, more responsible ones.

THE LIFE OF DIALOGUE

In *Between Man and Man,* Buber expresses his basic distinction in terms
of the contrast between "dialogue" and "monologue." Dialogue may be
silent, and monologue may be spoken. What really matters in genuine
dialogue is my acceptance of the "otherness" of the other person, my
willingness to listen to him and respond to his address. In monologue,
by contrast, I only allow the other to exist as a content of my experience. Not only do I see him primarily in terms of his social class, his
color, his religion, his I.Q., or character neurosis, but I do not even leave
myself open to him as a person at all.

Values as a philosophical or idealistic abstraction fill the air of the
world of "It" and are often, in fact, the favorite subject matter of those
given to monologue, whether it be the principles they expound, the code
by which they live, or the "moral" standards by which they judge others.
Values as a living human reality, however, exist only in the "life of dialogue," in the direct, reciprocal relation between man and man, for there
alone are we able to know and respond to the other in his uniqueness.
Buber says, "The life of dialogue is not one in which you have much to
do with men, but one in which you really have to do with those with
whom you have to do." And it is only when I "really have to do" with
the other that I can really be responsible to him. "The idea of responsibility is to be brought back from the province of specialized ethics, of an
'ought' that swings free in the air, into that of lived life," Buber explains.
"Genuine responsibility exists only where there is real responding."
Responsibility, to Buber, means the response of the whole person to

what addresses him in the "lived concrete"—his full concrete situation. No abstract code is valid in advance of particular situations. None has universal validity, because value does not exist in the universal at all, but in the particular, the concrete, the "interhuman." This does not mean that moral codes are of no use; they can be useful if they are recognized as what they are—abstractions, generalizations, rules of thumb that may be helpful in pointing us back to the concrete values that men have discovered in real meeting. But they cannot take the place of our discovering for ourselves, each time anew, what the right direction is in a particular situation. The movement of values, therefore, is from the concrete situation and the deep-seated attitudes that one brings into that situation to the response and decision producing the moral action. Buber declares:

No responsible person remains a stranger to norms. But the command inherent in a genuine norm never becomes a maxim and the fulfillment of it never a habit. Any command that a great character takes to himself in the course of his development . . . remains latent in a basic layer of his substance until it reveals itself to him in a concrete way . . . whenever a situation arises which demands of him a solution of which till then he had perhaps no idea. Even the most universal norm will at times be recognized only in a very special situation. . . . In moments like these the command addresses us really in the second person, and the Thou in it is no one else but one's own self. Maxims command only the third person, the each and the none.

The "ought" that arises in the concrete situation is not the pure I–Thou but what Buber calls the *quantum satis*—the sufficient amount of what one can do in that hour and in that situation. Just because real values arise in the concrete situation and in terms of the particular person confronted with that situation, the "ought" must include and be based on the real concrete person and all the limitations and resources that he brings with him into the situation.

PHILOSOPHICAL ANTHROPOLOGY

Buber's philosophy of dialogue has found its most thoroughgoing philosophical base in the philosophical anthropology that Buber has developed in his later years. Philosophical anthropology is concerned with the uniqueness of man, with what makes man a problem to himself. Man is an animal, yet man differs from all other animals, and he cannot understand himself as man apart from this difference. No approach to the problem of human society that is content to carry over an organic biological analogy from the life of animals without dealing with the specific problematic of man can claim our serious attention as a contribution to the understanding of man. The suggestiveness of such organic analogies is deceptive; their appeal is often based on the desire to escape from the problem of man, the desire to reduce man to the safer general categories that biological science has discovered for all animals, the desire of the scientist to escape responsibility, in fact, for his participation even as knower in what he is seeking to know—human existence.

Buber establishes the focus of the problem of man in the "interhuman," the "sphere of the between." Man, essentially, is neither a gorilla nor a termitary, neither a self-sufficient, primarily isolated individual, as Freud saw man, nor an organic collectivity. The fundamental fact of human existence is man with man, the genuine dialogue between man and man. The psychological or psychic stream of happenings within each man is only the accompaniment of the dialogical event. It is not itself the reality or aim of human existence. "All real living is meeting," Buber maintains. Individuation is not the goal, only the indispensable way to the goal. This point is absolutely central to Buber's thought and it cannot be emphasized too strongly. Many psychotherapists and psychologists, such as Erich Fromm and Carl Rogers, who today recognize the essential importance of mutual relations between men, still see these relations largely as the function of the individual's becoming and the means to that end. As long as dialogue is entered *merely* as a means to the end of health, maturity, integration, self-expression, creativity, "peace of mind," "positive thinking," or richness of experience, it will not even produce those things, for it will no longer be true dialogue and will afford no real meeting with the other.

DISTANCE AND RELATION

Buber's book *The Knowledge of Man* (1963) provides us with the latest and most important stage of his philosophical anthropology. Through contrasting man with the rest of nature, Buber derives a twofold principle of human life consisting of these basic movements: "the primal setting at a distance" and "entering into relation." The first movement is the presuppposition for the second, for we can only enter into relation with being that has been set at a distance from us and, thereby, become an independent entity opposite us. Only man can perform this act of setting at a distance because only man has a "world" (*Welt*)—a continuum that includes not only all that he and other men know and experience but all that is knowable now and in the future—while an animal merely has an environment or realm (*Umwelt*). "Only the view of what is over against me in the world in its full presence, with which

I have set myself, present in my whole person, in relation—only this view gives me the world truly as whole and one," says Buber.

Once distance has been given, man is able to enter into relation with other beings (I–Thou) or to enlarge, develop, accentuate, and shape the distance itself, turning what is over against him into his object (I–It). An animal cannot see its companions apart from their common life nor ascribe to the enemy any existence beyond his hostility. Man sets man at a distance and makes him independent. He is, therefore, able to enter into relation, in his own individual status, with those like himself.

THE INTERHUMAN

In 1905 Buber used the term "the interhuman" to indicate the social-psychological area in general, "the life of men together in all its forms and actions" and "the social seen as a psychological process." Half a century later he restricted the use of this term to the element in human life that provides the basis for direct dialogical relations. Buber now differentiates the "interhuman" from the sphere of the "social" in which many individual existences are bound into a group with common experiences and reactions but not necessarily with any personal relation between one person and another. The distinction between the "social" and the "interhuman" is of great significance in an intellectual climate in which the importance of "interpersonal relations" and the "social self" is increasingly recognized, and at the same time these aspects of association are indiscriminately confused with dialogue and the I–Thou relationship. The social includes the I–It relation as well as the I–Thou: many interpersonal relations are really characterized by one person's treating the other as an object to be known and used. Most interpersonal relations are, in fact, a mixture of I–Thou and I–It, and some are almost purely I–It. Both George Herbert Mead and Harry Stack Sullivan include something of what Buber calls the interhuman in their treatment of the social self and the interpersonal relation, but, unlike Buber, neither man singles out the interhuman as a separate, qualitatively different, and essentially significant dimension.

The unfolding of the sphere of "the between" Buber calls the "dialogical." The psychological—what happens within the soul of each—is only the secret accompaniment to the dialogue. The meaning of this dialogue is found in neither one nor the other of the partners, nor in both added together, but in their interchange. This distinction between the "dialogical" and the "psychological" constitutes a radical attack on the psychologism of our age. It makes manifest the fundamental ambiguity of those modern psychologists who affirm the dialogue between man and man but who are unclear as to whether this dialogue is of value in itself or is merely a function of the individual's self-acceptance and self-realization. "Individuation is only the indispensable personal stamp of all realization of human existence," writes Buber in *The Knowledge of Man*. "The self as such is not ultimately the essential, but the meaning of human existence given in creation again and again fulfills itself as self." By pointing to dialogue as the intrinsic value and self-realization as only the corollary and by-product rather than the goal, Buber also separates himself from those theologians and existential psychotherapists who tend to make the I–Thou relationship just another dimension of the self, along with one's relation to oneself and to one's environment.

The interhuman is the I–Thou relationship insofar as that relationship refers to the dialogue between man and man, but it is not synonymous with that relationship, since, according to *I and Thou*, man can also have an I–Thou relationship with nature and with art. In *The Knowledge of Man*, however, Buber has emphasized the difference between our knowledge of other persons and our knowledge of things, as he has not in *I and Thou*. This does not mean that he has come to reject the I–Thou relation with nature and art, but as he once told me, if he were to write *I and Thou* again, he would seek different categories to make clearer the distinction between the I–Thou relationships with nature and art and the dialogue between man and man. Man has in common with every thing the ability to become an object of observation, but it is the privilege of man, through the hidden action of his being, to be able to impose an insurmountable limit on his objectification. Only as a partner can man be perceived as an existing wholeness. To become aware of a man means to perceive his wholeness as person defined by spirit: to perceive the dynamic center that stamps on all his utterances, actions, and attitudes the tangible sign of oneness. Such an awareness is impossible if and as long as the other is for me the detached object of my observation, for he will not, thus objectified, yield his wholeness and its center. This yielding is only possible when he becomes present for me.

The essential problematic of the sphere of the between, writes Buber, is the duality of being and seeming. The man dominated by being gives himself to the other spontaneously without thinking about the image of himself awakened in the beholder. The "seeming man," in contrast, is primarily concerned with what the other thinks of him and produces a look calculated to make himself appear "spontaneous," or "sincere," or whatever he thinks will win the other's approval. This "seeming" destroys the authenticity of the life between man and man and thus destroys the authenticity of human existence in general. The tendency toward seeming originates in man's need for confirmation and in his desire to be confirmed falsely rather than not to be confirmed at all. To give in to this tendency is the real cowardice of man, writes Buber; to withstand it his real courage.

This distinction between "being men" and "seeming men" is central to Buber's anthropology; it enables him to substitute for the older notions of man's natural goodness or badness the more modern realization that even though some men appear to be entirely determined by seeming, it is only their successive layers of deception that give the illusion that they are "seeming men" by their very nature. "I have never met any young man who seemed to me hopelessly bad," writes Buber. "Man is, as man, redeemable."

CONFIRMATION AND "IMAGINING THE REAL"

"The basis of man's life with man is . . . the wish of every man be to confirmed as what he is, even as what he can become, by men; and the innate capacity in man to confirm his fellow men in this way. . .," Buber writes in *The Knowledge of Man*. "Actual humanity exists only where this capacity unfolds."

This mutual confirmation of men is most fully realized in what Buber calls "making present," an event that happens partially whenever men come together, but in its essential structure only rarely. Making the other present means to "imagine the real," to imagine quite concretely what another man is wishing, feeling, perceiving, and thinking. The particular pain I inflict on another surges up in myself until, paradoxically, we are embraced in a common situation. It is through this making present that we grasp another as a self, an event that is only complete when he knows himself made present by me. This knowledge induces the process of his inmost self-becoming, "for the inmost growth of the self is not accomplished, as people like to suppose today, in man's relation to himself." An animal does not need confirmation because it is unquestionably what it is. A man needs confirmation because he exists as a self, at once separate and in relation, with unique potentialities that can only be realized when he is confirmed in his uniqueness. Buber puts it this way: "Sent forth from the natural domain of species into the hazard of the solitary category, . . . secretly and bashfully man watches for a Yes which allows him to be and which can come to him only from one human person to another."

Buber describes "imagining the real" as a "bold swinging" into the life of "the particular real person who confronts me, whom I can attempt to make present to myself just in this way, and not otherwise, in his wholeness, unity, and uniqueness." "Imagining the real" is crucial for genuine ethical responsibility in which one's response is not to a subjective interest or to an objective moral code but to the person one meets. It is also essential for friendship and love in which each member of the relationship is made present by the other in his concrete wholeness and uniqueness. But imagining the real is also essential for all the helping relationships—pastor and parishioner, teacher and student, therapist and patient. If we overlook the real otherness of the other person, we shall not be able to help him, for we shall see him in our own image or in terms of our ready-made categories and not as he really is in his concrete uniqueness. But if we allow him to be different and still accept and confirm him, then we shall have helped him realize himself as he could not without us. No amount of knowledge on the part of the teacher and no amount of scientific technique on the part of the doctor and the psychotherapist can make up for the failure to experience the relationship from the side of the other as well as from our own.

Buber's teaching of confirmation is of the greatest importance for his philosophy of dialogue in general and for its application to education in particular. To appreciate its importance we must make a distinction— that many have failed to make—between acceptance or affirmation of the other and "confirmation." For Buber, confirmation means that while I accept the other as a person, I may also wrestle *with* him against himself. This is how he describes it:

I not only accept the other as he is, but I confirm him, in myself, and then in him, in relation to this potentiality that is meant by him and it can now be developed, it can evolve, it can answer the reality of life. . . . Let's take, for example, man and wife. He says, not expressly, but just by his whole relation to her, "I accept you as you are." But this does *not* mean "I don't want you to change." But it says "I discover in you just by my accepting love, I discover in you what you are meant to become." . . . . There are cases when I must help him against himself. He wants my help against himself. . . . The first thing of all is that he can trust me. . . . What he wants is a being not only whom he can trust as a man trusts another, but a being that gives him now the certitude that "there *is* a soil, there *is* an existence." And if this is reached, now I can help this man even in his struggle against himself. And this I can only do if I distinguish between accepting and confirming.

THE ESSENTIAL WE

The relation between man and man takes place not only in the I–Thou relation of direct meeting but also in the "We" of community. Just

as the "primitive Thou" precedes the consciousness of individual sepa-
rateness, whereas the "essential Thou" follows and grows out of this
consciousness, so the "primitive We" precedes true individuality and
independence, whereas the "essential We" only comes about when independent people have come together in essential relation and directness.
The essential We includes the Thou potentially, for "only men who are
capable of truly saying *Thou* to one another can truly say *We* with one
another," Buber points out. This We is not of secondary or merely
instrumental importance; it is basic to existence, and as such it is itself a
prime source of value. "One should follow the common," Buber quoted
Heraclitus, that is, join with others in building a common world of
speech and a common order of being. "Man has always had his experiences as I, his experiences with others and with himself; but it is as We,
ever again as We, that he has constructed and developed a world out
of his experiences," Buber emphasizes. Thus amid the changes of world
image, "the human cosmos is preserved, guarded by its moulder, the
human speech-with-meaning, the common logos."

The importance for education of Buber's concept of the common
world as built by the common speech-with-meaning can hardly be overestimated. Speech, from this point of view, is no mere function or tool,
but is itself of the stuff of reality, able to create or destroy it. Buber said,
"Man has always thought his thoughts as I, . . . but as We he has ever
raised them into being itself, in just that mode of existence that I call
'the between.' " Speech may be falsehood and conventionality, but it is
also the great pledge of truth. Whether he takes refuge in individualism
or collectivism, the man who flees answering for the genuineness of his
existence is marked by the inability any longer really to listen to the voice
of another. The other is now only his object that he observes. But true
dialogue, as Franz Rosenzweig pointed out, means that the other has
not only ears but a mouth. He can say something that will surprise one,
something new, unique, and unrepeatable for which the only adequate
reply is the spontaneous response of the whole being and nothing that
can be prepared beforehand. Only if real listening as well as real talking
takes place will the full possibility of education be present in group discussion, for only thus, and not through any mere *feeling* of group unity,
will the full potentiality of the group be realized. "He who existentially
knows no Thou will never succeed in knowing a We," Buber said. One
should follow the common, and that means that lived speech, "speech-
with-meaning," is itself a value. Values are not just the content or the
building-blocks of speech. They exist, in the realest sense, in the "between," in the dialogue between man and man.

THE WORD THAT IS SPOKEN

The concern of the modern logical analyst for clarification of concepts is not new. In Western thought it goes back to Socrates and in Eastern thought to Confucius. There is a story in Confucius' *Analects* about a disciple who spent some time at the court of one of the kings "clearing up designations." As long as designations were unclear, everything in the kingdom was doubtful. The reason why designations are problematic is not, as so many think, that there are no single, agreed-on definitions. Buber says: "They are problematic because they do not show a concrete context that can be controlled. Every abstraction must stand the test of being related to a concrete reality without which it has no meaning. This revision of designations entails a necessary destruction if the new generation is not to be the life-long slave of tradition."

Our goal is not agreement or unanimity. We clarify designations only in order that we may discuss them and relate to each other in terms of them, whether in cooperation or opposition. Dialectic may lead to discovering basic agreement or disagreement if it takes place in genuine dialogue but not if it becomes a dialectical exercise within the mind of a single thinker. Such *ratio* is one of the things that distinguishes man from animal, but it is not the decisive factor, as Plato thought. Nor is man understandable simply as the symbol-making animal, as Ernst Cassirer and Suzanne Langer hold. Basic to man as man is language, and language is, in the first instance, living speech between man and man.

Living speech presupposes the distancing that gives man the possibility of a world. It also presupposes the synthetic apperception whereby the world becomes one for us. But above all it presupposes that men become selves in relation with each other. Language is neither the unmediated cry of the animal nor the universal Platonic idea; it is the mediate-immediate dialogue between two persons each of whom recognizes himself as a self when he is speaking to the other person and the other person as a self even when he is speaking of himself. Our common world is, therefore, as Heraclitus pointed out, a *cosmos* built upon *logos* —the common "speech-with-meaning." It is through this speech between man and man that we are confirmed as selves. It is through it too that we build up a world of language—of potential speech that again and again becomes actual in the spoken word. And it is through speech, finally, that we create a world of categories within which we think, communicate with one another, and develop our civilization. The true civilizing tool is not Prometheus' fire but speech.

Yet language remains curiously ambiguous—being born, dying, going over from lived speech to conventional phrase, from genuine dialogue to technical interchange, from interhuman contact to mass social manipulation. We must distinguish, therefore, between the word as direct dialogue, the word as category pointing back to the immediacy of lived speech, and the word that no longer points back but instead points out toward a world of technical interaction. It is this last word that leads toward the ultimate consummation of objectified, monological thought, the electronic brain, an invention that fits Descartes' definition of man as a "thinking thing" as no human being ever has!

Useful as precision and definition are for the exact sciences, the true humanity and the very meaning of language depend on its being brought back to the fruitful disagreement of lived speech between men whose meanings necessarily differ because of the difference of their attitudes, their situations, their points of view as persons.

GUILT AND GUILT FEELINGS

The centrality of man's existence as We is basic to Buber's distinction in *The Knowledge of Man* between "groundless" neurotic guilt—a subjective feeling within a person, usually repressed and therefore unconscious —and "existential guilt"—an ontic, interhuman reality in which the person dwells in the truest sense of the term. True guilt does not reside in the human person but in his failure to respond to the legitimate claim and address of the world. Similarly, the repression of guilt and the neuroses that result from this repression are not merely individual psychological phenomena but events between men. Existential guilt, writes Buber, is "guilt that a person has taken on himself as a person and in a personal situation." Certainly there is purely social and even neurotic guilt derived from a set of mores and taboos imposed upon the individual by parents and society and incorporated into an internalized "superego." But there is also real guilt, guilt that has to do with one's actual stance in the world and the way in which one goes out from it to relate to other people. Real guilt is neither subjective nor objective. It is dialogical—the inseparable corollary of one's personal responsibility, one's answerability for authenticating one's own existence and, by the same token, for responding to the partners of one's existence, the other persons with whom one lives. Where there is personal responsibility, there must also be the possibility of real guilt—guilt for failing to respond, for responding inadequately or too late, or without one's whole self. Such guilt is neither inner nor outer. One is answerable for it neither to oneself alone nor to society apart from oneself but to that very bond between oneself and others through which one again and again discovers the direction in which one can authenticate one's existence. If a relation with another cannot be reduced to what goes on within each of the two persons, then the guilt that one person has toward a partner in relationship cannot be reduced to the subjective guilt he feels. "Existential guilt," writes Buber, "occurs when someone injures an order of the human world whose foundations he knows and recognizes as those of his own existence and of all common human existence." Hence existential guilt transcends the realm of inner feelings and of the self's relation to itself. But the order of the human world that one injures is not an objective absolute: it is the sphere of the "interhuman" itself. This sphere and the guilt that arises in it cannot be identified with the taboos and restrictions of any particular culture and society. "The depth of the guilt feeling is not seldom connected with just that part of the guilt that cannot be ascribed to the taboo-offense, hence with the existential guilt," Buber observes.

Guilt is an essential factor in the person's relations to others: it performs the necessary function of leading him to desire to set these relations to rights. It is actually here, in the real guilt of the person who has not responded to the legitimate claim and address of the world, that the possibility of transformation and healing lies. In Archibald MacLeish's play *J. B.*, J. B. demands of his "comforters" that they show him his guilt. He is answered instead in generalities—by the Marxist who removes guilt into history, by the psychoanalyst who reduces it to the unconscious, by the priest who universalizes it in original sin. It is Martin Buber's great merit that he has given us a philosophical ground for understanding guilt in its particular, existential reality, that he takes guilt as seriously as he takes the unique, unrepeatable person and the unique, unrepeatable situations in which that person is addressed and must respond. "Original guilt consists in remaining with oneself," writes Buber. If the being before whom this hour places one is not met with the truth of one's whole life, then one is guilty.

Many modern thinkers see guilt as arising primarily from failing to fulfill one's self and realize one's potentialities. One's potential uniqueness may be given, however, but the direction in which one authenticates one's existence is not; one discovers it in constantly renewed decisions in response to the demands of concrete situations. When we are guilty, it is not because we have failed to realize our potentialities, which we cannot know in the abstract, but because we have failed to bring the resources we find available to us at a given moment into our response to a particular situation that calls us forth. This means that we cannot be guilty by presumption in relation to any ideal conception of the self but only by actualization in relation to those chances to authenticate our selves that come to us moment by moment in concrete situations. Buber writes in *Pointing the Way*: "What is possible in a certain hour and what is impossible cannot be adequately ascertained by any foreknowledge. One does not learn the measure and limit of what is attainable in a desired direction otherwise than through going in this direction. The forces of the soul allow themselves to be measured only through one's using them." Our potentialities cannot be divorced from the discovery of our personal direction, and this comes not in the meeting of man with himself but with other men. The order of existence that one injures is one's own order as well as that of the others because it is the foundation and the very meaning of one's existence as self.

EDUCATION AS DIALOGUE

Education means a conscious and willed "selection by man of the effective world," writes Buber in *Between Man and Man*. The teacher makes himself the living selection of the world, which comes in his person to meet, draw out, and form the pupil. In this meeting the teacher puts aside the will to dominate and enjoy the pupil, for this will more than anything else threatens "to stifle the growth of his blessings." Buber wrote, "It must be one or the other: either he takes on himself the tragedy of the person, and offers an unblemished daily sacrifice, or the fire enters his work and consumes it." The greatness of the educator, in Buber's opinion, lies in the fact that his situation is completely unerotic. He cannot choose who will be before him but finds him there already. Buber describes the teacher's view thus: "He sees them crouching at the desks, indiscriminately flung together, the misshapen and the well-proportioned, animal faces, empty faces, and noble faces in indiscriminate confusion, like the presence of the created universe; the glance of the educator accepts and receives them all."

The teacher is able to educate the pupils whom he finds before him only if he is able to build real mutuality between himself and them. This mutuality can only come into existence if the child trusts the teacher and knows that he is really there for him. The teacher does not have to be continually concerned with the child, but he must have gathered him into his life in such a way "that steady potential presence of the one to the other is established and endures." Buber urges, "Trust, trust in the world, because this human being exists—that is the most inward achievement of the relation in education." But this means that the teacher must be really there facing the child, not merely there in spirit. Buber emphasizes, "In order to be and to remain truly present to the child he must have gathered the child's presence into his own store as one of the bearers of his communion with the world, one of the focuses of his responsibilities for the world."

What is most essential in the teacher's meeting with the pupil, according to Buber, is the act of inclusion, or experiencing the relationship with the pupil from the other side. If this experiencing is quite real and concrete, it removes the danger that the teacher's will to educate may degenerate into arbitrariness. This "inclusiveness" is of the essence of the dialogical relation, for the teacher sees the position of the other in his concrete actuality yet does not lose sight of his own. Unlike friendship, however, this inclusion must be largely one-sided: the pupil cannot be *expected* to understand the teacher's point of view without the teaching relationship being destroyed thereby. Inclusion must return again and again in the teaching situation, for it not only regulates but constitutes it. Through discovering the "otherness" of the pupil the teacher discovers his own real limits; also through this discovery he recognizes the forces of the world in which the child needs to grow and he draws those forces into himself. Thus through his concern with the child, the teacher educates himself.

Buber's philosophy of education points to a genuine third alternative to the either-or of conflicting modern educational philosophies. The two attitudes of the "old" and the "new" educators that Buber cited in an essay written in 1926 are still dominant in educational theory and practice today. On the one hand, there are those who emphasize the importance of so-called objective education to be obtained through the teaching of Great Books, classical tradition, or technical knowledge: on the other, there are those who emphasize the subjective side of education and view it as the development of creative powers or as the ingestion of the environment in accordance with subjective need or interest. Like idealism and materialism, these two types of educational theory represent partial aspects as being the whole. Looking at education in terms of the exclusive dominance of the subject-object or I–It relationship, they picture it either as the passive reception of tradition poured in from above— in Buber's terms, the "funnel"—or as drawing forth the powers of the self—the "pump." Only the philosophy of dialogue makes possible an adequate picture of what in fact takes place: the pupil grows through his encounter with the person of the teacher and the Thou of the writer. In this encounter the reality that the teacher and writer present to him comes alive for him: it is transformed from the potential, abstract, and unrelated to the actual, concrete, and present immediacy of a personal and even, in a sense, a reciprocal relationship. This means that no real learning takes place unless the pupil participates, but it also means that the pupil must encounter something really "other" than himself before he can learn. This type of educational relationship is no compromise combination of subjectivity and objectivity. It is rather the dialogical relation between the I and the Thou in which the I takes part as a whole being and yet recognizes the genuine otherness of the Thou.

It is not freedom and the release of instinct that are decisive for education, Buber writes, but the educative forces that meet the released instinct. Proponents of the old, authoritarian theory of education do not understand the need for freedom and spontaneity. But proponents of the new, freedom-centered educational theory misunderstand the meaning of freedom, which is indispensable but not in itself sufficient for true education. The opposite of compulsion is not freedom but communion, according to Buber, and this communion comes about through the child's first being free to venture on his own and then encountering the real values of the teacher. The teacher presents these values in the form of a lifted finger or subtle hint rather than as an imposition of the "right," and the pupil learns from this encounter because he has first experimented himself. The action of the teacher proceeds, moreover, out of a concentration that has the appearance of rest. The teacher who interferes divides the soul into an obedient part and a rebellious part, but the teacher who has integrity integrates the pupil through his actions and attitudes. The teacher must be "wholly alive and able to communicate himself directly to his fellow beings," but he must do this, insofar as possible, with no thought of affecting them. He is most effective when he "is simply there" without any arbitrariness or conscious striving for effectiveness, for then what he is in himself is communicated to his pupils. Intellectual instruction is by no means unimportant, but it is only really important when it arises as an expression of a real human existence. As Marjorie Reeves has shown in her application of Buber's I–Thou philosophy to education, the whole concept of the objectivity of education is put into question by the mediation of our knowledge of things through the minds of others and by the occurrence of real growth "through the impact of person on person."

In his essay on "Education of Character" in *Between Man and Man,* Buber makes it particularly clear that the task of the educator is to bring the individual face to face with God through making his responsible for himself rather than dependent for his decisions upon any organic or collective unity. Education worthy of the name is essentially education of character, wrote Buber. The concern of the educator is always with the person as a whole both in his present actuality and his future possibilities. This education cannot be carried out merely as a conscious aim, however, for "only in his whole being, in all his spontaneity can the educator truly affect the whole being of his pupil." The teacher's only access to the wholeness of his pupils is through their confidence, won by his direct and ingenuous participation in their lives and by his acceptance of responsibility for this participation. Feeling that the teacher accepts him before desiring to influence him, the pupil learns to *ask*. This confidence does not imply agreement, however, and it is in conflict with the pupil that the teacher meets his supreme test. He may not hold back his own insights, yet he must stand ready to comfort the pupil if he is conquered or, if he cannot conquer him, to bridge the difficult situation with a word of love. Thus the "oppositeness" between teacher and pupil need not cease, but it is enclosed in relation and so does not degenerate into a battle of wills. Everything that passes between such a teacher and a pupil may be educative, for "it is not the educational intention but . . . the meeting which is educationally fruitful."

There are two basic ways by which one may influence the formation of the minds and lives of others, writes Buber in *The Knowledge of Man*. One of these is most highly developed in propaganda, the other in education. In the first, one imposes one's opinion and attitude on the other in such a way that his psychic action is really one's own. In the second, one discovers and nourishes in the soul of the other what one has recognized in oneself as the right. Because it is the right, it must also be living in the other as a possibility among possibilities, a potentiality that only needs to be unlocked—unlocked not through instruction but through meeting, through the existential communication between one who has found direction and one who is finding it.

Genuine dialogue, like every genuine fulfillment of relation between men, involves acceptance of otherness. This means that although one may desire to influence the other and to lead him to share in one's relation to truth, one accepts and confirms him in his being this particular man made in this particular way. One wishes him to have a different relation to one's own truth in accordance with his individuality. Influencing the other is not injecting one's own "rightness" into him but is using one's influence to let what is recognized as right, just, and true take seed and grow in the substance of the other and in the form suited to his individuation.

The manipulator of propaganda and suggestion, in contrast, wishes to make use of men. He relates to men not as to independently other beings but as to things. The propagandist is not really concerned with the person whom he wishes to influence. Some of this person's individual properties are of importance to him, but only insofar as they can be exploited for his purposes. The educator, on the other hand, recognizes each of his pupils as a single, unique person, the bearer of a special task of being that can be fulfilled through him and through him alone. He has learned to understand himself as the helper of each in the inner battle between the actualizing forces and those opposing them. But he cannot desire to impose on the other the product of his own struggle for actualization, for he believes that the right must be realized in each man in a unique personal way. While the propagandist does not trust his cause to take effect out of its own power without the aid of the loudspeaker, the spotlight, and the television screen, the true educator does believe in the power that is scattered in all human beings in order to grow in each to a special form. The educator has confidence that this growth needs only the help that he is at times called to give through his meeting with this person who is entrusted to his care.

The significance for education of Buber's distinction between propaganda and legitimate influence can hardly be overestimated. The ordinary positions on this problem have tended to be anxious and unfruitful. One of these is the desire to safeguard the student by demanding of the teacher an illusory objectivity, as if the teacher had no commitment to a certain field of knowledge, to a method of approaching this field, and to a set of attitudes and value assumptions embodied in his questions. Another is the desire to safeguard the student by such impossible distinctions in content as what is "progressive" and what is "reactionary," what is "patriotic" and what is "subversive," what is in the spirit of science and what is not. These are in essence distinctions between the propaganda of which we approve and the propaganda of which we disapprove. They betray a lack of real faith in the student as a person who must develop his own unique relation to the truth. The true alternative to false objectivity and to standards set from the outside is not, of course, a subjectivity that imprisons the teacher within his own attachments nor is it the absence of any value standards. The true alternative to which Buber points is the teacher's selection of the effective world and the act of inclusion, or experiencing the other side.

The real choice, then, does not lie between a teacher's having values or not having them, but between his imposing those values on the student or his allowing them to come to flower in the student in a way appropriate to the student's personality. One of the most difficult problems that any modern teacher encounters is cultural relativism. The mark of our time, writes Buber, is the denial that values are anything other than the subjective needs of groups. This denial is not a product of reason but of the sickness of our age; hence it is futile to meet it with arguments. All that the teacher can do is to help keep the pupil aware of the pain that he suffers through his distorted relation to his own self and thus awaken his desire to become a real and whole person. The teacher can do this best of all when he recognizes that his real goal is the education of great character. Character cannot be understood in Dewey's terms as a system of interpenetrating habits, writes Buber in *Between Man and Man*. The great character acts from the whole of his substance and reacts in accordance with the uniqueness of every situation. He responds to the new face that each situation wears despite any similarity to others. The situation "demands nothing of what is past," Buber says. "It demands presence, responsibility; it demands you."

The teacher is not faced with a choice between educating the occasional great character or educating the many who will not be great. It is precisely through his insight into the structure of the great character that he finds the one way by which he can influence the victims of collectivism. He can kindle in them the desire to resume responsibility by bringing before them "the image of a great character who denies no answer to life and the world, but accepts responsibility for everything essential that he meets."

Just how this attitude toward the education of character functions in practice is best shown by Buber's own application of it to adult education. He conceives of adult education not as an extension of the professional training of the universities but as a means of creating a certain type of man demanded by a certain historical situation. The great need in the state of Israel today is the integration into one whole of the peoples of very different backgrounds and levels of culture who have immigrated there. To meet this need Buber set up and directed an institute for adult education that devoted itself solely to the training of teachers to go out into the immigration camps and live with the people there. To produce the right kind of teacher the institute developed a method of teaching based on personal contact and on living together in community. Instruction was not carried on in general classes but individually in accordance with what each person needed. The education of these future teachers toward the task ahead of them would have been impossible if their teacher were not in a position to get to know them individually and to establish contact with every one of them.

The curriculum of these classes must arise from the social, political, and cultural reality of life at this historical juncture, writes Buber, and the inferences to be drawn from this curriculum must occur in the minds of the students of their own accord. In order to be able to teach in immigration camps, the students had to learn to live with people in all situations of their lives, and for this reason the teachers at the institute were prepared to deal with the personal lives of the students. This emphasis on the students' personal lives was not at the expense of academic studies in the classics, Jewish and otherwise, but the students did their academic learning in order that they might become whole persons able to influence others and not for the knowledge itself. "Adult education is concerned with character," says Buber, "and character," he adds, "is not above situation, but is attached to the cruel, hard demand of this hour."

DIALOGUE, DIALECTIC, AND ORGANIC DEVELOPMENT

Buber would agree with Jacques Maritain and Robert M. Hutchins that the conception of "what man is" is basic to the philosophy of education. But in their conception of man and of the education proper to man, Hutchins and Maritain have carried forward the Platonic dualism of soul and body in a way that Buber could not accept. To both, man is essentially defined as a rational animal; to both, the essential function of education is the development of man's rational faculty. Liberal education, writes Hutchins, conforms to "the conception of man as . . . an animal who seeks and attains his highest felicity through the exercise and perfection of his reason." Buber, in contrast, has continually protested against a one-sided intellectualism cut off from the totality of life and from personal responsibility. "This intellectualization isolates man," writes Buber, "for the bridge of direct community only spans from man to man and so from spirit to spirit, but not from thinking apparatus to thinking apparatus." The definition of man as a rational animal, moreover, is radically erroneous in its core, even as it is radically harmful in its consequences. Buber writes: "Man is not a centaur. He is man through and through. . . . Even man's hunger is not an animal's hunger. Human reason is to be understood only in connexion with human nonreason."

Buber's criticism of the classical mind-body dualism is shared by the educational school of John Dewey. But, for Dewey, the denial of this dualism rested upon an experimental naturalism emphasizing man's organic continuity with his natural environment and the development of man's reasoning powers as a natural product of organic evolution. Dewey's conception of mind as the conscious adaptation of the organism to the social and natural environment falls almost exclusively into Buber's I–It relationship of knowing and using. "Meaning," writes John L. Childs, paraphrasing Dewey's educational philosophy, "signifies that knowledge of operations, or of the behavior of events, which makes significant prediction and control possible." Dewey insisted on the education of "the whole man"—the integration of thought and emotion, of learning and experience, but his conception of the individual's potentialities and wholeness falls short of a real understanding of personality. The Deweyite approach to education has often tended to confuse personality with individuality, to look on the "person" as merely a collection of potentialities and to view the education of the person as the development of these potentialities. Buber writes: "The genuine educator does not merely consider individual functions of his pupil. His concern is always the person as a whole, both in the actuality in which he lives before you now and in his possibility, what he can become." Personality, for Buber, is the wholeness of man, what he becomes in the I–Thou relation with other real selves; individuality is the necessary substratum of personality comprising the partial factors—mental and material—that are needed before his wholeness can come into being but that do not add up to this wholeness. Personality is the I of the I–Thou relation; individuality is the I of the I–It. It is only in the I–Thou relation that one becomes whole, becomes a person, and it is only in this reciprocal relation that the teacher can really make the student's wholeness present to himself and can aid in the growth of this wholeness.

A corollary of this issue of the education of the "rational man" or of "the whole man" is the famous controversy between educators who take the Great–Books approach stressing a uniform classical education to correspond to a universal and timeless human nature and educators who take the developmentalist approach stressing an education for immediate needs. Hutchins writes in *The Conflict of Education in a Democratic Society*: "I do not deny the fact of individual differences. I deny that it is the most important fact about men or the one on which an educational system should be erected. . . . The great productions of the human mind are the common heritage of all mankind. They supply the framework through which we understand one another." According to John Dewey, this call for the pure classics isolates the literary products of man's history from their connection with the present environment. He advanced, in contrast, the idea of education as a "continuous reconstruction of experience." "Principles and universals grow out of the subject matters of the everyday world and are of the nature of means for ordering empirical affairs," writes Professor Childs in the Dewey volume of *The Library of Living Philosophers*. "They are not a priori, and they cannot be learned effectually apart from their use in social and natural contexts."

Buber, like Dewey, opposes a uniform education and proposes instead an education that will produce the particular type of man who is able to respond to the demands of his particular historical situation. The realm from which the educative material should be drawn, however, is no special one. Buber writes in *Pointing the Way*:

Basically it includes everything. But what is taken from it at any particular time is not determined by any universal principles; what is decisive here is our present situation. It alone furnishes the criterion for selection: what the man who shall there withstand this situation—what our growing generation needs in order to withstand it—that and nothing else is the educative material of our hour. Here the universal and the particular properly unite and mix.

A classic can only attain the quality of immediacy for us through our present encounter with it into which we enter as a whole person with *all* our faculties and from the standpoint of our present concrete situation. One certainly begins with what Buber calls a "real text"; the meaning, however, is not already in the text but comes into being in the moment when a voice speaks to us from the text and we respond—in the present.

Martin Buber proposes an "education that is aware of the age and directed toward it, the education that leads man to a lived connection with his world and enables him to ascend from there to faithfulness, to standing the test, to authenticating, to responsibility, to decision, to realization." At first glance, this statement would seem to place Buber squarely on the side of Dewey in opposition to Hutchins. But in fact, Buber is as far from Dewey on the one hand as from Hutchins on the other. Responsibility, to Buber, means responding, but no responding is possible unless one relates to what one meets as present, as unique, as Thou. Verification for Dewey means the objective empirical verification that enregisters what one perceives in general categories; to Buber it means the authentication of one's truth in the whole of one's personal life—in the faithful meeting with the reality that one finds "over against" one. Only the teacher who has authenticated his truth in his own existence can impart it to his students in such a way that they too can gain a real relationship to it. "Human truth can be communicated only if one throws one's self into the process and answers for it with one's self," Buber declares.

Buber's plea for the re-establishment of true dialogue calls for an education that brings together individuals with seemingly incompatible world views. He describes it thus:

The work of education unites the participating groups . . . into a model of the great community: not the union of the like-minded, but genuine living together of men . . . of differing minds. Community is the overcoming of *otherness* in living unity. It is not a question of exercising "tolerance," . . . or of a formal apparent understanding on a minimal basis, but of an awareness from the outside of the other's real relation to the truth.

Buber, like Hutchins, urges a Socratic clarification of concepts. The use of concepts without a clear knowledge of their significance, Buber writes, leads to confusion and empty talk that disrupt society. Teachers should inculcate responsibility concerning concepts and speech, and classrooms should be turned into experimental laboratories where concepts have their reliability tested. "This applies especially in the realm of the humanities, and with particular force to the social sciences," Buber emphasizes. "It is here that the Socratic system begins to hold sway." But, as Matti A. Sainio has pointed out, clarification of concepts is only the first stage on the way to understand between men. This stage is not yet education in the proper sense of the word but is only the creation of the presuppositions for education. Buber does not accept the view of those who would reduce the teacher's function to that of asking Socratic questions. His demand for genuineness in the educational relationship requires that a teacher not ask questions to which he already knows the full answer. True otherness is not just otherness of views and minds but of persons. Dialogue that does not recognize this is really monologue. Real personal contact, that is, the confronting of one human entity by another, is the root and basis of education, according to Buber. He writes: "What is wanted is true reciprocity through the interchange of experiences between the matured mind and the mind that is in the process of formation. . . . What is sought is a truly reciprocal conversation in which both sides are full partners." The teacher leads and directs this conversation and enters it without any restraint. The teacher should ask genuine questions, and the student in turn should give the teacher information concerning his experiences and opinions. Conversely, when the teacher is asked a question by the student, his reply should proceed from the depths of his own personal experience.

Men understand one another not through finding some universal element that they share in common but through the establishment of a living communication. This communication does not abolish the other's differences but recognizes from his side his real relation to the truth. The meaning that emerges from such dialogue is not located in the objective or in the subjective but in the *between*. The interpreter does not *possess* the meaning of a work, Buber points out in *Pointing the Way*. He must rediscover it anew in genuine meeting, and it is through just such discovery that the teacher is able to communicate the meaning of a text to his students. Buber explains it this way:

Perhaps I am discussing a text from the Bible. It has been interpreted countless times and in countless ways. I know that no interpretation, and now not even mine, coincides with the original meaning of the text. I know that my interpreting, like every other, is conditioned through my being. But if I attend as faithfully as I can to what it contains of word and texture, of sound and rhythmic structure, of open and hidden connections, my interpretation will not have been made in vain—I find something, I have found something. And if I show what I have found, I guide him who lets himself be guided to the reality of the text. Him whom I teach, I expose to the working forces of the text that I have experienced.

Buber's approach to education can be put into practice more easily in a modern progressive college than it can in the old system of straight lectures, enormous classes, objective examinations, and fragmented and overspecialized curriculums. Small classes, class discussions, the participation of the teacher in the discussion, the individual conference, the emphasis upon what the student really learns—all these make possible real dialogue for the teacher whose true aim is to establish it. Yet, as Buber's dialogue may not be confused with Socratic dialectic, neither may it be confused with "individual education" as it first took shape in progressive schools. Liberal educators at their best assert both that the curriculum should be adapted to the development and interests of the student and that it should be an expression of the interests and values of the teacher. Yet they lack any principle to reconcile these two criteria. It is not the expression of individual interests that produces such a mutually meaningful curriculum and teaching situation, as so many liberal educators think. This is produced by the reciprocal contact between teacher and student, the teacher's selection in his own person of the effective world, and the teacher's act of experiencing the other side.

In the chapter on education in the Buber section of *Philosophical Interrogations*, Martin Buber agrees with Robert Hutchins that it is a "fateful error" to see the educational task as "adjusting the student to his environment." Rather, he says, we have to take our stand toward the changing situations and master them. We cannot foresee the specific situation the student will have to confront, Buber explains, but "we can and should teach our students what a situation means for the mature and courageous man." This underscores the point that "the idea receives its reality from situations in which it has to authenticate itself." Principles have been imparted by the older generation but not the capacity to let practice be determined by situations in a way that is faithful to these principles. To impart this capacity we must change education, and that necessitates educating the educators.

The teacher is, of course, superior to the students both in learning and experience. There can be no question of "full partnership" between them. Yet to restrict their partnership to the "search for truth," as Hutchins suggests, is not enough. The personal experiences that the student has had and that he communicates directly or indirectly are unique material that the teacher can and must learn from the student. Buber says. "Every teacher who has ears and a heart will willingly listen to such reports, . . . but he will also help the student to advance confidently from the individual experience that he has now had to an organic knowledge of the world and life." Though such an interchange cannot be a full one, it is nonetheless, a dialogical one.

The educational value of "Great Books" cannot be doubted, says Buber, but it cannot replace the dialogue between teacher and student—the simple human meeting that in its immediacy helps the student to become what he is called to become. Neither can the Socratic dialectic be accented as the decisive educational method. Its questions are part of a dialectical game that has as its goal revealing that the student does not know what he thinks he knows. The teacher who asks a real question, in contrast, desires a real answer—"a nuance of experience that is perhaps barely conceptually comprehensible." Buber explains:

The teacher will awaken in the pupil the need to communicate of himself and the capacity thereto and in this way bring him to greater clarity of existence. But he also learns himself through teaching thus; he learns ever anew to know concretely the becoming of the human creature that takes place in experiences, he learns what no man ever learns completely, the particular, the individual, the unique.

Those who have spent their lives as educational administrators will object that there are too few good teachers for this sort of dialogue, and they are right. There are far too few. But what follows from that? Buber confronts the question and answers: "Just this, that our most pressing task is to educate educators." The dialogue and "experiencing the other side" that Buber sees as the heart of education are not objective techniques, such as so many teachers' colleges seem to hold dear, nor are they a form of "artistry," as Sir Fred Clarke and Sir Herbert Read suggest. They are a one-sided but nonetheless concrete form of the life of dialogue, based on mutual contact, mutual trust, and the teacher's selection of the effective world in terms of his understanding of the student's side of the teaching-learning relationship. The teacher must be ready to give of himself—his knowledge, his imagination, his technical mastery, and his person—in order that the student may become what—in his created uniqueness and his existential situation—he is called to become.

BIBLIOGRAPHICAL NOTE

For general expositions of the life of the dialogue, the following works by Martin Buber are recommended.

I and Thou, Second Edition with Postscript by the author, translated by Ronald Gregor Smith. Scribner's Paperbacks, New York, 1960.

Between Man and Man, translated by Ronald Gregor Smith. Beacon Paperbacks, Boston, 1955.

Pointing the Way, edited and translated and Introduction by Maurice Friedman. Harper Torchbooks, New York, 1963.

The Knowledge of Man, edited with an Introductory Essay by Maurice Friedman, translated by Maurice Friedman and Ronald Gregor Smith. George Allen & Unwin, London; Harper & Row, New York, 1965.

For primary writings by Buber on education, the following are suggested.

"Education," and "The Education of Character," in *Between Man and Man*.

"Education and World View," in *Pointing the Way*.

"Elements of the Interhuman," in *The Knowledge of Man*.

"Adult Education in Israel," edited by Maurice Friedman, *The Torch*, The Magazine of the National Federation of Jewish Men's Clubs of the United Synagogue of America, Vol. 11, No. 3, Spring 1952.

"A New Venture in Adult Education," *The Hebrew University in Jerusalem, Semi-Jubilee Volume*. The Hebrew University, Jerusalem, April 1950, p. 117 ff.

"Martin Buber Section," edited by Maurice Friedman, in *Philosophical Interrogations*, Sydney C. Rome, editor, Chapter III. Holt, Rinehart & Winston, New York, 1963.

For other sources, the following are available.

Maurice Friedman, *Martin Buber: The Life of Dialogue*. Harper Torchbooks, New York, 1960. (Especially Chapter XX, "Education.")

Maurice Friedman, "Martin Buber's Philosophy of Education," *Educational Theory*, Vol. 6, No. 2, April 1956.

Maurice Friedman, "Martin Buber and Religious Education," *Religious Education*, Vol. 54, No. 1, January–February 1959.

Ernst Simon, "Martin Buber, the Educator," in *The Philosophy of Martin Buber*, edited by Paul Arthur Schilpp and Maurice Friedman, *The Library of Living Philosophers*. The Open Court Publishing Co., Wilmette, Ill., 1954.

Sir Herbert Read, *Education through Art*, Second Edition. Pantheon Books, 1945, pp. 279–289.

Sir Fred Clarke, *Freedom in the Educative Society*, in the series Educational Issues of Today, edited by W. R. Niblett. University of London Press, London, 1946, pp. 53–68.

Matti A. Saino, *Pädagogisches Denken bei Martin Buber*, Jyvaskylan Kasvatusopillisen Korkeakoulun Jukaisuja XII, Acta Academiae Paedogigicae Jyvaskylaensis XII, Jysvaskylan Ylipistoyhdistys, 1955.

Gerhard Huber, *Menschenbild und Erziehung bei Martin Buber*, Pamphlet No. 108 of the *Eidgenössische Technische Hochschule Kultur-und Staats-wissenschaftliche Schriften*, edited by Gerhard Huber and Guido Calgari, Polygraphischer Verlag AG., Zurich, 1960.

🦡 B. F. SKINNER (1904–   ) was born in Susquehanna, Pennsylvania. He was graduated from Hamilton College in 1926 and received the M.A. in 1930 and the Ph.D. in 1931 from Harvard. He has taught at the University of Minnesota and at Indiana University where he was chairman of the department of psychology. In 1947 he returned to Harvard where he is presently Edgar Pierce Professor of Psychology. Eschewing theory, Skinner practices a strict positivism and insists upon a descriptive approach to behavior. He seeks what he calls a "functional analysis of behavior" through the establishment of relationships among variables by means of highly controlled experimental techniques. Skinnerian techniques are widely accepted by a growing number of psychologists. Some of his disciples have recently established their own periodical, *Journal for the Experimental Analysis of Behavior*. Skinner is best known for his research on the control of behavior by scheduled reinforcement. Much of his work has been done with animals. During World War II he developed a training program whereby pigeons learned how to guide missiles to their targets. Professor Skinner has also been interested in the control of human behavior. He has invented and marketed commercially an automatized baby-tending device. Less radical, perhaps, has been his work in the area of "teaching machines" and programmed instruction. He presented his views on the control of human behavior in his widely discussed utopian novel *Walden Two*. A more academic discussion of the implications of science for human affairs is contained in *Science and Human Behavior*. A collection of his papers, recently published, is entitled *Cumulative Record*.

15

THE PLANNED MAN: *Skinner*

BY MARY JANE McCUE ASCHNER

It is the plan of this chapter to examine a conception of the educated person that may one day become an actuality. Professor B. F. Skinner of Harvard University is recognized as the foremost proponent of strict behaviorism in contemporary psychology. Educators report that his influence upon current developments in educational theory and practice is growing, especially through his contributions to the field of programmed instruction. And since his utopian novel *Walden Two* appeared in 1948 —with its philosophy of determinism, its re-examination of "free will," and its vision of the good life for man in a planned society—Skinner has become a significant and controversial figure in contemporary social thought. His works in psychology, education, and social theory represent an impressive synthesis of three major foci upon the role of education in shaping man's future.

Skinner has never offered a description of "the ideally educated man," nor would he be inclined to do so. Unlike some of his predecessors in this volume, such as Locke or Rousseau, his view of education does not concentrate narrowly upon the tutored upbringing of a young man to become a member of a given social class or to fulfill a particular social role. Skinner's educational thought centers upon mankind—upon men and women alike—as an evolving species for whose continued survival on this planet he has a profound and somewhat anxious concern.

Still, it is possible to call forth some fairly authentic representations of the variety of individuals whom Skinner would consider to be optimally educated human beings. Accordingly, the first three parts of this chapter are designed to give the reader a background of information about Skinner's work, his thinking, and his purposes; in the fourth part, the reader, thus familiarized with Skinner's theories, will meet representatives of a new version of our species: Planned Man. Following the meeting, a discussion will inquire into how welcome such people might be to those who have not been educated according to plan and whether

389

—welcome or not—planned people might be the only members of the human species fit to survive the tests of the future.

Behaviorism, for Skinner, is "not the scientific study of behavior but a philosophy of science concerned with the subject matter and methods of psychology."[1] His own interpretation of this philosophy has matured in more than thirty years of research, teaching, and writing; its lineage is traceable to Pavlov, Thorndike, Watson, and Dewey.[2] Skinner would be identified, actually, not with a philosophy of science but with the science of behavior. This allies him with a five-decade tradition of positivistic, experimental psychology. These psychologists have been alternately praised for conceptual rigor and laboratory ingenuity and damned for being more preoccupied with the peculiarities of rats than with the problems of men. But Skinner would not call himself a behaviorist.

Yet, despite his so-called "radical behaviorism" and his long years of close association with rats and pigeons, Skinner's preoccupation was from the outset and has remained with the problem of man—with the question of why people behave as they do. More specifically, he seeks to discover the laws of human behavior. For in Skinner's view of the physical universe, human beings are as wholly subject to the governance of natural law as are any other physical phenomena—from gametes to galaxies.

Skinner's earlier research undertook the initial development of his methodology for the scientific study of animal and human behavior. And in the course of these studies, he also worked out the well-known principles and techniques of operant conditioning, as described in his *Behavior of Organisms*, published by Appleton-Century-Crofts, New York, in 1938.[3] These principles and techniques represent a systematic and versatile elaboration upon Thorndike's "Law of Effect." In later studies Skinner applied his methodology and experimental techniques to the manipulation and design of certain arbitrarily selected patterns of behavior in pigeons—such as, for example, pecking, head bobbing, bowing, etc. The striking results of these experiments attracted widespread attention. After all, it is no mean feat to turn the familiar addlepated

---

[1] B. F. Skinner, "Behaviorism at Fifty," *Science*, Vol. 140, No. 3570, May 31, 1963, p. 1.

[2] Skinner's kinship to Dewey is suggested in Dewey's essay, "The Reflex Arc Concept in Psychology," written in 1896. (See Wayne Dennis, editor, *Readings in the History of Psychology*, Appleton-Century-Crofts, New York, 1948.) Here, Dewey not only foreshadowed the notion of "feedback"; he also approximated Skinner's concept of reinforcement, as an effect upon the organism arising from the consequences of its own behaviors.

[3] We shall discuss the techniques and principles of operant conditioning later.

pigeon into a precocious Ping-pong player. Even more remarkably, Skinner's pigeons learned so well how to guide air-to-ground missiles on a project during World War II that, six years after these feathered veterans were retired from active duty, tests showed that the pigeon "will immediately and correctly strike a target and will continue to respond for some time without reinforcement."[4] And today, although he is chiefly concerned with the educational and social applications of his research and its results, Skinner is generally recognized to be a leading figure in contemporary psychology, respected both for and despite his own special version of behaviorism.

PSYCHOLOGY AND EDUCATION

In Skinner's opinion, psychology has a long way to go before becoming a genuine science. If psychology were a science comparable, say, with physics, it would rest upon a comprehensive body of knowledge drawn from the *direct* observation and measurement of animal and human behavior. Cumulative data on constant relationships found among behavioral phenomena would then permit the systematic formulation of certain laws of behavior. With such a grounding and superstructure, psychology could rightly be called an empirical science. And as a science, psychology could begin making theoretical progress at last; for it would then possess the explanatory force and predictive fertility that it so greatly lacks at present.

Skinner proposes the development of a genuine science of behavior. The scientific study of behavior should proceed by means of what he calls a "causal or functional analysis."[5] In such an analysis, every instance of the organism's behavior is to be treated as a function of a set of antecedent conditions. In other words, whatever a pigeon does on a given occasion—raising the head, for example—is taken to be an effect of the circumstances or conditions attending the act of head raising. Antecedent conditions (including prior behaviors of the organism) are referred to as "independent variables"; observed behaviors are termed "dependent variables." By systematic manipulation of antecedent conditions,

---

[4] Skinner, "Pigeons in a Pelican," *American Psychologist*, January 1960. See Skinner, *Cumulative Record*, Enlarged Edition, Appleton-Century-Crofts, New York, 1959, 1961, p. 426.16.
For other details on this remarkable study, see Skinner's article, "Stimulus Generalization in an Operant: A Historical Note," in David I. Mostofsky, editor, *Stimulus Generalization*, Stanford University Press, Stanford, 1964.
[5] Skinner, *Science and Human Behavior*, The Macmillan Company, New York, 1953, p. 35.

together with observation of corresponding changes in the behaviors under study, cause-effect linkages may be identified. The greater the control attained over the antecedent conditions, the greater the precision with which lawlike cause-effect relationships may be specified among behavioral phenomena and the conditions that produced them. Moreover, control over the causal conditions of behavior entails control over behavior itself.

A functional analysis proceeds step by step from one observed instance of behavior to the next and relies exclusively upon direct observation rather than inference. Skinner holds that only *external* variables need be held in account. In other words, there is no need to posit "intervening variables," that is, constructs about what goes on *inside* the organism, such as memory, imagery, or libido, for example. Each step in this kind of analysis is suggested by the cumulative record of preceding observations. There is no need to formulate hypotheses as guidelines for research. Skinner does not deny the existence of inner states or processes. Quite contrary to his critics' claims, Skinner asserts the presence of such events. But until the science of behavior develops adequate techniques for observing inner events directly, they must remain inferential. It is in this sense that "private events" are therefore presently irrelevant to any causal, functional analysis of behavior.

Psychology, according to Skinner, is still at the stage of gathering observational data preliminary to the identification of behavioral laws. And no science can make fruitful use of hypothetical or theoretical constructs until it has established a systematic set of lawlike relationships among at least some of the phenomena in its chosen field of investigation. Therefore, Skinner would hold, theories and hypotheses are presently just so many impedimenta delaying rather than advancing the progress of psychology toward establishment as a science.[6]

Skinner's critics decry his position as antitheoretical. But here they misunderstand; Skinner would be the last person to deny the potential value of theory in the service of a well-grounded empirical science. His present insistence that theories are not useful to psychology seems more accurately to reflect his belief that the science of behavior must progress much further along the road to scientific status before theory can serve its purposes to some avail.

In much the same vein, Skinner criticizes the widespread practice of

---

[6] Skinner, "Current Trends in Experimental Psychology," in *Current Trends in Psychology,* University of Pittsburgh Press, Pittsburgh, 1947. "Are Theories of Learning Necessary?" *Psychological Review,* Vol. 57, 1950, pp. 193–216. "The Flight from the Laboratory," in *Cumulative Record.* "The Operational Analysis of Psychological Terms," pp. 272–286, in *Cumulative Record.*

analyzing research data by means of elaborate and esoteric statistical techniques. Their usefulness is limited at best. The long-hallowed learning curves, drawn from the data recorded on memory drums or from rat mazes, for example, are not only misleading but also fail to warrant the very generalizations which they invite one to make. Skinner wrote:

They summarize the arbitrary and often accidental consequences which arise when complex and largely unanalyzed conditions of reinforcement act upon large samples of behavior. There are probably as many learning curves as there are apparatuses for the study of learning, and mathematicians will strive in vain to pull a useful order out of this chaos ("Reinforcement Today," *American Psychologist*, Vol. 13, No. 3, March 1958, pp. 94–99; also *Cumulative Record*, p. 134).

Nor do generalities about the "average" behavior of a large population offer any information or knowledge about the laws governing and explaining such behavior. And if our ability to induce learning depends upon knowledge of the actual processes of learning and upon gaining control over their necessary conditions, then, Skinner wrote in "The Flight from the Laboratory" (*Cumulative Record*, p. 252), "Psychologists should recognize that with proper techniques one can see *learning take place*, not in some inner recess removed from the observable performance of the organism, but as a change in that performance itself." Accordingly, the utility of psychology—as an aid to education, for example—is fostered neither by present-day theoretical preoccupations nor by the sophisticated wizardry of modern statisticians.

Operant Conditioning

Skinner and his colleagues have worked out the set of techniques and principles for the manipulation and control of behavior generally referred to as operant conditioning. An operant, according to Skinner, is a class of behaviors, a *kind* of thing that an organism does, not just an instance of the doing. He says, "The term emphasizes the fact that the behavior *operates* upon the environment to generate consequences" (*Science and Human Behavior*, p. 65). This is a kind of behavior that is emitted (initiated) by the organism rather than elicited from it. An operant is *not* paired with a particular stimulus. But we can make the occurrence of an operant contingent upon prior behavior even when we cannot identify any particular prior stimulus. When the operant becomes contingent upon some prior (antecedent) behavior, then the operant is said to be conditioned. It was necessary to develop such a set of practices in order to isolate and identify constant relationships between independent and dependent variables in the functional analysis of behavior. Operant conditioning provides the technological means by which Skinner would see his educational and social planning put into effect. His interest in the scientific study of behavior has never been "merely scientific," but ultimately practical, in the same sense that the work of engineering is practical.

Skinner introduced his discussion of operant conditioning by reference to Thorndike's pioneer studies of animal learning. In *Science and Human Behavior* (p. 60), he wrote: "The fact that behavior is stamped in when followed by certain consequences, Thorndike called 'The Law of Effect.' What he had observed was that certain behavior occurred more and more readily in comparison with other behavior characteristic of the same situation." What makes a cat begin, say, to pull at a latchstring in the puzzle box more often than it will scratch at a corner or bump its head against the top? Thorndike studied the escape efforts of a number of cats—each of which had been placed in a puzzle box several times—in a series of "trials." For each cat the situation was the same every time it was put into the box: the cat wanted to get out, and getting out depended on doing one particular thing rather than anything else—pulling down the latchstring that would release the bolt and open the door of the box.

What Thorndike noted—and Skinner found most interesting—was that although the situation remained the same, the cat's behavior began to change over the series of trials in the box. Nothing was being done to the cat; that is, no extraneous distracting stimuli were added to the situation. The cat could engage in any number of behaviors and usually did, in its first experience inside the box. Of course, the box was "rigged" so that only one kind of behavior, latch pulling, would afford escape. But getting out was left up to the cat. Soon the cat's activity would begin to lose its random, trial-and-error characteristics; some behaviors dropped out, while others grew more frequent and appeared more quickly after the cat was placed in the box. Finally, among the surviving behaviors, there remained only the series of actions that the cat performed in moving immediately and directly toward the latchstring and pulling it. Of course, some cats were smarter and learned faster than others how to get out of the box.

Thorndike concluded that learning occurred in the cat when some act, say, that of pulling a latchstring, became firmly associated with a *consequence*, such as getting out of the box. The association was established by repeated experience, or practice, in solving the same problem. He went on to measure graphically the rate of learning, in terms of how rapidly irrelevant behaviors were eliminated until only the one effective behavior remained. What intrigued Skinner about Thorndike's experiments were not the quantitative measurements of progress in learning, but the striking changes in the "topography of behavior" *under unchanging circumstances.* The definite effect of the consequences of behavior upon the behavior itself—the greater likelihood of its recurrence under the same conditions—was clear. But how these consequences related to the eventual *selection* of a particular response by the organism *acting on its own* was not clear. And it is to the study of this problem that Skinner has devoted his career.

Response selection is the key to operant conditioning. An organism may appear to select its own responses in a given situation. Thorndike's cat clawed the latchstring on its own; nobody pushed its paw down upon the string loop. Yet the cat made no inner "decision" to act. Nor was its performance of this kind of operation *elicited* by means of some form of "reflex" reaction-triggering mechanism, such as an electric shock. As Skinner describes it, the cat *emitted* the response. However, he would go on to say that this instance of operant behavior (pulling down on an object) was selected—but *not* by the cat, and *not* by Thorndike. (The cat could have curled up in a corner and sulked, instead). The cat's response was selected by the set of variables at work in that situation.

Ultimately, Skinner maintains, all behavior is externally caused and externally controlled. The selection and emission or elicitation of a given response are functions of the controlling variables. Some of these are constituted by the behaving organism itself: its species characteristics; its past history; its present state of deprivation or satiation relative to the primary biological reinforcers—food, water, and sexual contact. Other controlling variables come from the environment, one feature of which may be the experimenter in a laboratory situation.

Reinforcers—events tending to strengthen, that is, to increase the probable frequency of a given kind of behavior—cannot be identified, Skinner said in *Science and Human Behavior* (p. 72), "apart from their effects upon a particular organism." To illustrate, suppose we put another cat into the puzzle box. This time it is hungry.[7] Through the bar of its prison, the cat sees and smells food. Now if the operation of pulling down the string loop lets our cat out of the box, his behavior will have produced two consequences, escaping and eating. Escaping confinement and eating food are powerful reinforcers both in this situation and potentially in many others. Reinforcement here consists in

---

[7] Thorndike used hungry cats in his experiments, with food placed in range of the subject's sight and smell. See his "Animal Learning," written in 1898, reprinted in *Readings in the History of Psychology,* cited previously.

whatever strengthening effects the consequences of this instance of latch-string pulling may have upon possible future latchstring pulling by this cat. In our example the reinforcement is such that the probability is greatly increased that this kind of response will be *selected*—out of the cat's total repertoire of possible behaviors—for recurrence the next time our cat finds itself back in the box. And since latch pulling has now become an operant instrumental for escape the next time the cat is boxed in, the cat will probably emit this form of escape behavior whether it is hungry, thirsty, or sex-starved.

What is to be noted in Thorndike's procedure is his control of the stimulus situation by keeping its conditions constant while permitting the responding behaviors of the organism to vary freely. Moving from this point, Skinner took a step toward the development of operant conditioning when he began to wonder what would happen if the behaviors of the organism were allowed to vary freely, as before, while the stimulus situation was controlled in a different way. Instead of holding initial stimulus conditions constant, the experimenter would subtly and systematically vary them in accord with observed changes in the form and frequency of the organism's behavior.

The upshot of Skinner's modification of Thorndike's technique was the achievement of precise control over the behavior of an organism— effected without any direct elicitation or manipulation of the behavior itself. By manipulation of the initial situation, behaviors could be created, designed, shaped, and changed almost at will. By taking as given the present behavioral repertoire of the organism, it was becoming possible to produce behavior—whole patterns and sequences of action—of forms so varied as to seem limited only by the generic and physical structure of the organism. What might be the limits to which behavior so controlled could extend? And what might be the limits of the control itself? No one is more acutely aware than Skinner himself of the danger and threat that are potential in the possession and exercise of a control so powerful. Yet, so far, few seem to share his vision of the enormous benefit that is potential for mankind in this same capacity to control behavior.

PRINCIPLES OF CONDITIONING. For all its power and precision, operant conditioning is little more than a subtle refinement and application of certain principles of control over behavior that men have been using on each other ever since man began. There are two ways to produce and modify behavior and one surefire way to stamp it out. When the consequences of an instance of behavior are *rewarding*, that kind of behavior is more likely than before to recur in the behaviors of the organism. Punished behavior recurs, too, although usually under circumstances allowing punishment to be avoided. Behavior is affected—shaped, changed, redirected—through feedback. Feedback informs the organism through the channels of perception of the consequences of its acts. In the absence of feedback, behavior dies out; it is extinguished.

First consider extinction. Take the example of the wise teacher and a tattling child. Tim has recently started telling his teacher about the misbehaviors of his classmates. The teacher considers this undesirable behavior and decides to extinguish it. On the playground next day, Tim comes up to the teacher and begins his latest tale—about the naughty words he heard Billy saying to Ted. She listens attentively to Tim as he speaks, but she does not react. She shows no sign of approval, no sign of disapproval, only that she has heard what he said. For Tim there has been no feedback. His experience is akin to that of shouting down a barrel and waiting, in vain, for the echo. Tim may repeat this attempt to carry tales to teacher more than once over the next few days. But if the teacher consistently fails to supply feedback to his tale-bearing behavior, it will eventually cease—extinguished.

Reinforcement is the key to the production and control of behavior. Reinforcement is an effect upon the organism brought about by the consequences of some action; the consequences, conveyed by feedback, are such that the future career of the kind of action will itself be affected. Reinforcement is either positive or negative; its absence entails extinction. *Positive reinforcement* increases the likelihood that a given kind of behavior will be more and more often repeated; positively reinforced behavior can, under certain conditions of reward, become part of the organism's most highly probable kind of behavior. For example, if a student experiences the consequences of diligent study promptly and invariably as a sense of delightful excitement and growing interest and curiosity concerning the subject of study—whether this be astronomy or gastronomy—the chances are that the student will pursue his study with increasing diligence and fervor.

Negative reinforcement also increases the likelihood that a given kind of behavior will be repeated. For instance, look at that sunbather reclining on the sands of the Bahamas. After some time, the heat of the sun seems to be getting too much for him. Despite his evident intent to deepen his tan, he rises and moves into the cooling shade of a palm grove nearby. *Negative reinforcement follows the removal of an unpleasant*—an aversive—*stimulus.* The behavior likely to recur in this case will be that of moving from open sunlight to a place of shade in order to escape the burning pain of an overheated skin. This will be done whenever similar circumstances arise. In negative reinforcement, a pattern of *escape behavior* is learned.

PUNISHMENT. In Skinner's terms, punishment involves either the introduction of an aversive stimulus or the withdrawal of a positive reinforcer. Punishment is usually thought of as something done by somebody to someone else in order to halt unwanted behavior. Well, punishment *can* stop behavior; it can deflect behavior; it can even suppress behavior—for a time. But contrary to the hopes of parents and pedagogues down the dreary aeons of discipline, punishment rarely if ever extinguishes behavior. Punishment can be instructive, too. The punished organism learns to *avoid* the circumstances that brought on the punishment; it does not "unlearn" the behavior that was punished!

Consider the case of Johnny and his puppy. A slap on the stern abruptly deflects Johnny from his endeavors to separate his puppy from its tail. Johnny flees howling from the room. For Johnny, an unmistakably aversive stimulus was introduced; the punished behavior ceased; another kind of behavior—escape from the source of punishment—replaced it. But Johnny may pull his puppy's tail again when he is unobserved and can avoid being punished for it. Therefore Johnny should be put on a "competing schedule of reinforcement." He should be rewarded and encouraged to be gentle with his pet. For unless some redirection of Johnny's behavior is begun, his tail-pulling activity may recur time and time again, once he has learned how to avoid getting punished for it.

The sad story of Jane at the prom illustrates the other kind of punishment, the withdrawal of a positive reinforcer. Jim is Jane's date for the evening; his admiring attention is a most desirable and reassuring reinforcer for Jane. Then Judy arrives. Judy's beauty attracts all eyes to her graceful grand entrance. Jim's attention is drawn from Jane and transferred with undisguised fervor to Judy. The punishing effect of Jim's sudden loss of interest could be described in the ordinary way as a blow to Jane's self-confidence and her feminine pride. All her life she has been conditioned to seek and need the admiring attention of young men. And suddenly, she just "isn't there" in Jim's eyes. That hurts. So, Jane departs for the powder room. For Jane, the punished behavior was that of having a good time at the dance and being the center of Jim's admiring attention. Her retreat from the scene was her escape to fend off further blows to her injured ego.

The kind of punishment that Jane experienced at the prom can lead to one of two different kinds of future dating behavior, depending upon Jane's personality and her previous experiences in similar situations.

Jane may become progressively shyer, ever more reluctant to enter the boy-girl arena, until eventually she becomes a wilted wallflower. Or Jane may decide to regroup her defenses and bring up the artillery (new hair-do, dress, figure, new set of attraction tactics) and come forth ready once more to meet the competition and regain her self-confidence.

Operant conditioning, to sum up matters, consists in the systematic manipulation of situational variables so that the *consequences* of a given instance of behavior become the *locus of control* over that kind of behavior, controlling both its strength and its "topography." Situational variables are arranged according to a complicated system of "schedules of reinforcement"; a schedule is designed to bring about the strength (degree of resistance to extinction) and the performance characteristics of the behavior selected in the organism that is being conditioned, Skinner explained in *Science and Human Behavior*. The key to the success of operant conditioning lies in the precision with which a given type of reinforcement can be made *contingent* upon the organism's emission of a certain kind of response. For example, the receipt of food by a hungry organism depends entirely upon the performance of some specified kind of action by that organism. Consider hungry Tim and his mother who wants him to come to meals with clean hands. Tim has no other source of food. So, for Tim, the situation is airtight: clean hands, then dinner; no clean hands, then no dinner. In other words, Tim's eating dinner is *contingent* upon his presenting a clean pair of hands when he arrives at table.

Of course, Tim's mother may find it harder to control her hungry son than Skinner finds controlling his pigeons in the laboratory. But she is on the right track. If her resolve is firm and Tim's food supply is kept completely under her control over a long enough series of hand-washing and dinner sequences, then Thorndike's Law of Effect will go into operation. In time, Tim will begin coming regularly to the table with well-scrubbed hands; soon neither Tim nor his mother will give the matter a second thought. For now, this contingency of the receipt of food upon the presentation of clean hands is a conditioned operant in Tim, firmly stamped into Tim's behavior, and built into the total Tim-mother-meals situation.

Programmed Instruction

During the past decade, educators and school people have expressed growing interest in Skinner's views on education. They are not yet aware, for the most part, of Skinner's educational philosophy or of the over-all educational import of operant conditioning. Rather, their interest in

Skinner's work and their conception of his educational position, too, derive mainly from his contributions in the field of teaching machines and programmed instruction. Programmed instruction offers, after all, one workable solution to an immense and imminent practical problem. The current and forseeable rate of population growth threatens to outdistance our best efforts to build schools, let alone recruit and prepare teachers to serve the millions of children and youth whom we are pledged to educate. And when teachers and schools are in short supply, teaching machines can greatly extend the range of a single teacher's effectiveness. In crowded classrooms machines can take over aspects of instruction in which the teacher's function is not essential. This frees the teacher to enter those phases of the instructional process in which his personal participation is indispensable.

Skinner cites Pressey as the true prophet of the technological revolution in education, and of the teaching machine. His contributions to this field of educational technology, dating back to the middle and late 1920s, were so far ahead of the times that they were almost completely ignored (*Cumulative Record*). Acknowledging our collective debt to Pressey, Skinner and his colleagues set out to develop machines and programming techniques for use in classroom instruction. They have worked out a programming system that is designed to accommodate the individual. Each child proceeds at his own pace; each step ahead in learning is accomplished by the child on his own and is accompanied by that powerful reinforcer—success. In this way, teaching machines can counter the detriments resulting from the dwindling opportunities of the teacher personally to shepherd each pupil along his own best path to learning. Moreover, such teaching machines serve three major educational objectives: provision for individual differences; self-directed learning; and learning giving impetus to further learning.

Today, programmed instruction has become "big business." All sorts of enterprising individuals and organizations have entered the field in pursuit of the profits so clearly promised by the rising demand for teaching machines and programs to put into them. Consequently, this new educational enterprise is hampered by slipshod, hasty, and inept production, while at the same time it is hailed from all sides by an uncritically enthusiastic consumer market. Nevertheless, the principles that underlie responsibly designed and programmed teaching machines today—for instruction in all kinds of skills and subject matters from rhythms to syllogisms—derive largely from the work of Skinner and his students.

One feature of Skinner's "image" in the contemporary educator's mind is a result of his impact upon the field of programmed instruction. He is quite commonly viewed as the man who will not consider what goes on inside the person, as the mechanistic psychologist, the would-be manufacturer of human robots. And while nothing could be more remote from the truth, it is not altogether surprising that so many educators have formed this narrow, incomplete picture of Skinner and of his potential influence upon the future of education in this country. It does seem unusual and not to be expected that an experimental psychologist of Skinner's stripe should also and simultaneously be a practical man, fond of human beings, and a social philosopher at heart.

CONTEMPORARY SOCIAL PHILOSOPHY

So long as he stuck to his laboratory and his pigeons, and so long as he pottered about with his teaching machines, few misgivings were voiced concerning the enormous scope and power of control over behavior that Skinner's behavioral technology promises to wield. After all, who cares about the rights of rats or the personality problems of pigeons? If teaching machines keep pupils busy and happy and teach them what we want them to learn, why worry over what makes the machines work? Then came *Walden Two* (published by the Macmillan Company, New York, in 1948). Speaking here as a novelist to a cold-war, postwar world, Skinner portrayed a utopia in which men not only designed and planned their own society but also planned and designed the members of that society. His message was this: Man has reached the point of ultimate choice in his career on this planet. With the possibility of nuclear obliteration of the human species now at the fingertips of competing world powers, mankind can either anticipate self-destruction or take steps to avert it.

Only by gaining control over himself and his deep-seated destructive tendencies can man hope to survive. This control depends on his obtaining precise and intimate knowledge of the causes of human behavior and then putting his knowledge about himself to fruitful use. Men could create better societies and better men than we have ever known. Whole cultures could flourish, in which people could be healthy, happy, secure, productive, and creative.[8] In this connection, Skinner pointed out that the community depicted in *Walden Two* is but one version of many ways in which societies so planned and so peopled could be brought into being. And Skinner would urge there is no time to spare: The causes of human behavior must become the immediate object of intensive

---

[8] Carl R. Rogers and B. F. Skinner, "Some Issues Concerning the Control of Human Behavior," *Science*, Vol. 124, No. 3237, November 1956. Reprinted in *Cumulative Record*. Skinner, "The Design of Cultures," *Daedalus*, Summer, 1961.

scientific study, and human beings the chief subjects of observation and of experimentation aimed ultimately at the production and control of human behavior.

Much is already known and has been known for centuries about how to control human behavior in all manner of subtle ways. Skinner believes that it is neither possible nor desirable to restrict the continuing advance of such knowledge. For this reason he insists that *all* present and future knowledge about the causes and control of human behavior must be made entirely public, accessible to all men in order that all men may have a voice in how this knowledge is to be used or not used. Repeatedly he warns that unless all such potent knowledge is kept public, it could easily fall into the hands of those bent upon enslaving mankind.[9]

Public reaction to *Walden Two*, with its proposal for planned man, was initially slow. But eventually Skinner found himself at the storm center of a controversy that has scarcely abated to this day. Philosophers and psychologists charged into the latest jousting match in the perennial tourney between proponents of determinism and defenders of free will. Social seers and literati, pundits and political buffs entered the lists. Skinner was denounced as proposing to abolish individual freedom and the democratic way of life, and damned for a modern Machiavelli intent upon banishing human rights and dismissing the dignity and unique worth of the human individual. So it came about that although nobody boggled at his earlier demonstrations of the precision with which animal behavior could be "engineered," reaction to Skinner's proposal that human behavior could and should also be engineered resembled sheer purblind panic.

In his later work, *Science and Human Behavior* (published by The Macmillan Company, New York, in 1953), Skinner set forth a definitive and scholarly exposition of the views advanced in *Walden Two*. Evidently some of the knights–errant who have attacked Skinner's position have remained unacquainted with his later publication. This is regrettable, since it does take a close reading of *Walden Two* to recognize Skinner's own conception of the self-controlling and self-determining individual—the kind of person he would most welcome into his planned society. Perhaps Skinner as an amateur novelist embroiled in problems of plotting and characterization, lacked the literary skills that might have enabled more of his readers to distinguish his own point of view from those represented and expressed by his characters. At any rate, it is apparent that Skinner's actual deep regard for the unique worth, dignity, and rights of the human person was not communicated as clearly in *Walden*

---

[9] Skinner, *Walden Two, Science and Human Behavior, Cumulative Record.*

Two as it has been in his later writings. If some of Skinner's more quixotic critics had studied these later works, they might have found themselves bereft of windmills against which to tilt.

In a recent, arresting study, *Utopia and Its Enemies*, George Kateb devoted considerable attention to Skinner's version of utopia and to its critics.[10] In discussing Skinner's commitment to the search for and disclosure of man's innermost nature and to the making public of all information thus obtained, Kateb examined the position taken by the distinguished litterateur Joseph Wood Krutch in his book *The Measure of Man*.[11] Krutch has been among Skinner's sharpest and most hostile critics. Kateb dealt ably with some of the points that seem most often to mark the clash of views. Krutch, Kateb said:

. . . gave voice to what must be a widespread sentiment indeed: the feeling that there is something indecent or unclean about the whole enterprise of studying human nature with an end to employing the fruits of that study in the task of upbringing and education. It is clear that Krutch intends to defend human dignity by shielding humanity from the probings of scientific psychologists. What is not clear is precisely why Krutch thinks that human dignity is necessarily bound up with ignorance or uncertainty about the facts of human nature. Krutch fears, as all men must fear, the possibility of psychological knowledge coming into the hands of the wicked; but he does not rest satisfied with expressing that fear. In good hands or bad, psychological knowledge, for Krutch, is a danger; is, in fact, poisonous (*Utopia and Its Enemies*, p. 148).

Now it is by no means the intent of this essay to defend Skinner, or to preach in behalf of his views. The central purpose here is to bring out Skinner's conception of the educated person. However, since education is the basis upon which Skinner would build a planned society designed to serve the ultimate values of humankind, it is necessary to examine his educational views within this broader social context. Otherwise it would seem hardly feasible to arrive at a responsible estimate of their potential significance. It is thus also necessary to examine Skinner's position on its own grounds before undertaking to evaluate it.

As a philosopher, Skinner reveals a close kinship to John Dewey. Both Dewey and Skinner conceive of a physical reality in which mankind and nature are all one, with and in each other. Both men have built philosophic systems that attempt to make clear man's place in nature, to establish his relation both to his physical and his social environment,

---

[10] George Kateb, *Utopia and Its Enemies*, The Free Press of Glencoe, Collier, Macmillan Ltd., London, New York, 1963.
[11] Joseph Wood Krutch, *The Measure of Man*, Charter Books, New York, 1962. (Copyright by Joseph Wood Krutch, 1953, 1954.)

and to point out the direction in which mankind should optimally move in concert with an evolving universe. Both men urge commitment to the experimental method as the means by which to identify, test, and eventually to realize human values, individual and social. Both men see education as the life source of human growth and progress. And upon their mutual commitment to a pragmatic experimentalism, both men would, I believe, base their view that planned social reconstruction is the best means to ensure man's evolution toward a world flourishing in peace—a world in which at last human understanding would grow apace with human knowledge.

Skinner conceived an ideal society, and Dewey did not—but this in no way detracts from the remarkable congruence of their views. It is immaterial whether one or the other chose to spell out his hopes for mankind in a utopian image. Perhaps the one major difference between the two philosophies is that Skinner's methodology is grounded in laboratory research. For despite Dewey's admirable command of psychology and grasp of its relevance to social theory, he was in his time hardly in a position to offer an already tested behavioral technology for setting mankind on the path of progress.

BEDROCK PREMISES OF SKINNER'S PLAN FOR MAN[12]

The present section seeks to prepare the reader for Skinner's view of a planned society and its planned people by outlining the basic premises of Skinner's position. These include his conceptions about physical reality, the scope and limits of knowledge, and the values to be sought in the service of human survival and progress.

Physical Reality

AN ORDERLY, DETERMINED UNIVERSE. The structure and processes of physical reality are orderly, as evidenced by the regularity in both the form and mode of occurrence of natural phenomena. Life in all its forms is part of physical nature and as such is subject to the rule of natural

---

[12] The following account represents the writer's distillation of Skinner's position. It is derived mainly from Walden Two, Science and Human Behavior, Parts I and II of Cumulative Record, and from a recent, extended series of conversations with Professor Skinner. The views represented here have been stated or implied earlier in this essay; Skinner has expressed or implied them in his own way throughout a variety of contexts among the sources noted. Their brief, somewhat stark exposition here is made in the interest of succinctness. Any inadequacy of statement is to be attributed to the present writer, not to the works of Skinner.

laws. Every event is externally caused; it occurs as a function of a set of antecedent, causal conditions. No event occurs spontaneously, accidentally, or "by chance." Causation relates events through the *contingency* of one event upon the occurrence and interplay of other events. For contingency to be determined between events, they must be observable as discrete events—discriminable from one another. Otherwise, cause-effect relationships will not be ascertainable. Multiple causation is the rule: any series or set of events can become causal determinants of other series and sets of events. In this wholly determined and orderly universe, no Prime Mover, or any first or final cause or purpose, is postulated.

THE EVOLUTION OF SPECIES.[13] All life forms are subject to the principles and processes of organic evolution. The principles of variation, natural selection, and adaptation to environmental conditions determine the emergence, survival, and extinction of species. Adaptability to environmental change is the condition of selection and survival (instead of extinction) for both individual and species. Species adaptability is contingent upon the following elements: a hardy and prolific population, limited only by the availability of nourishment and shelter in the environment; a wide variability in both genetic composition and experience among the membership of a species—individual differences, if you will; and the degree of control achieved and maintained by the species as a whole over its environment.

Environmental control is taken to be the most potent adaptation factor favoring species selection and survival. While a species competes, in effect, with its environment, cooperation rather than competition among individuals and groups within a species tends to extend the species' scope of environmental control. In primitive life forms, however, the individual's generic capacity to cope with its environment often varies directly with that of its species; yet, at this stage of evolution, once procreation is effected, neither individual nor species seems to be interdependent in any further way in the general struggle for survival (microorganisms, lower forms of aquatic life, are examples).

MAN AND EVOLUTION. The human species is thought to be the most rapidly evolving of all life forms on earth. Man also exceeds all other species in the scope and power of his control over the environment. As man's environmental control extends, so also does the human environment expand in range, variety, and complexity.

---

[13] Evolutionary processes are treated in far greater detail here than in Skinner's own discussions of the subject. But, because so much of his conception of Planned Man is addressed to the survival and evolutionary advancement of the human species, it is believed that the present elaboration will serve to clarify much of Skinner's position.

Human beings possess a set of generic traits that seem to have played a large part in putting man at the top of the evolutionary ladder, for the present, at least. Man is typically inquisitive, exploratory, and venturesome. He is intrigued by novelty and commonly prefers change and variety over uniformity in his environment. Man is a manipulatory creature, too. He likes to handle things, to exert effects upon things, to make or change things, to make a difference, to work his will upon the environment through his own actions. Thus he is also a controller by inclination.

In the evolutionary career of humankind, men learned to cooperate with other men, although they have been for the most part equally inclined toward competition. Nevertheless, man's current sway over the environment probably issues more from cooperation among individuals and groups than from competitive activities. Cooperation is presumably based on mutual interdependence. But as group control over the environment extends, so also is increased the power of the individual to be independent of others in controlling his environment. For example, thanks to public education, the individual in our society is normally able to make his own place and his own way in the world. He enjoys a range of control over his environment—through our technological advances— that now permits one man to harvest in one day a crop of grain that would have required the labors of several men for several days less than a century ago. (The question of the scope of an individual's control over his physical and social environment in a megalopolitan society is not so simply answered. But we must forego its exploration here, since our wordspace is limited.)

In a cooperative, mutually interdependent species (or society), the well-being of the total group depends in no way upon the fate or actions of any one or a few individuals—even though the individual may be very much dependent upon his group. But with the increased power and independence of the individual (through knowledge and intelligence), the relationship between individual and group (in species or society) may shift. The future well-being of a society may now be greatly affected by the fate of one individual (for example, the death of John F. Kennedy). And the fate of the human species as such may depend upon the actions of one or a few persons (for instance, the one or two men who can push the one or two buttons that would blast humanity from the face of the earth).

I have diverged here from Skinner's way of looking at the processes of species evolution. Implicit in my analysis lies the assumption that the kind of control necessary for human survival is a matter of power, in the competitive sense. Men have used power and force far more often than they have used peaceful persuasion in their efforts to influence other men. This is the way we tend to view the world "realistically" today. But Skinner would say that this view of the conditions for human evolution is neither logically necessary nor consonant with now-evolving social and technological conditions to which mankind must adapt for continuing survival. The old tooth-and-claw belligerent struggle for survival simply will not work at this stage of human evolution. I am inclined to agree with Skinner.

The intricate realities of the evolutionary process pose the human paradox: How may mankind survive to continue evolving toward further levels of intellectual and social development as a species while cherishing and earnestly fostering the fullest development and self-realization of the human individual—when an essential condition for the latter is the self-dependence, self-control, and self-direction of that individual? For may not independence prompt competitive efforts to extend one's own domain of control?

Knowledge

All knowledge originates in observation either through direct, physical sense perception or by means of instruments to aid observation and measurement. Abstract knowledge of whatever kind—mathematics, logic, linguistics, etc.—derives from empirical knowledge, knowledge based on experience and observation. Empirical knowledge is established by scientific procedures of verification and validation. Scientifically grounded knowledge is then put to use in two ways: to extend empirical knowledge through experiment and prediction and to apply established knowledge to practical and technical problems.

The human perceptual apparatus, however magnified in receptivity by the aid of instruments, is limited as to what can be perceived; the limits of human perception limit human knowledge. Another limit upon what man may come to know is revealed by Heisenberg's "Principle of Indeterminacy." In his analysis, the very act of observation—made within the dynamic context of the universe as a whole—changes both the observer and the observed. As Skinner put it in *Science and Human Behavior* (p. 17), if the scientist "chooses to observe one event, he must relinquish the opportunity of observing another." So we are at sea in a shifting, elusive universe, fated to live with the unknowable—some indeterminate residue of reality forever beyond our ken.

This condition of indeterminacy—paradoxically not incompatible with the postulate of absolute determinism in physical nature—obliges us to accept uncertainty and give up our cherished hope of absolute, certain knowledge. We are consequently obliged to resort to probabilistic reasoning and to deal with observable events in terms of their relative probabilities and of the relative accuracy with which we can predict and control their occurrence.

On Human Values

Since *Walden Two,* Skinner's social-value commitments have been the source of much controversy in sociological literature. Here follows the writer's effort to set forth Skinner's fundamental value premises as he would affirm them.[14] Regarding ultimate human ends and the means for their realization, Skinner has declared his commitment without reservation to two basic premises:

The ultimate *survival of mankind* must be served. It is humanity's primary, unquestionable goal or *end.*

Experimentation, scientifically conducted, is the one best *means* to obtain the knowledge that is needed in order to serve man's ultimate *end.*

In defense of these premises, Skinner said:

Do not ask me why I want mankind to survive. I can tell you why only in the sense in which the physiologist can tell you why I want to breathe. Once the relation between a given step and the survival of my group has been pointed out, I will take that step. *And it is the business of science to point out just such relations* ("Some Issues Concerning the Control of Human Behavior," p. 9, italics added).

For his commitment to serve human survival, Skinner offers no philosophically rational defense—only his option, unabashed, *for* the continuity of human life and *against* man's death in the extinction of his kind on earth.

However, as a pragmatist to the core, Skinner would defend his second premise on both rational and practical grounds. Man has no source of knowledge other than his own experience. Only science can yield dependable, empirically grounded knowledge. No other basis exists on which to decide what values may best serve man's continuity as a species. Value judgments (whether of means or of ends) are nothing more than bets or guesses, until they are tested. Only value judgments that pass the

---

14 The reader who prefers that Skinner speak for himself is referred to "Some Issues Concerning the Control of Human Behavior," previously cited. Here, in reply to the thoughtful criticisms of psychologist Carl Rogers, Skinner states his value position flatly and unequivocally.

test of experimental application in actual practice can become established values. With human survival at stake, we cannot depend on guesses. We must base decisions on *facts*—about what works to man's advantage and what does not—in our efforts to realize the good life.

Skinner frankly places his bets. Of the human society most likely to survive, he said in "Some Issues Concerning the Control of Human Behavior" (p. 9), "Other things being equal, I am betting on the group whose practices make for healthy, happy, secure, productive, and creative people." There would be no slaves and no masters, no submissive followers, no power-wielding leaders in such a society. Each individual would be free to be himself and to realize his own best way of life within a society that would cherish him and that he would cherish in turn, seeing his own interests and concerns as identical with those of his community.

Skinner bets further that this survival-prone society can become a reality only if man takes over rational and scientifically guided control of himself and his behavior. Such control would require the following conditions: that all social decisions on plans and policies be made on the basis of scientifically tested and grounded values; that education become a community enterprise, with no discontinuity between school and society; that all individuals be educated in the methods and skills of learning, of self-control, and of critical, reflective, and productive thinking; and that no individual seek or value personal gain or influence for its own sake or at the expense of others.

DIALOGUE CONCERNING PLANNED PEOPLE

What would planned people be like? *Walden Two* portrayed a community of first-generation immigrants from our own supposedly unplanned society. We need some idea of how Skinner's plan for man would be embodied in a planned society that has existed for several generations. Fortunately, this is not an impossibility, thanks to recent developments in modern physics that just might let us tamper with space-time.

The following episode in the lives of three people occurs in the very near future. You the reader, R, and I the writer, W, have just met T, a traveler whose arrival we have been awaiting at Boston's newest aerospace port. He agreed some time ago to meet us upon his return from a tour of Walden *n* and to tell us how things are going there. Walden *n* is a planned society, already six generations old, in a neighboring space-time continuum. T is the first official visitor from our space-time. He has just passed through customs; now we are seated over coffee in a conference room off the main lobby of the port building, comfortable and ready for conversation.

T: Well, after six weeks out there, I've got so much to tell, I hardly know where to begin. I've brought a lot of material—films, tape recordings, and a batch of documents. But why don't you start off with some questions? And I'll try to come up with the information you want.

W: Is Walden n anything like Walden Two? I mean, is it running pretty much as Skinner would have planned it—with managers and so forth, and everybody working at some kind of community maintenance job for only four hours a day?

T: Well, yes, they're running fairly close to Skinner's original plan. But they've advanced well beyond the life he pictured in Walden Two, especially in their social engineering and their control over environmental resources. Also, they're fairly big now, with the population nearing 6,000.

R: How about the people themselves, with all this planning and social engineering? What are they like?

T: Actually, in many ways they aren't so different from ourselves as you might think when you get your first look at them. Still, they are planned people, they're descended according to plan from planned people, and they're busy planning the next generation even while they're raising the current crop of young ones.

T dims the lights and turns on his motion-picture projector. A sweeping panorama comes into view, apparently filmed from some nearby elevation. Walden n is laid out like a small, tidy town. Its buildings are grouped, campus-like, around summer-green quadrangles, with more walkways than streets in view. People move about everywhere; while there is much activity, we see no signs of hurry or crowding. Seated and reclining figures dot lawns and benches. Athletic fields and swimming pools abound, alive with people at play. A few cars and trucks ply the four streets of the town. The streets, at right angles to each other, lead out from a central plaza and link the town to highways that disappear beyond the surrounding, neatly patterned farm and forest lands. As the camera sweeps further, another, similar town appears in the distance.

R: What's that place out there—another Walden?

T: No, that's their experimental town—where they try out new technological and social planning schemes. It's also the place where differences of opinion, competing points of view, and proposals for social change are settled—by experimental test. (He smiles.) They call it "Terra-Try"—territory for trying out things—for the scientific exploration and testing of new ideas.

R: What's this—disagreement, competition? I thought everybody was con-ditioned to agree with everybody else in that kind of place, and that any idea of competition was just bred out of people altogether.

T: No, that's a common misinterpretation of what Skinner had in mind when he said . . .

W: (*Interrupting*) Why don't we hold that question for now—until we've got a better notion of what these people are like and how they live? Besides, our main purpose here is to find out about their educational setup—about the kind of person they would consider to be ideally educated.

R: Okay, I'll buy that. But since you *say*, Mr. T, Walden *n* has disagree-ment and competition, that's something I'll definitely want to see.

T: Fine, because that's what we're going to find out. First, let's take a closer look at Walden *n*. Then in the next reel you'll see me in confer-ence with some of their managers. We'll be discussing a description I wrote about the people I had met and observed during my visit in their community, and what I had come to see as their ideally or optimally educated person. Then you'll get some answers to your questions, I think.

Now we are down in the town, scanning the scene on one of the streets. There is much talk among passers–by; the sound track is a babble of voices. People of all ages stroll the walks—singly, in pairs, and in groups. All are dressed for summer. Clothing is light, colorful, and simply styled, in most cases. Yet there is great variety in costume and grooming—much greater than we would ever see on our own summer-thronged streets. One little lady swishes by attired in the fashion of 1910, complete from ground-sweeping skirt to pompadour hair-do and pert parasol. A young man strides along sporting a full beard, hair tightly plaited in a blonde braid down his T-shirted back. Girls and women appear in all manner of dress, including a few in work coveralls like those we see among the men. A number of older men swing past in knee-length kilts, reminiscent of ancient Gaelic garb. Children scamper about clad in scanty shorts and playsuits.

There is an air of camaraderie—as if everybody knew, and really liked, everybody else. There is much laughter and calling back and forth. Children dart among the grownups. A tiny girl seizes a man by the hand and skips along at his side. A small boy reaches out to carry a woman's bundle and walks along, chatting with her. Amid all this bustle and intermingling of adults and children, we see not a look or gesture of impatience or displeasure.

R: (*Amused*) Look at those getups, will you—what a bunch of individual-ists! I was expecting to see a mob of drab conformists, like Orwell's proles!

T: No, they're not conformists, and they aren't nonconformists either. Individuality is part of the picture there, and there's no subtle pressure toward conformity. Of course, they have group standards of conduct, but not in matters of purely personal preference and taste.

W: What an uninhibited lot! Look at all that public show of affection!

T: (*Chuckling*) Yes, I see what you mean. They are much more open in expressing feelings than we are. But there it's the natural thing to do. Besides, they are truly fond of each other—nobody is unloved; everybody cares. So people grow up emotionally secure; nobody feels left out. "Love thy neighbor" is a *fact* for those folks, not just a pious maxim.

R: Yeah, but what about someone who wants to be let alone—in a mood to be by himself?

T: Oh, that's part of loving your neighbor, there. A central tenet of their Code says: "Regard your neighbors' feelings as you would have others regard yours." Look (*he points*), see there—how some people are quite alone; nobody pays them any attention. Well, you see, everyone is observing a convention they have, for just your reason. Eyes cast downward are "the signal" that someone wishes to be alone. Nobody is offended; nobody intrudes. (*The film ends; T halts the projector and turns up the lights.*)

W: Something else I noticed—they come in all shapes and sizes and colors, don't they?

T: Yes, indeed—though you won't see any obese or any very thin people. They're quite a healthy lot. But as to color and size, these folks come from every kind and combination of racial and ethnic stock. They've been genetically planned for over four generations, with careful blendings of racial and ethnic lines. Segregation, as we know it, was ruled out of Walden *n* right from the start.

R: How about economic segregation—social class lines drawn between the "haves" and the "have nots"?

T: There are no poor people there, and everyone is as rich as he wants to be. They've attained such control over the environment that their resources are nearly limitless. Everything—atomic energy, man power, brain power, water, food, metals, minerals, land—they're even controlling the weather. So nobody has to strive for economic security—it's there in abundance. Also, since nobody ever feels himself superior or inferior to anybody else, the concepts of "class" or "social status" just don't exist.

R: (*Looking skeptical*) What about "vested interests"—or genuinely public-minded interests that can arise within and between subgroups of Walden *n*? Do groups ever fall into conflict, there?

T: Very seldom. And when they do, they talk things over until all are clear. And then, if they still disagree, they take the matter out to Terra-Try.

Now T passes papers to R and W. He says: "Here is the description I mentioned. I prepared it as a basis for the discussion you'll see in this next reel. Why don't you glance over it while I change reels?" R and W look over the paper, exchanging low-voiced comments. Then T says: "Ready now? By the way, I want you to know that this discussion was *not* rehearsed. The managers you'll meet had all read the paper in advance. But otherwise, the conversation was on its own." He dims the lights and starts the film.

The scene is a large, airy room, apparently in one of the central community buildings. Several men and women sit in a semicircle around a conference table with T. All appear relaxed and at ease, except T who shuffles papers nervously. He opens with the conventional introductory remarks and amenities, and then:

T: (*On screen*) All right, let's begin with goals. Here is what I have come to view as your basic aim of education (*reads*), "To produce individuals who will maintain the well-being of Walden *n* and ensure the continuous advancement of its people toward their optimal organic and social evolution." As Chief Education Manager, would you agree, Mr. Tickner?

Mr. Tickner: Yes, Mr. T, you have stated our goal. Everything we do here is planned for that purpose. For us, you see, education and community life are one and the same process. Skinner—and before him, your late philosopher John Dewey—had the same thing in mind. Schooling—curriculum and instruction—is but one aspect of the whole process. And from what we know about education in your society, ours seems to be much more individualized and much less standardized than yours.

T: All right, Mr. Tickner, then what is the place—the value, if you will—of the individual in Walden *n*? This is an important question in our society. You agree that your basic aim is the continuity of your society, with all your people planned to that end. But this makes the individual's own development seem merely instrumental—as if he were just a tool of Walden *n*.

Mr. Tickner: Well, you've already seen for yourself how we treat the individual. But for the benefit of your—uh, sponsors (*smiles broadly at the camera, then looks serious*), let me say this, very emphatically. *The individual is and must be our first concern.* The strength and viability of any society *depend entirely* on the strengths and capabilities of its members. A society is nothing other than what they together make of it. So it is *because* we want Walden *n* to grow and flourish that our primary interest *is* the individual and his optimum development.

T: You make that clear, Mr. Tickner, and it leads us to the next big question. What goes into the optimum development of the individual in Walden *n*? In your answer to that question, I believe we'll have your conception of the optimally educated person—which is mainly what I came to find out. I've already noted that you draw no lines between the sexes; there is no "educated man" and no "educated woman." Right?

Mr. Tickner: Right! But let us be very clear on another thing, too. There is no such individual as *"the* educated person of Walden *n.*" Variety is the rule here—across sex lines, in physique and personality structure, in abilities and skills, in experience and social outlook. Wide variation among individuals favors our collective flexibility and adaptability in the event of unpredictable environmental change. And no matter how far we extend the scope of our environmental control, there always remains the possibility that some drastic or catastrophic change may occur.

T: Well, that makes sense to my people, too. But then, with all that planning, haven't you possibly eliminated some variations you might actually need, when social survival is at stake? How can you be sure you haven't?

Mr. Tickner: We can't be *sure*—that's something we can't know, until the time comes. All we can do is make some educated guesses on the basis of what we've learned so far. And so far, things have worked out very well.

T: But that means that some of your guesses—your value judgments, as Skinner himself calls them—must always remain *untested* until something comes up you can't foresee or predict. (*Tickner nods agreement.*) Well, let's leave that for the moment.

During my stay among you I have observed an enormous range of individual differences. But, as you have seen in my paper, I've also found quite a number of basic traits you all seem to have in common—at least among your adults. Granted, they vary, as you indicated, in abilities, experience, and so forth—but what about personality structure? I found certain marked uniformities in this respect. Would the Assistant Education Manager in charge of Personality Development care to comment on my list of these traits?

Miss Dalrymple: Yes, that's my department, Mr. T, so I'll take over. I'd say your list is complete and correct. But you must remember that even though we do build certain personality traits into everyone, these traits show up in very different "profiles," from one person to the next. No two personalities are alike here, any more than in your society. Each person is unique.

T: Well, I wonder about that. I'll admit, I have never in my life seen a whole society of people who seem so truly happy, emotionally secure, and productive. I've never met so many reasonable people—intelligent, reflective, and critical thinkers. I've never seen so much versatility—so many talented and truly creative people. And *never* have I seen such playful wit and sparking humor—such even temperaments and sunny dispositions. All these are wonderful to behold. But still, I am uneasy. I am uneasy—not so much about what you've *planned in* but about what you've *planned out* of your personalities. You'll see there some traits I've listed that I did *not* find.

Miss Dalrymple: (*Scanning T's paper solemnly*) Well, yes, we eliminated mental retardation. But that's what you've been *trying* to do, isn't it? (*T agrees.*) And of course we ruled out highly unstable and passionate types—people prone to violent mood swings or given to uncontrollable, unreasoning emotional commitments. All the evidence shows that the person most likely to survive—when life itself is at stake—is the one who is rational, self-controlled, and who has a high tolerance for shock, stress, frustration, and discomfort. So naturally you didn't meet any neurotic or psychotic personalities, as you'd call them. And we don't have your wild-eyed evangelists, your fanatics, your demagogues or superpatriots, either—not even any "eternal lovers," for that matter. But we've ruled out only the extremes, only personality types having a very *low* survival potential—as they seem also to have in *your* society. Mr. T.

T: (*Nodding agreement*) Well, on the face of it, Miss Dalrymple, you seem to make a pretty good case for what you've planned in and planned out of Walden *n* personalities. Still, I wonder—since the long-term survival of Walden *n* is your basic aim—if maybe you've invited a *contrasurvival* factor into your system. Perhaps the Genetics Manager or Research Manager would discuss the effects of limiting the range and scope of individual variability, instead of letting a random factor operate.

Mr. Ravin: In genetics, we're compensating for that factor by *breeding* innovation. As you saw at Terra-Try, we've produced quite a variety of mutants. Some of these may well extend our scope of variability without leaving us so vulnerable to random happenstance as you might think.

Mr. Pauling: Our Research Department thinks it's obvious, Mr. T, that we're far less subject to the fickle fingering of fate than *you* people are, back where *you* come from. (*Grins broadly, winks at the camera.*)

T: (*Equably*) Granted, sir, so it would seem. So let us turn now to your social dynamics and your system of behavioral engineering. Under the heading "Social Outlook," in my paper, I've listed a number of community-wide views—views I found rather strongly held in common throughout your adult population. Here's one (*reads*), "Sees community as extension of self; identifies self with all other individuals in the community." (*Looks up from his notes.*) Now it seems to me that the very size of your population—even at a mere 6,000—works against that. But on the other hand, I can see how three aspects of your social perspective reinforce this self-identification of the individual with society. First, the general assumption of mutual cooperation. Secondly, the readiness to accept "the facts" established by experimental tests as *settling* all disagreements over questions of value or opinion. And thirdly, the *total absence* of both coercion and competition as social concepts—no sign of their manifestation in either interpersonal or intergroup behaviors. May I ask Mrs. Chin, the Human Relations Manager, whether I am correct so far?

Mrs. Chin: Yes, Mr. T, you are correct. But what are you leading up to?

  T: Something I think may be important. It's this. Is there *always* harmony and *never* irreconcilable discord between the desires and purposes of an individual and those of his society? Is there never a rebel—one who refuses to abide by the "tested facts," who still insists on urging his own point of view, who *must* have his own way?

Mrs. Chin: (*Blandly*) But of course, Mr. T, there is always the possibility of such a case. But it would be *extremely* unlikely, at our stage of social development.

  T: (*Looking troubled*) How can you be so sure? And how would you handle such a case—individual, I mean—if he *did* take such a stand?

Mrs. Chin: As you say, we can't be "so sure." And I couldn't say offhand what we would do if something like that came up. But, you see, our system of behavioral engineering practically guarantees that no adult —unless he should suddenly become irrational, which is hardly likely— would ever take a flat stand against "the facts," let alone the group. It is not even likely that a child over six would act this way.

  T: Why? What makes you so confident that your individuals will always be so reasonable?

Mrs. Chin: (*Unruffled*) Let me explain. In the first place, no person is ever set apart or sets himself apart from his group. He has never known punishment, and he has never seen or experienced hostile behavior on the part of another person. This is due to the self-control of our people.

  T: Maybe, but even self-control must have limits, it seems to me.

Mrs. Chin: Not very narrow limits at all, Mr. T, if it is acquired early and becomes part of one's way of life. By the time one of our children is three years old, he no longer needs to be protected from injury by means of physical restraints on his actions. By six, through his regular training for self-direction and self-control, our youngster is usually in full command of himself in all his activities, including his social life. Also, he gets acquainted with all kinds of people from the very beginning— peers, older children, adolescents, adults, elderly people. They all show him love and give him guidance. Everyone makes him feel welcome and wanted as a worthwhile person. So the child grows emotionally secure at the same time he is becoming more and more closely identified with his community. This security and sense of identity as a self

THE PLANNED MAN: *Skinner* 🌼 417

and sense of identification with others are reinforced from all sides. (*She speaks with some fervor.*)

T: But isn't there *any* kind of negative or undesirable behavior that a child might see and be affected by it? This all sounds too pat for me.

Mrs. Chin: We planned *out* certain kinds of behaviors so long ago that our children simply never experience them—they have no idea that such behaviors could exist. Some of these behaviors *are* familiar ones in your society. You would call them ambitious, competitive, power-seeking, status-seeking. We have also planned out some things still favored in your world—such things as expressing gratitude, praising people, or giving them public recognition and acclaim. And we have also extinguished all forms of behavior that you would call ridicule, shaming, public censure, or sitting in moral judgment. We have deliberately ruled all these behaviors out because they tend one way or another to set the individual apart from his fellows. It is most unlikely that any one of our children would behave in a way that would put him out of harmony with the rest of us. But if a child *were* to act in such a way, his behavior would be automatically extinguished—there wouldn't be any "feedback," let alone any "pay-off," as you call it.

T: Well, you seem to have a lot of answers, Mrs. Chin. But the whole thing sounds pretty complicated to me. (*Shrugs, looking puzzled.*) I can't see how such a smooth, airtight control can be kept up all the time in a growing society, like yours.

Mrs. Chin: Actually, Mr. T, our behavioral engineering is fairly simple and straightforward. There is nothing strange or insidious about it. Everybody knows about it and how it's done; everybody learns to use it on himself and others. These are the rules. Never punish, never coerce. Reinforce, both positively and negatively, all desired behaviors. Extinguish all undesired behaviors. And everybody after the age of fifteen has a say in what is desirable and what is not. That's all there is to it, and it works. Granted, the techniques are complicated, but anybody can learn them. And whenever we hit any kind of problem, there's always Terra-Try to help us work it out.

T: Well, Mrs. Chin, in the face of your system of behavioral engineering, I must indeed concede that such a stubborn case as I proposed is a most improbable one. But all in all, I'm not sure that it is really as simple as you say—or that your system is really going to bring you to your ultimate social goals—whether or not it seems to be working so far. We'll certainly have a lot of thinking to do about that, when I return home with all these data.

Oh, there are so many other broader questions I'd like to ask—such as how Walden *n* is getting along with other, outside groups or societies. And I'd especially like to ask Mr. Case, your Manager of External Affairs, what you people would do if some hostile outside group tried to take over Walden *n* by force. But that will have to be on the agenda of our next filmed discussion. So that's all for now. (*Fade-out; film ends.*)

T stops the projector and turns up the lights. R and W sit back from the edges of their chairs, both clearly excited and concerned.

T: Well, now, what do you make of all this?

R: Can't say. I'll have to think it over for quite a while. And I certainly want to look over all the rest of the material you brought back.

W: Me, too. But now I've got to get home and write up my impressions of Skinner's ideas about the kinds of people who would compose the society he's betting on to survive. Well—my car is out in the lot—shall we head for Boston? (*All three gather up T's many items of luggage, and depart.*)

PLANNED MAN: A MODEST RECKONING

In view of what we have just seen of Skinner's views here in an interpretation, and what we know of his own statements of his views, it seems fair to ask certain questions. Is Skinner's system both logically and practically self-consistent? Are his means adequate to his avowed ends? To what extent does his bet—that the society most likely to survive is one in which people are happy, healthy, secure, creative, and productive—seem well placed? Frankly, it is hard to imagine a more desirable society. But will social planning and behavioral engineering of the kind Skinner advocates produce such a society? It seems to me that Skinner's program is feasible, and that it would be worth an experimental tryout. Whether or not a society representing Skinner's version of planned man would outlast any other social system is of course an open question.

The ultimate goal, *species survival*—our own, in this case—must be kept in mind. And control, obtained and exercised by rational and scientific methods, is *the* means to this end. Here doubts creep in. It seems quite possible that control could be carried too far, and that the mistake could be discovered too late. This possibility arises because in placing one's bets—even the most wisely reasoned estimates—one must risk something. Before a planned society could be brought into being, a number of sweeping social decisions would have to be made and enacted. Only then would the society's potential for survival be testable. But the test itself could eventuate only in circumstances putting the continued existence of that society—or species—literally at stake. And such circumstances must be unforeseen, hence by definition beyond the scope of control; otherwise, the question of survival would never come to issue. Yet, some of those prior sweeping decisions, hypothetically now in effect, may have been faulty; they might, therefore, contribute to our demise as a species instead of precluding it.

For instance, it might prove to be a bad idea to "plan out" people who are capable of unshakable, irrevocable commitment to something or someone or some group. It might well be that no society could ensure its own ultimate survival by making certain that every one of its members has optimal individual survival potential. Perhaps a society or a species needs some individuals who by their very nature are reckless of self and of others, in the original sense of "reck" (to care). It could be that only by the actions of these passionate, committed ones might the survival of the many be secured. Skinner is, of course, much too dedicated himself to the well-being of the individual ever to consider the idea of deliberately planning "expendables" to safeguard the future of society as a whole. That is, indeed, a horrid thing to imagine as part of any "master plan" for human survival. But perhaps, if we seek species survival, our calculations must include a reserve of "expendables." For so long as control can only narrow but never seal the crevices in man's protective armor against possible assault from the unknown, we must accept the enduring possibility of oblivion. One cannot stack his chips on any bet—even on what makes for the best kind of human society—without accepting the risk of losing that bet, once and for all.

Skinner's most important point, in my opinion, is his urgent plea that we adopt a more rational way of managing ourselves and our world—that we plan the future instead of letting it plan us. For we are not unplanned anyway, Skinner points out, and we never were unplanned. We are only haphazardly and irrationally planned, letting each other and the captious course of events shape us and our society. Yet, by this time we are in a position to take over the job of planning consciously and intelligently. Skinner's suggestion that we should at least do a bit of experimenting—to see whether something better could be achieved than what we are currently enduring—seems eminently sensible.

In conclusion, I suggest that it may be somewhat beside the point to charge Skinner with the task of holding his system—with its fresh and questing vision of a better world—under the relentless rein of logical symmetry. Granted, his proposed means may not serve the ends he seeks. Yet I doubt he would or ought to feel defeat in failing to meet this charge. And this entails no side-stepping of the issue. Rather, it introduces an earnest proposal on my part: We should waste no time in getting down to the job of actually doing some of the social planning and experimentation for which Skinner is calling. Unless we manage soon to gain further and more rational control over ourselves and our societies, it will matter not at all how or whether we place our bets on man's future. There will be no future.

BIBLIOGRAPHICAL NOTE

The Planned Man—the chapter title refers to B. F. Skinner's conception of the optimally educated person for a survival-prone society—may be for many of you a first meeting with the ideas and works of Skinner as an experimental psychologist and as a social thinker. If you wish to read further, let me suggest a plan. First, if for no other reason than the sheer fun of it, read Skinner's novel *Walden Two*, published by the Macmillan Company, New York, in 1948. Then, for a lucid and not too technically worded account of his systematic but practical methodology and his ideas concerning the science of human behavior, read Skinner's *Science and Human Behavior*, published by Macmillan in 1953. Finally, go exploring into the richly varied collection of Skinner's articles brought together in his *Cumulative Record*, Enlarged Edition, published by Appleton-Century-Crofts, New York, in 1959 and 1961. If you are interested in teaching machines and in Skinner's ideas on learning theory, for example, this volume offers ample material on both subjects.

Then you should be well prepared to enter the arena of controversy. Meet Skinner's critics. Carl Rogers is a thoughtful, serious, and responsible critic of Skinner's social philosophy—especially in terms of its view of the individual person. Joseph Wood Krutch is a hostile and vociferous critic of Skinner. Judge Krutch's views for yourself in his booklet *The Measure of Man*, published by Charter Books, New York, in 1962. George Kateb deals with Krutch and other critics of Skinner in his very interesting book, *Utopia and Its Enemies*, published by the Free Press of Glencoe, Collier, Macmillan Ltd., London and New York, in 1963.

Philosophers have also debated Skinner's behaviorism. Michael Scriven launched a logician's lance at Skinner in "A Study of Radical Behaviorism" that appeared in the *Minnesota Studies in the Philosophy of Science*, H. Feigl and M. Scriven, editors, published by the University of Minnesota Press, Minneapolis, in 1956. Scriven's thrust was deftly parried by Rochelle J. Johnson in "A Commentary on 'Radical Behaviorism'" that was published in *Philosophy of Science*, Volume 30, Number 3, in July, 1963. I, too, attacked Skinner's position, as a "push-button theory of conditioned behavior," in "The Language of Teaching," published in *Teachers College Record*, New York, in February, 1960. Intent at the time on scoring a point for my own position on verbal behavior, I reached a hasty and inaccurate conclusion regarding Skinner's views on the subject, which he set forth in *Verbal Behavior*, published by Appleton-Century-Crofts, New York, in 1957. This kind of misinterpretation arises for many, as it did for me, from the biased and superficial study of a subject that is far more complex than it appears to be at first glance.

Favorable appraisals of Skinner's social philosophy have been scarce, although there seems to be a rising tide of favorable interest among educators and psychologists today. One such appraisal worth reading is Matthew Israel's "A Science of Behavior," published in *The Humanist*, Volume 18, Number 1, for January-February, 1958. Israel is a former student of Skinner. He has been engaged in the development of educationally sound programs for teaching machines. Dr. Israel has also been associated with a number of individuals who have been seriously considering setting up a planned community in order to give Skinner's ideas a real trial run.